AF291338

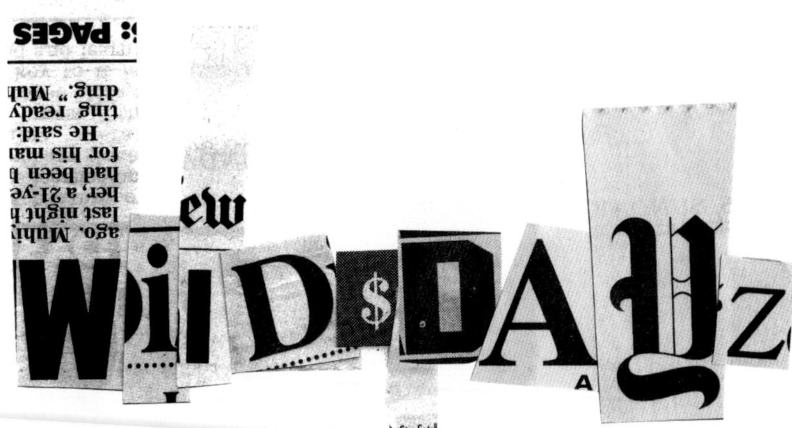

Photos by BEEZER

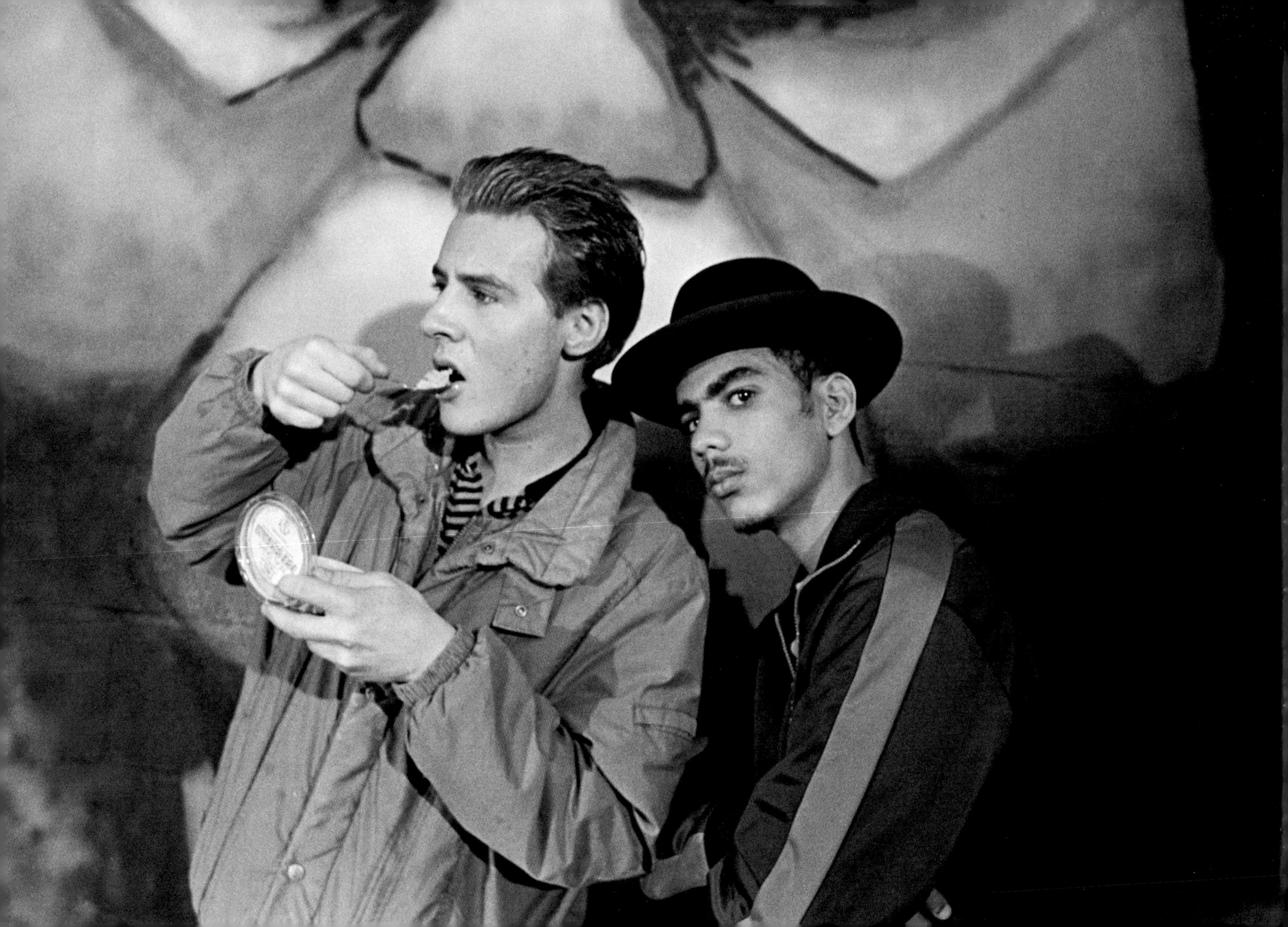

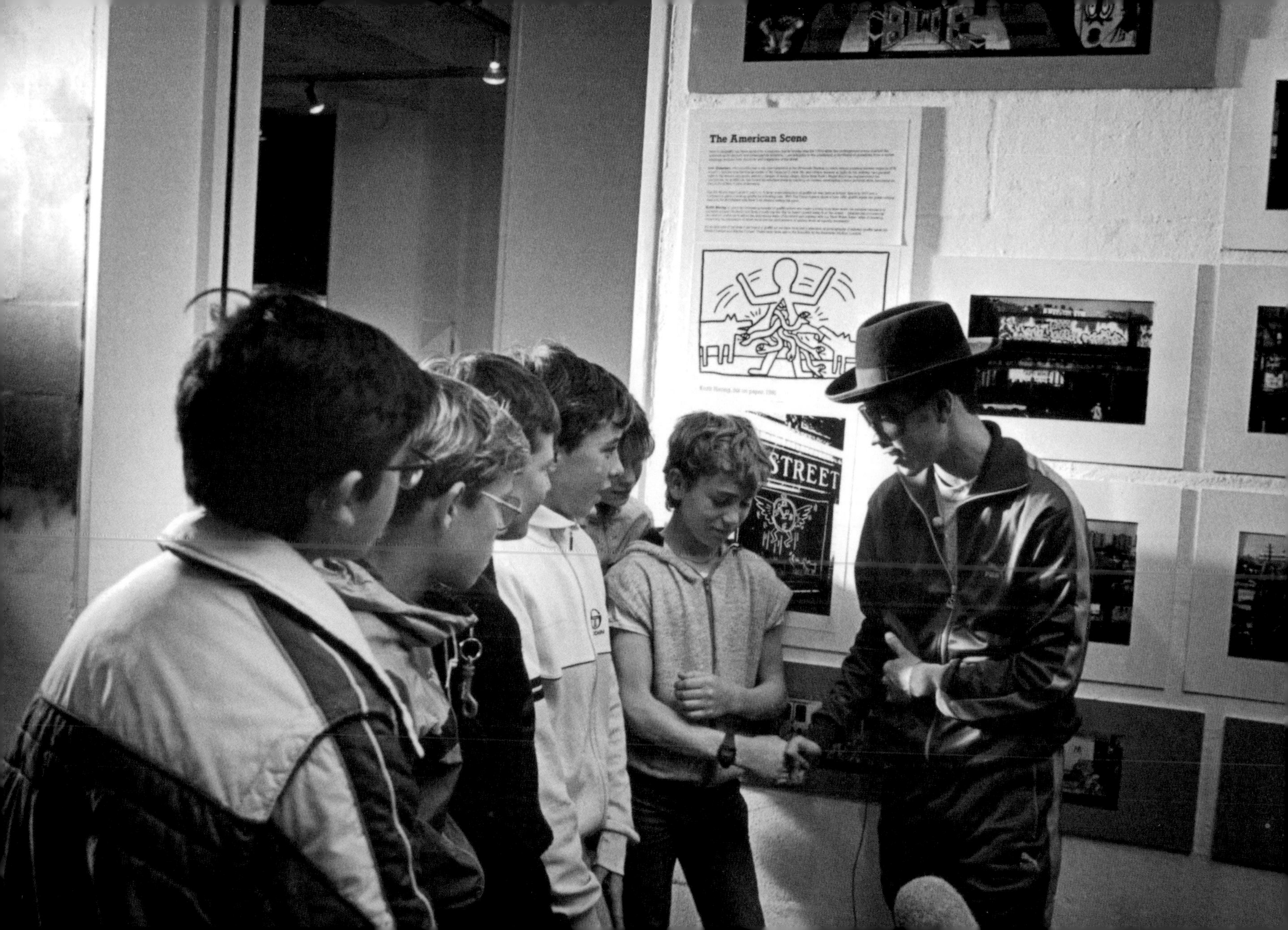
The American Scene
STREET

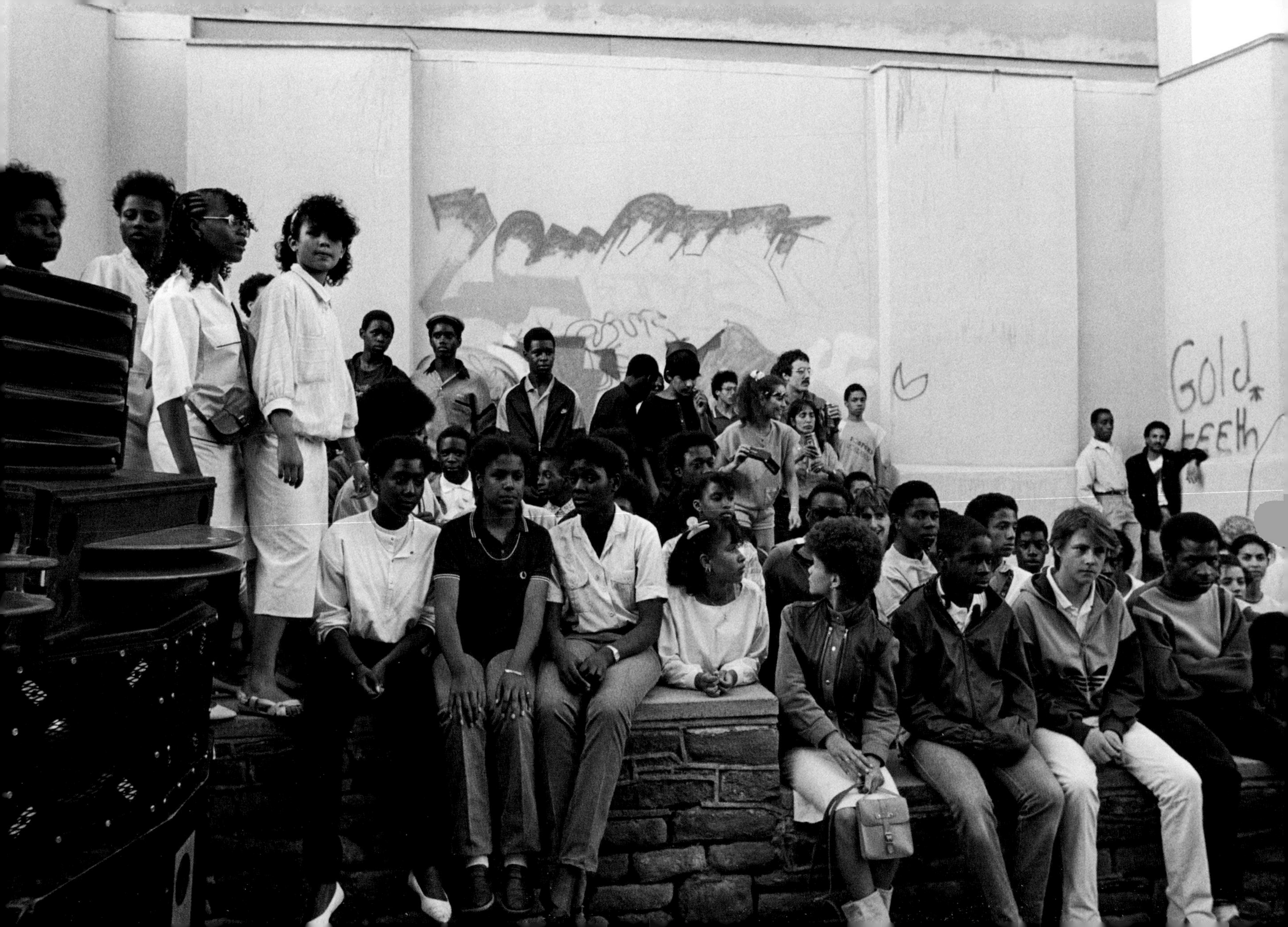

Gold
teeth

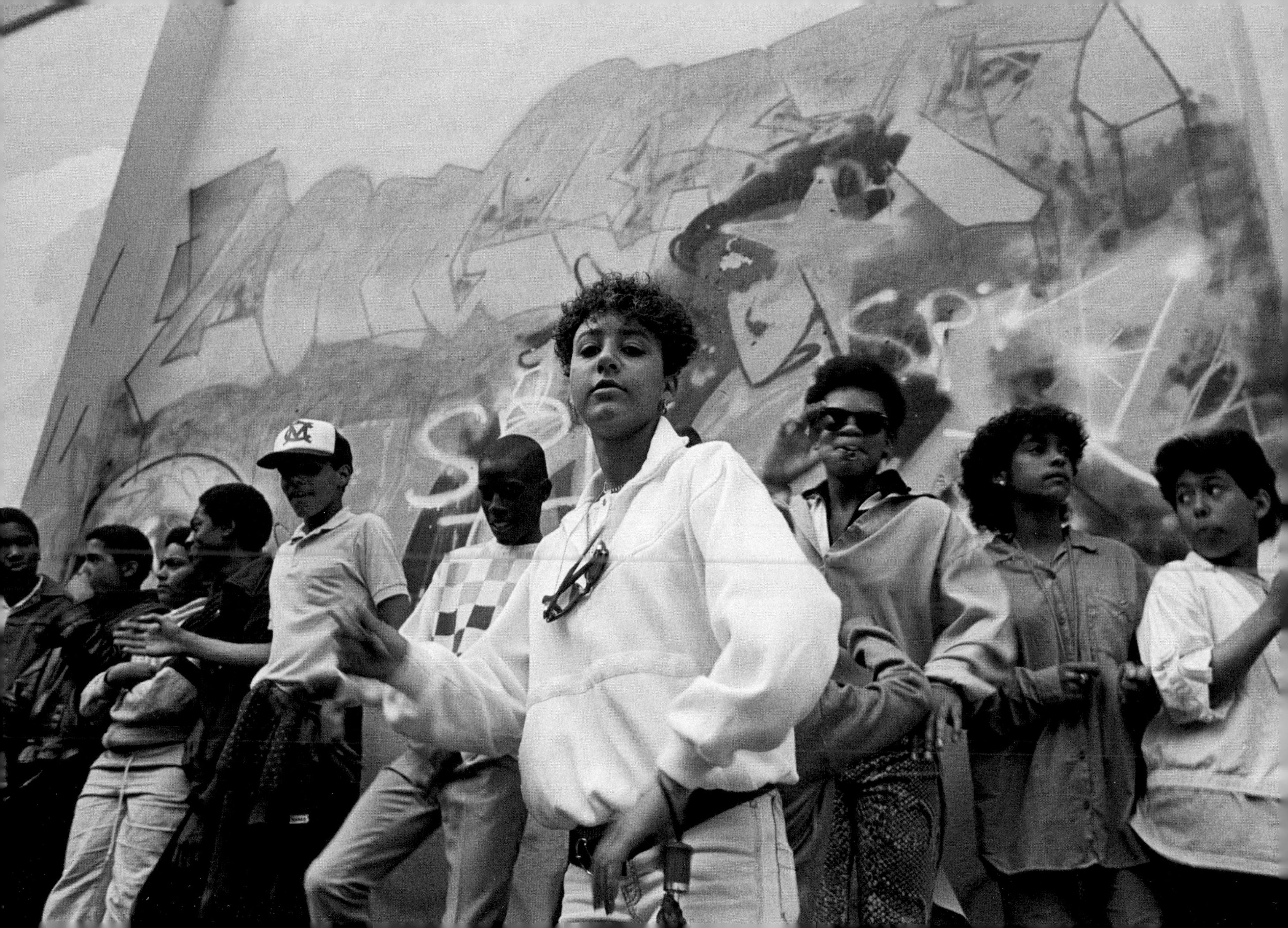

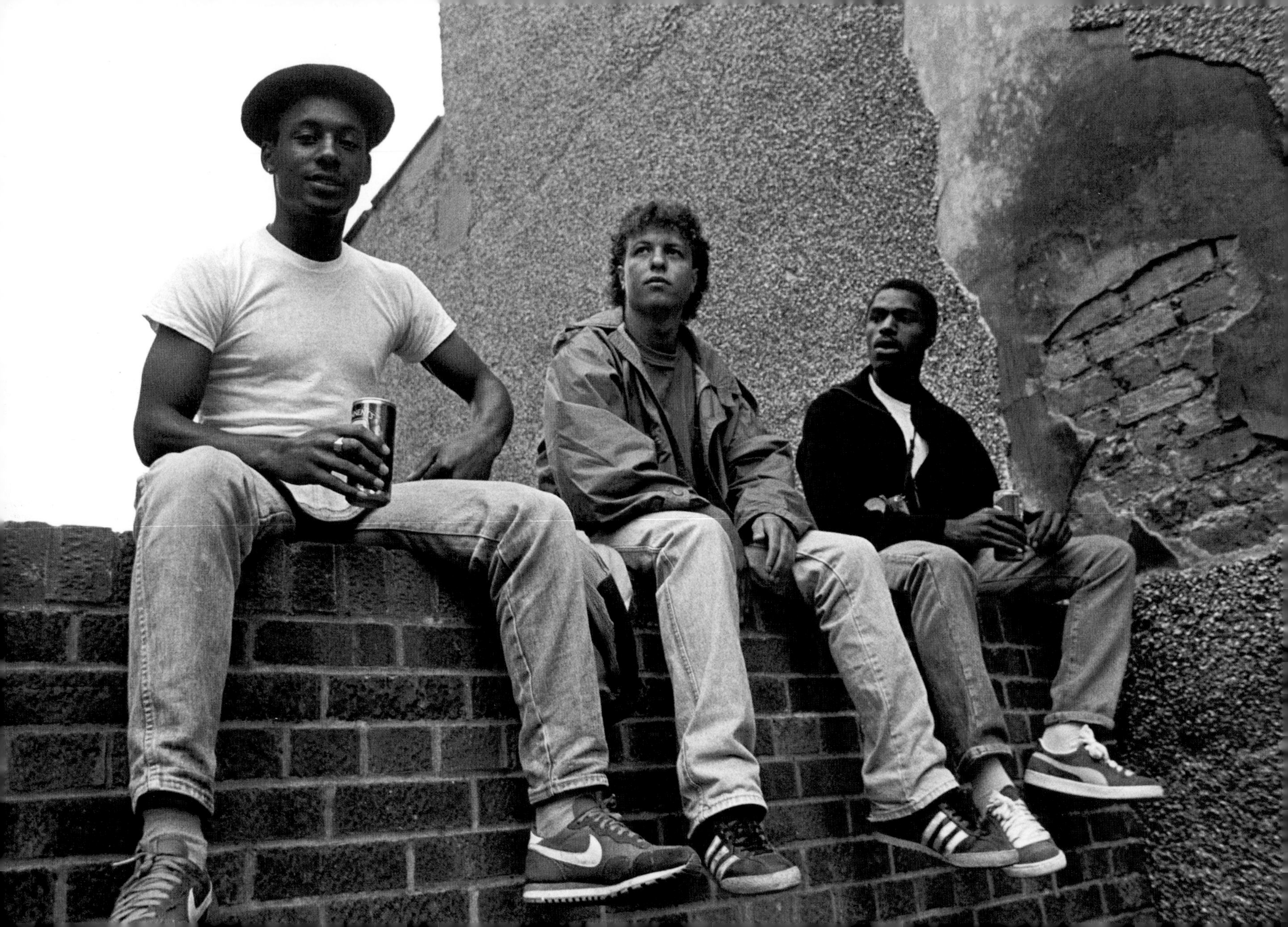

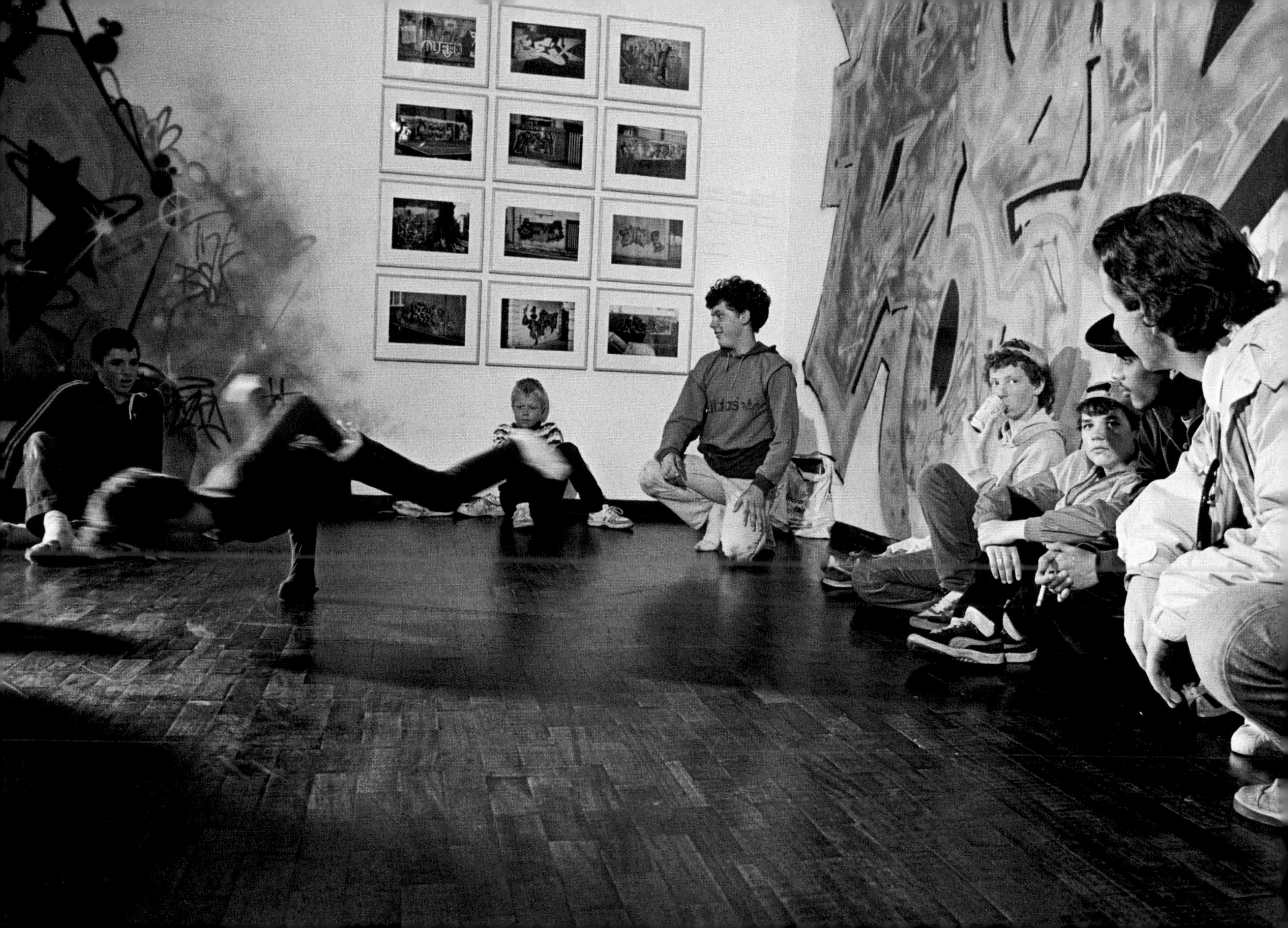

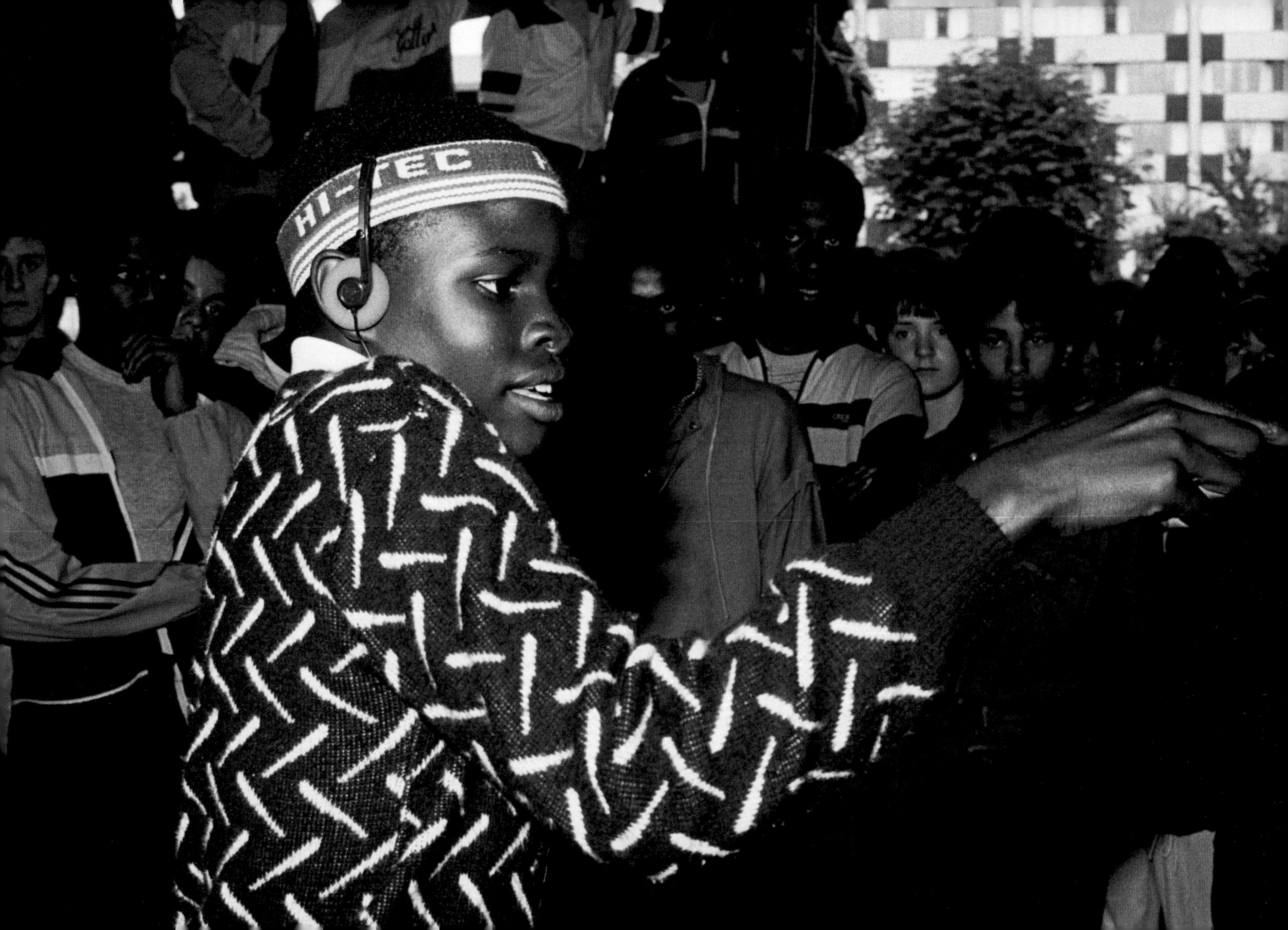

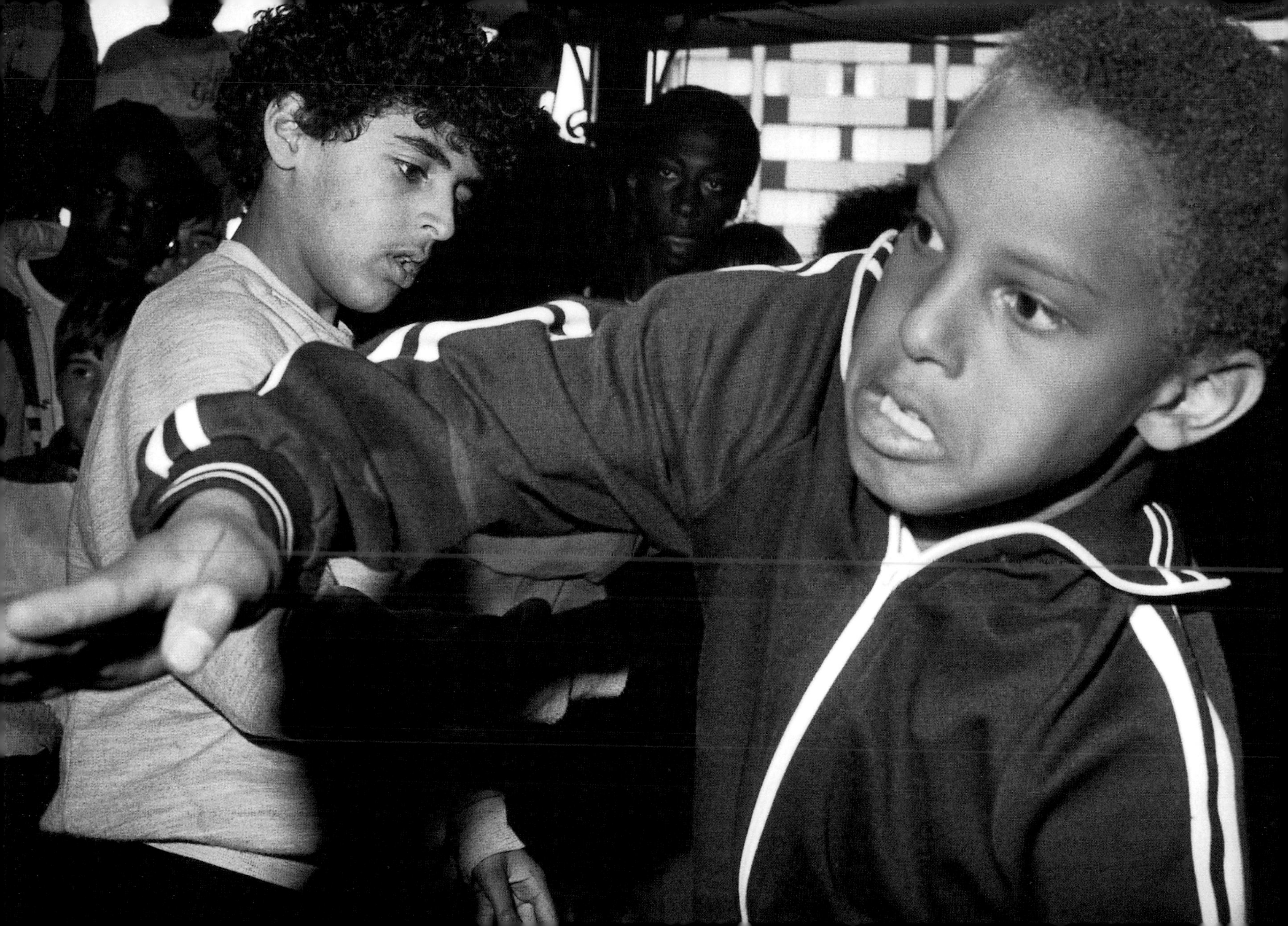

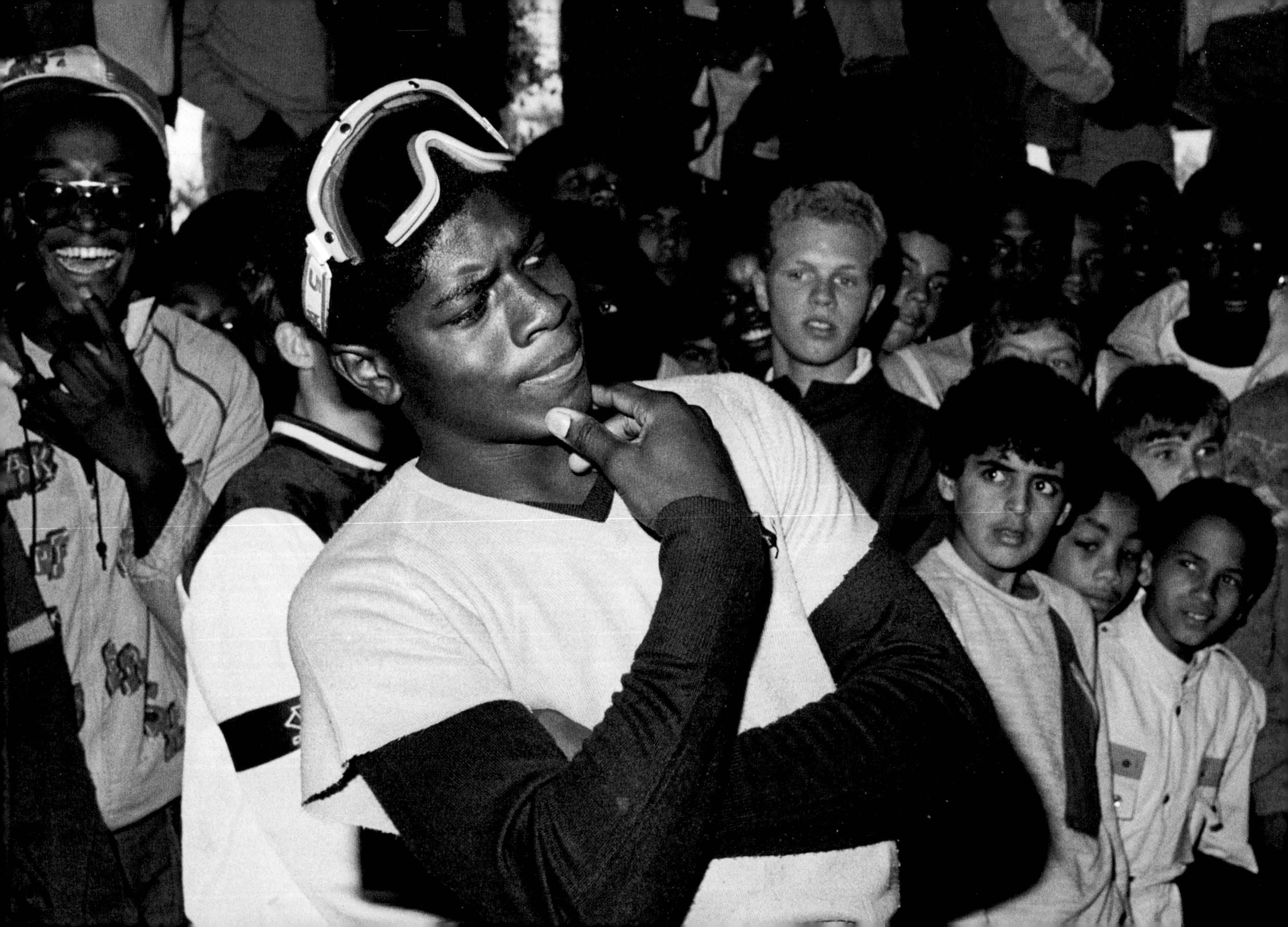

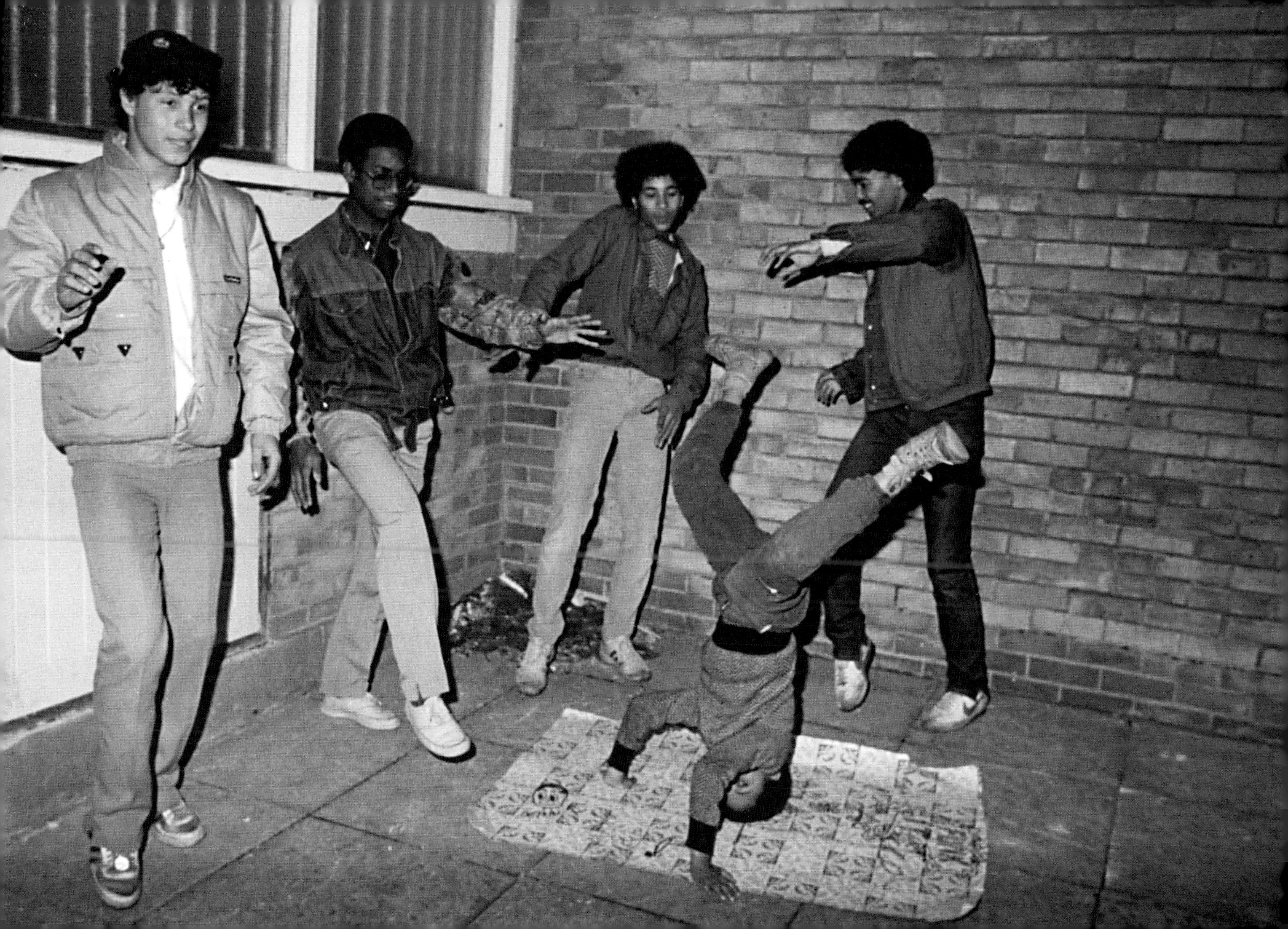

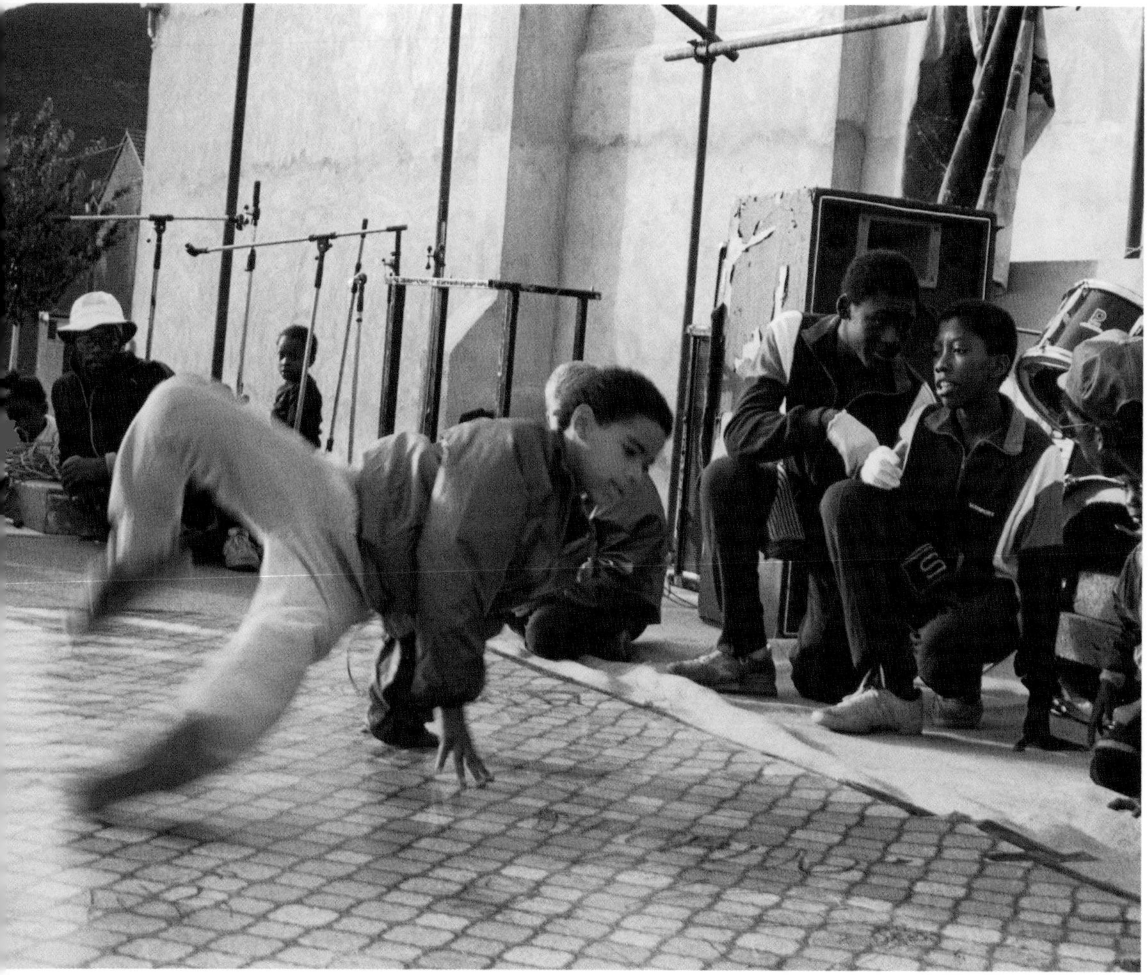

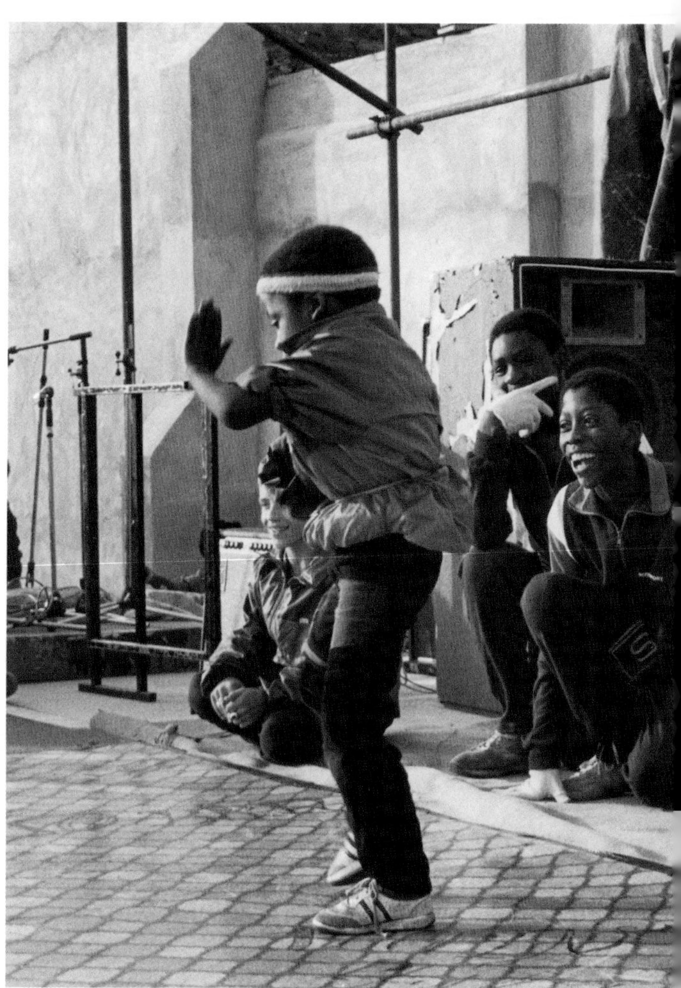

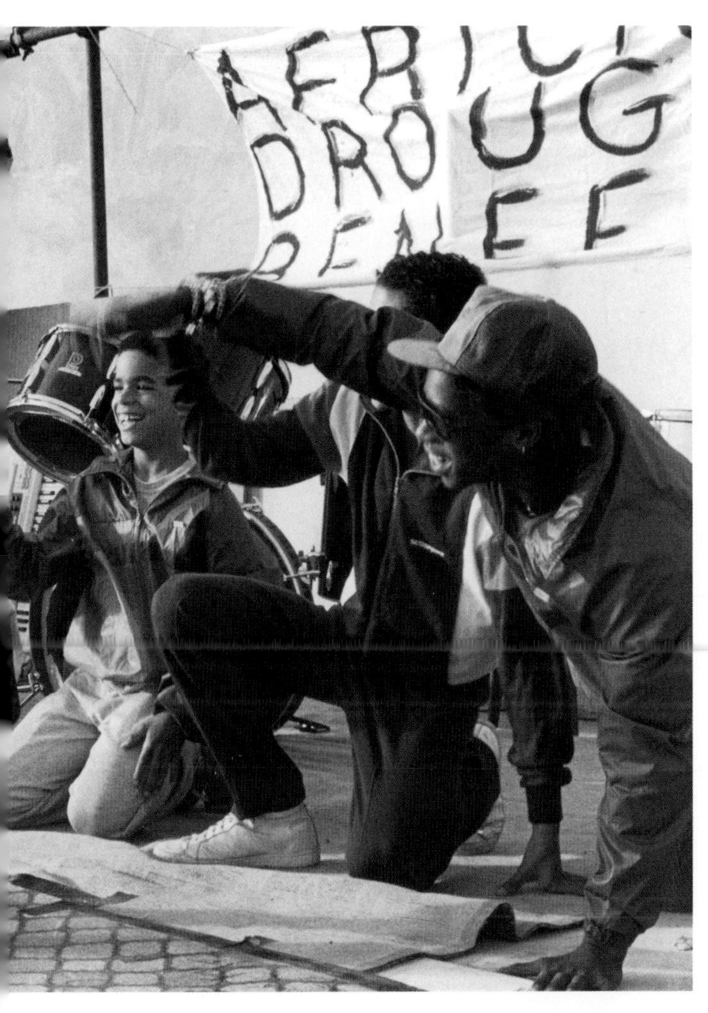
AFRIC
DROUG
RELIEF

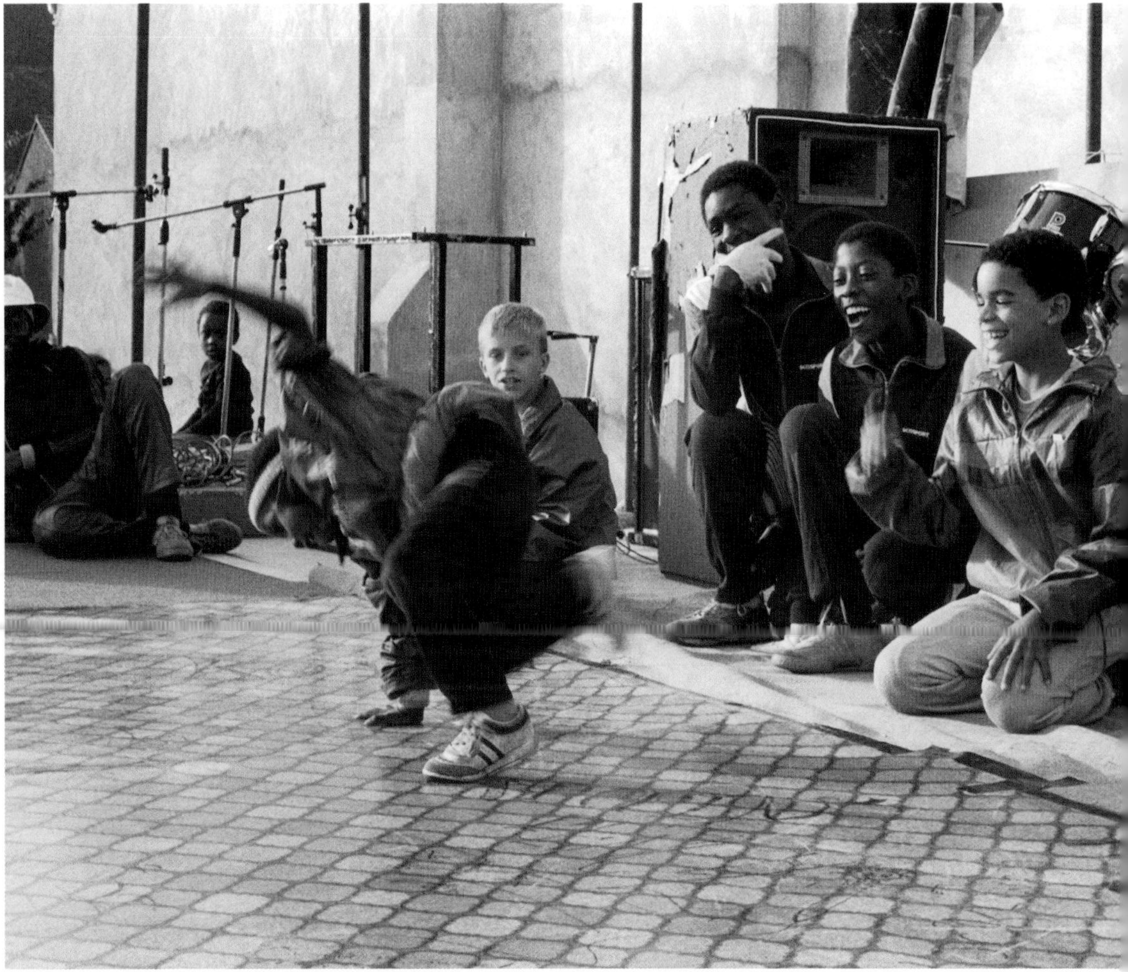

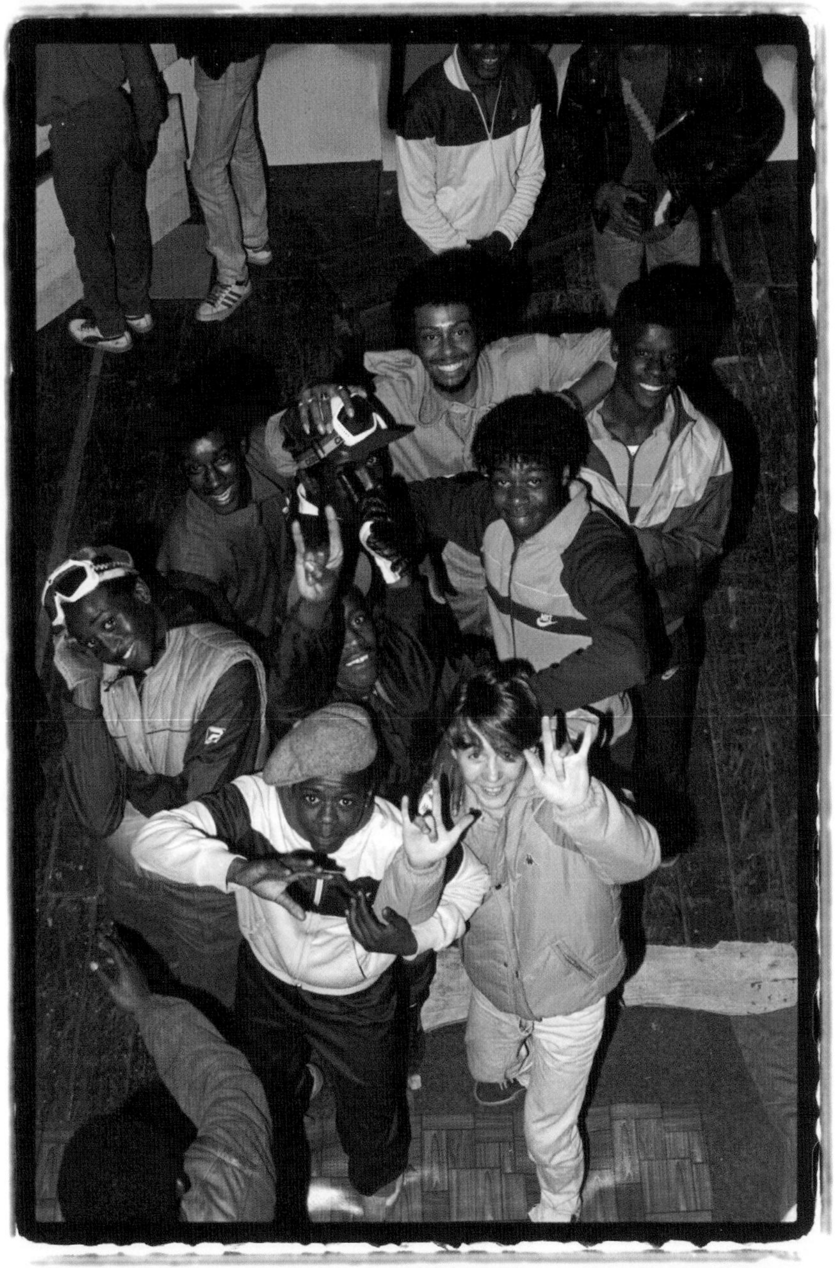

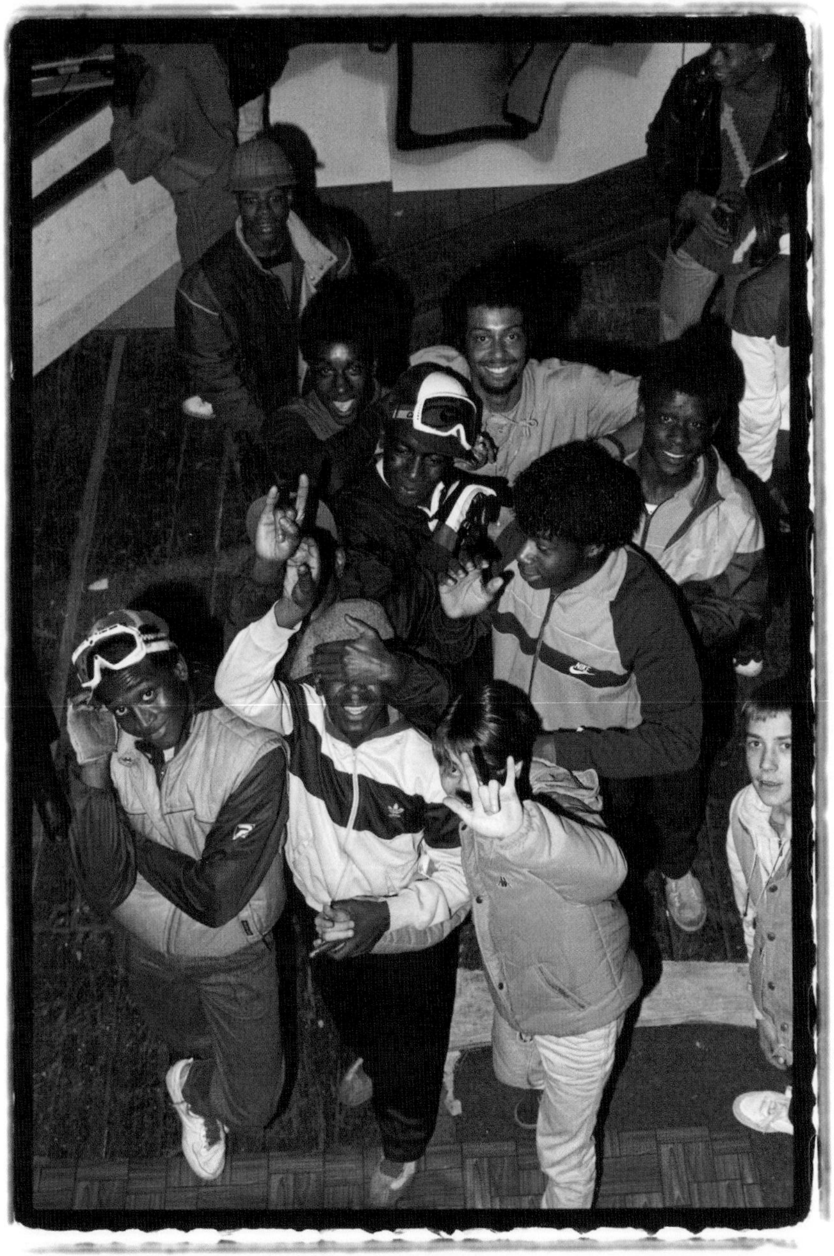

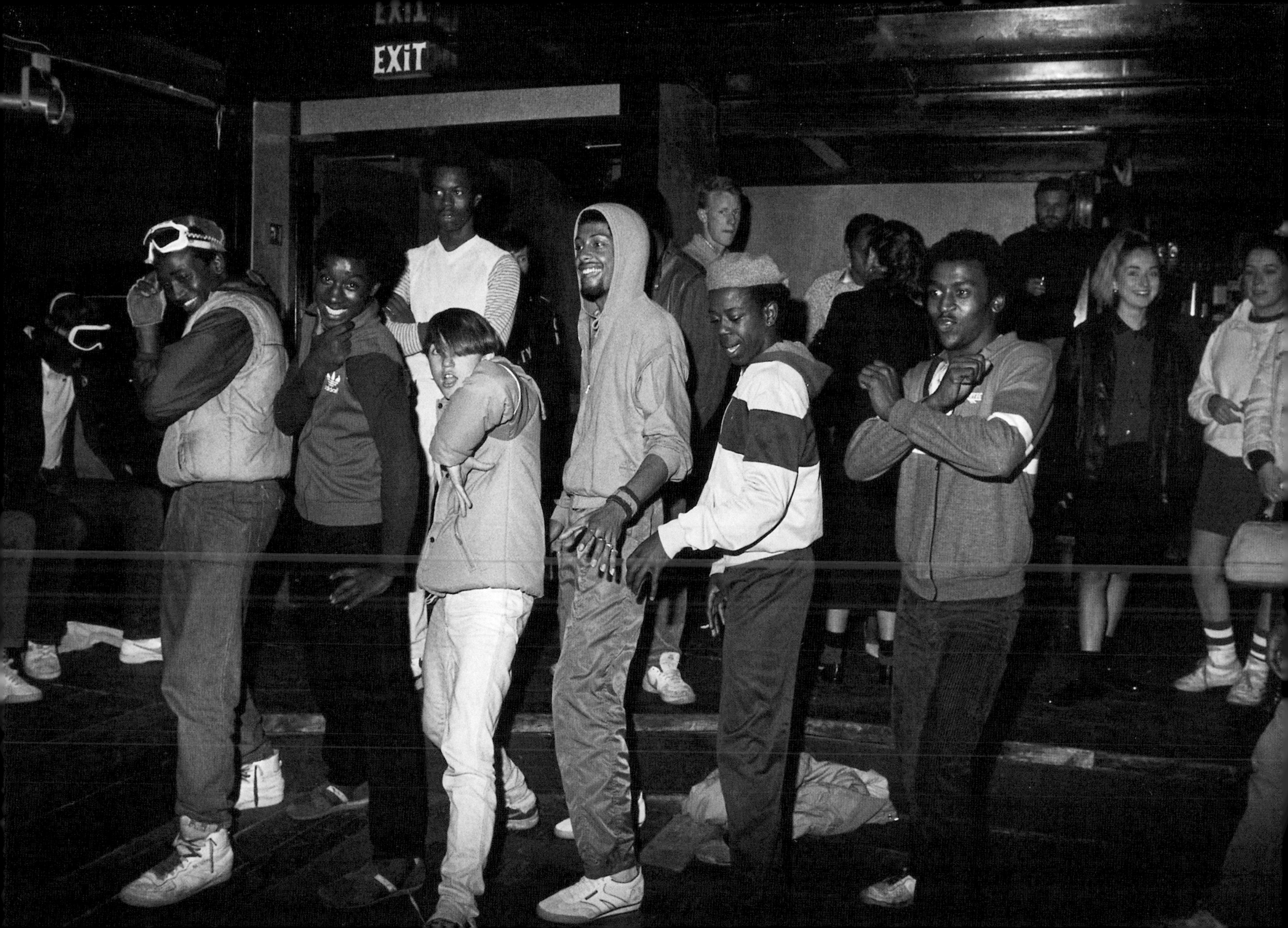
EXIT

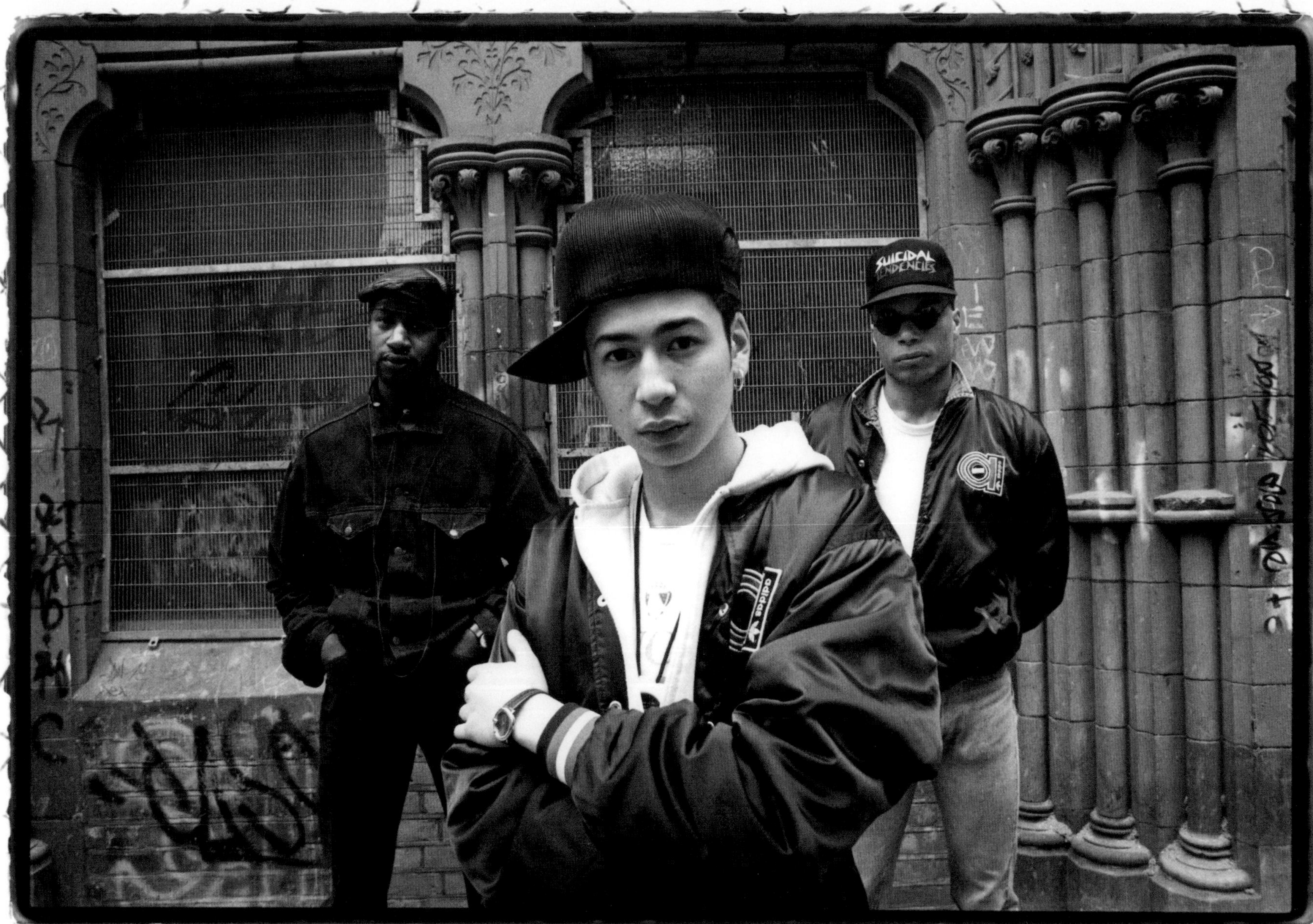

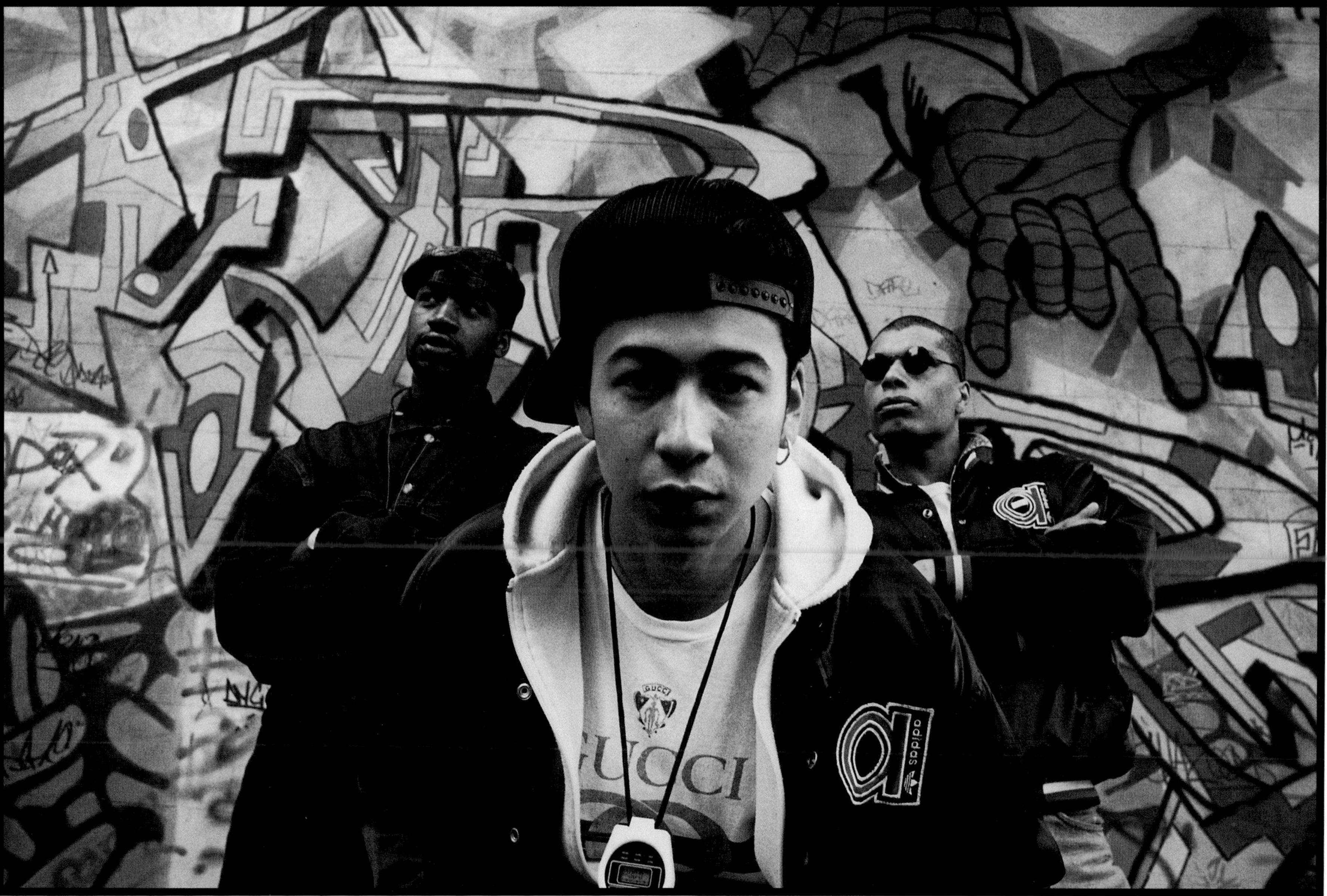

hit electro pop
falklands war
combat rock
radio clash
mix tapes
sign on Tuesdays
new wave/reggae/ska/
punk
7 electro hip hop/garage
house
dug out club
metal box
miners strike
futura 2000
sean and daze
rock steady crew
community service
walter negro & nicky
testo
ashton gate 8...
africa islam
fab five freddy
redhouse jam
brim/bio/mode2/goldie
mark roy r.i.p
special k's

adam & eve
mark stewart & the mafia
special brew
red leb
c.i.a in afghanistan
iran contra scandal
no religion
groove records
revolver
flyers
letraset
quickmixing
city rockers/Fbi/ud4
football tradgedy
£40 a week
fearless
oasis pa
ira/uda
wildstyle
new trainers
hiring generators
selling beer
buying import le...

shit electro pop
falklands war
combat rock
radio clash
mix tapes
sign on Tuesdays
new wave/reggae/ska/punk
/electro hip hop/garage house
metal box
futura 2000
rock steady crew
j walter negro & nicky tesco
africa islam
fab five freddy
dug out club
miners strikes
thatcher's britain
sean and daze
carplan paint
community service
stencil art
ashton gate 8
ajax blues
realistic mixer
redhouse jam
brim/bio/mode2/goldie
mark key r.i.p
special k's

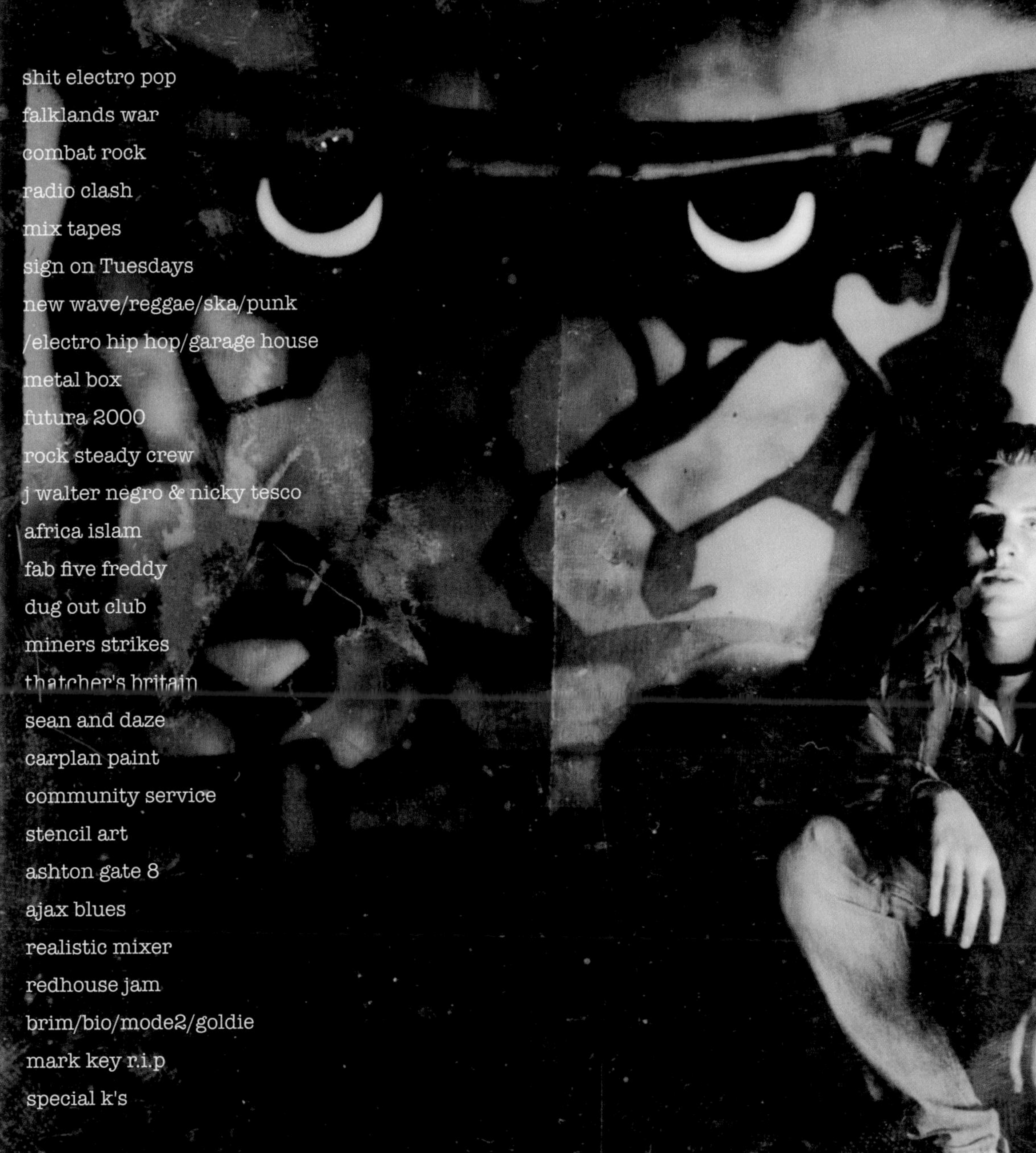

adam & eve
mark stewart & the mafia
special brew
red leb
c.i.a in afghanistan
iran contra scandal
no religion
groove records
revolver
flyers
letraset
photocopy shops
beezer
fearless 4
dug out club eternity
me & willi wee
dj box
quickmixing
city rockers/fbi/ud4
football tradgedy
£40 a week
oasis pa
ira/uda
wildstyle
new trainers
hiring generators
selling beer
buying import 12s

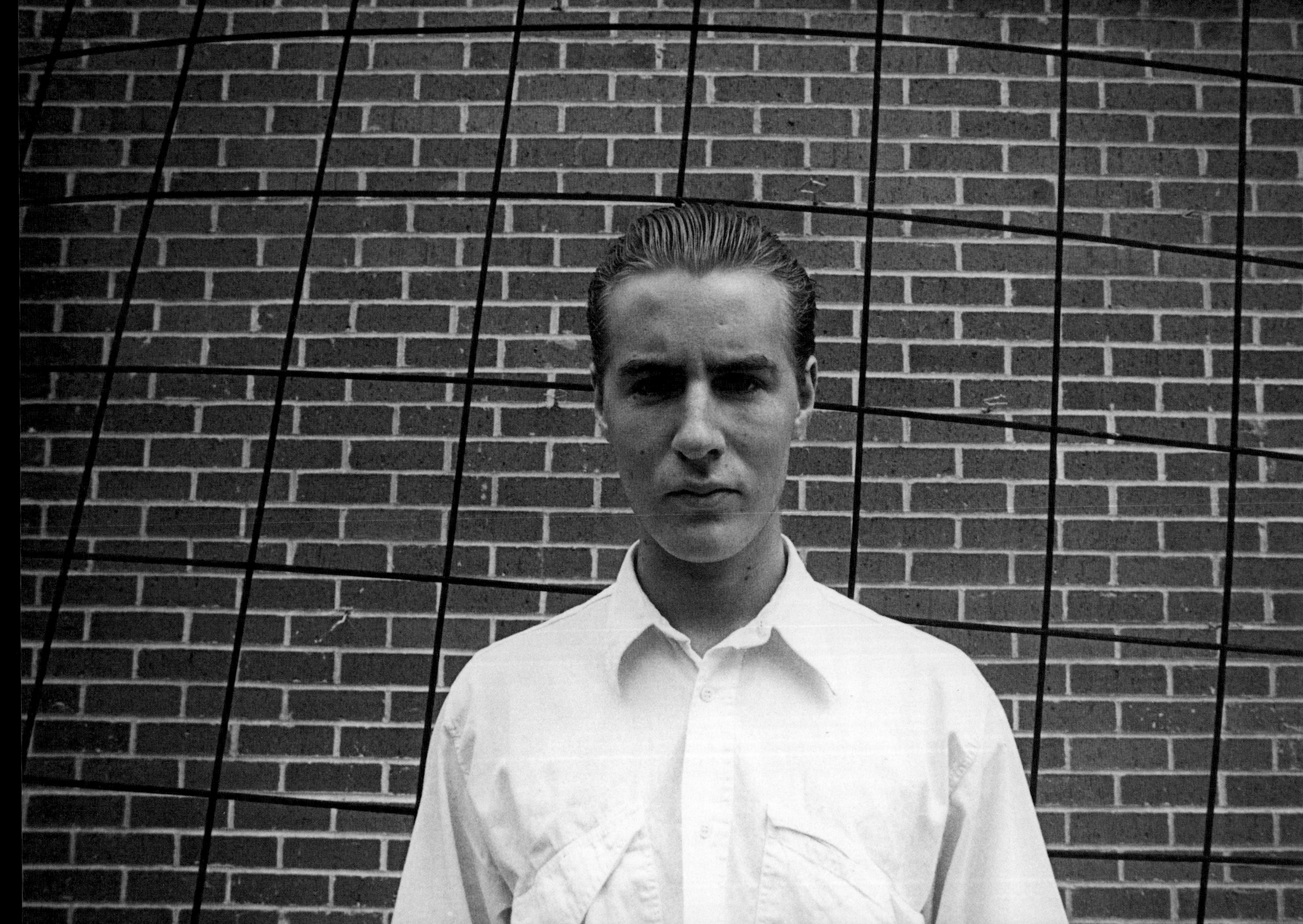

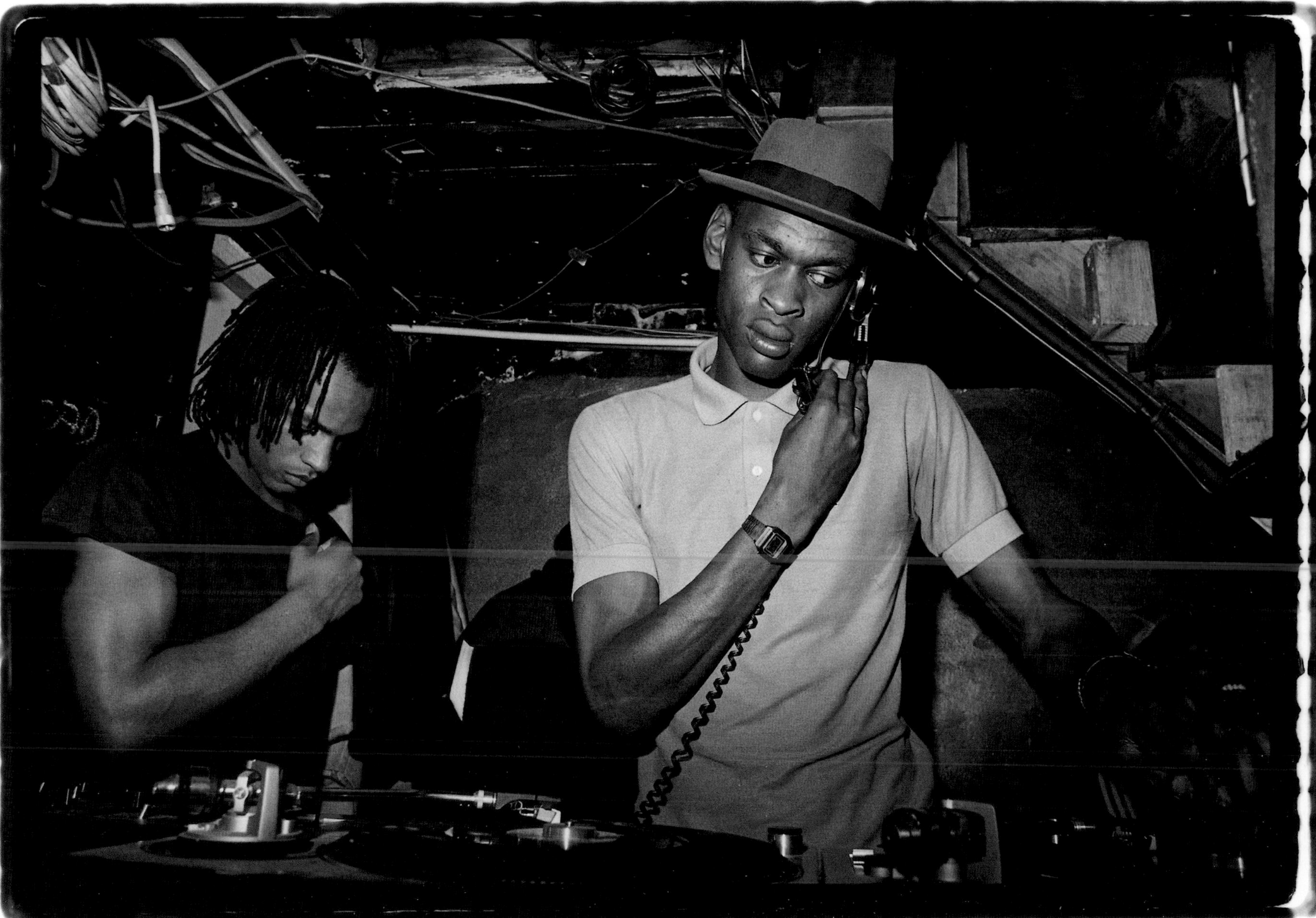

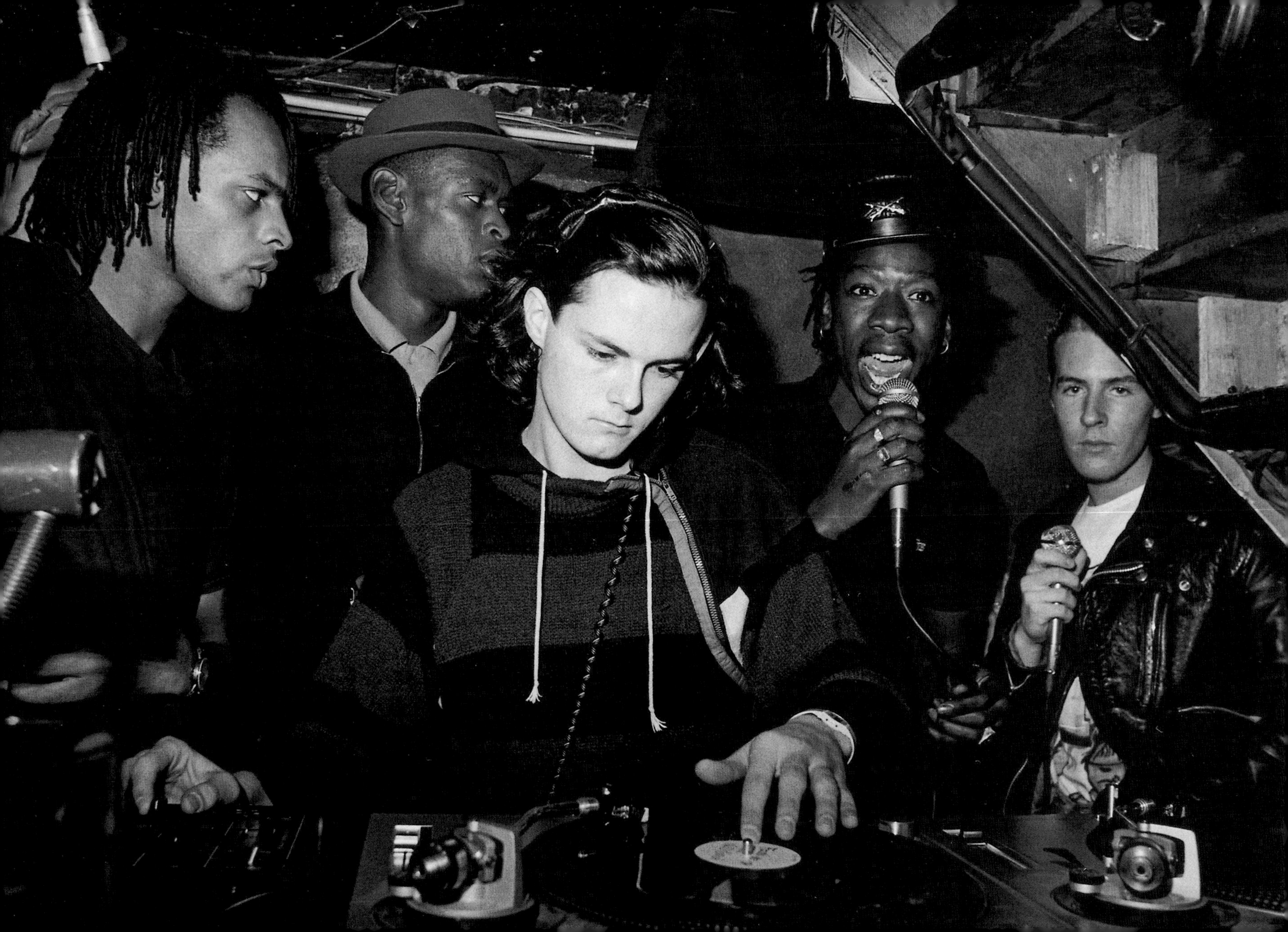

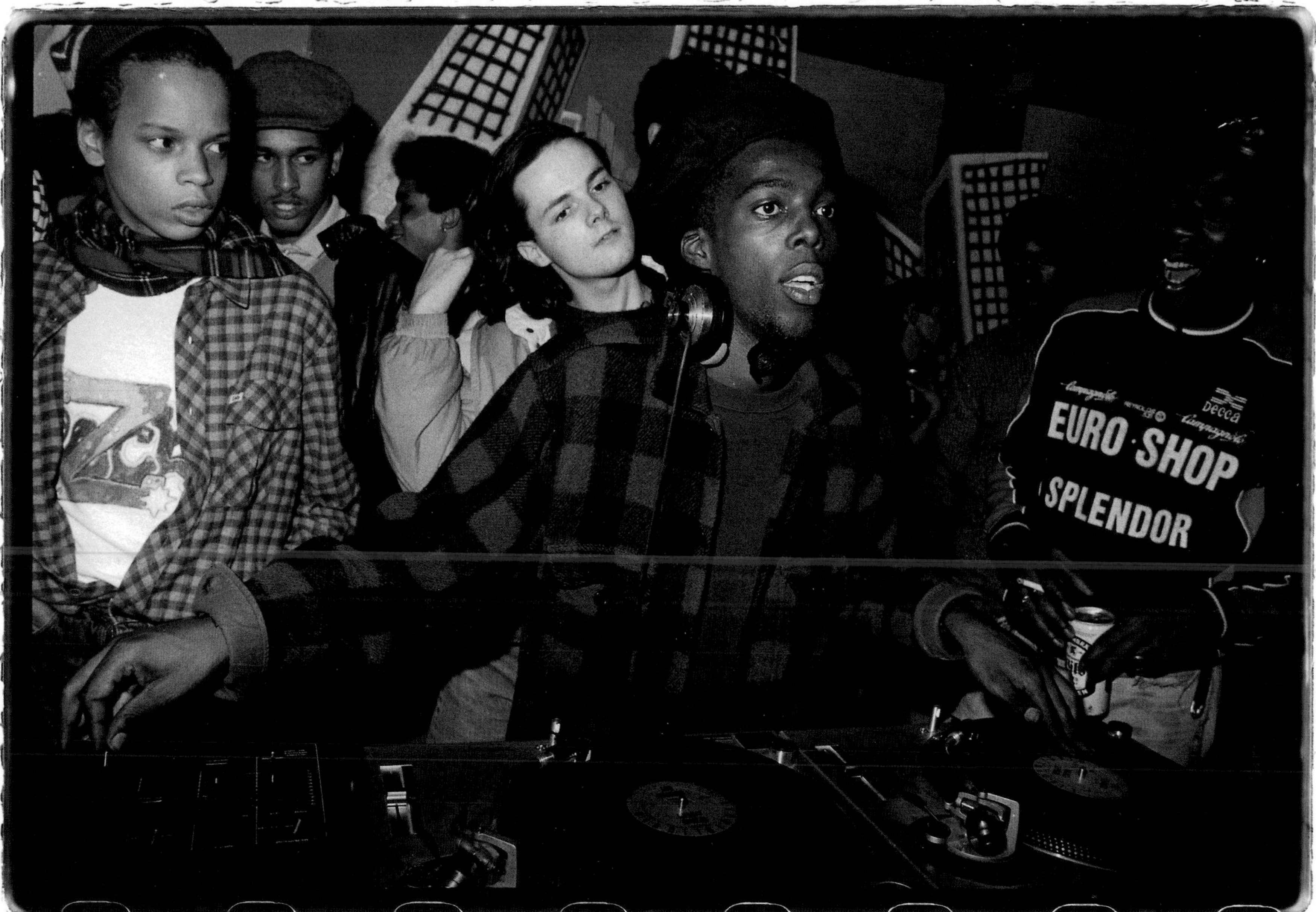

EURO·SHOP
SPLENDOR

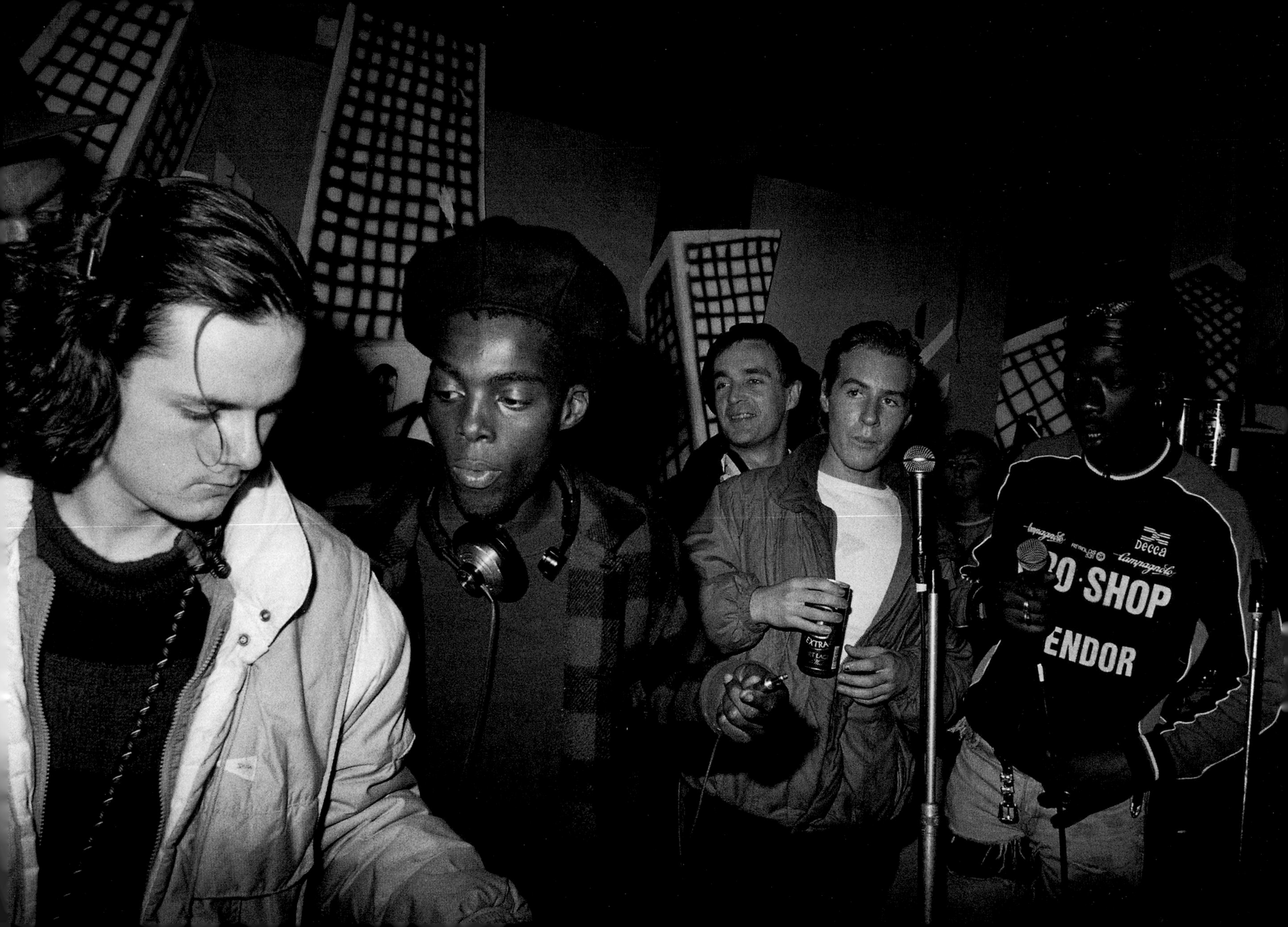

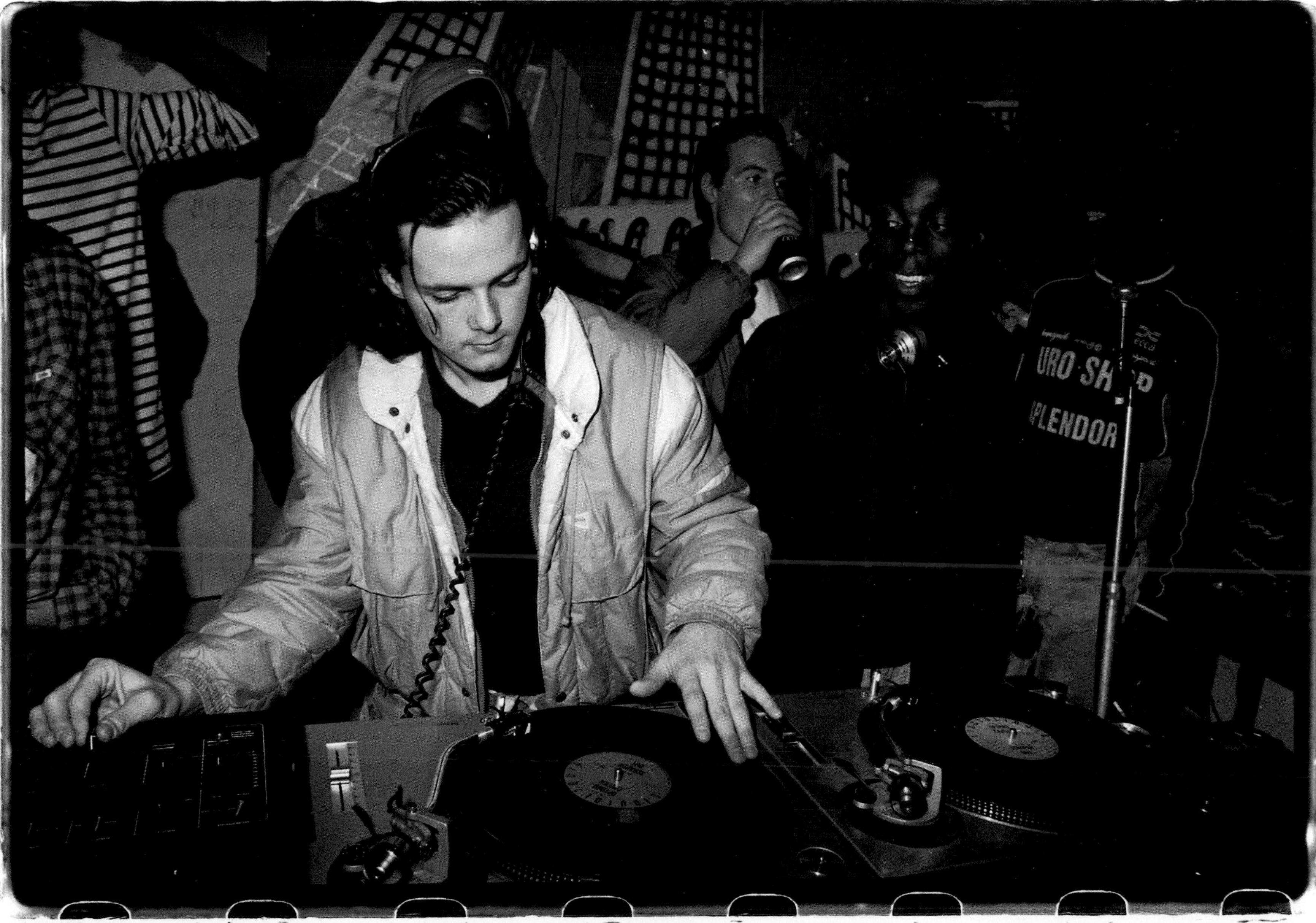

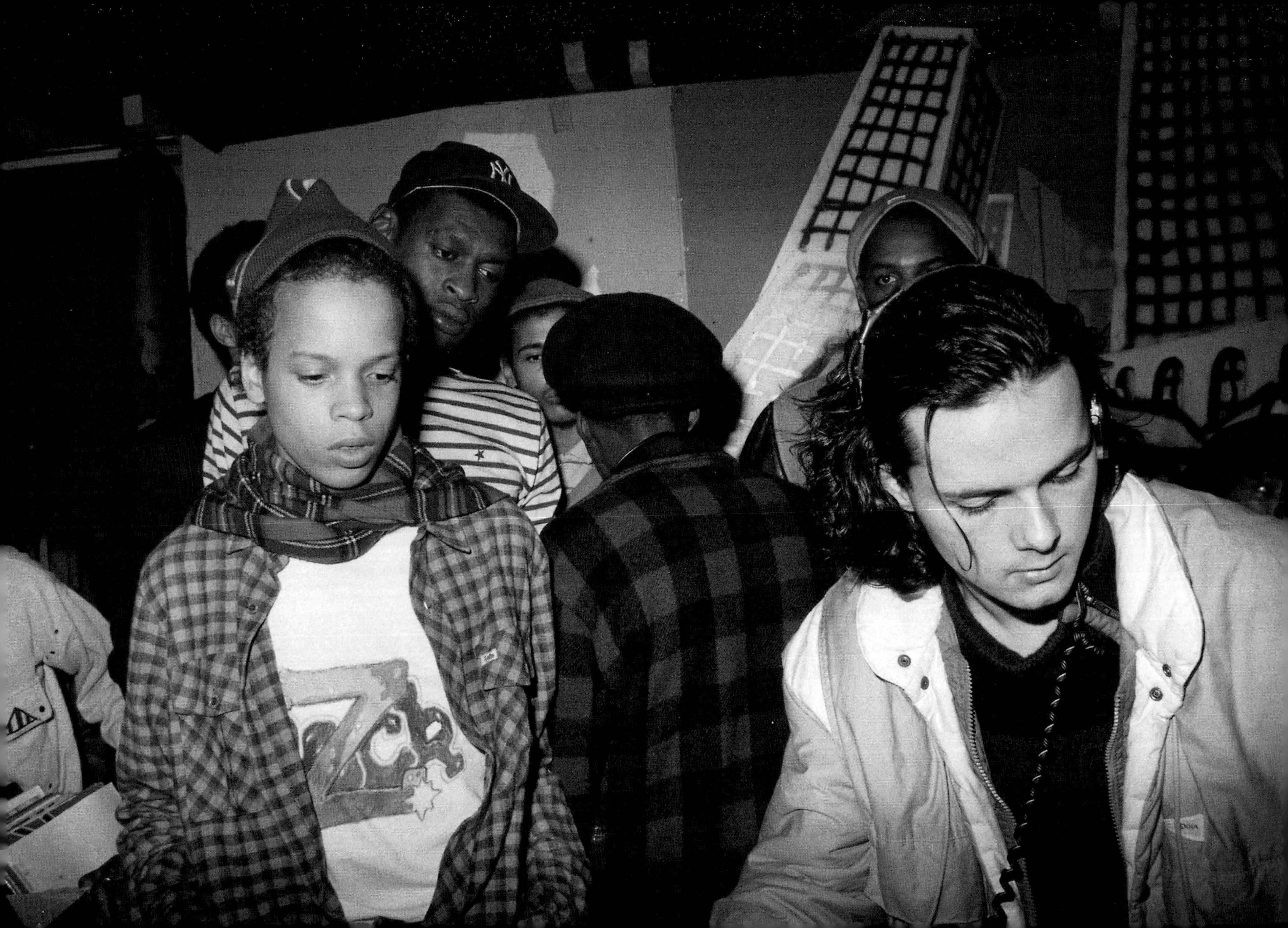

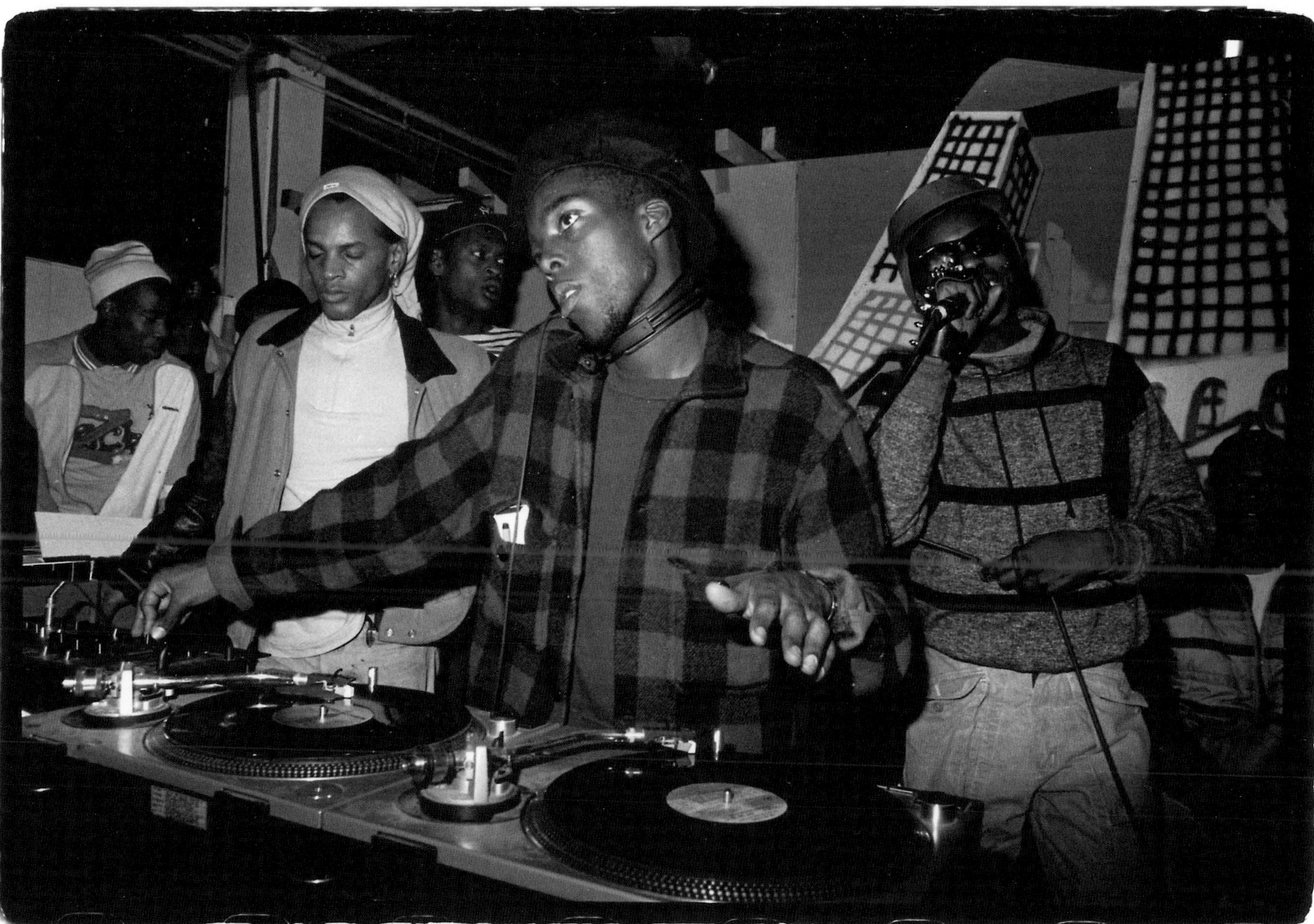

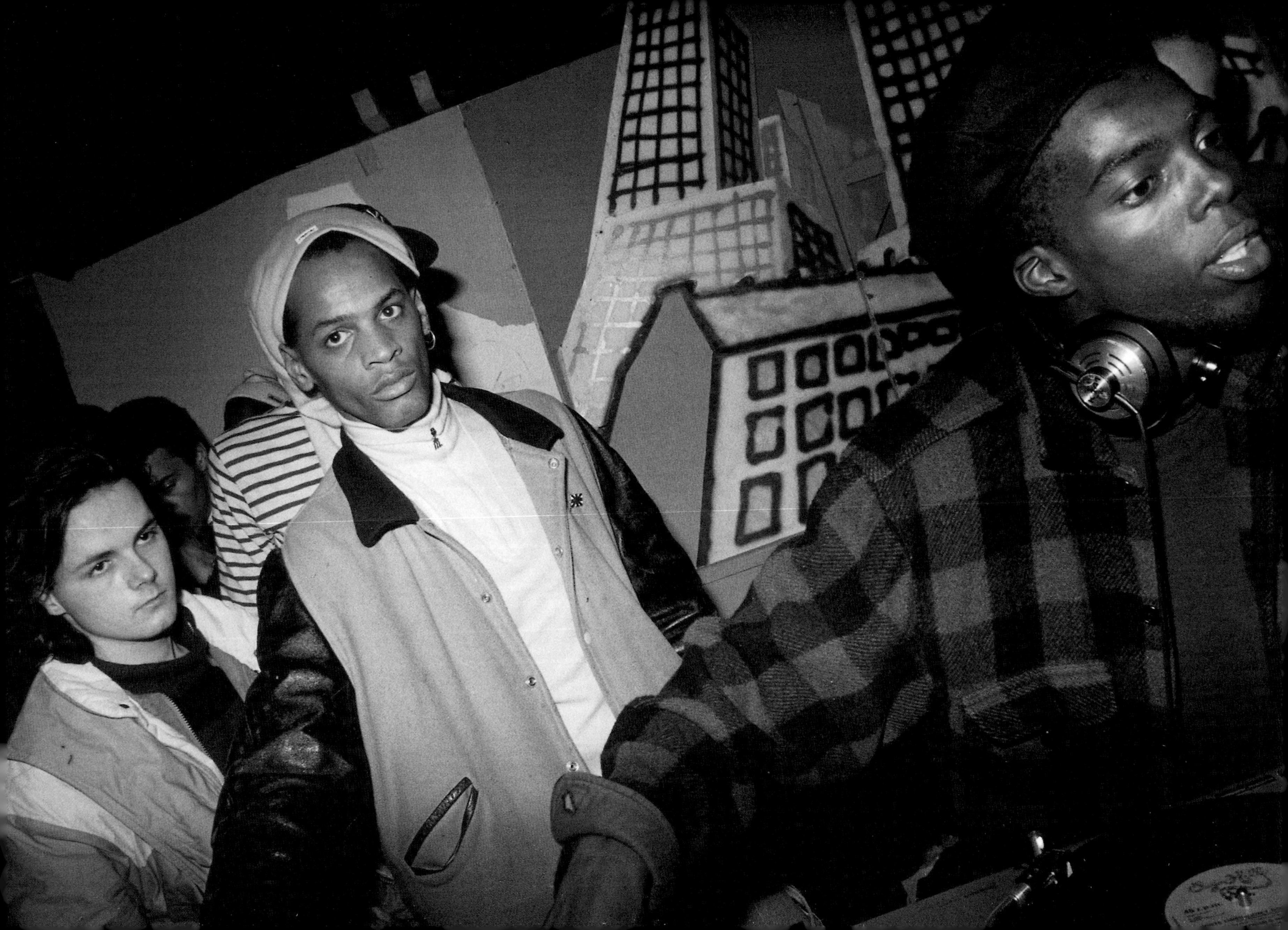

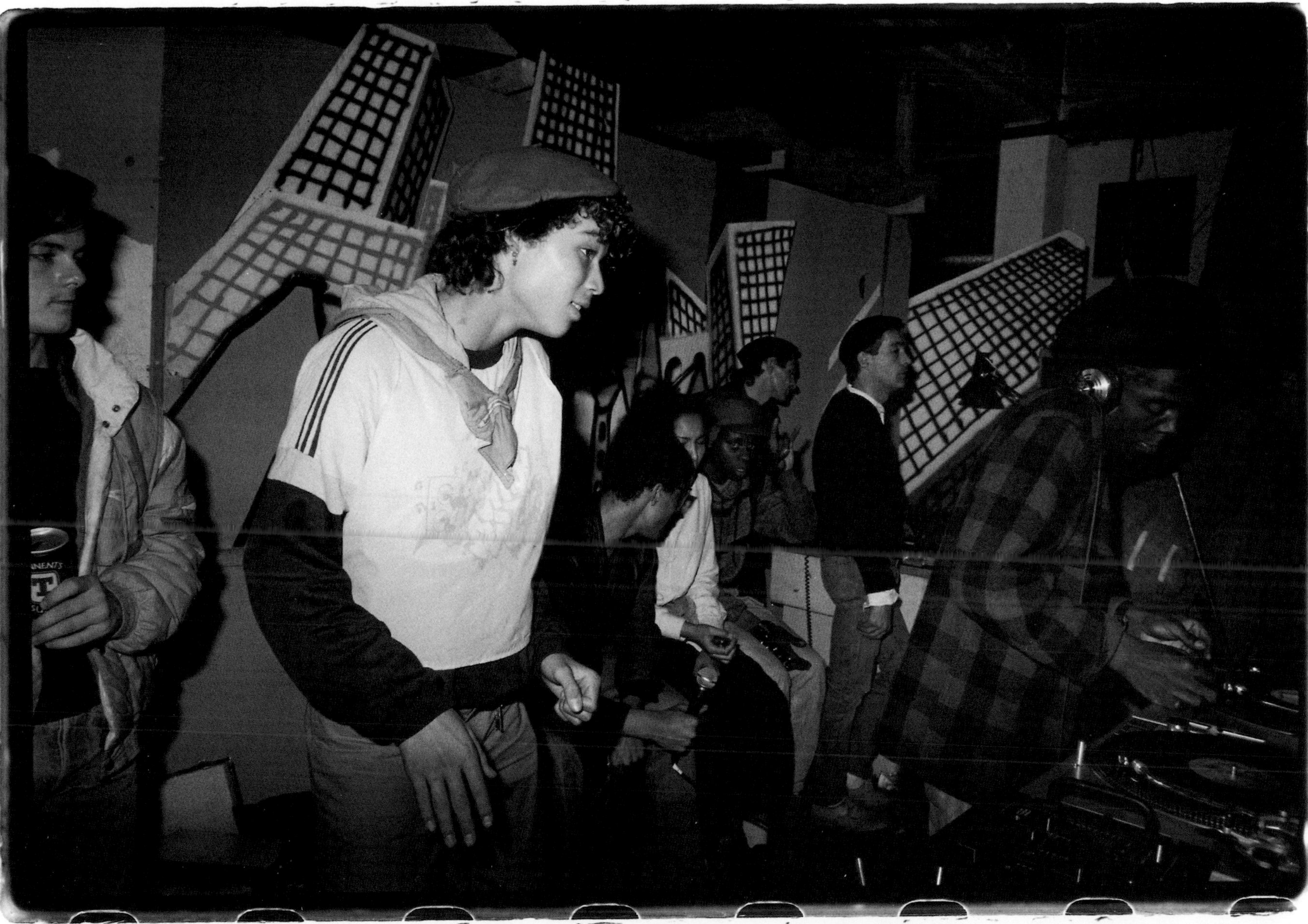

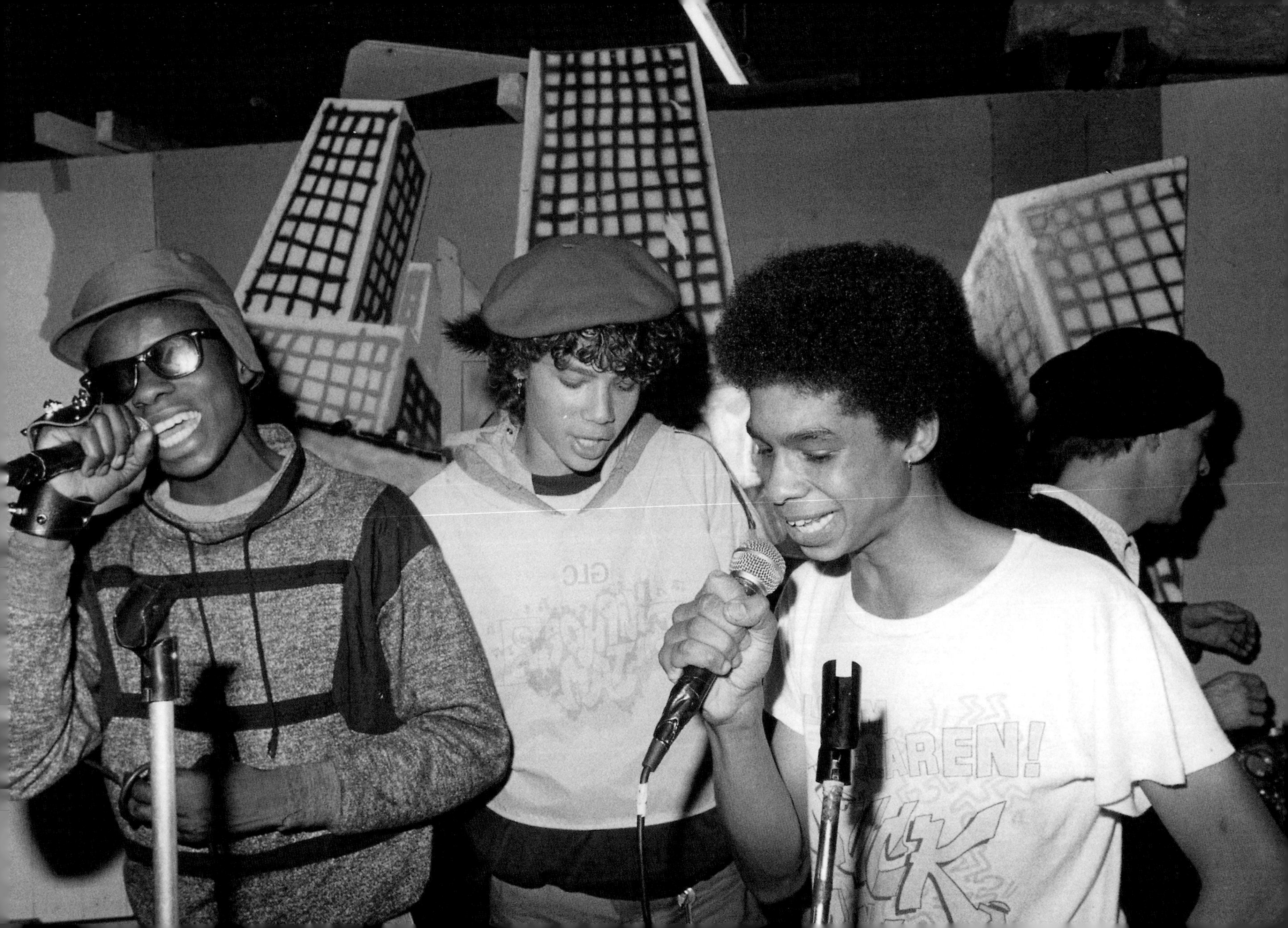

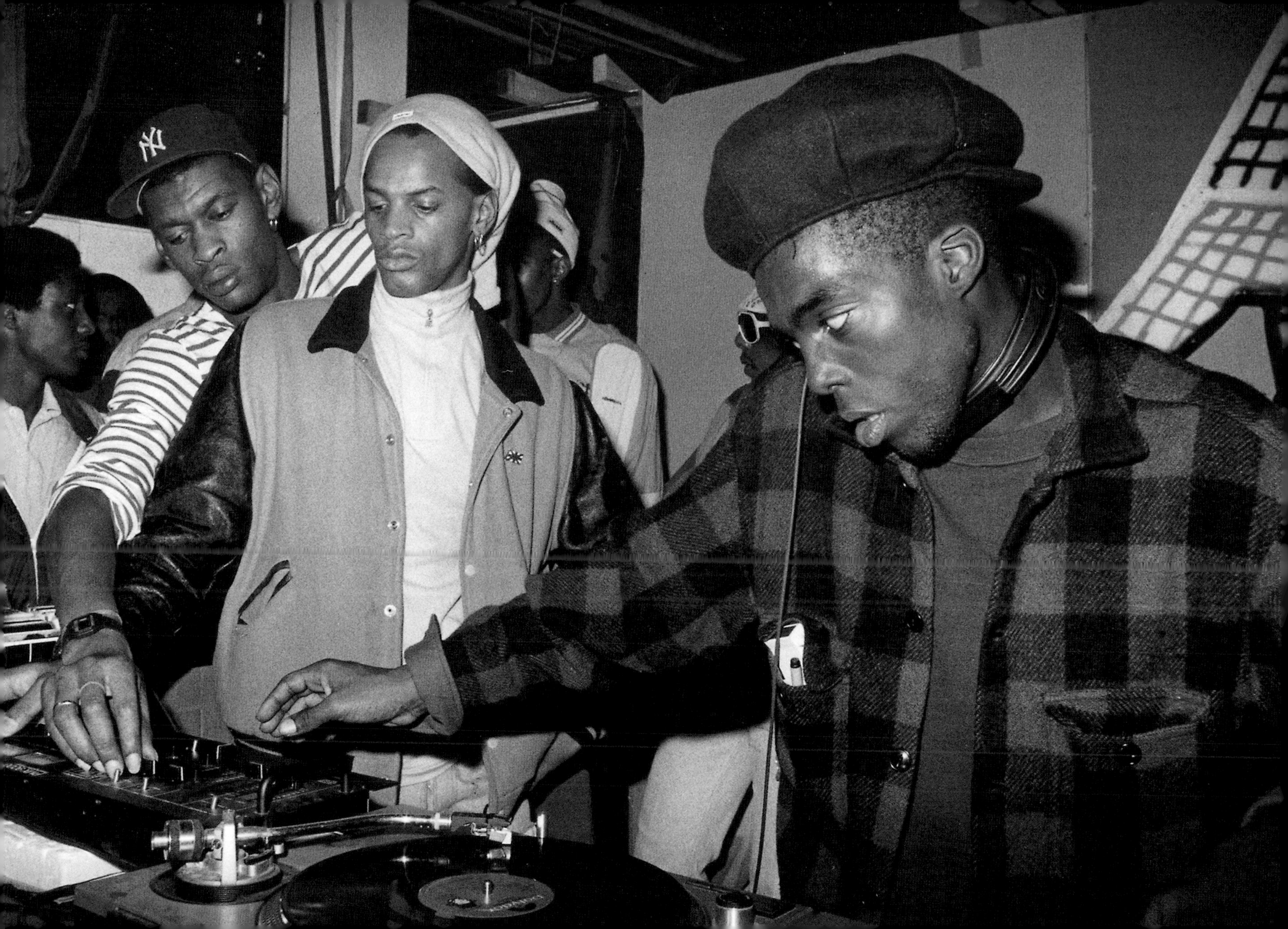

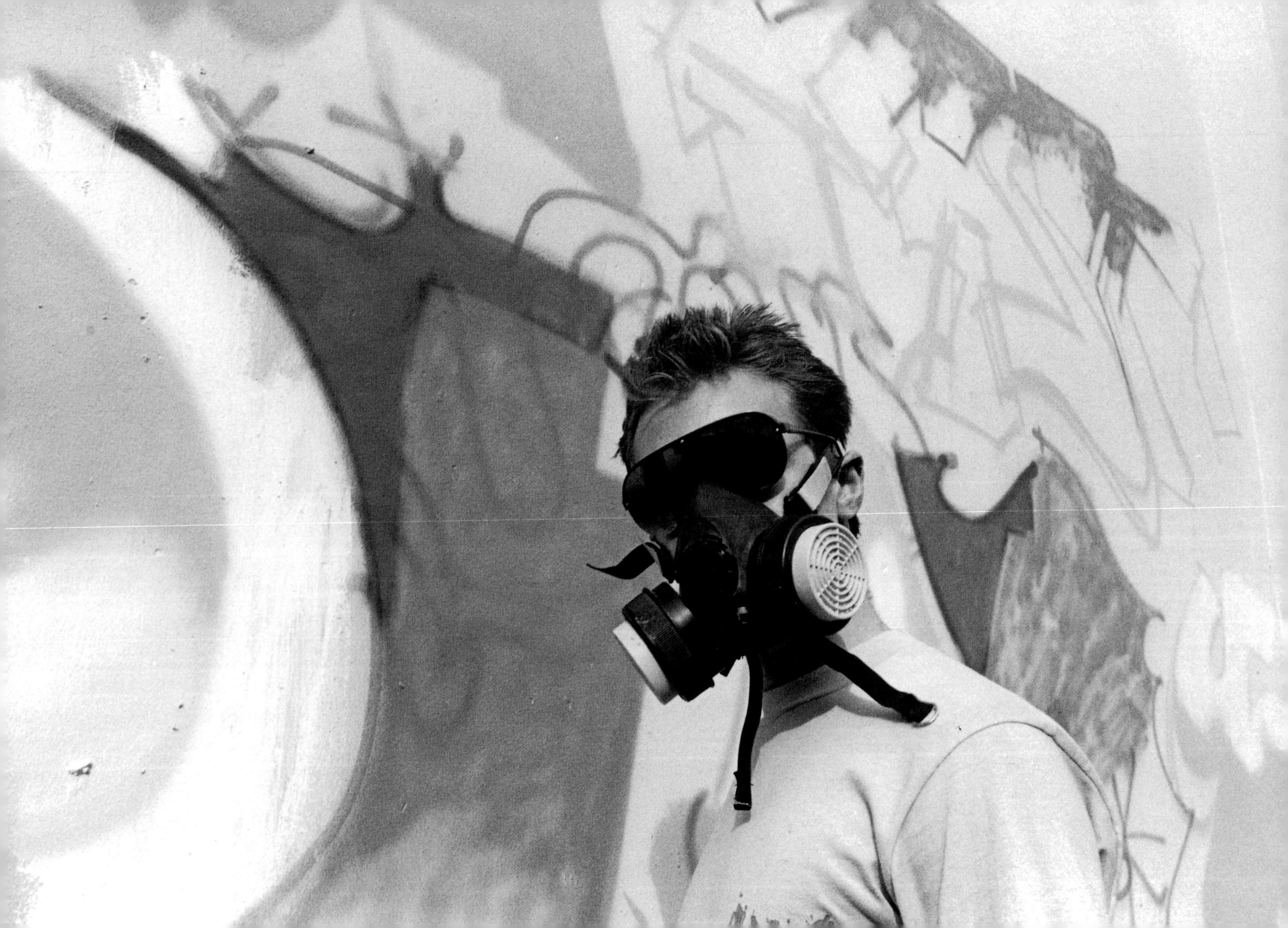

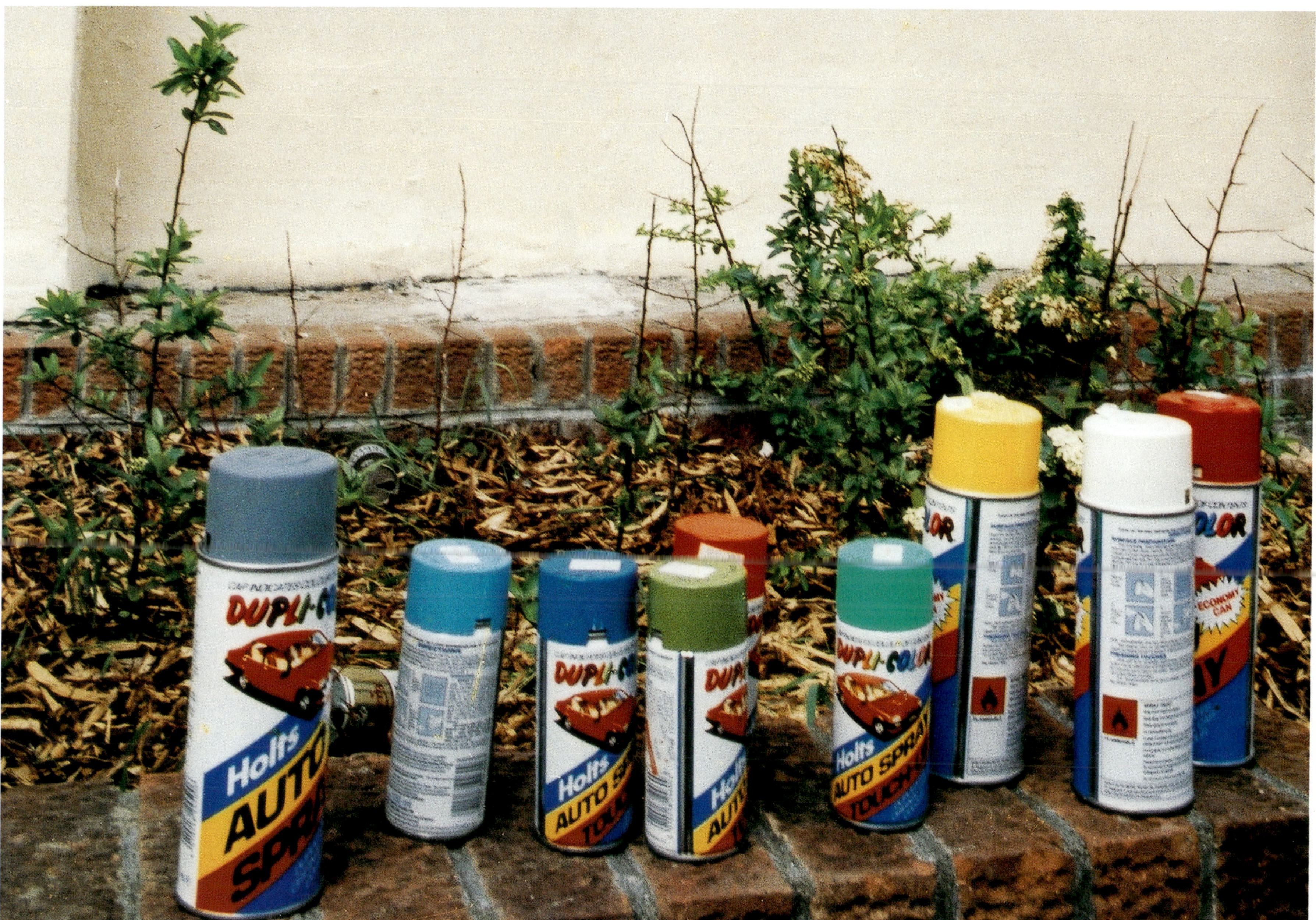

DUPLI-COLOR
Holts
AUTO SPRAY
DUPLI-COLOR
Holts
AUTO SPRAY
TOUCH
Holts
AUTO SPRAY
TOUCH
DUPLI-COLOR
ECONOMY CAN
ECONOMY CAN

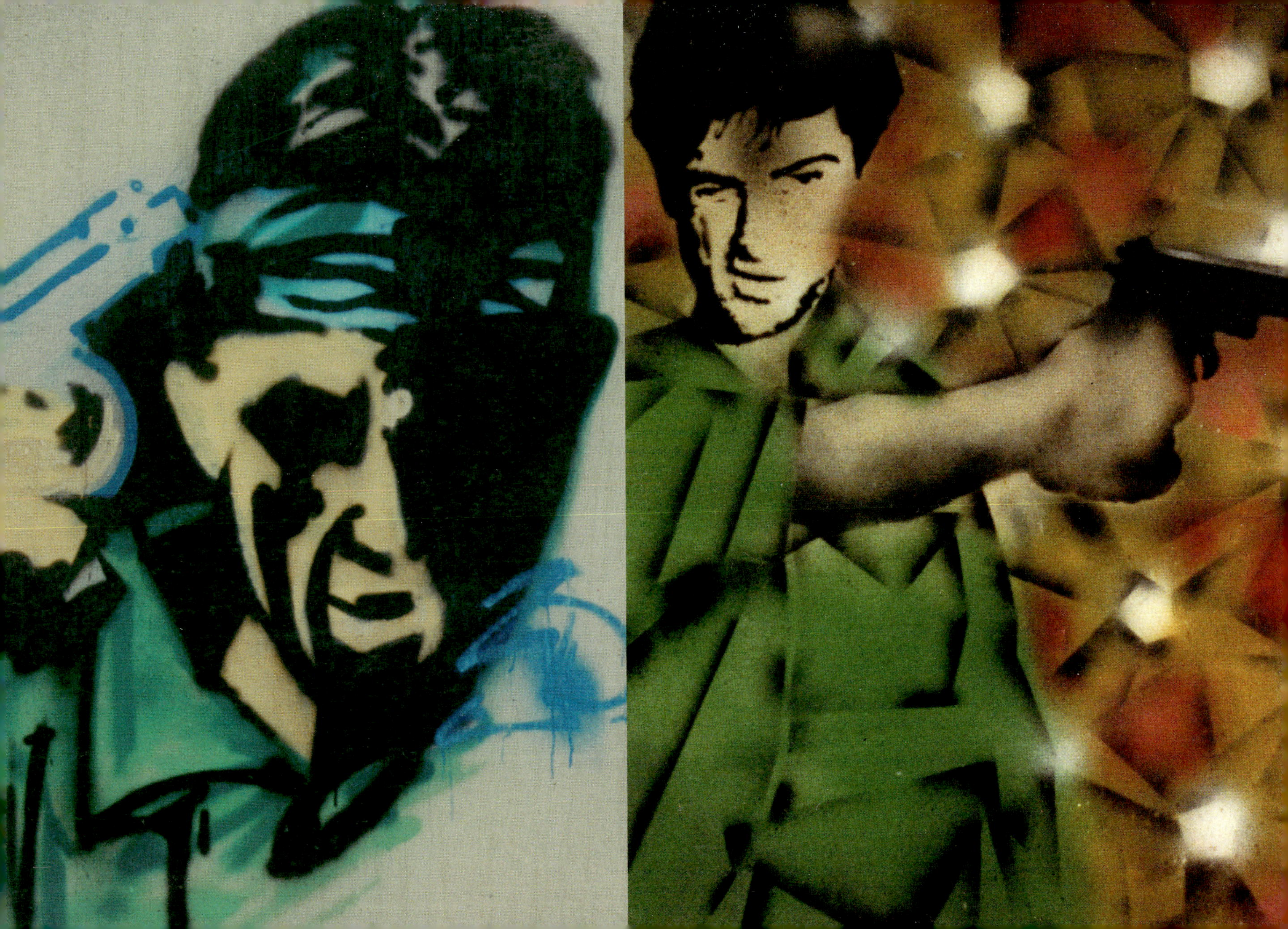

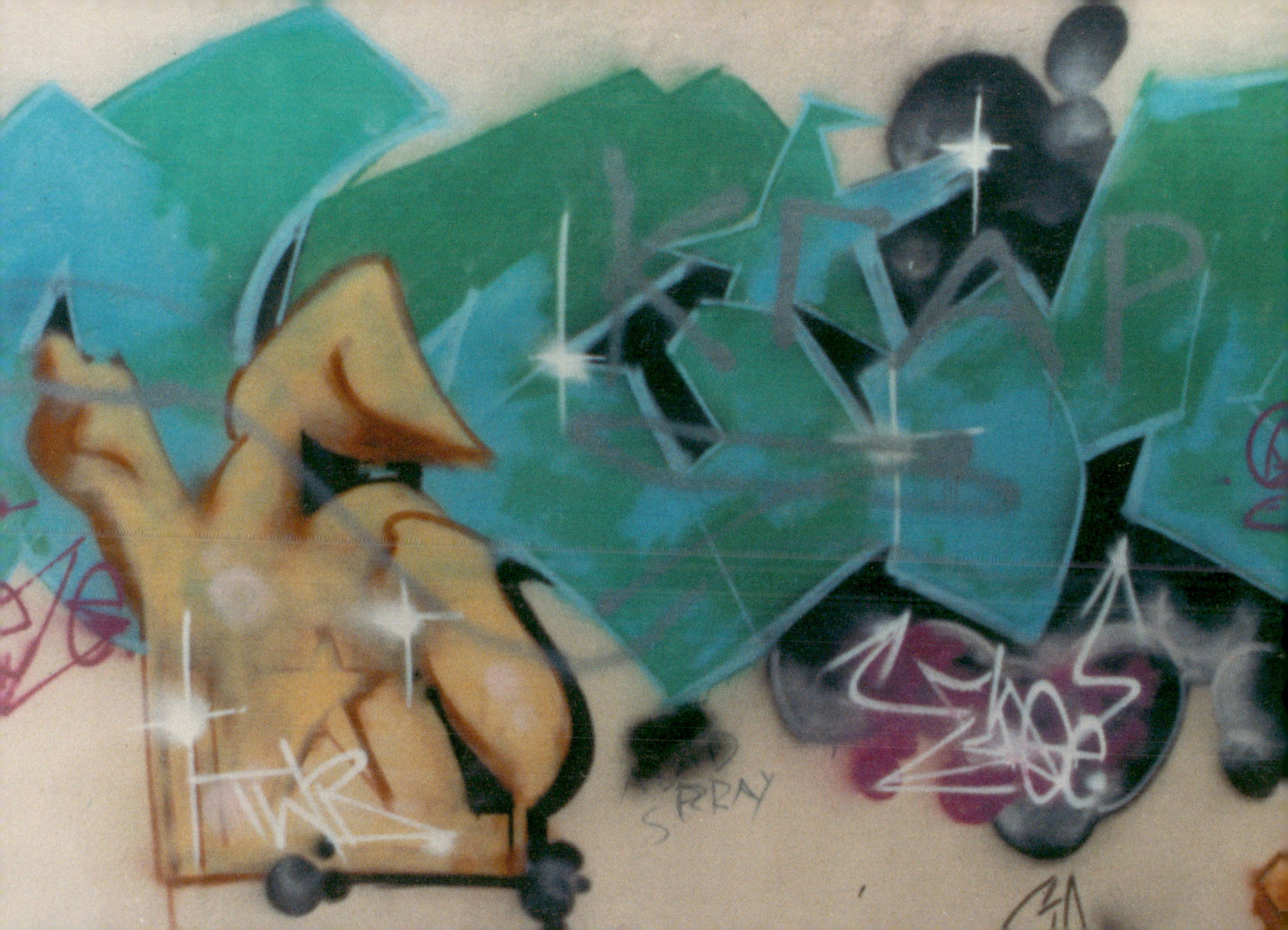

SPRAY

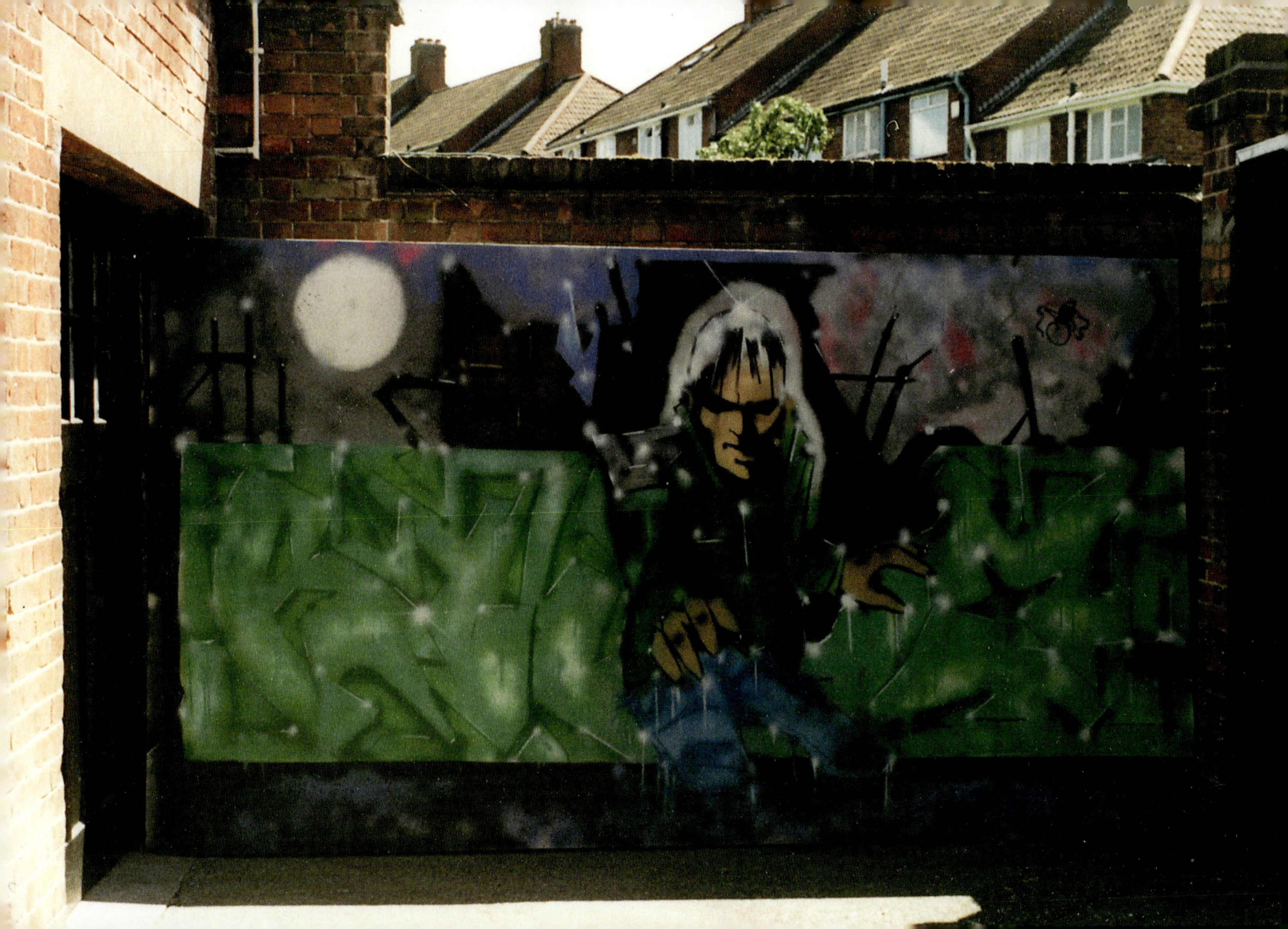

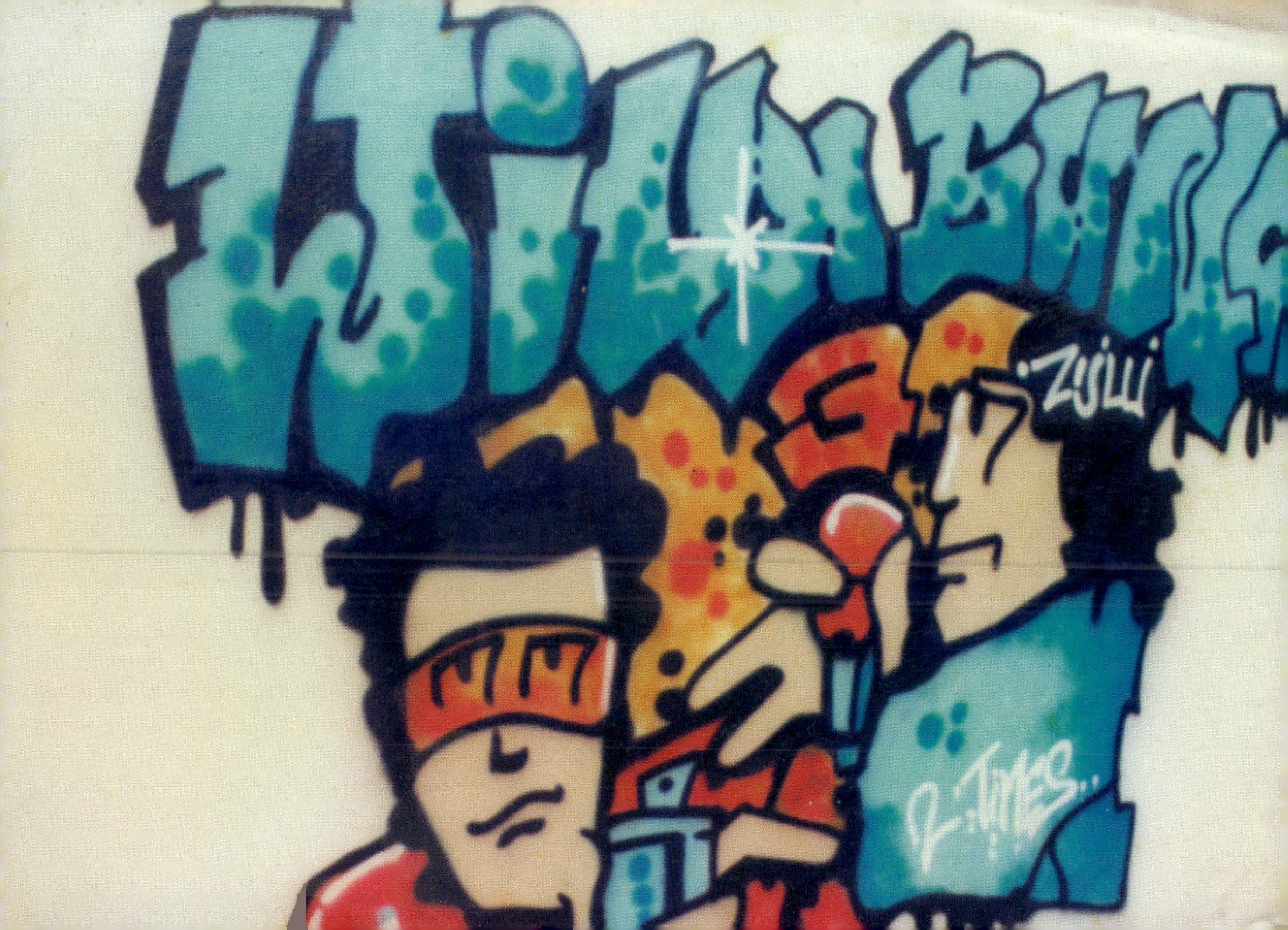
ZULU
R. JONES

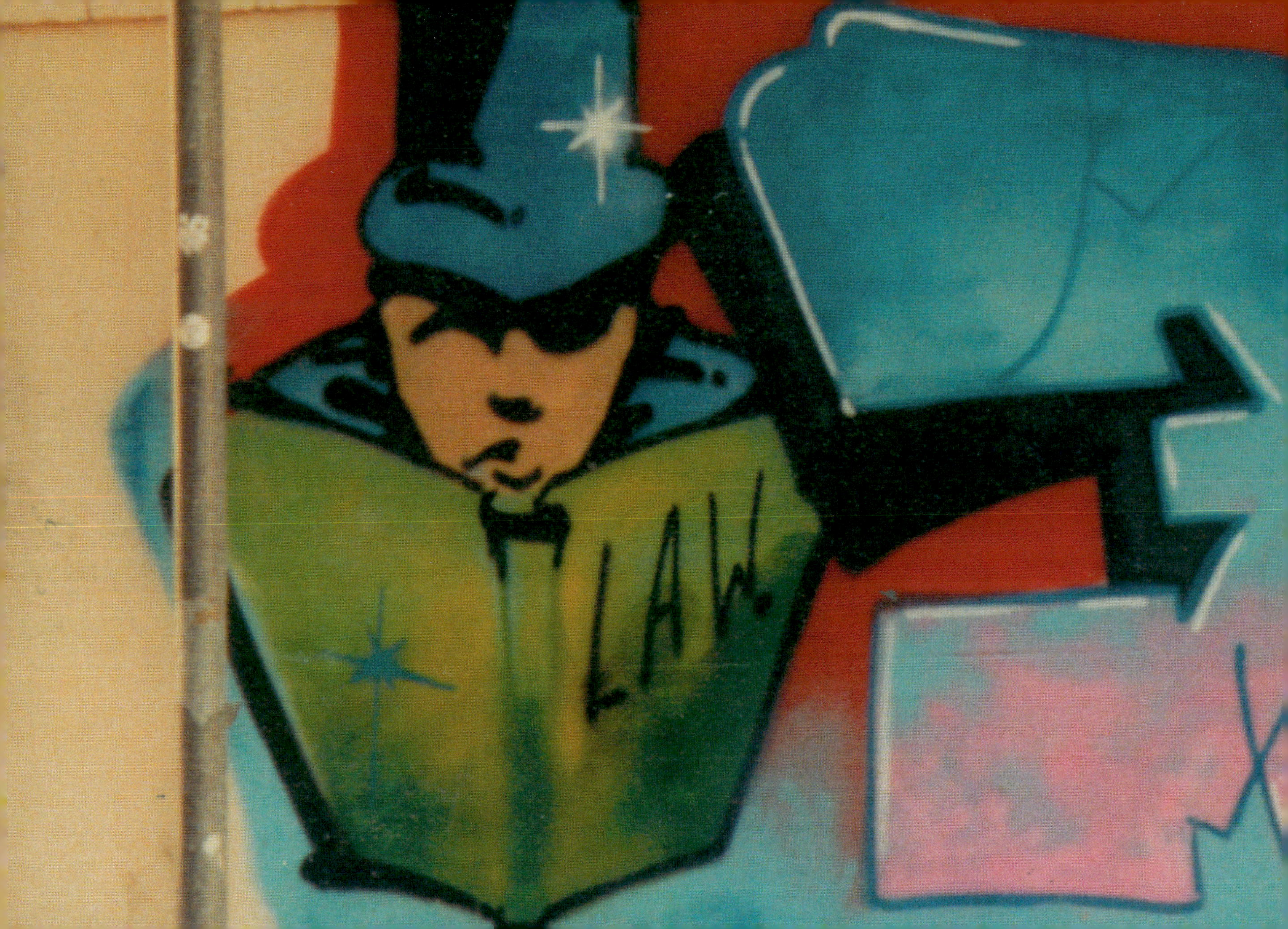

LAW

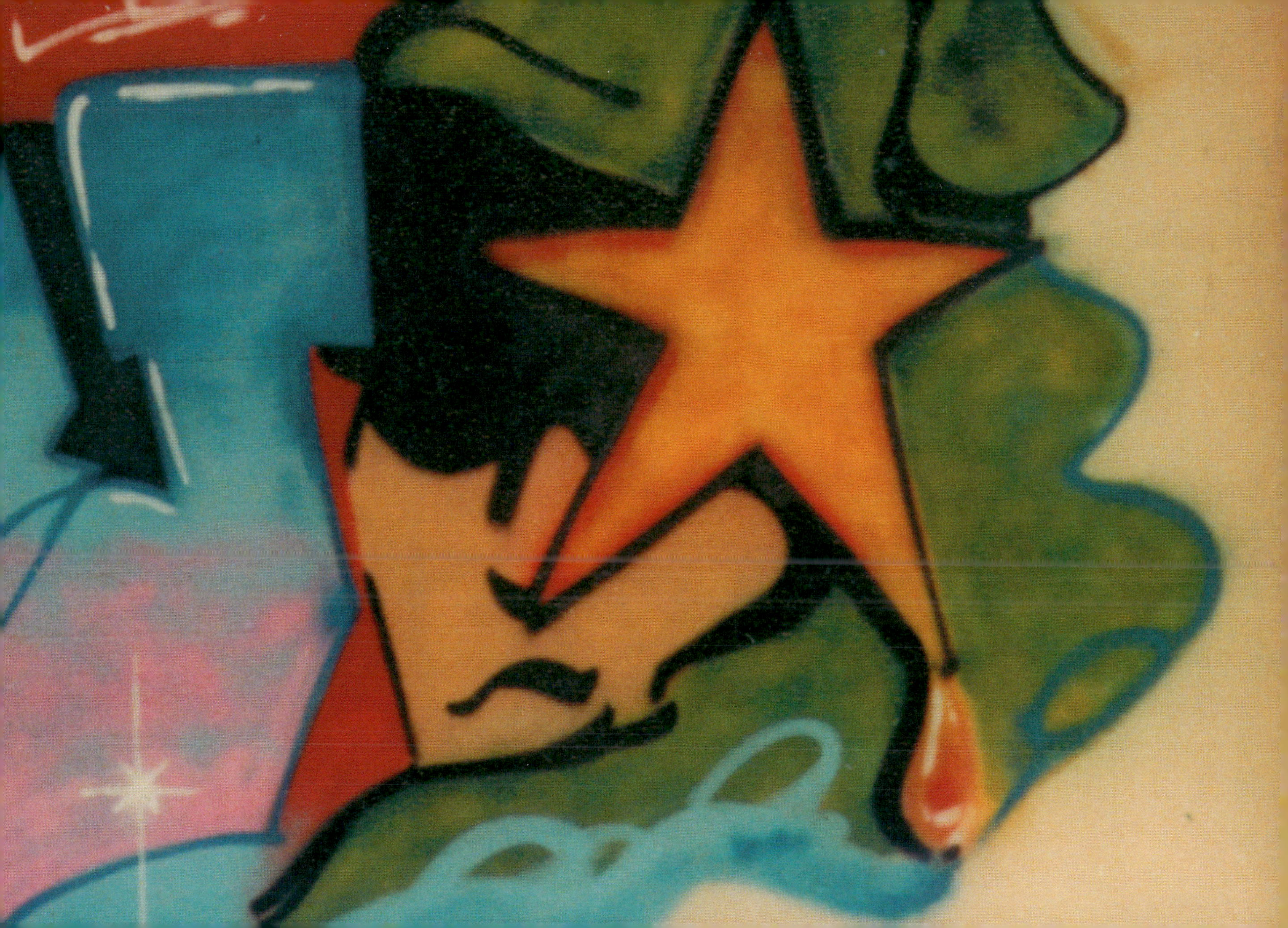

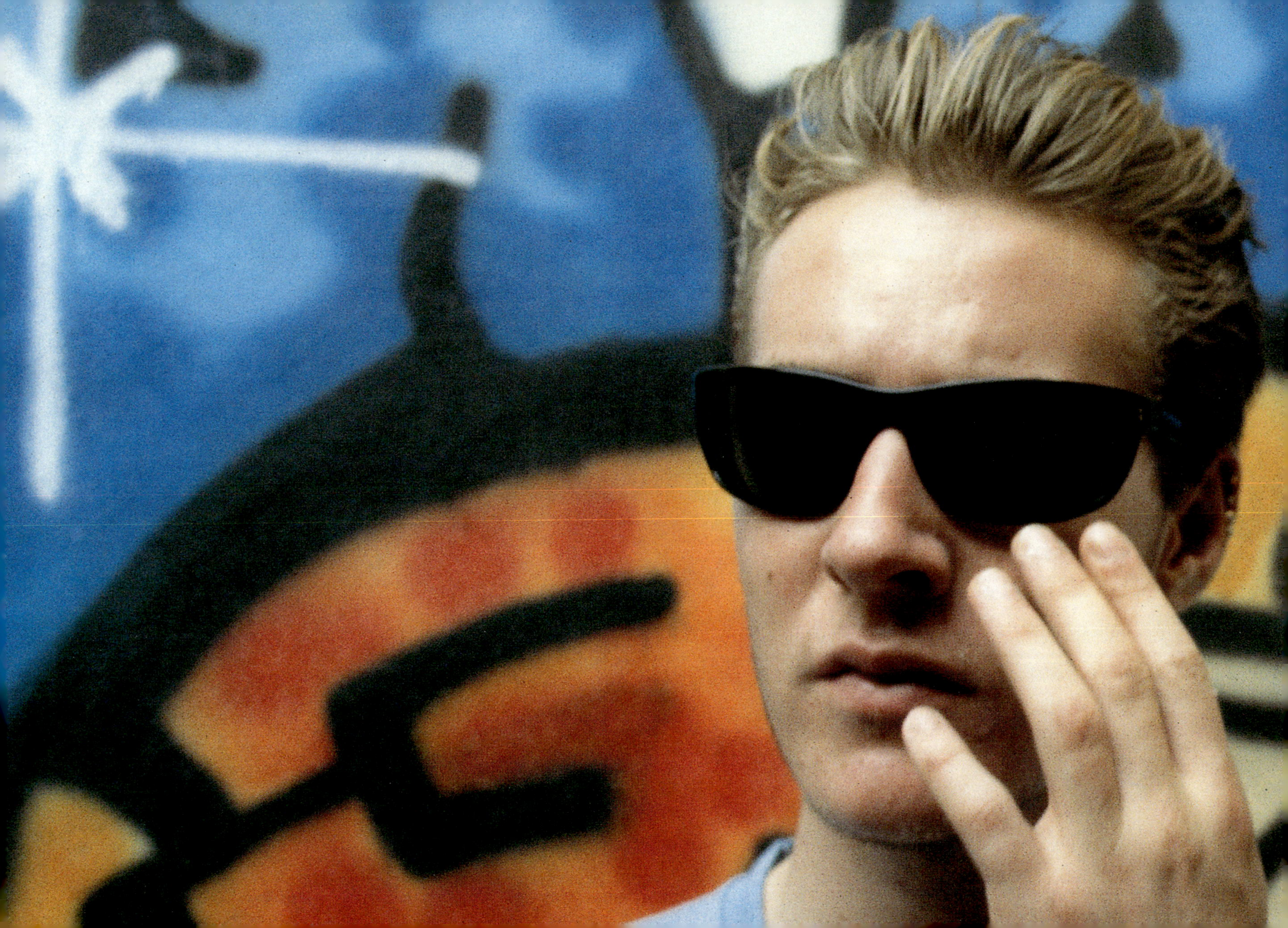

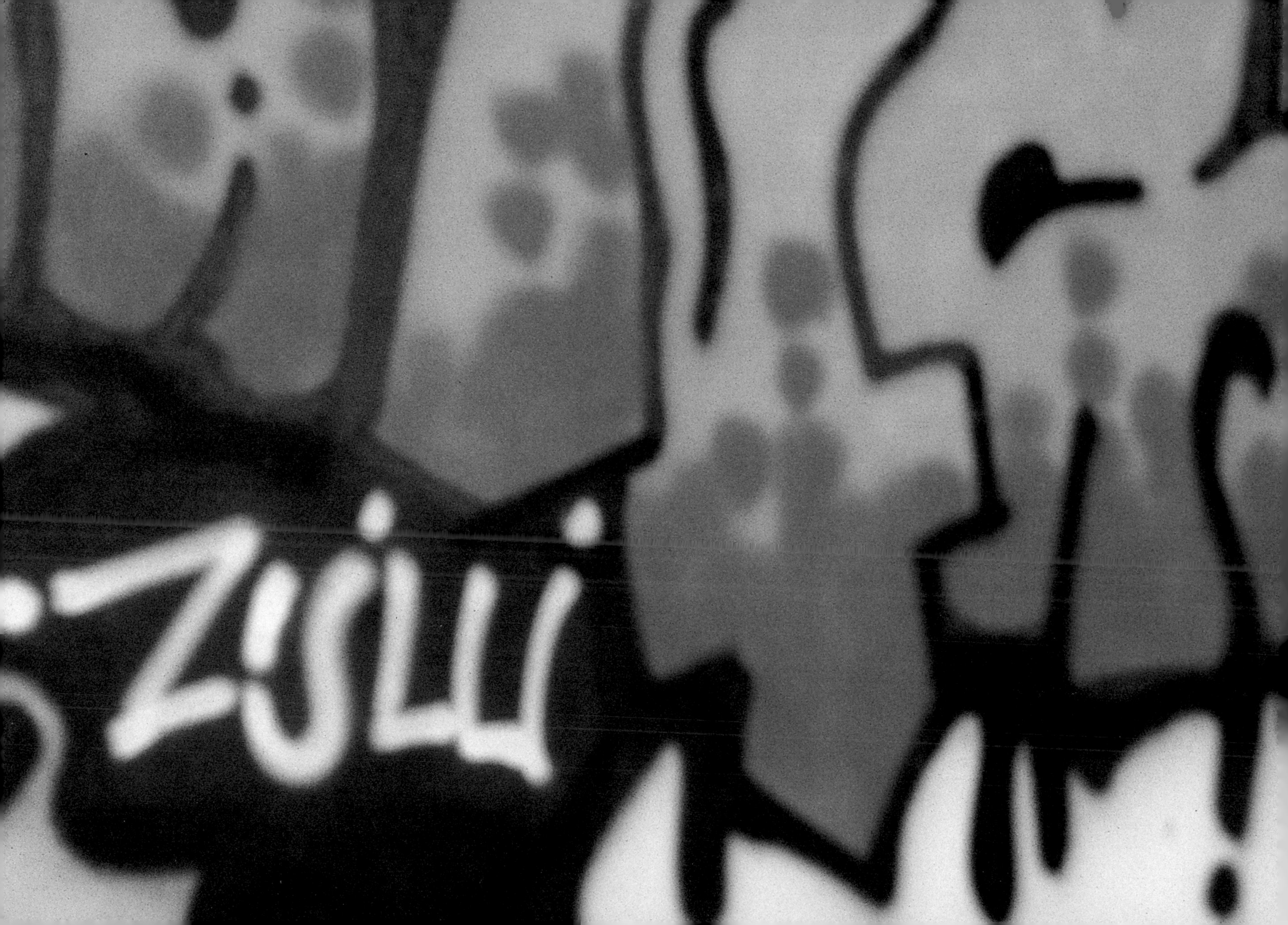
Zulu

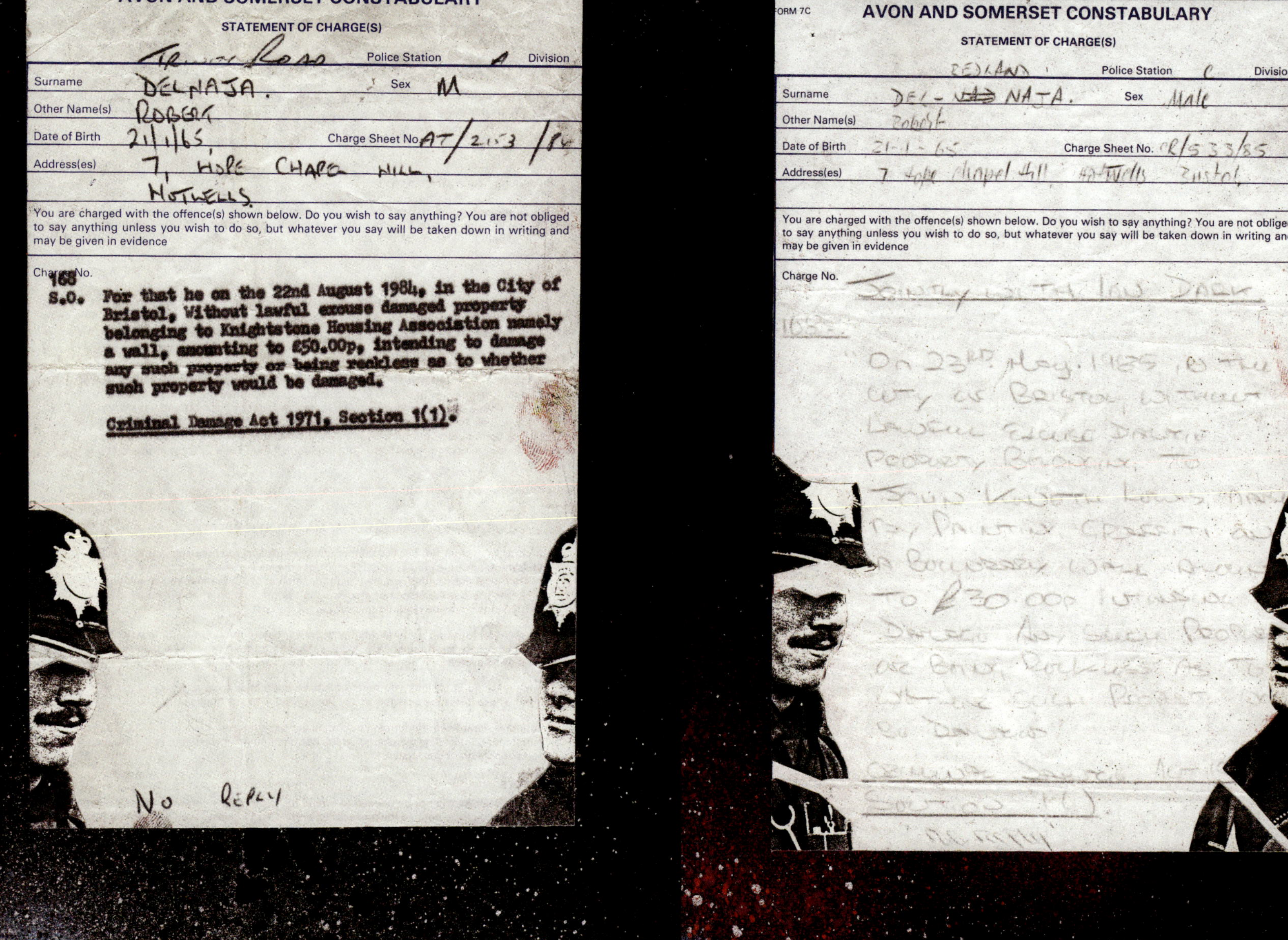

FORM 7C

AVON AND SOMERSET CONSTABULARY

STATEMENT OF CHARGE(S)

Trinity Road   Police Station   A   Division

Surname   DELNAJA.   Sex   M

Other Name(s) ROBERT

Date of Birth 21/1/65   Charge Sheet No. AT/2153/84

Address(es)   7, HOPE CHAPEL HILL,
               HOTWELLS.

You are charged with the offence(s) shown below. Do you wish to say anything? You are not obliged to say anything unless you wish to do so, but whatever you say will be taken down in writing and may be given in evidence

Charge No.

166
S.O.   For that he on the 22nd August 1984, in the City of
       Bristol, Without lawful excuse damaged property
       belonging to Knightstone Housing Association namely
       a wall, amounting to £50.00p, intending to damage
       any such property or being reckless as to whether
       such property would be damaged.

       Criminal Damage Act 1971, Section 1(1).

No Reply

FORM 7C

AVON AND SOMERSET CONSTABULARY

STATEMENT OF CHARGE(S)

Redland   Police Station   C   Division

Surname   DEL- NAJA.   Sex   Male

Other Name(s) Robert

Date of Birth 21-1-65   Charge Sheet No. CR/533/85

Address(es)   7 Hope Chapel Hill, Hotwells, Bristol,

You are charged with the offence(s) shown below. Do you wish to say anything? You are not obliged to say anything unless you wish to do so, but whatever you say will be taken down in writing and may be given in evidence

Charge No.   Jointly with John Dark

1053

"On 23rd May 1985, in the
City of Bristol, without
lawful excuse did
property damage, to
John Knightstone Housing
by painting graffiti on
a boundary wall amounting
to £30.00p intending to
damage any such property
or being reckless as to
whether such property
be damaged."

Criminal Damage Act
Section 1(1)

No Reply

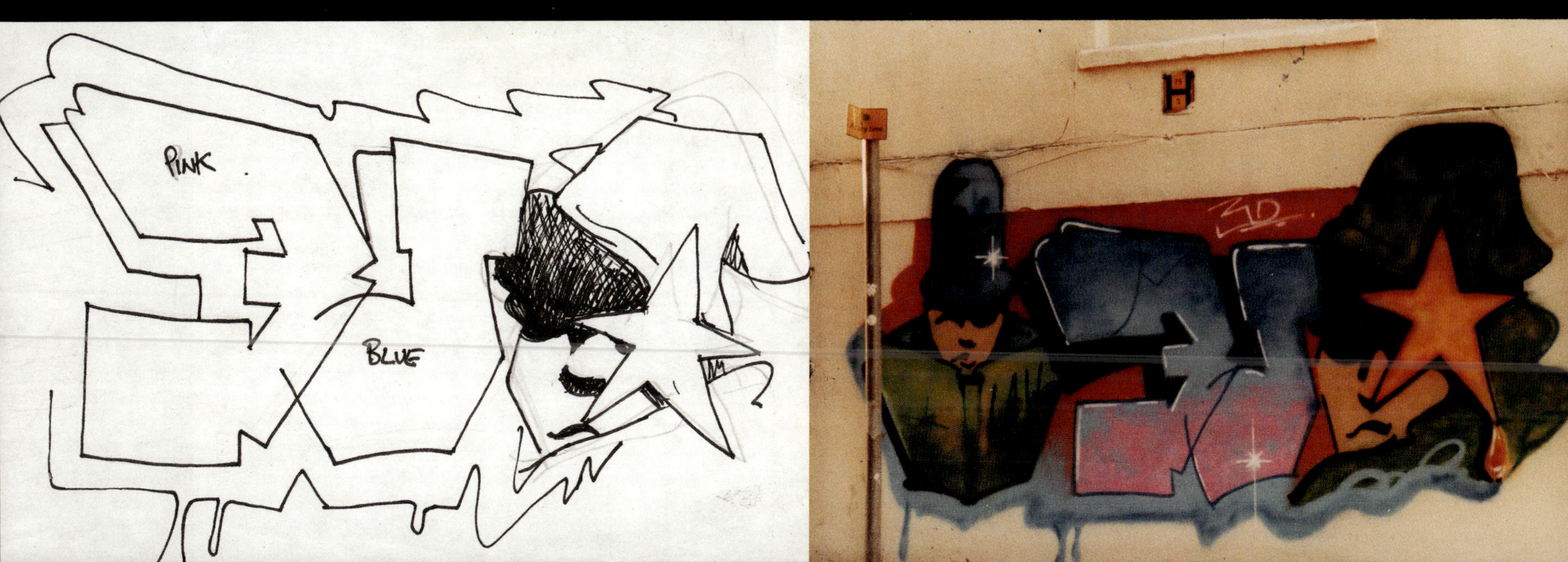
1984
PINK
BLUE

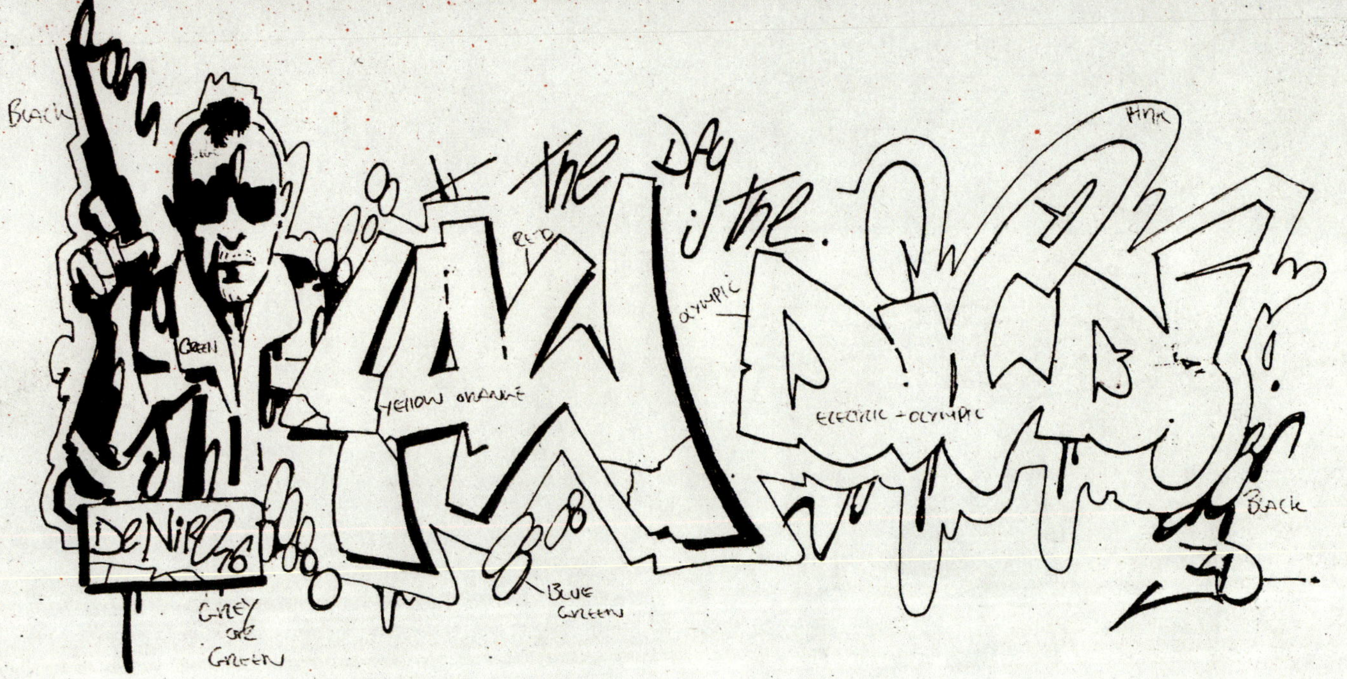

BLACK
PINK
RED
the DAY the.
OLYMPIC
ELECTRIC + OLYMPIC
YELLOW ORANGE
GREEN
BLACK
DeNiro 86
GREY OR GREEN
BLUE GREEN
The Day the law died!

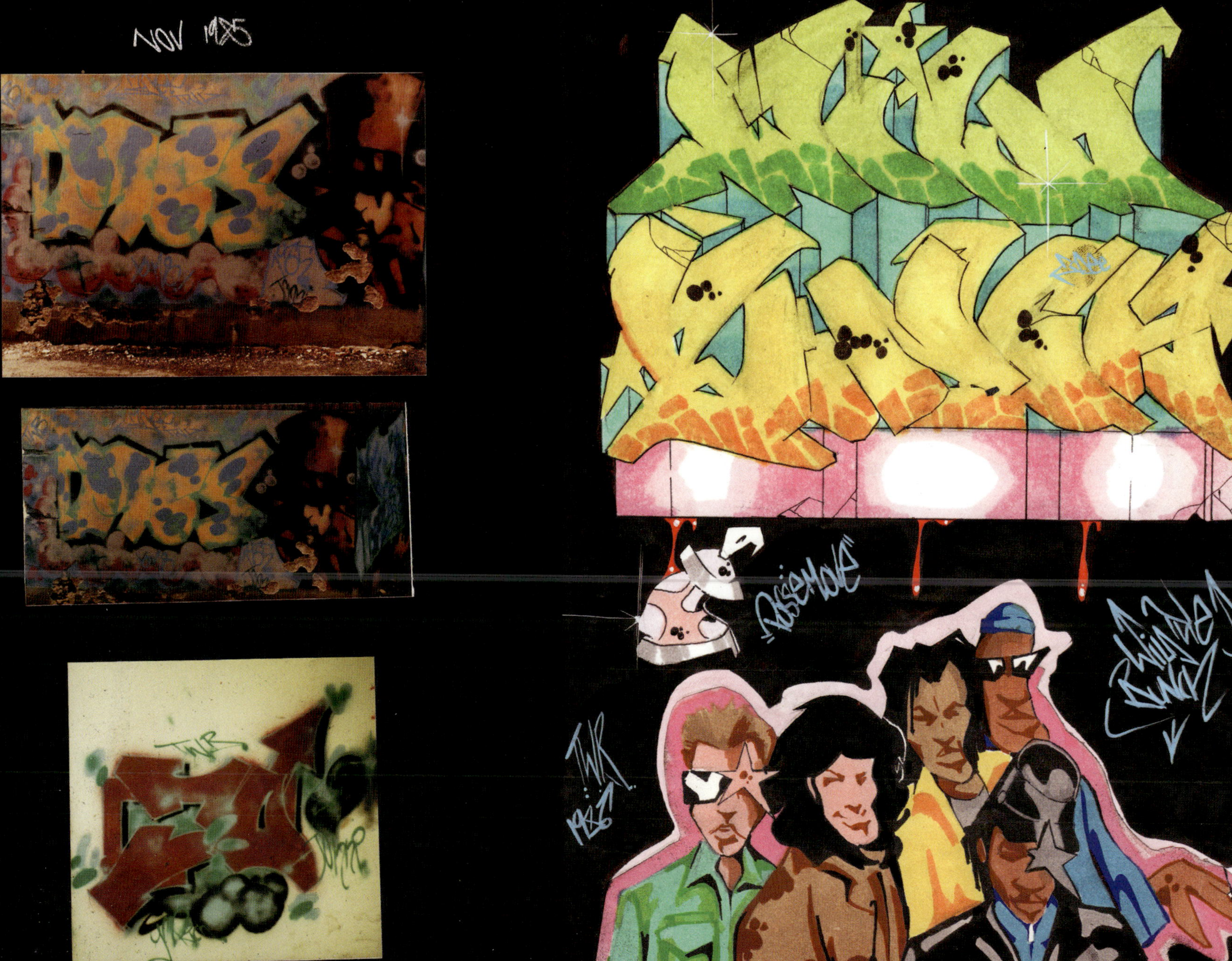
NOV 1995

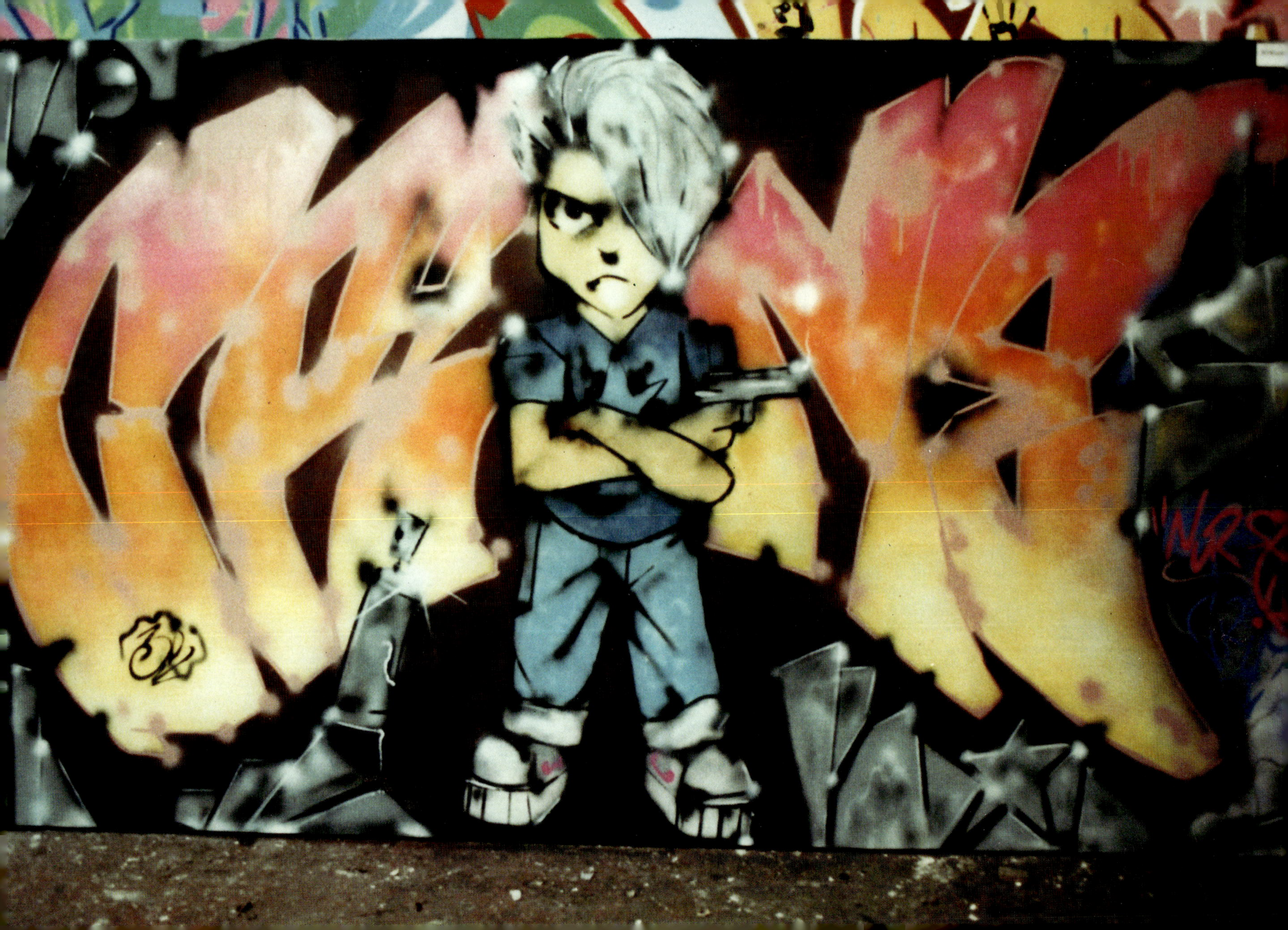

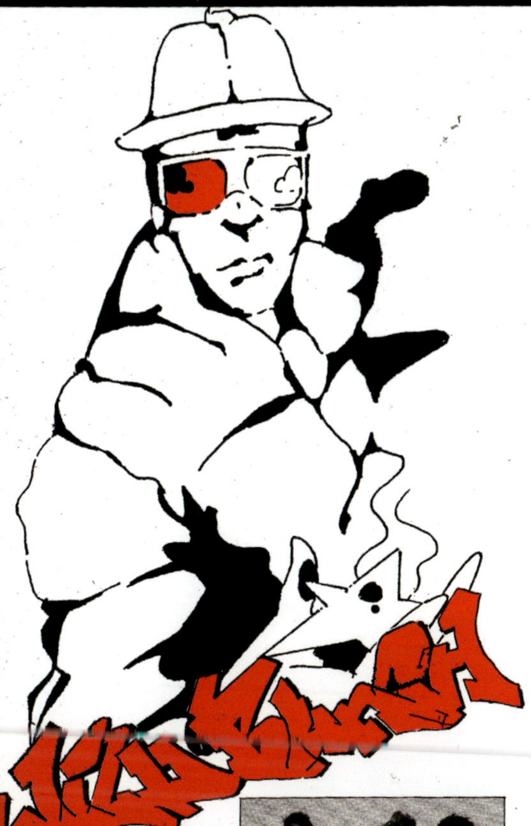

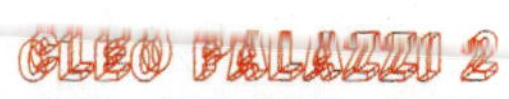

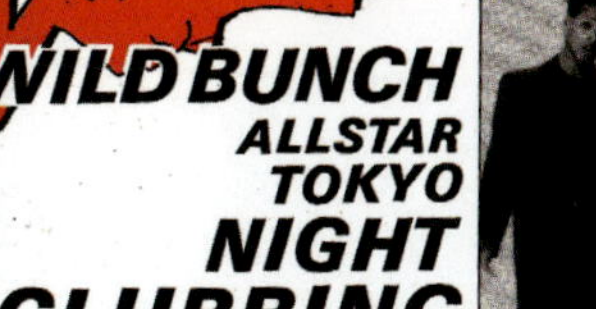

WILD BUNCH
ALLSTAR
TOKYO
NIGHT
CLUBBING

FEATURING

3-D "The Cool Breeze"
 Graffiti Outlaw Supreme
DJ Nellee
MC Willi Wee
 Master of Ceremonys
DJ Milo
Papa Gee "The Soul Daddy"

PRESTIGE

25 APRIL FRI
[HIP HOP NIGHT]
OPEN 17:00
START 20:00 23:00
03-589-4125
03-584-0021
CHARGE ASK

club D

1 MAY THU
OPEN 19:00
START 23:00
03-423-1471
CHARGE ASK

TSUBAKI BALL

9 MAY FRI
OPEN 17:00
START 21:00 23:30
03-478-0087
CHARGE ASK

CLEO PALAZZI 2

29 MAY THU
OPEN 20:00
START 22:00
03-403-4554
CHARGE ASK

TSUBAKI HOUSE

31 MAY SAT
OPEN 17:00
START 21:00
03-354-3236〜7
CHARGE ASK

WILD BUNCHに関する
お問い合せは各CLUBまたは
NITES 03-354-8981迄。

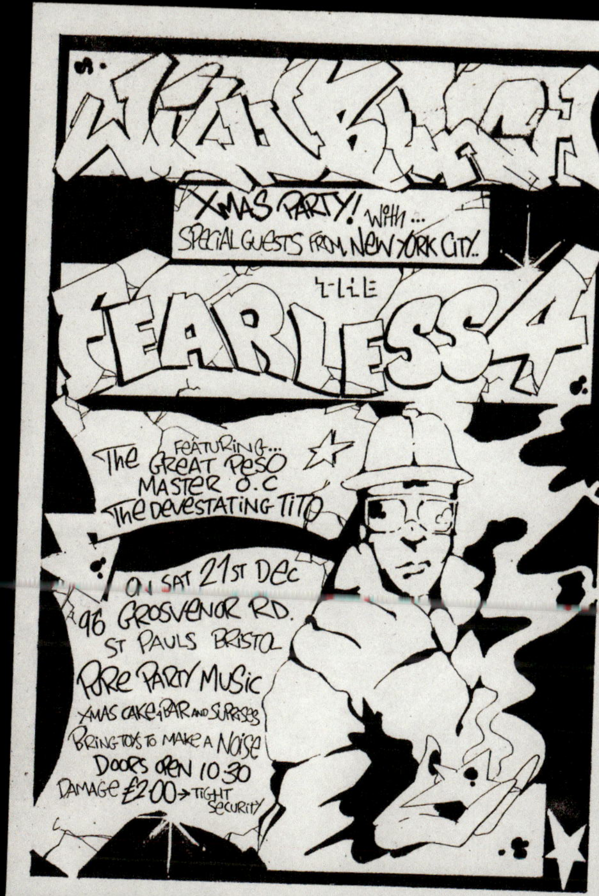

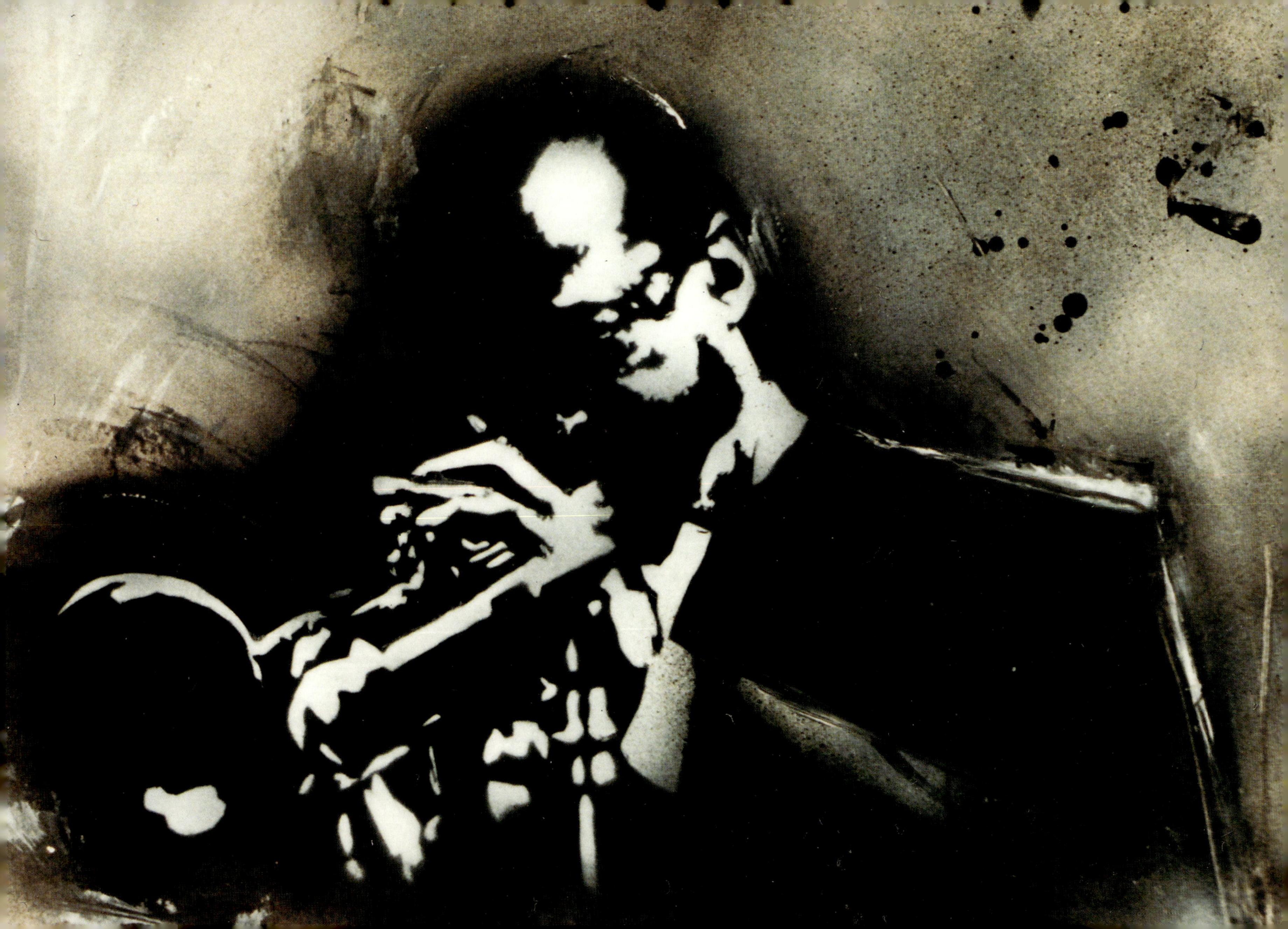

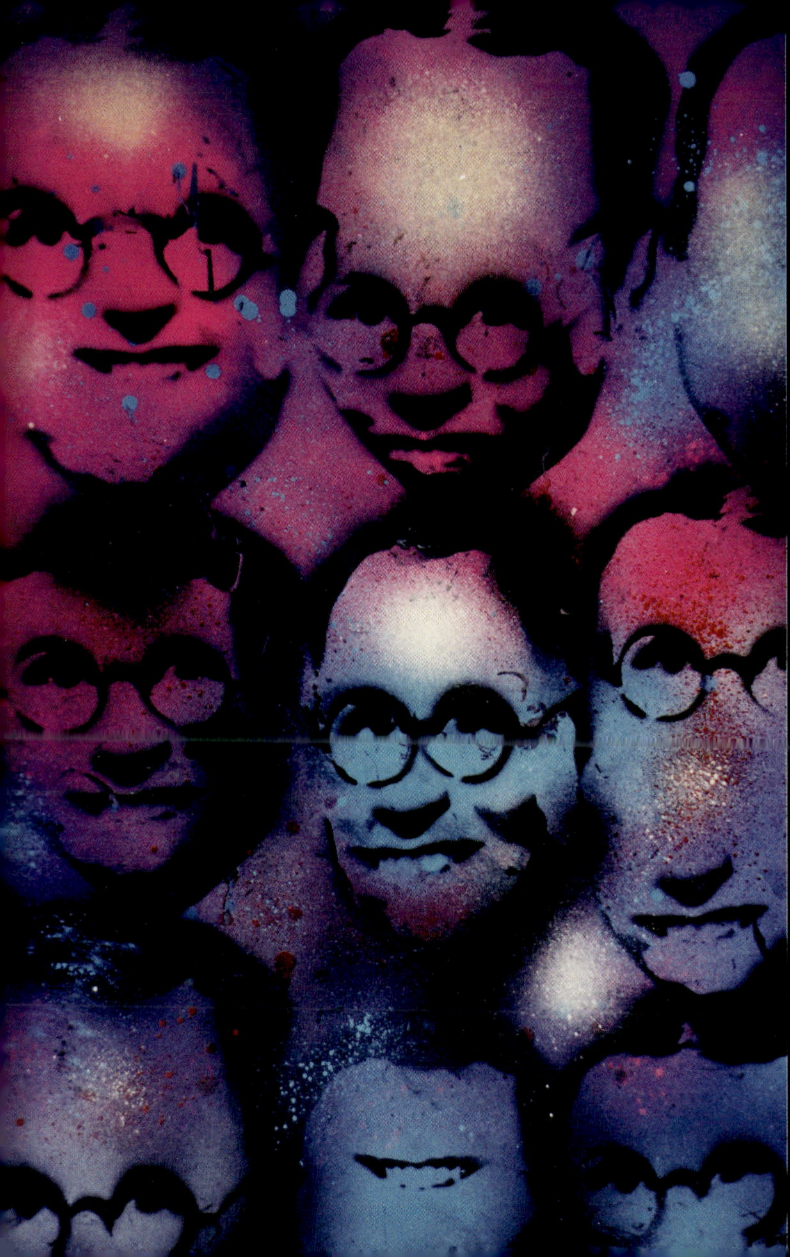

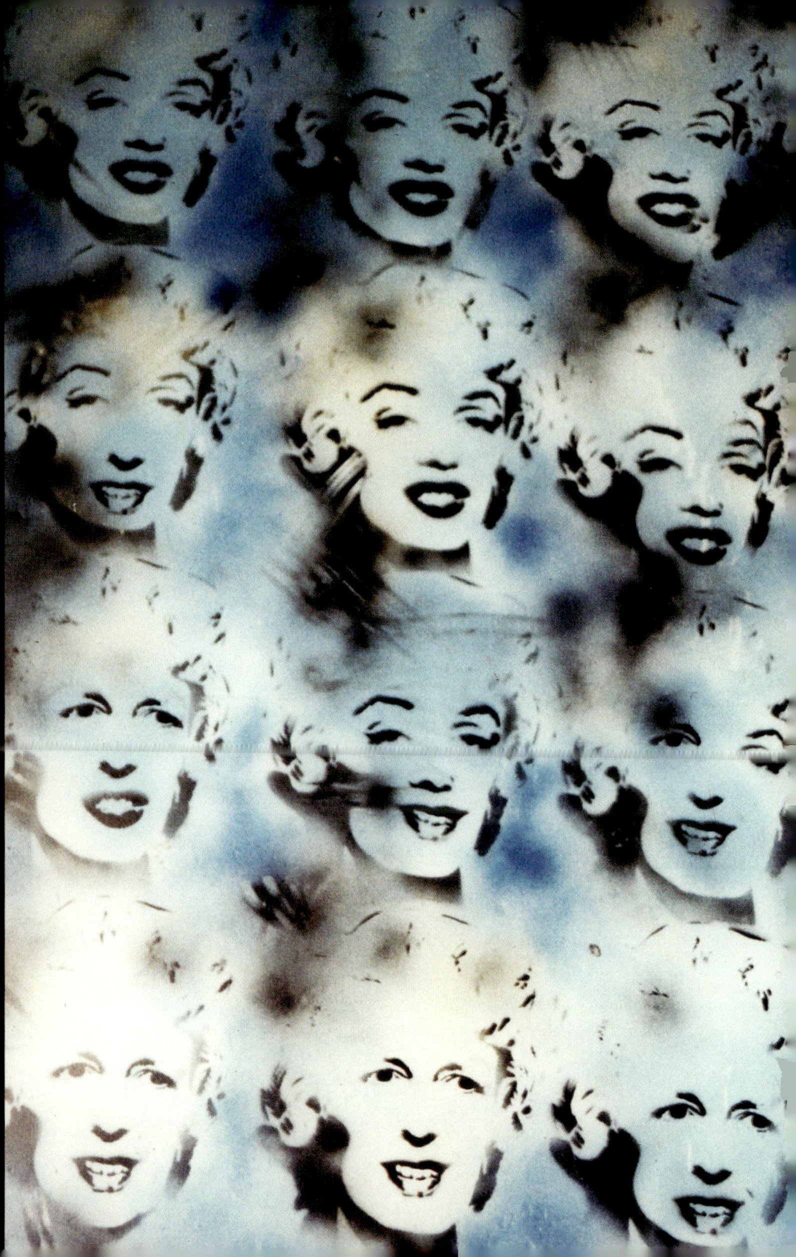

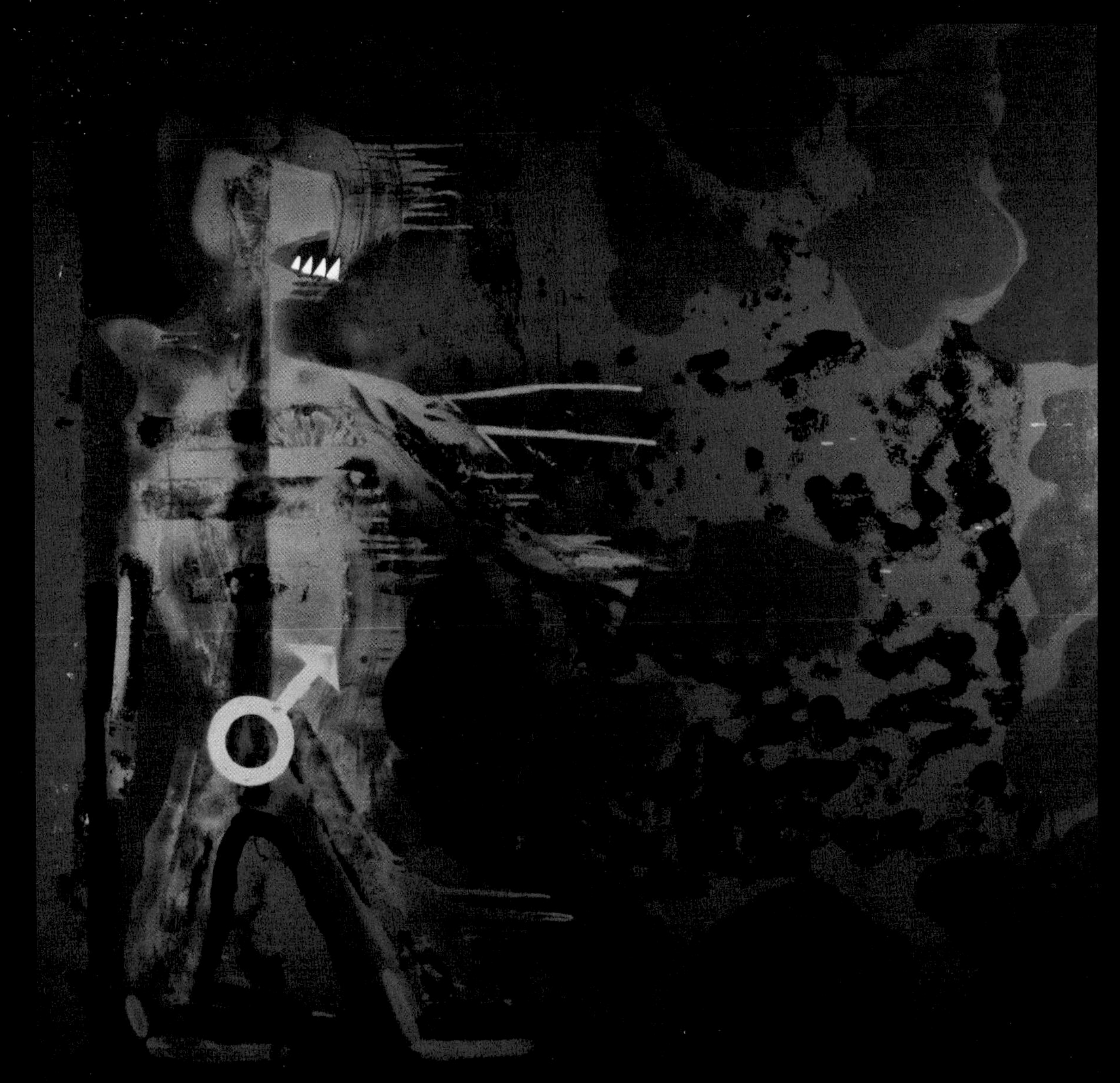

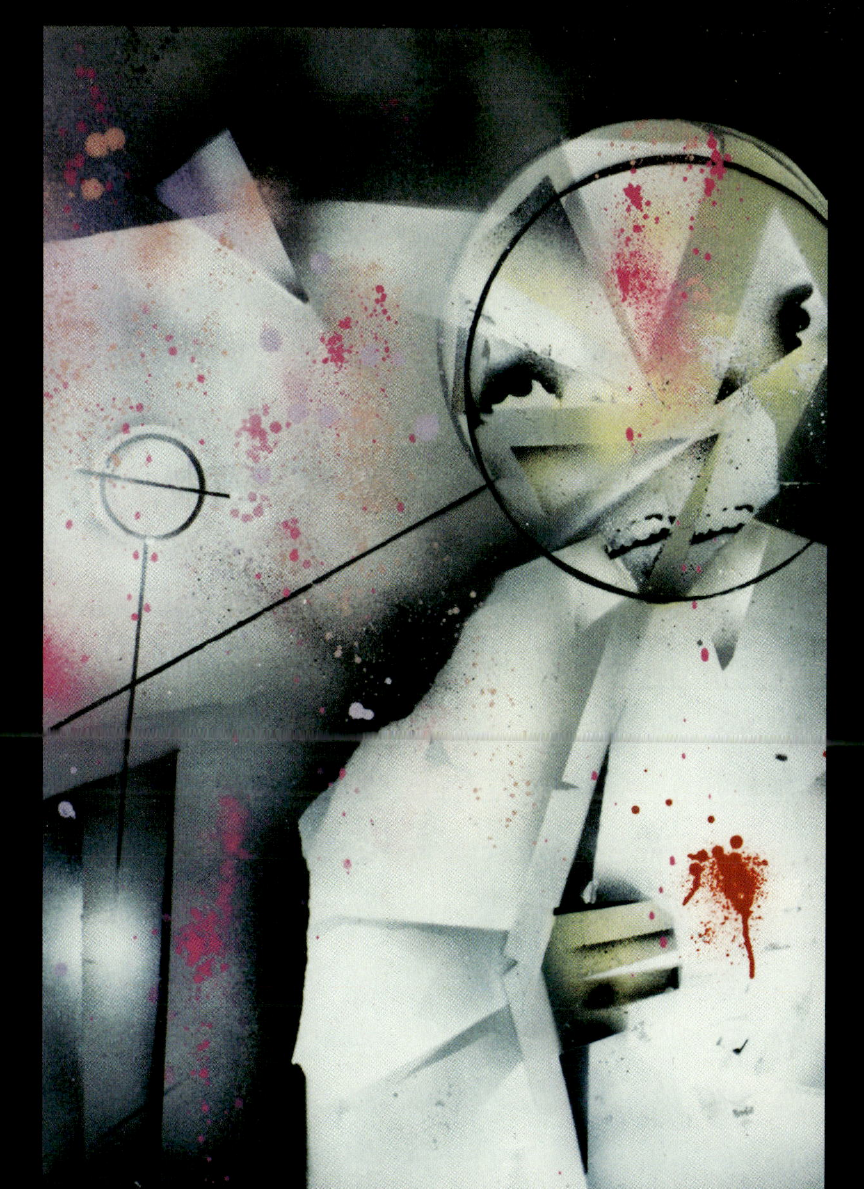

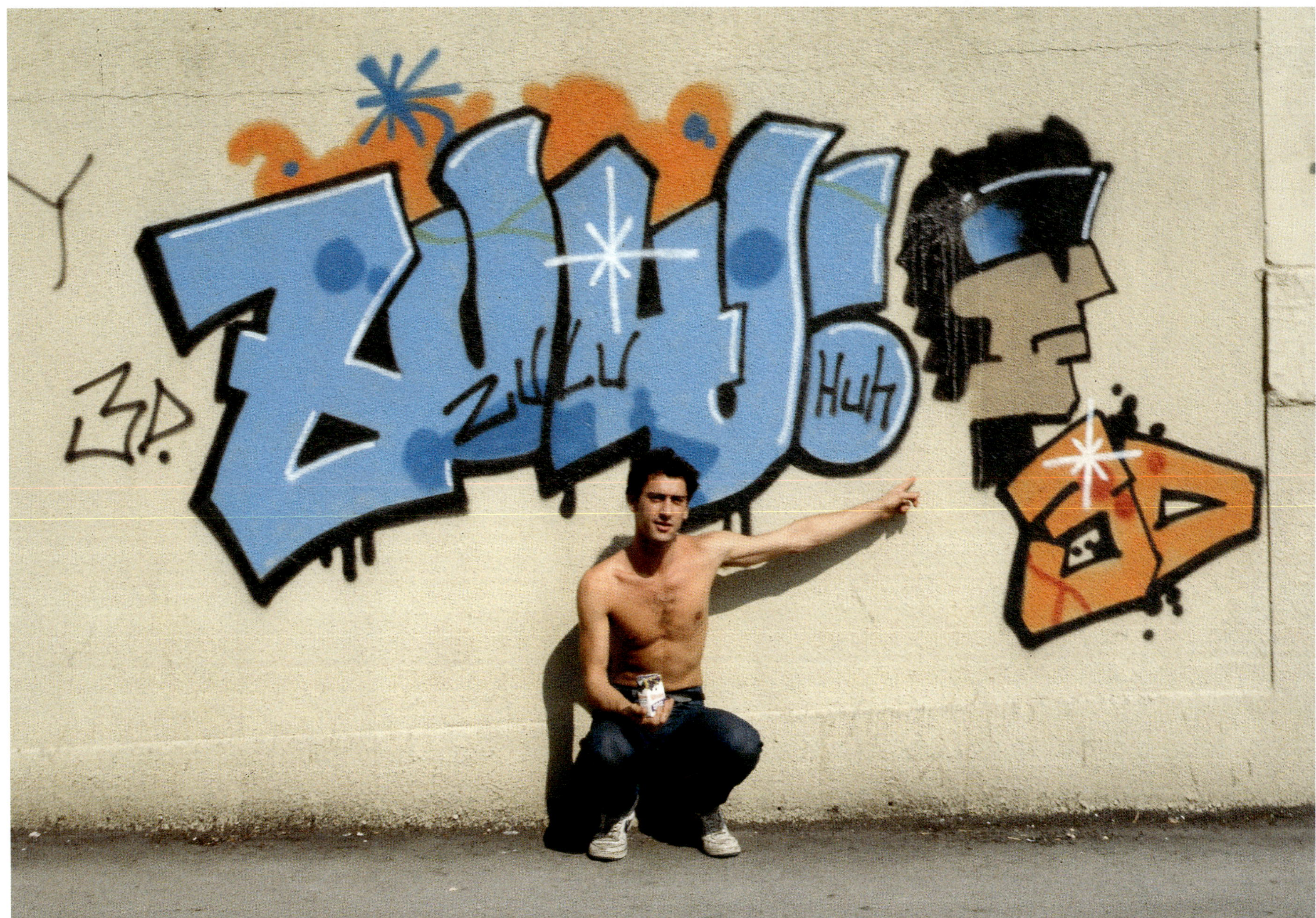

3D.
ZULU
Huh

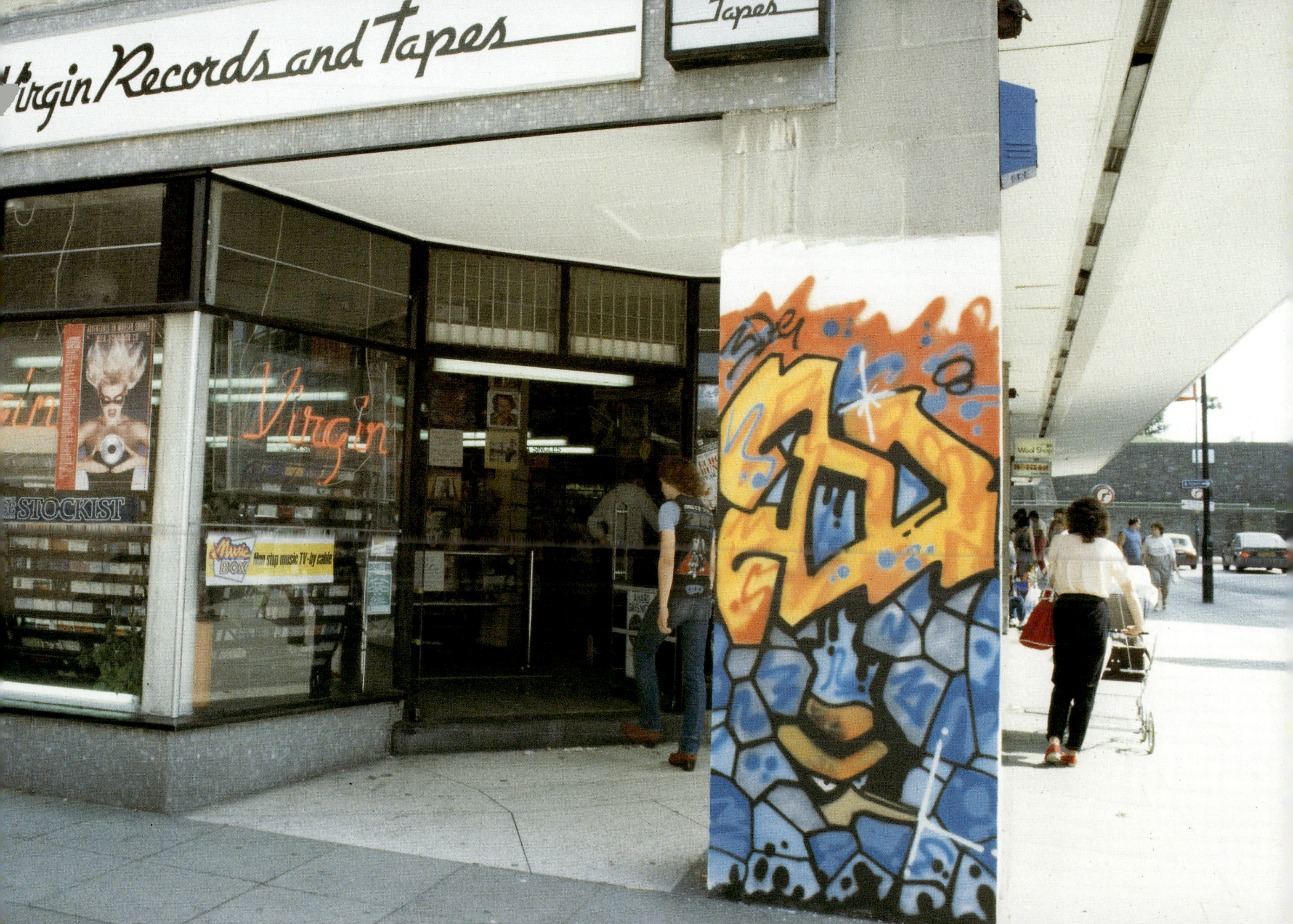

Virgin Records and Tapes
Tapes
Virgin
STOCKIST
Music BOX
Non stop music TV by cable
SINGLES
Wool Shop

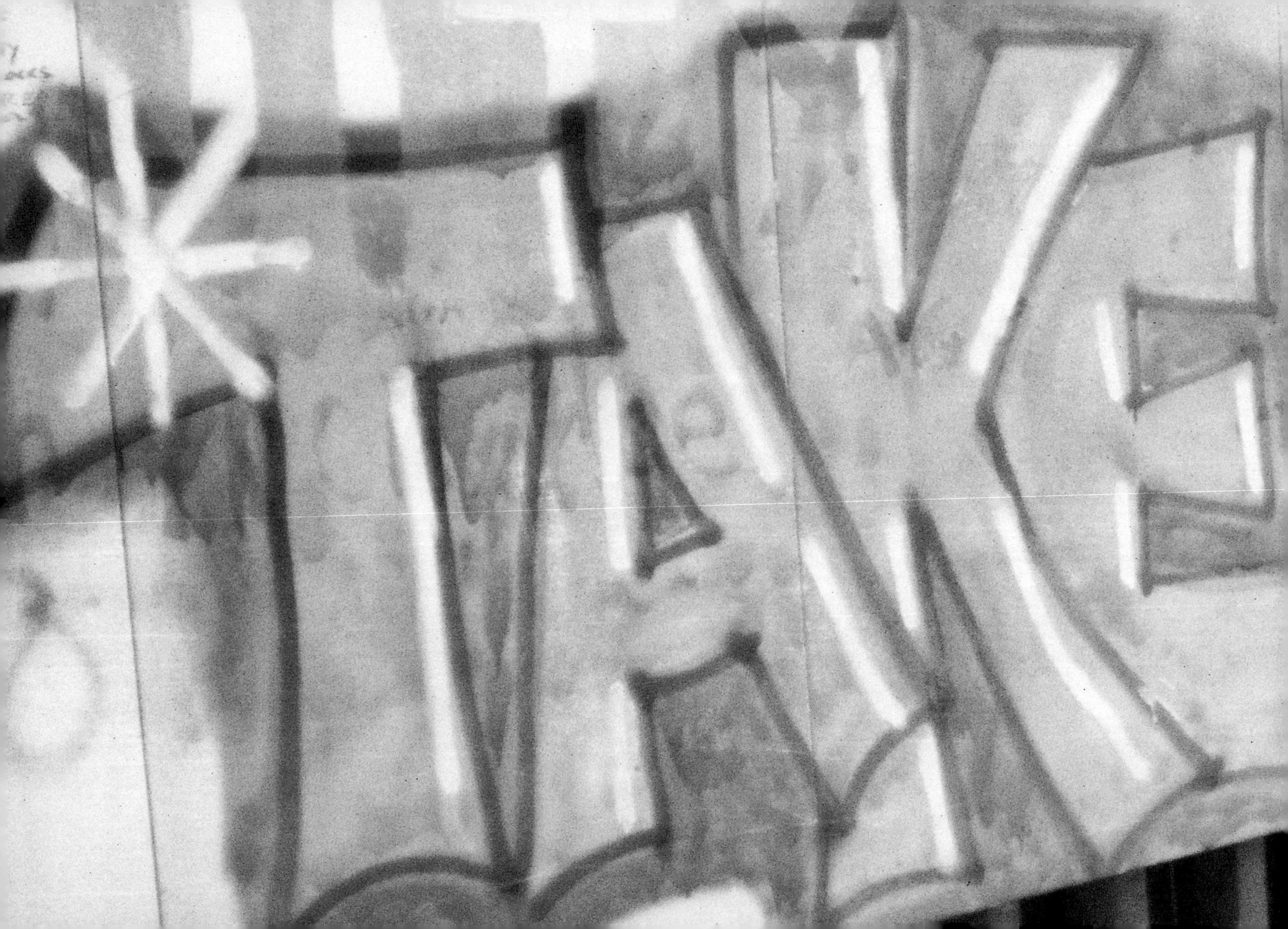

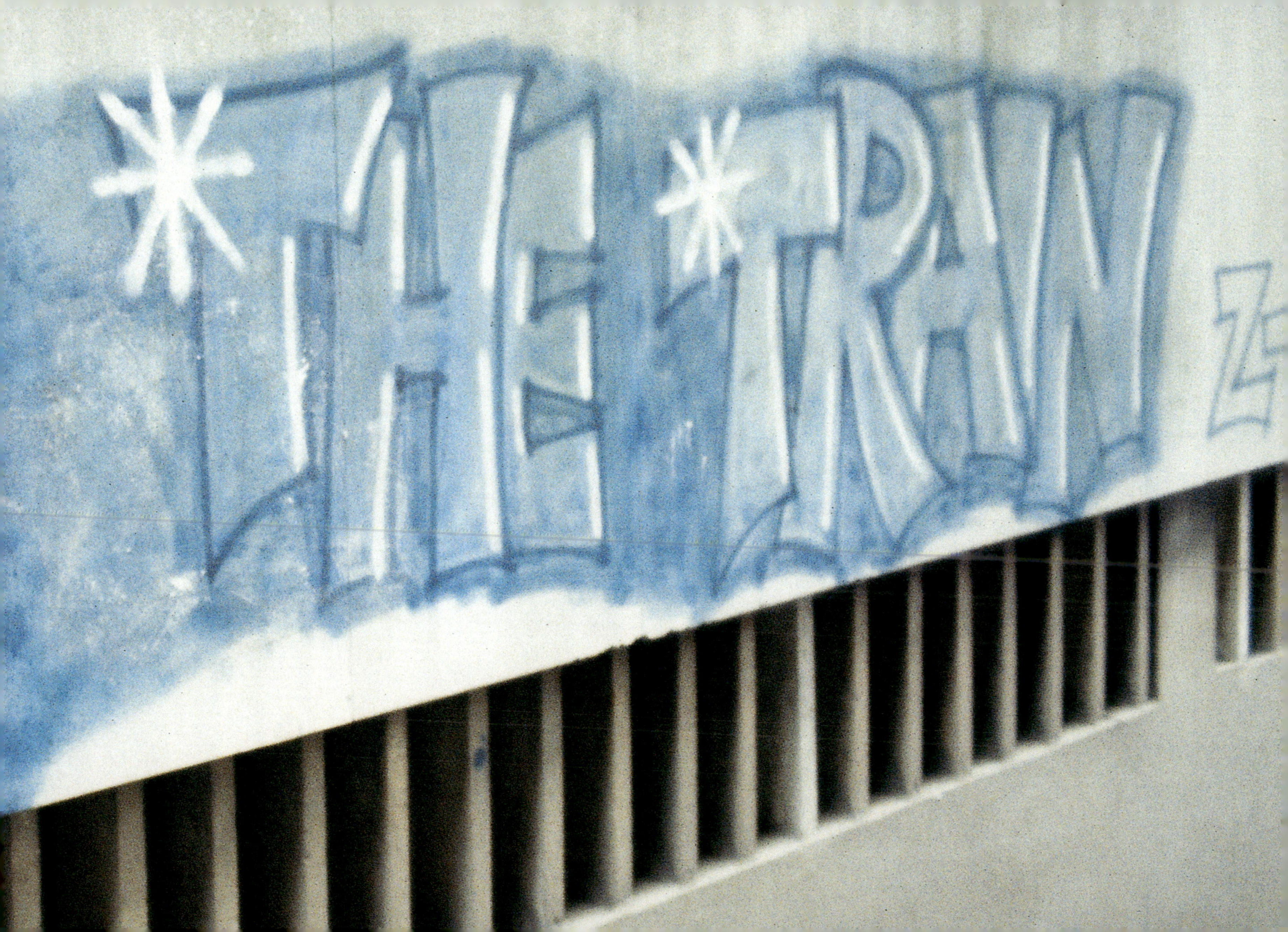
THE TRAW

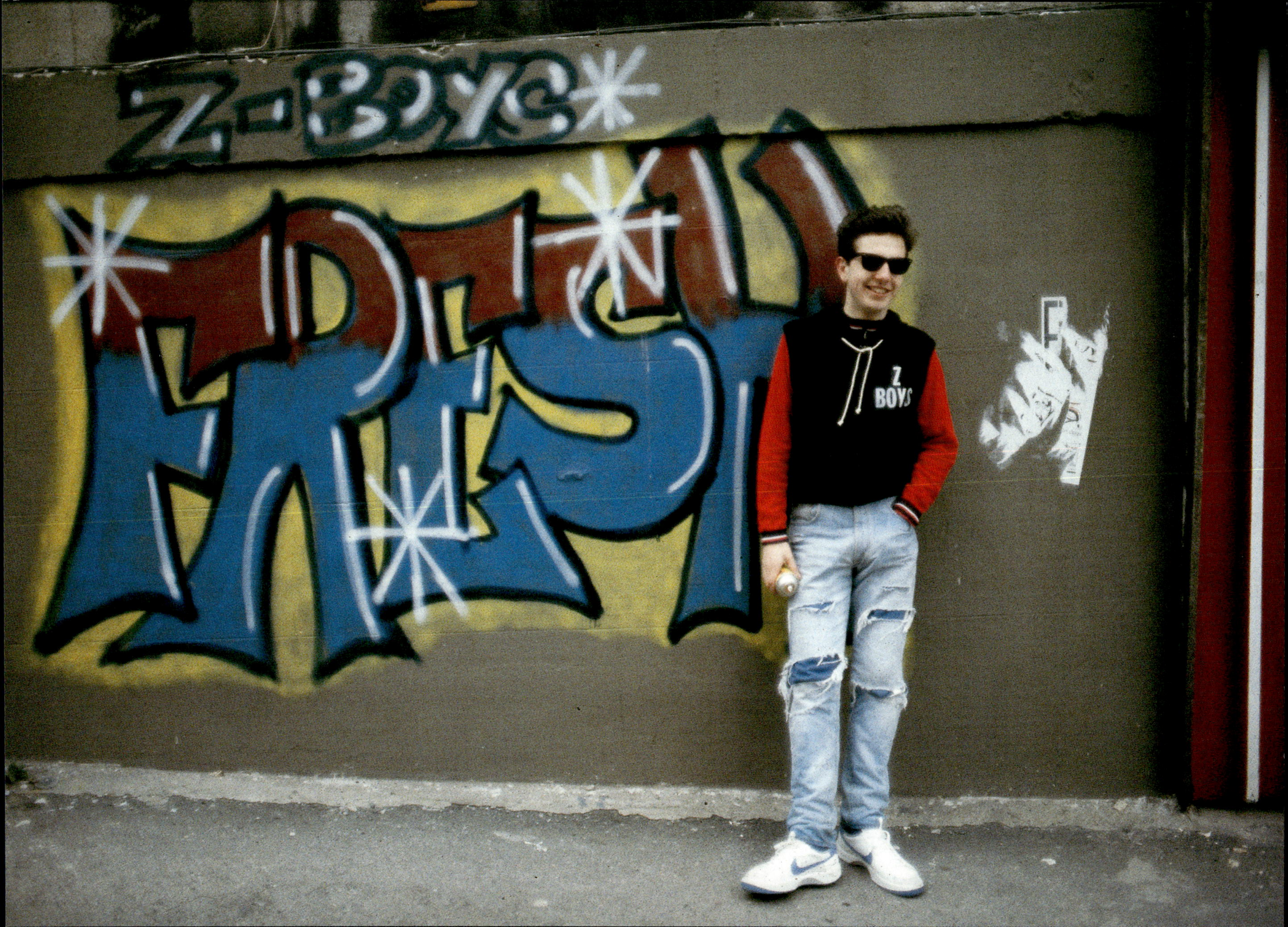
Z-BOYS
FRESH
Z.
BOYS

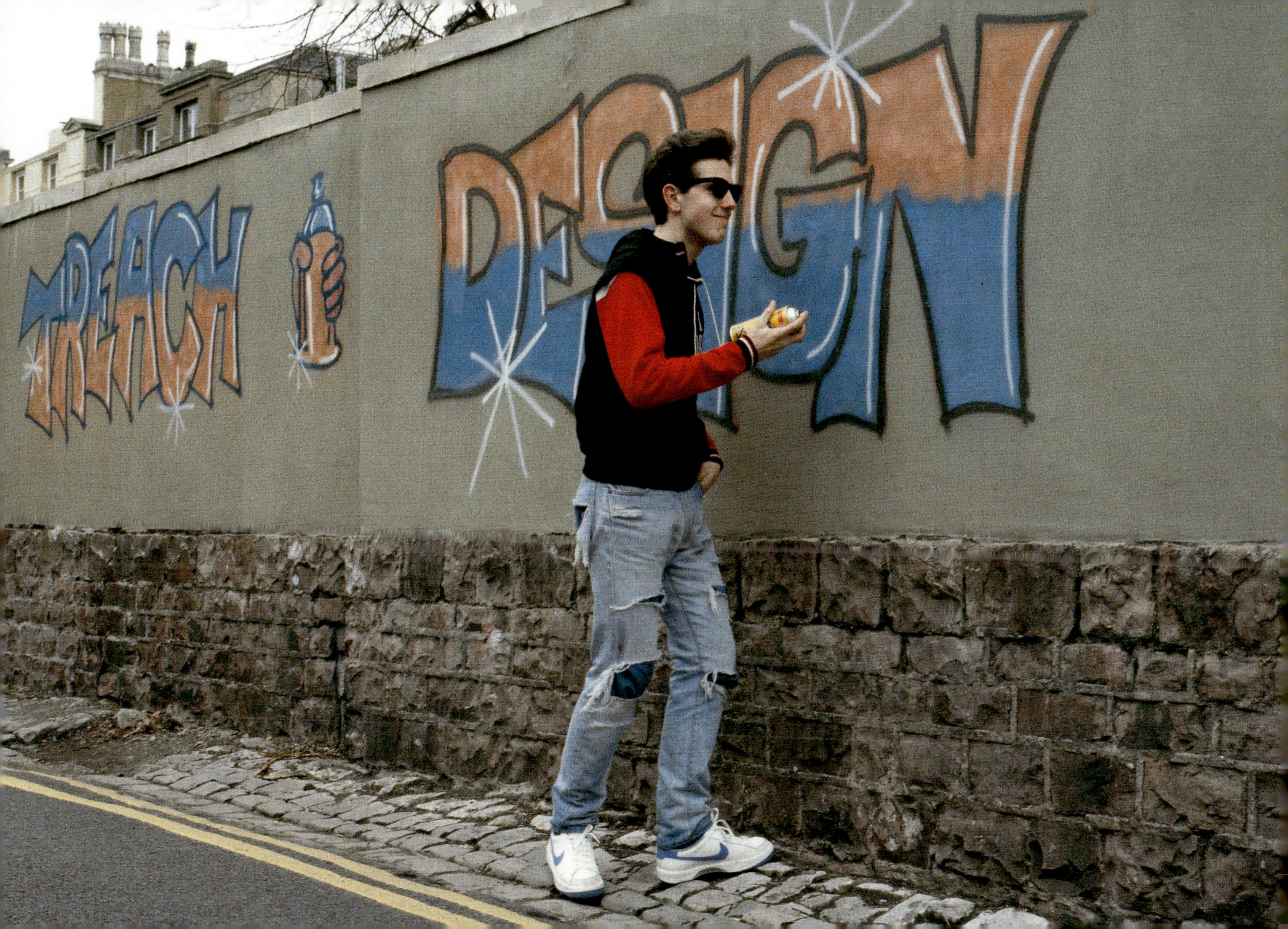
TREACH
DESIGN

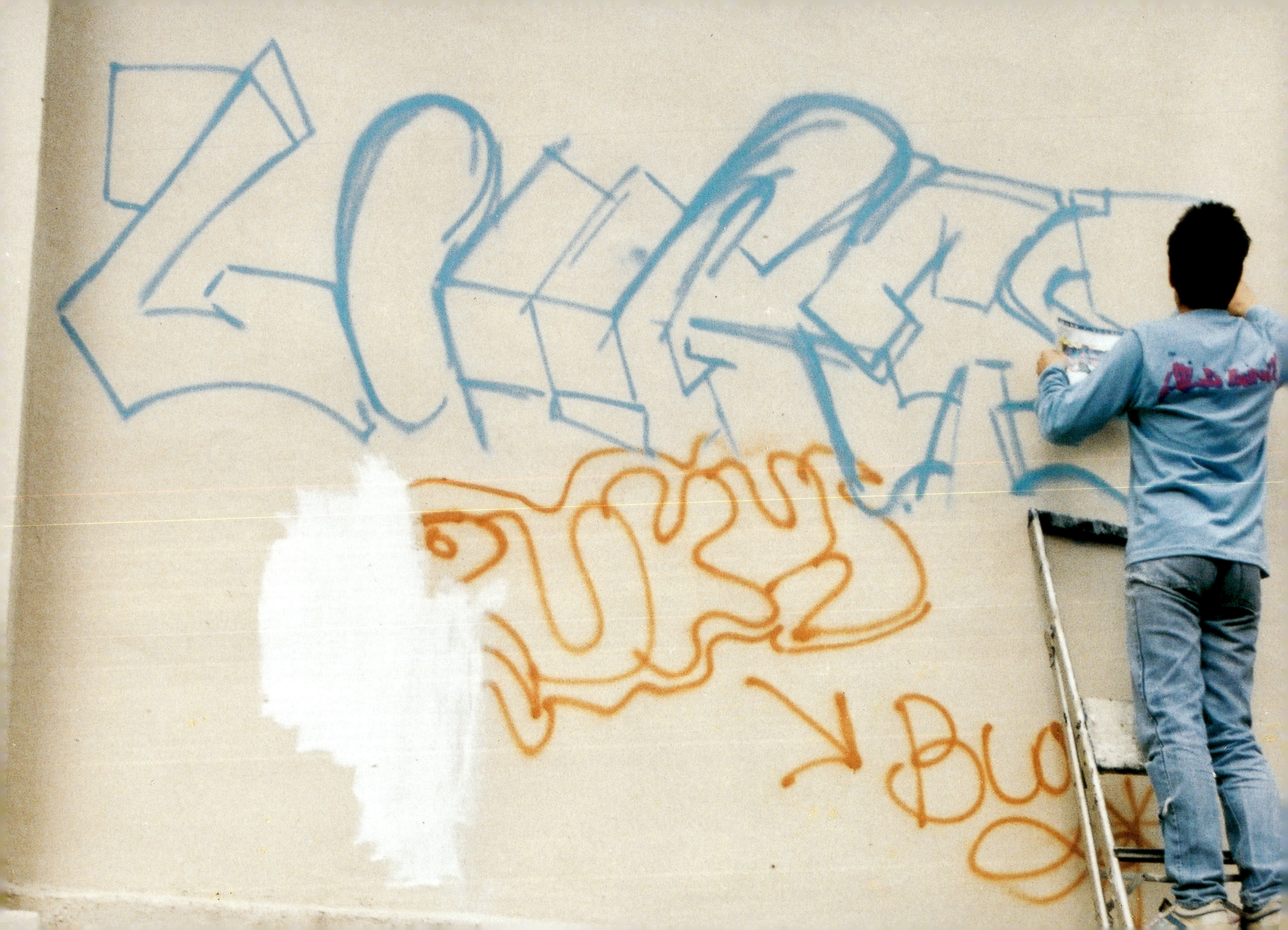

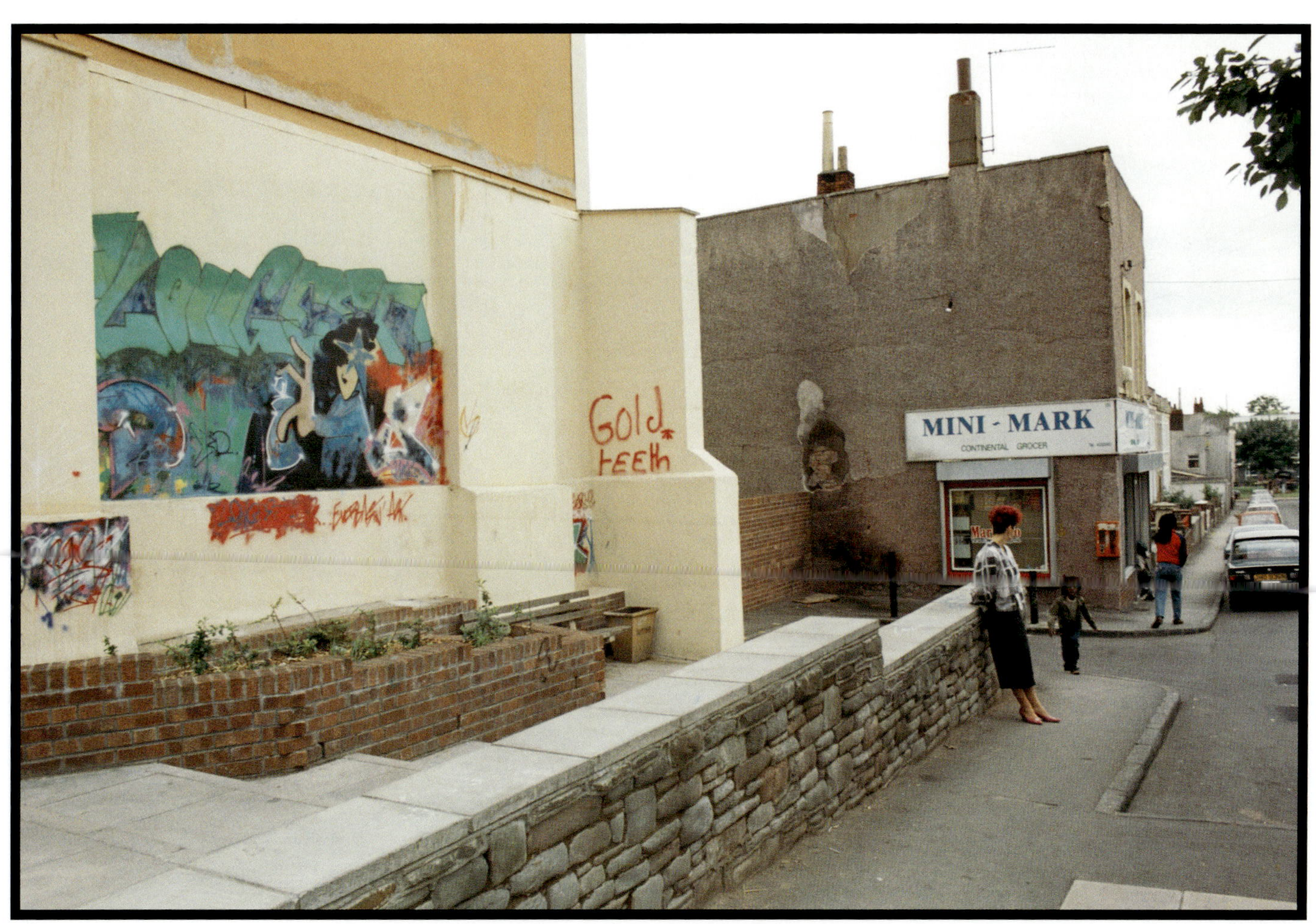

Gold
teeth
MINI - MARK
CONTINENTAL GROCER

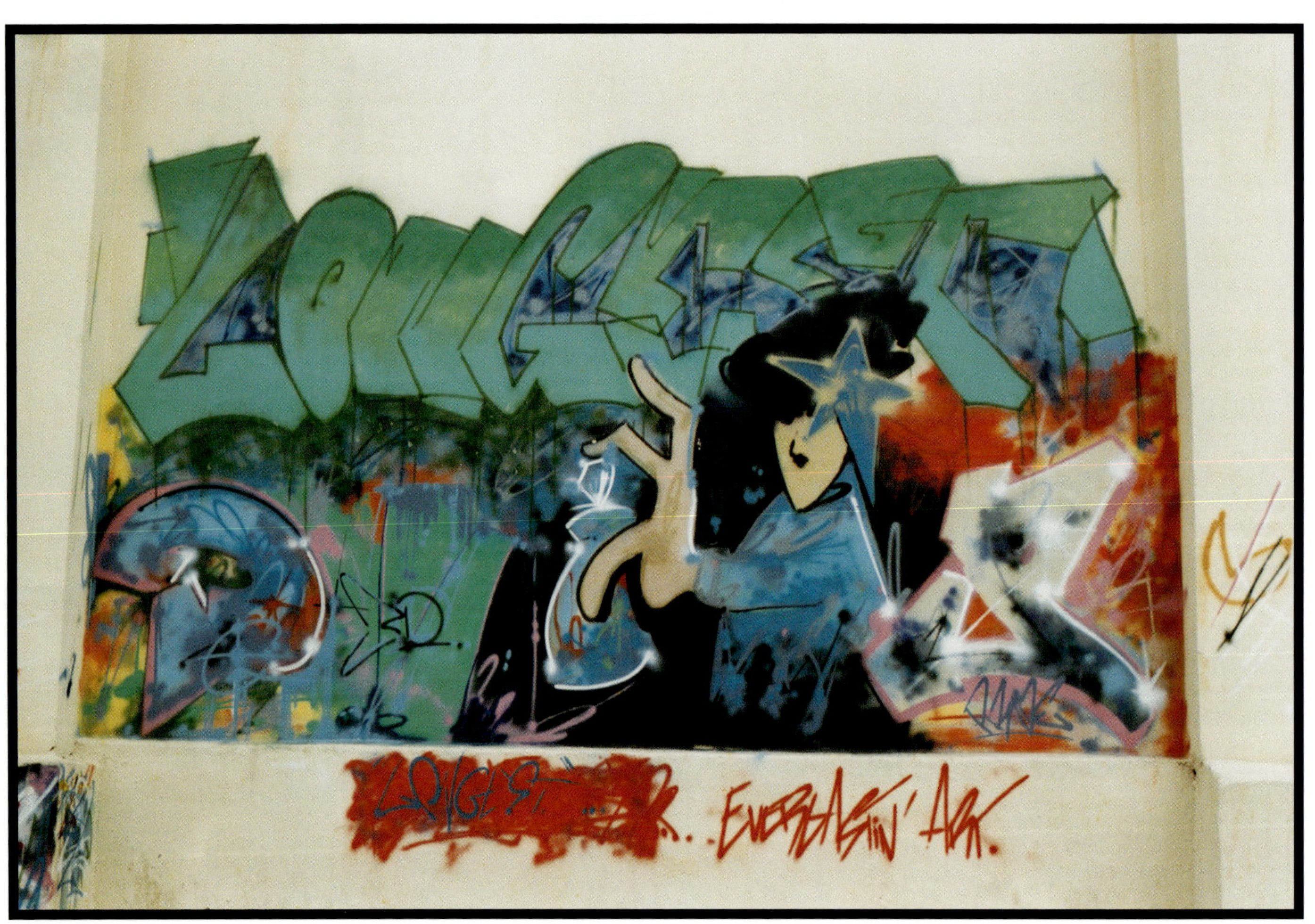

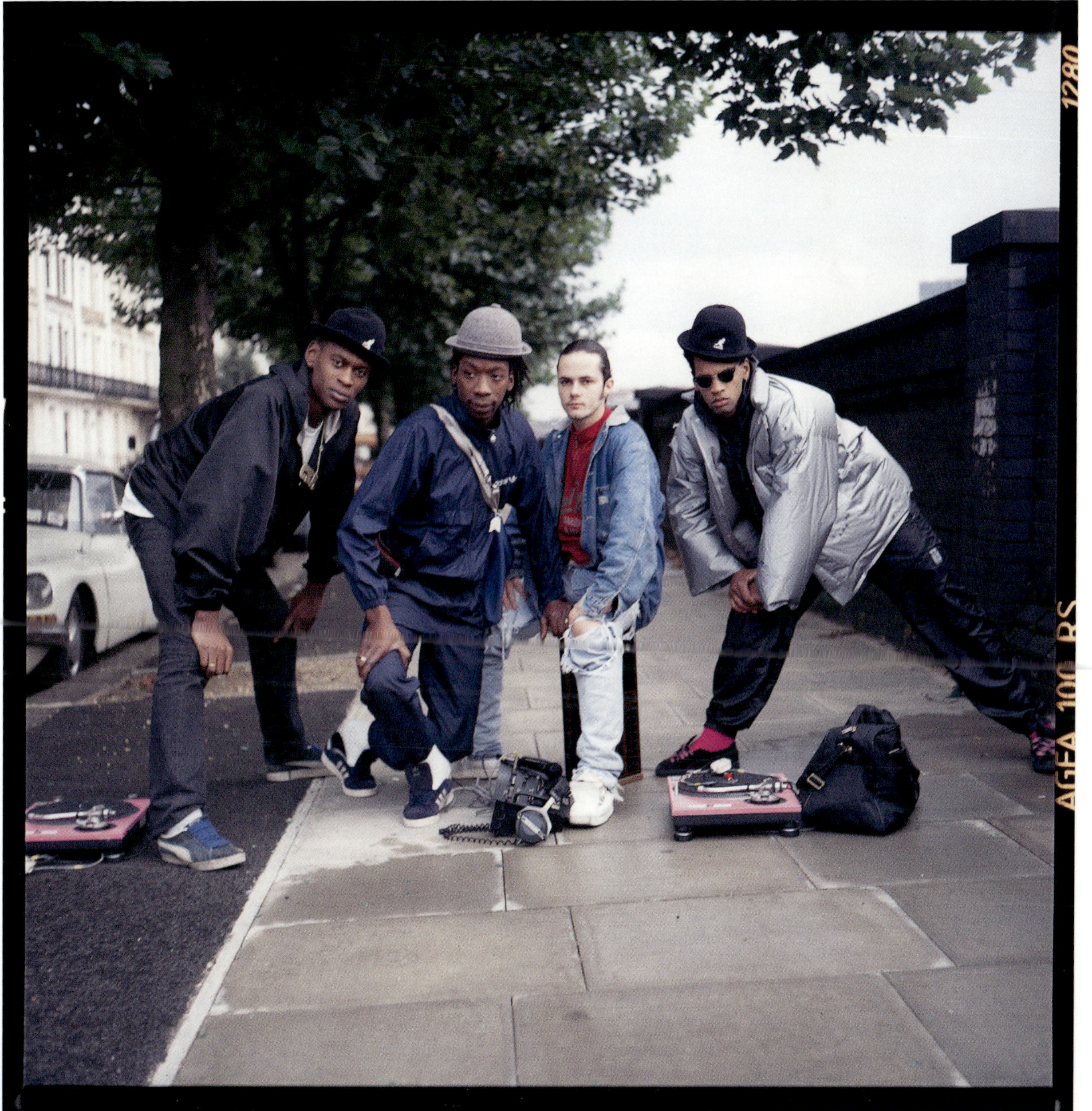

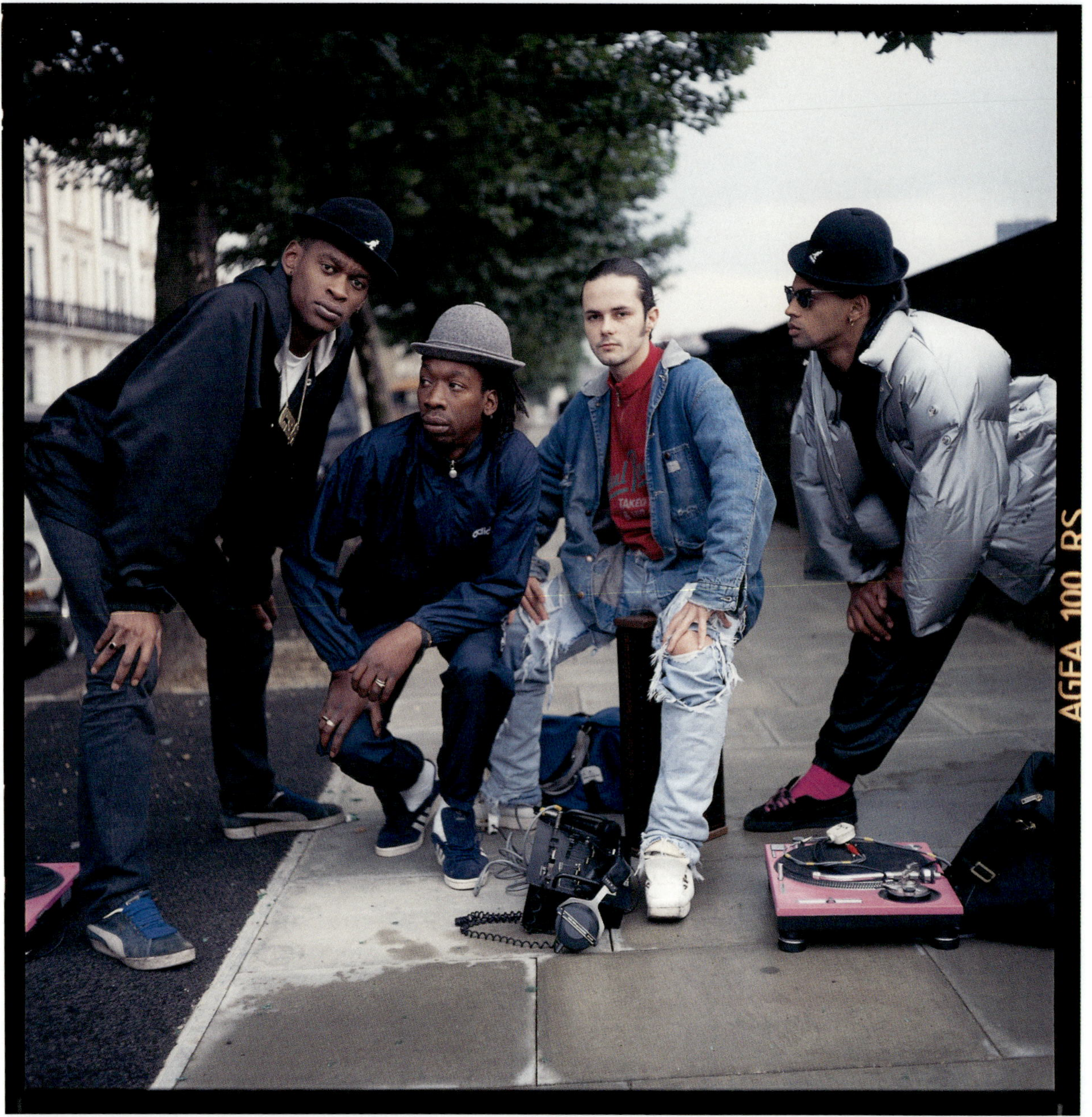

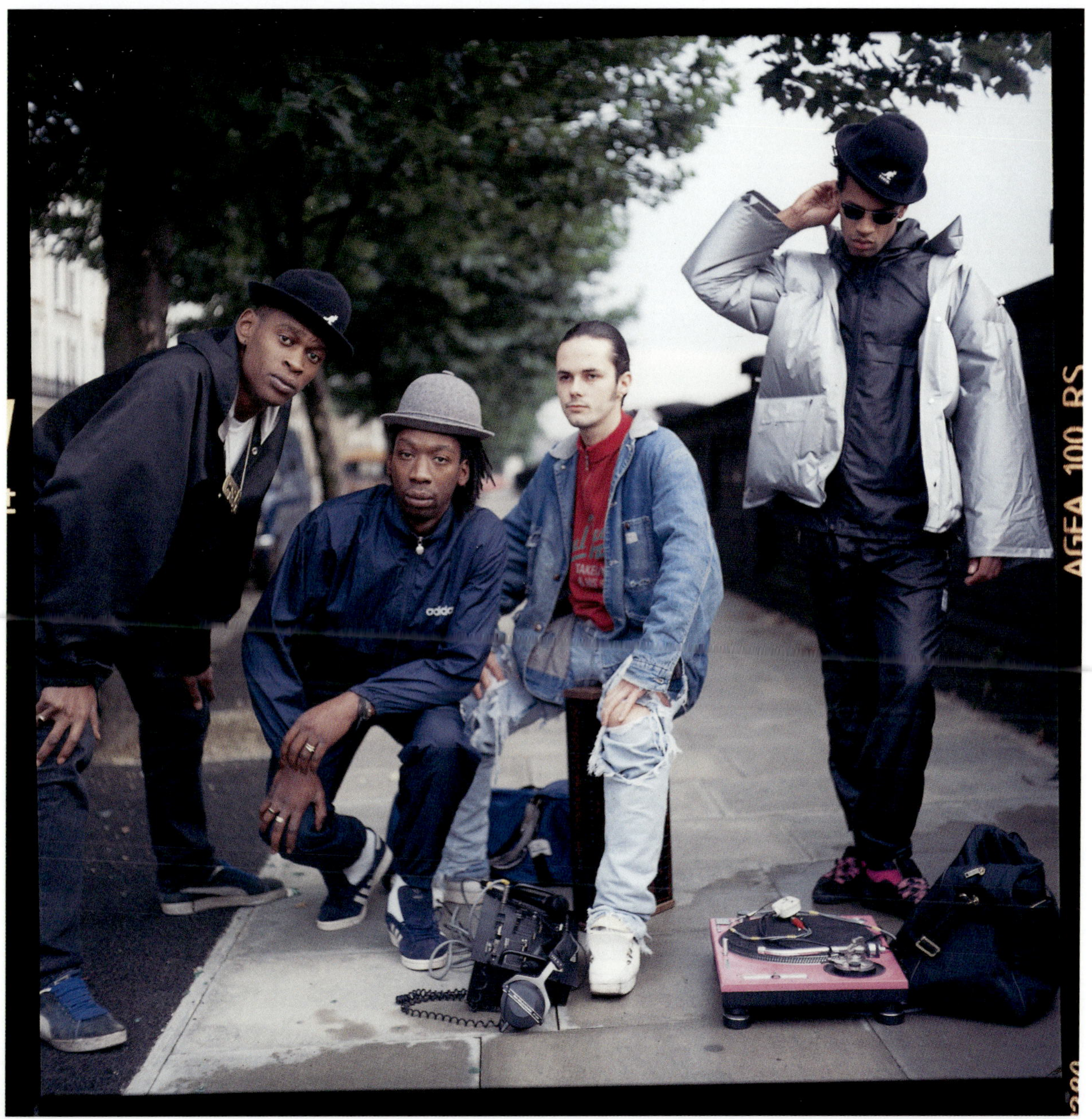
AGFA 100 RS

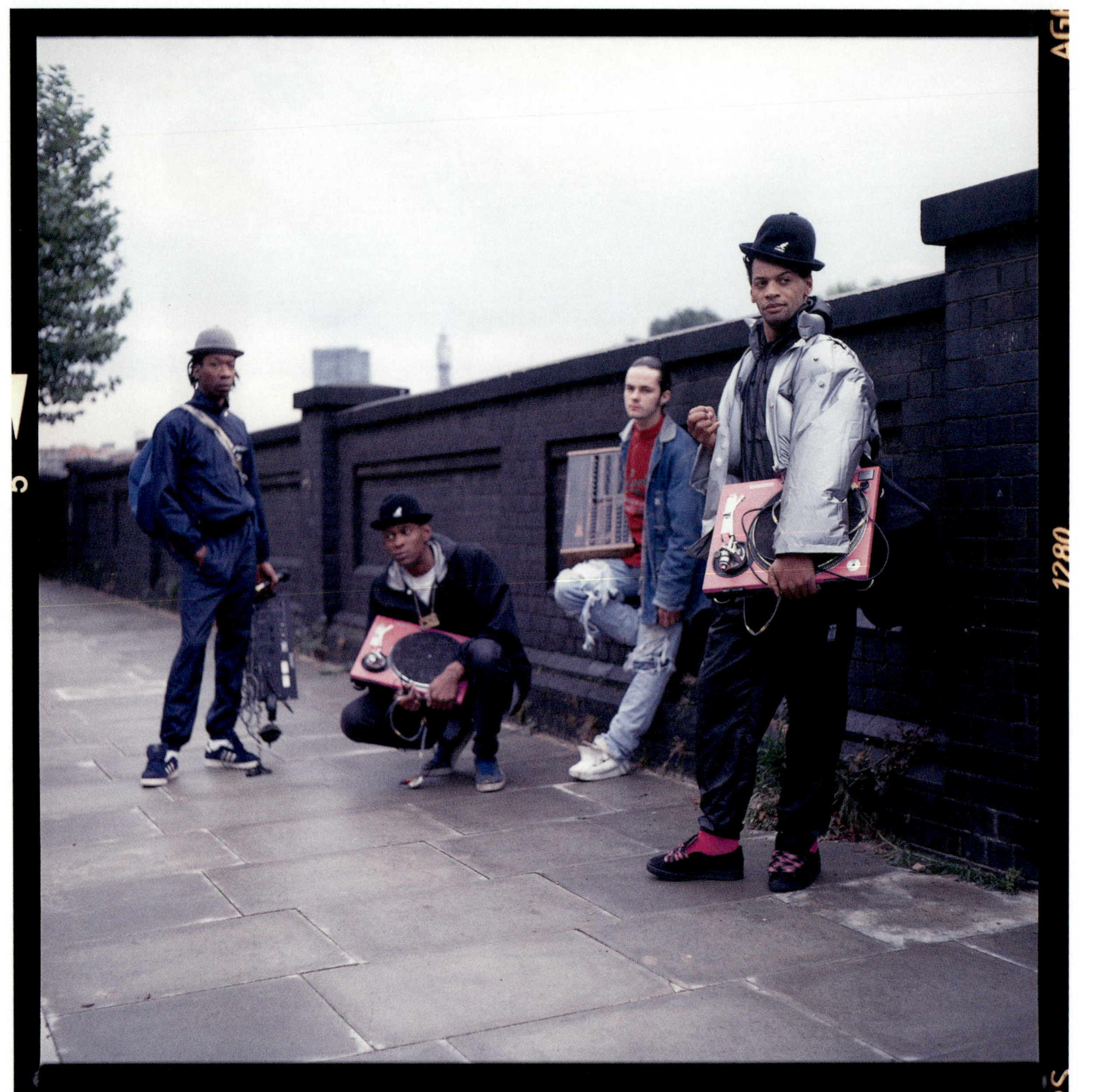

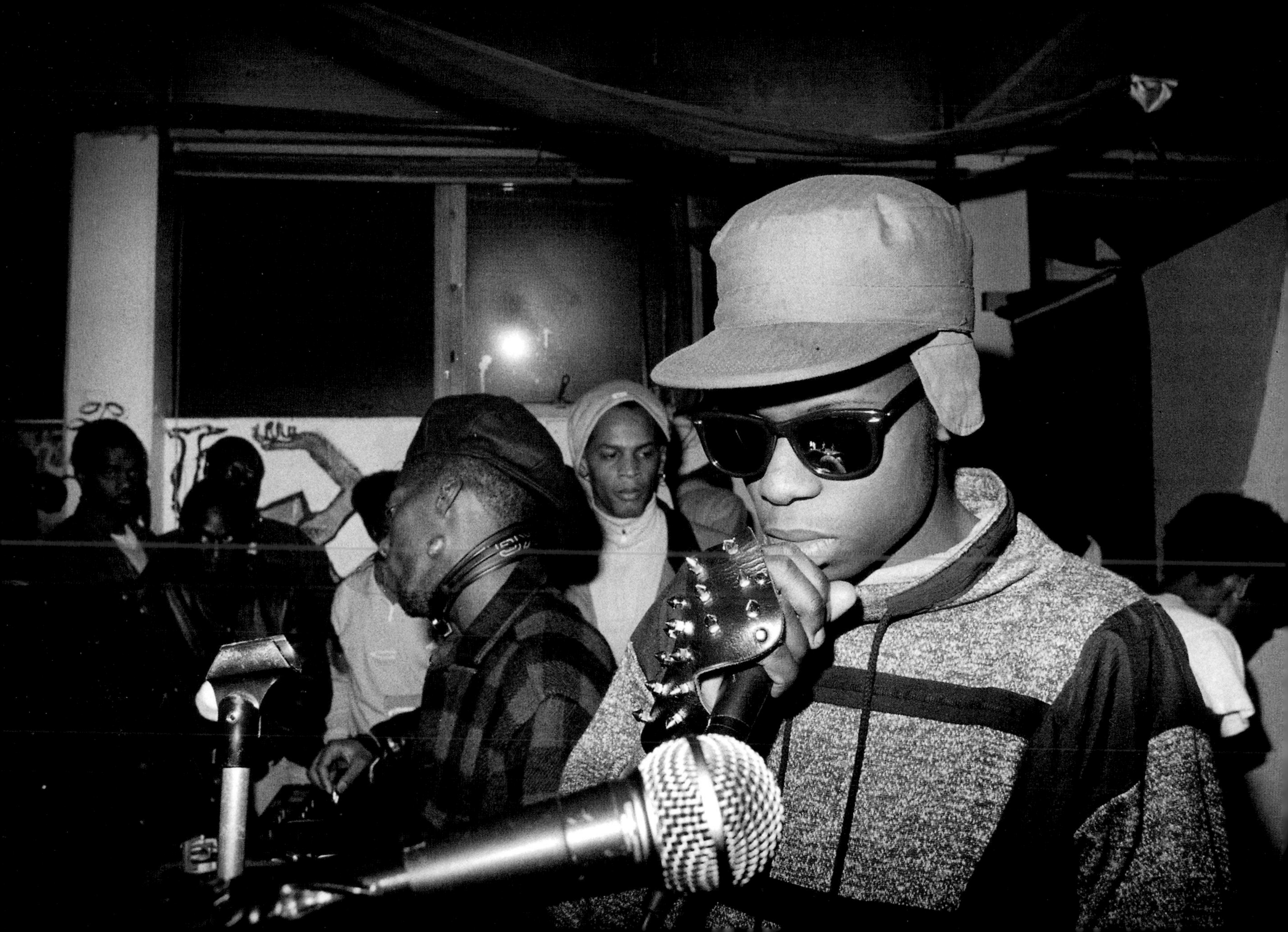

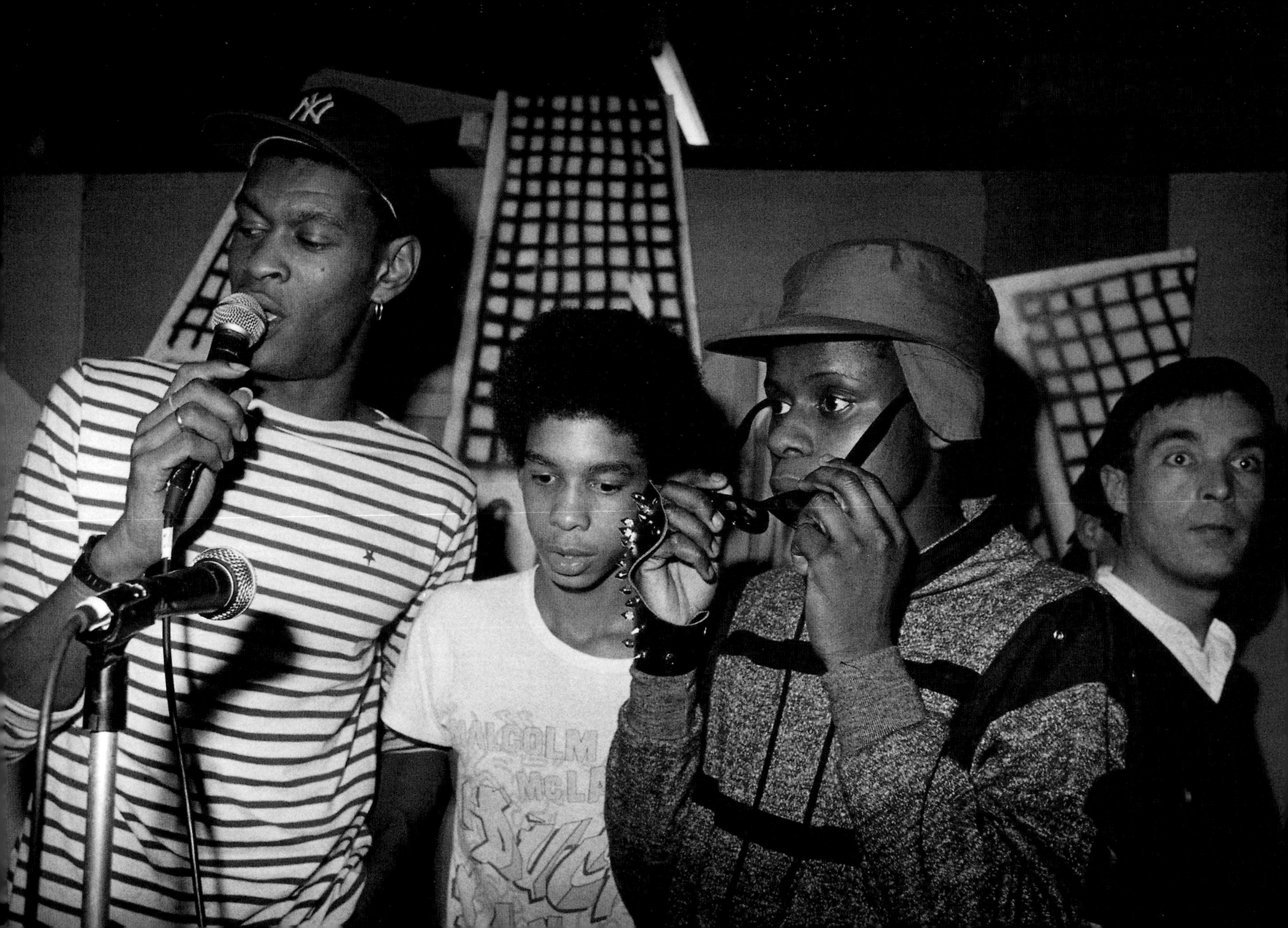

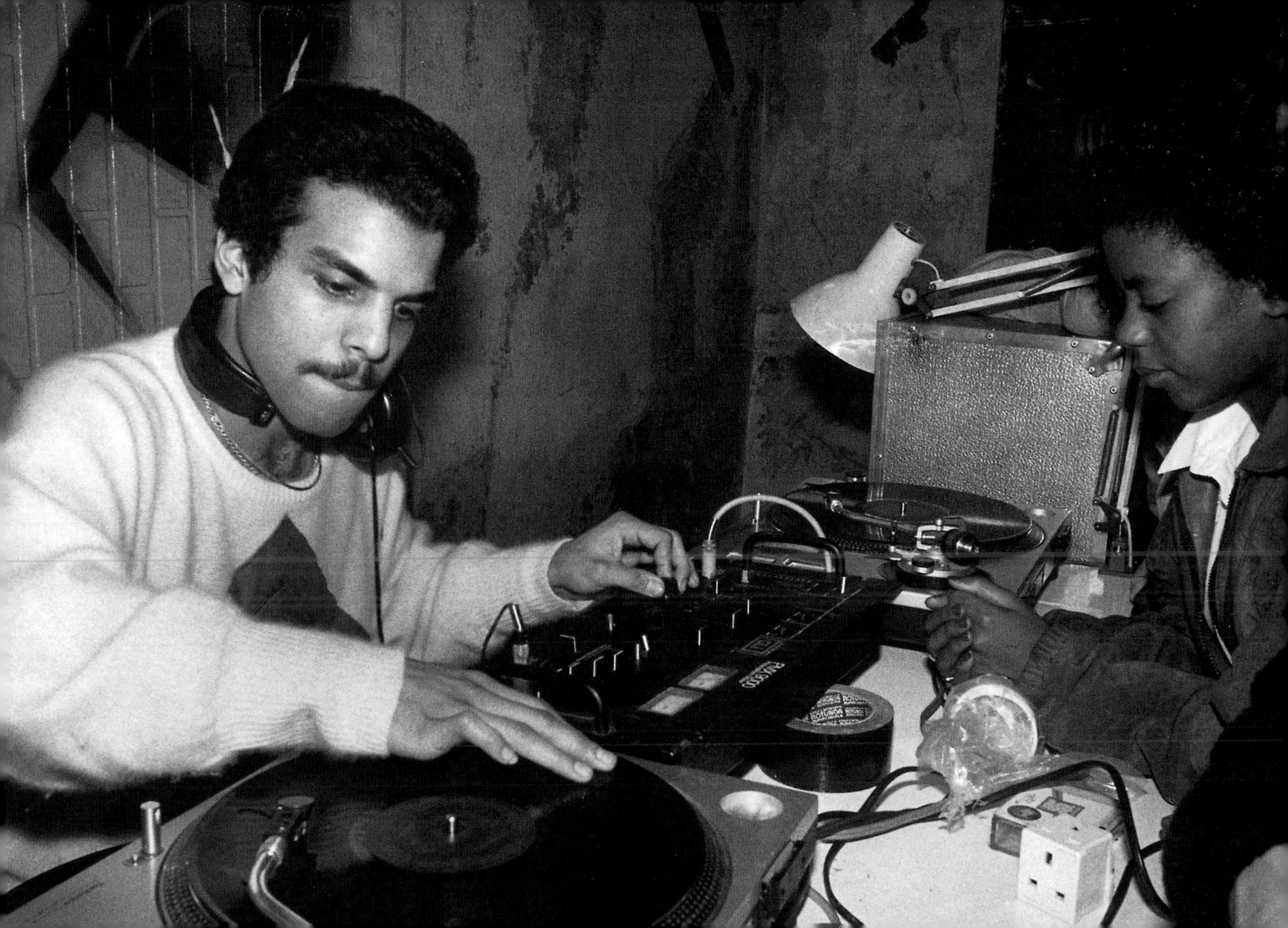

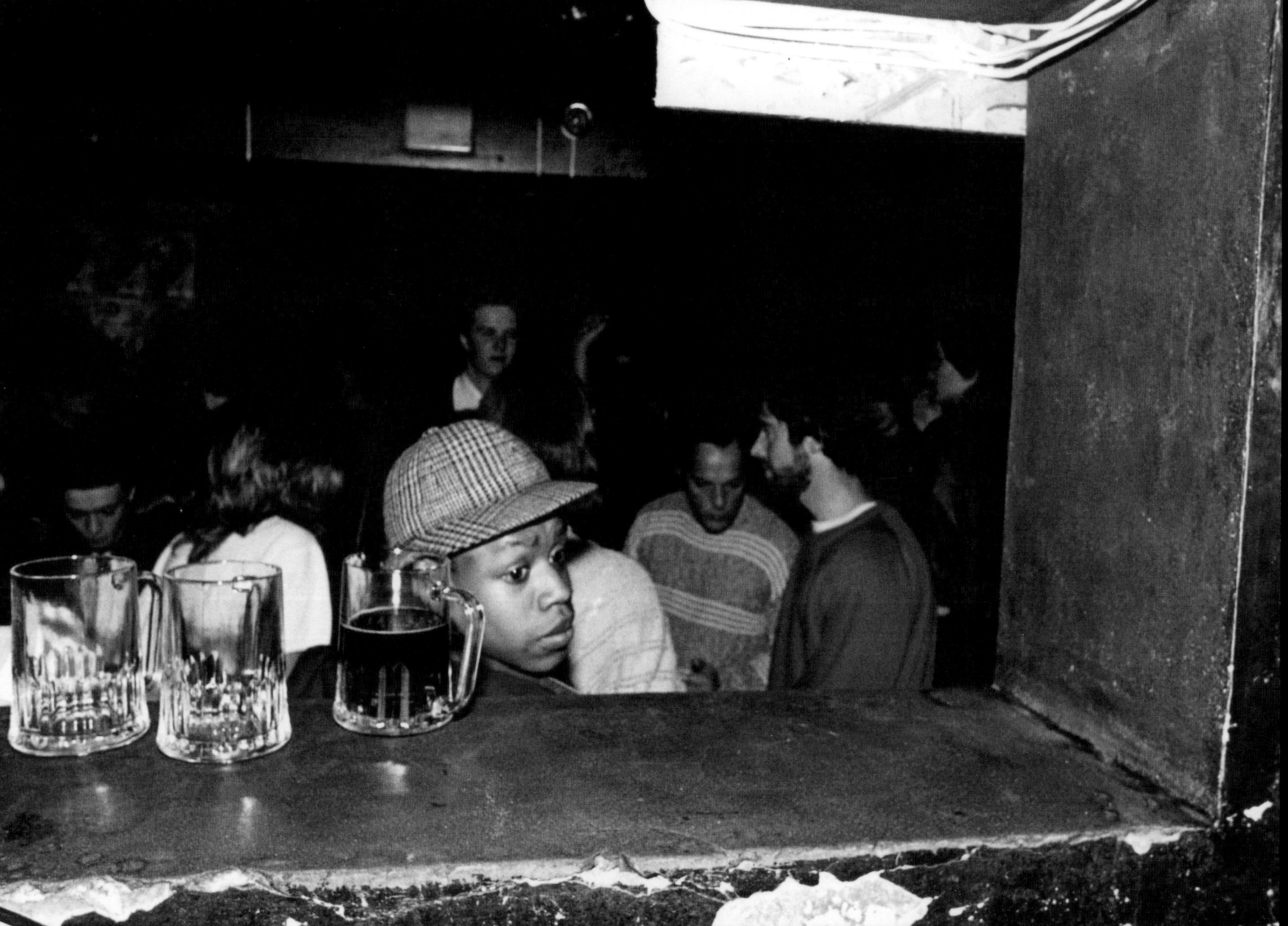

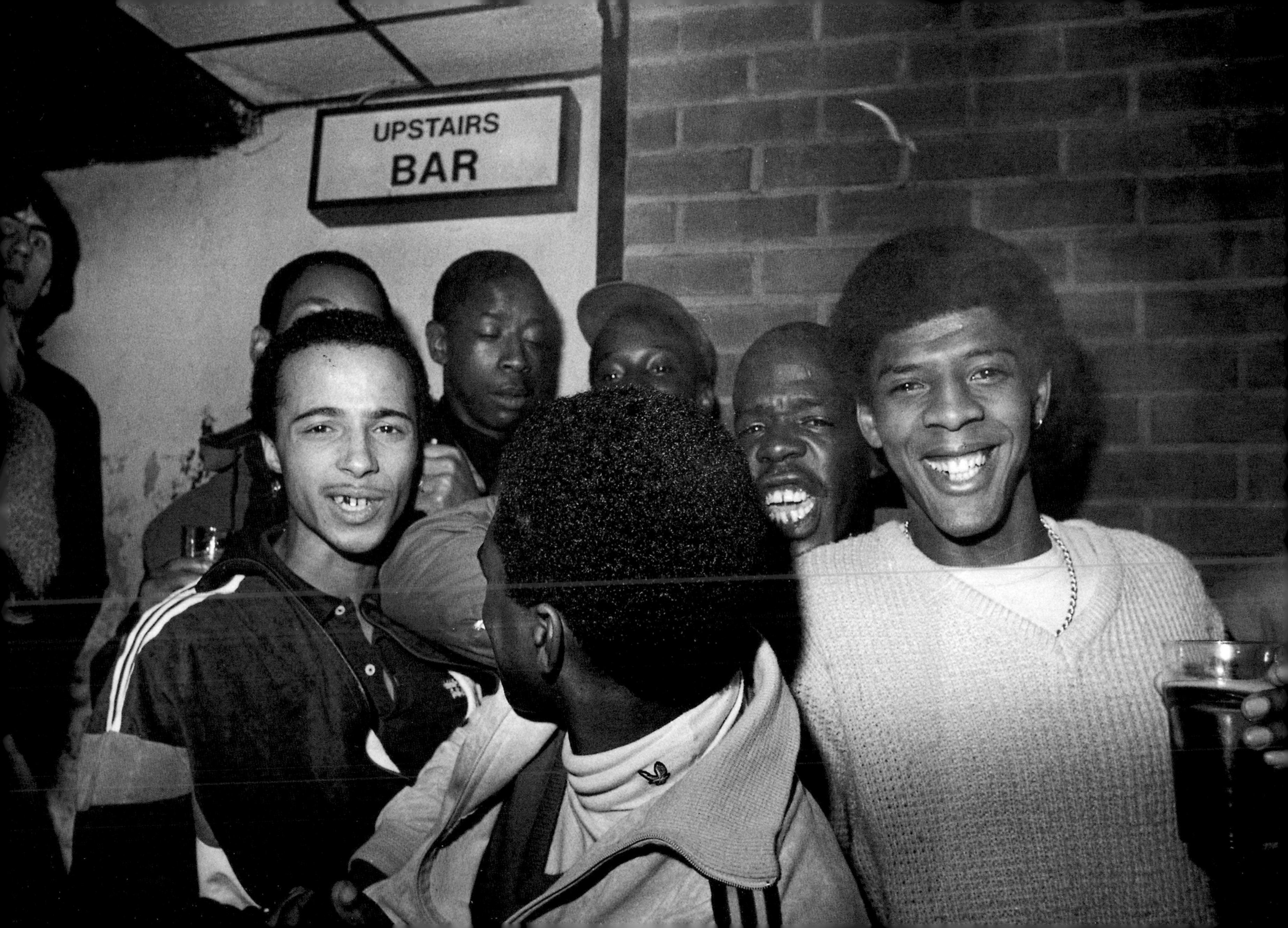
UPSTAIRS
BAR

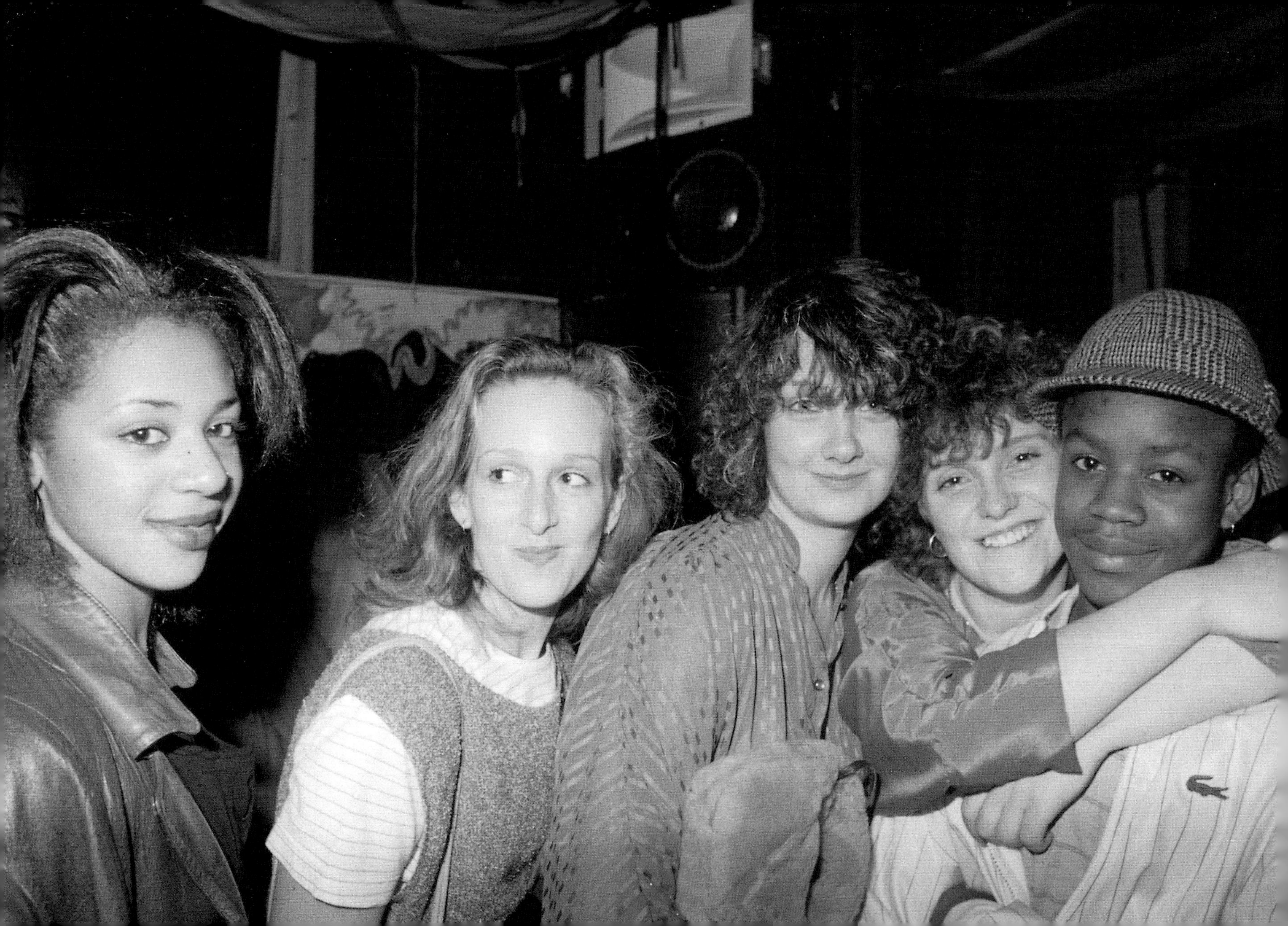

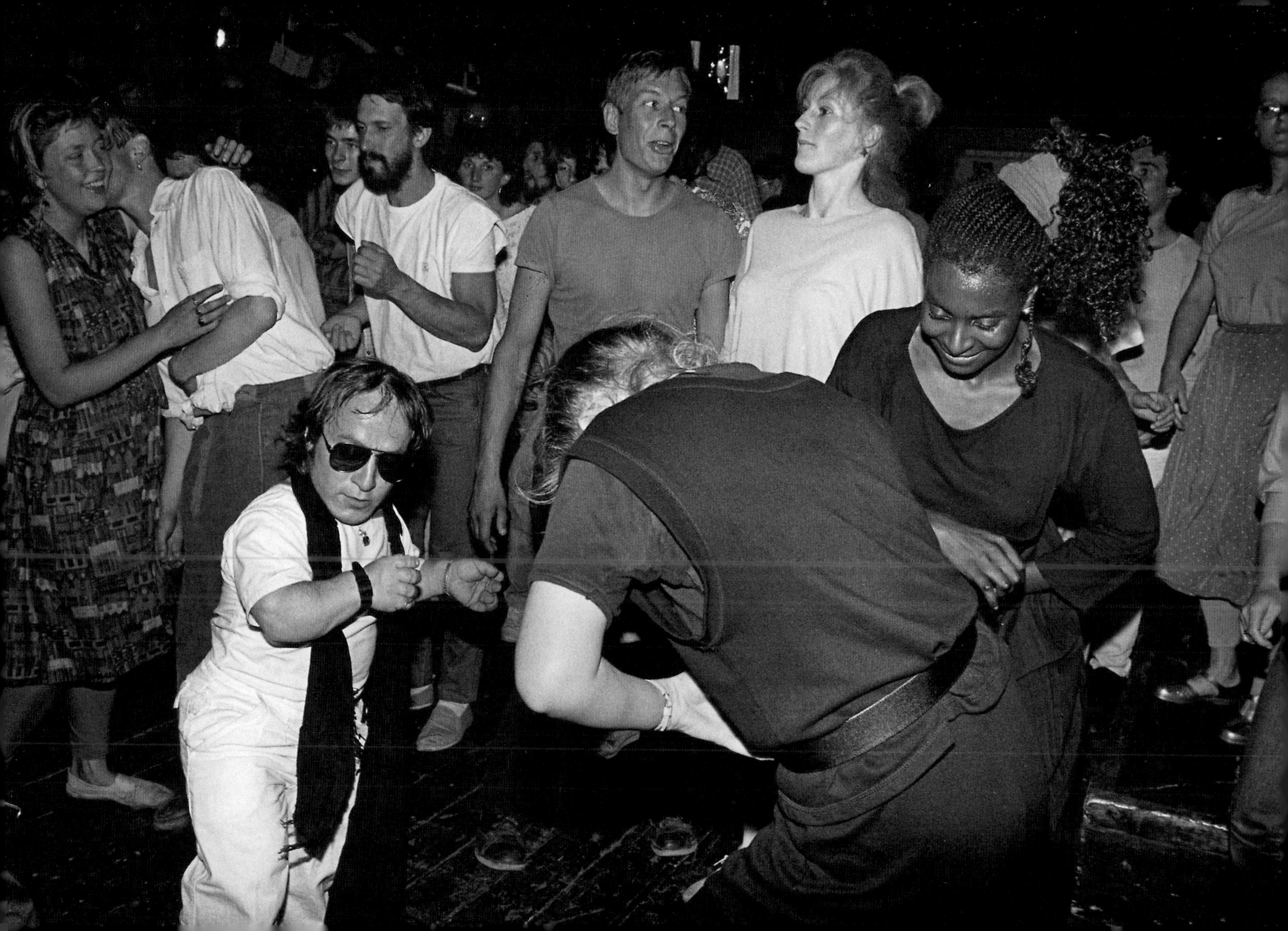

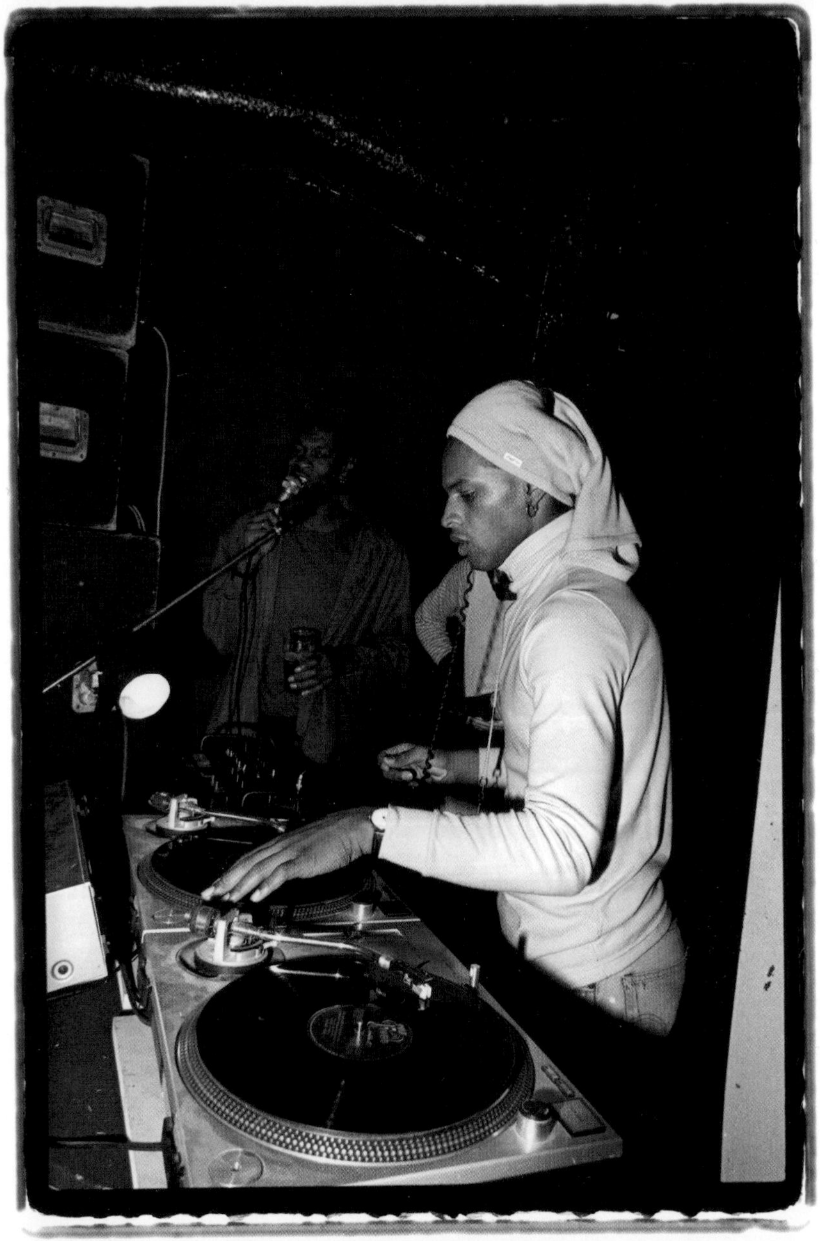

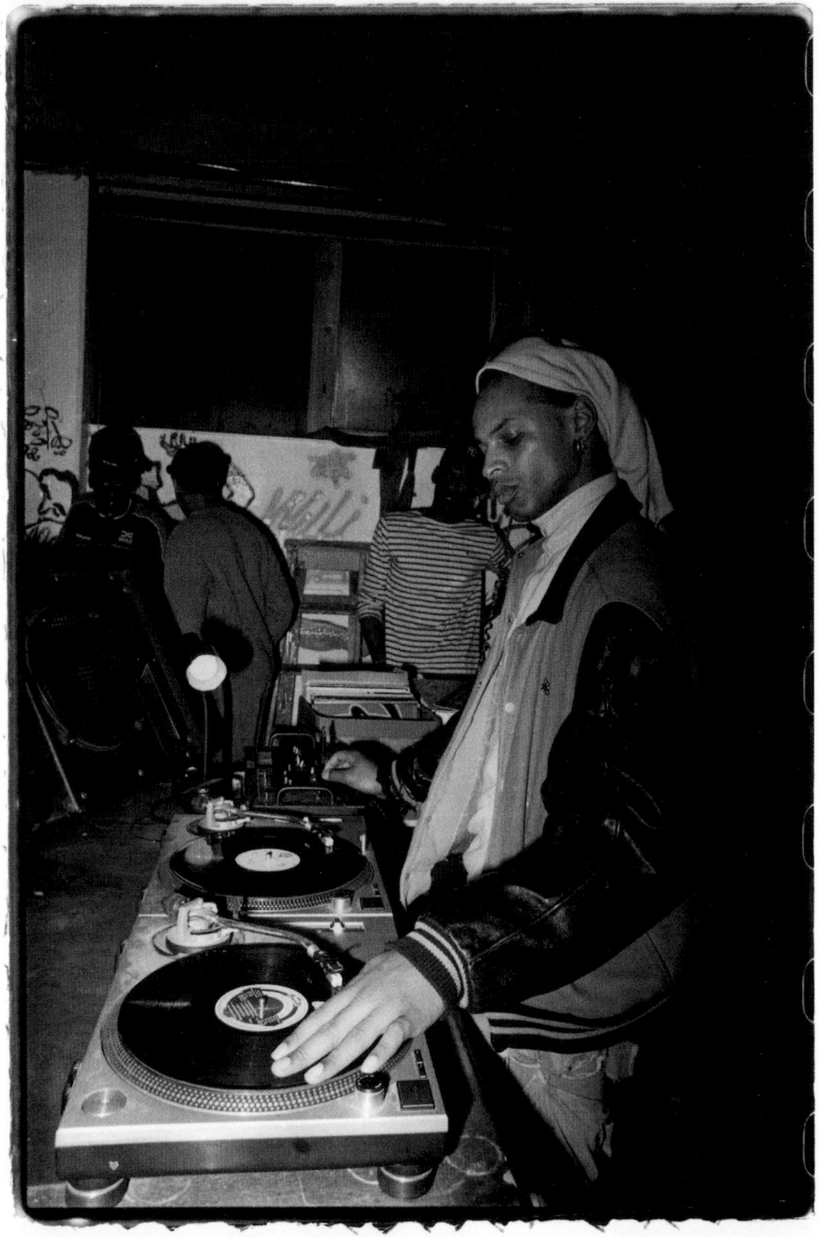

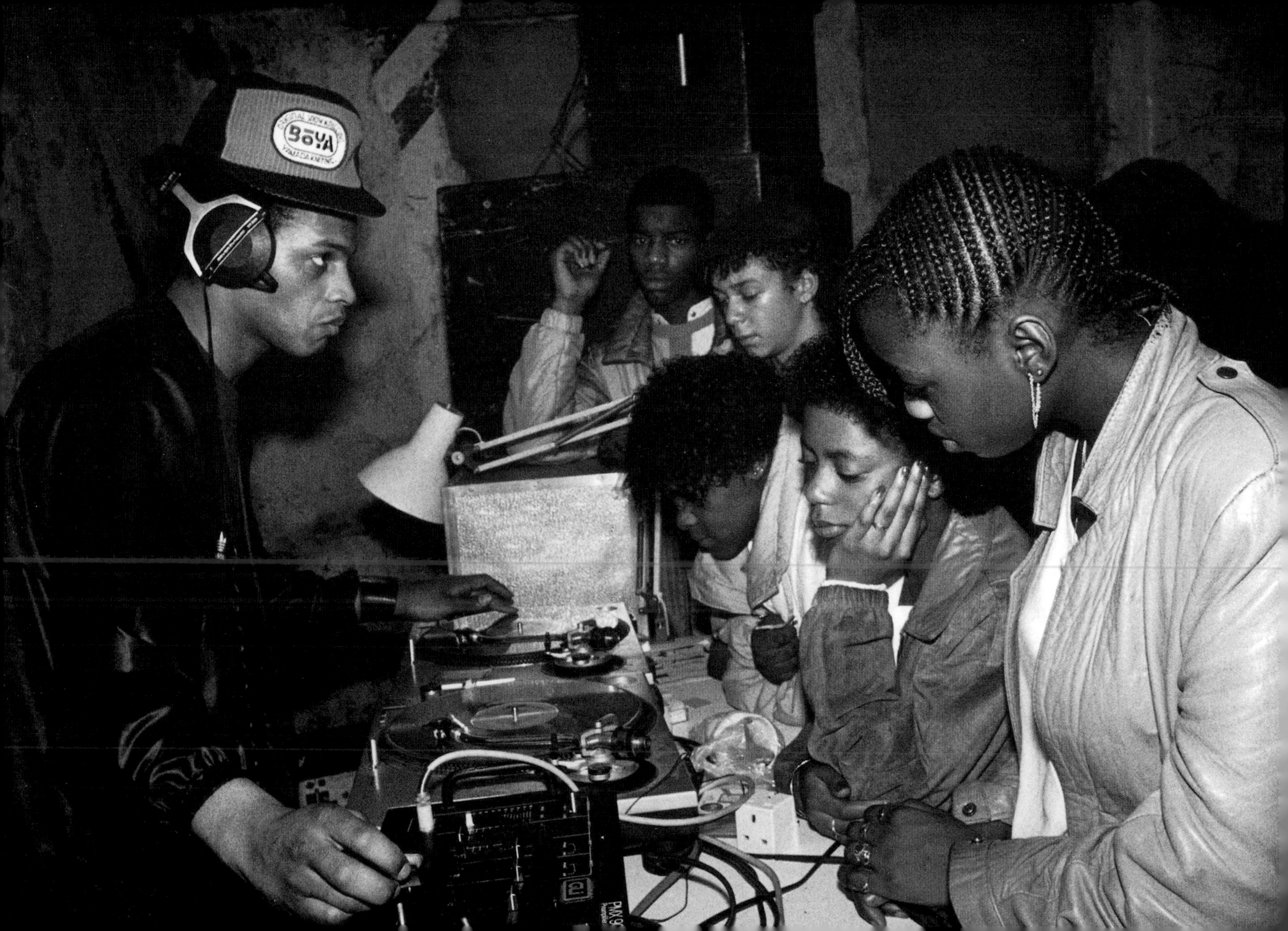

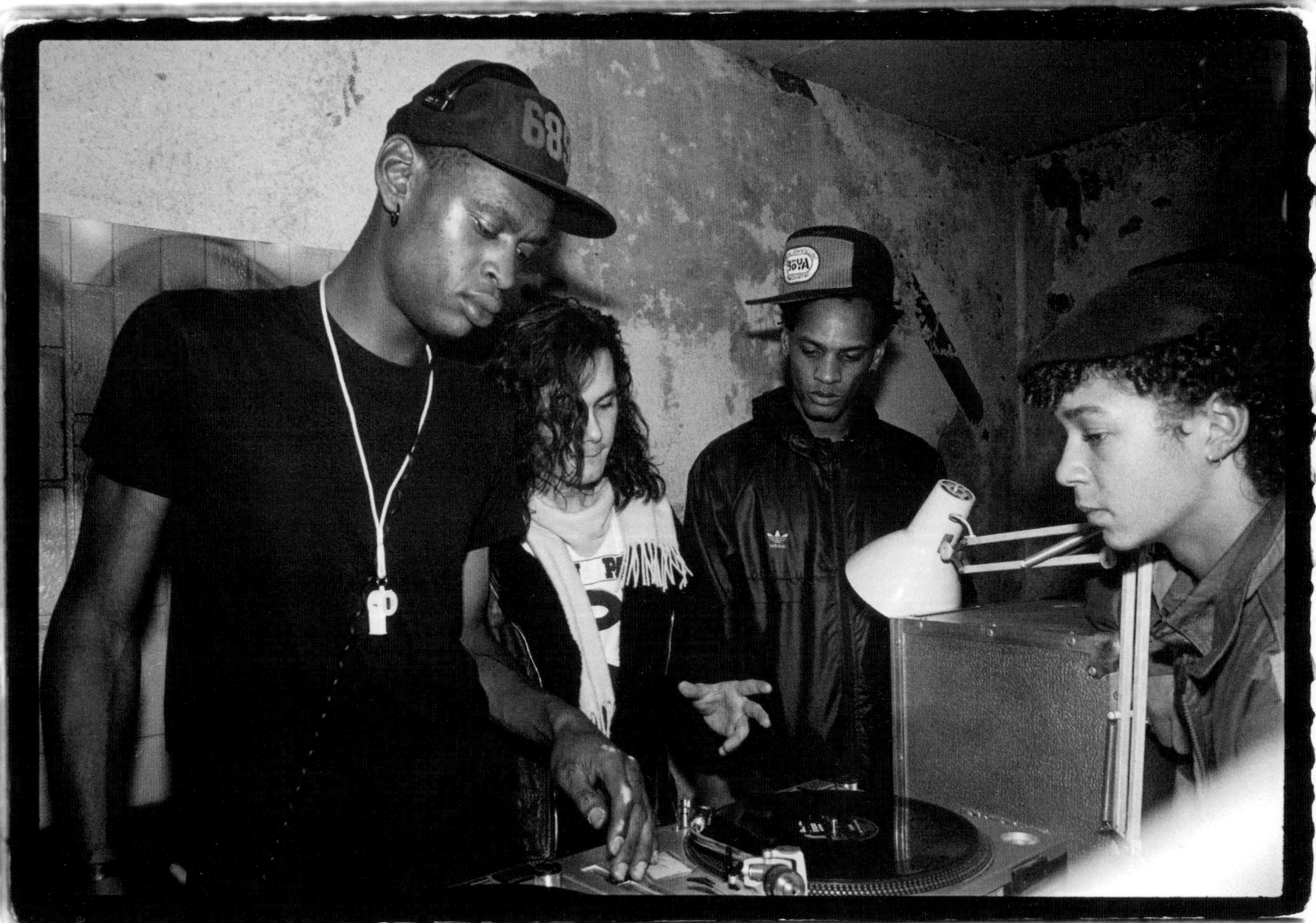

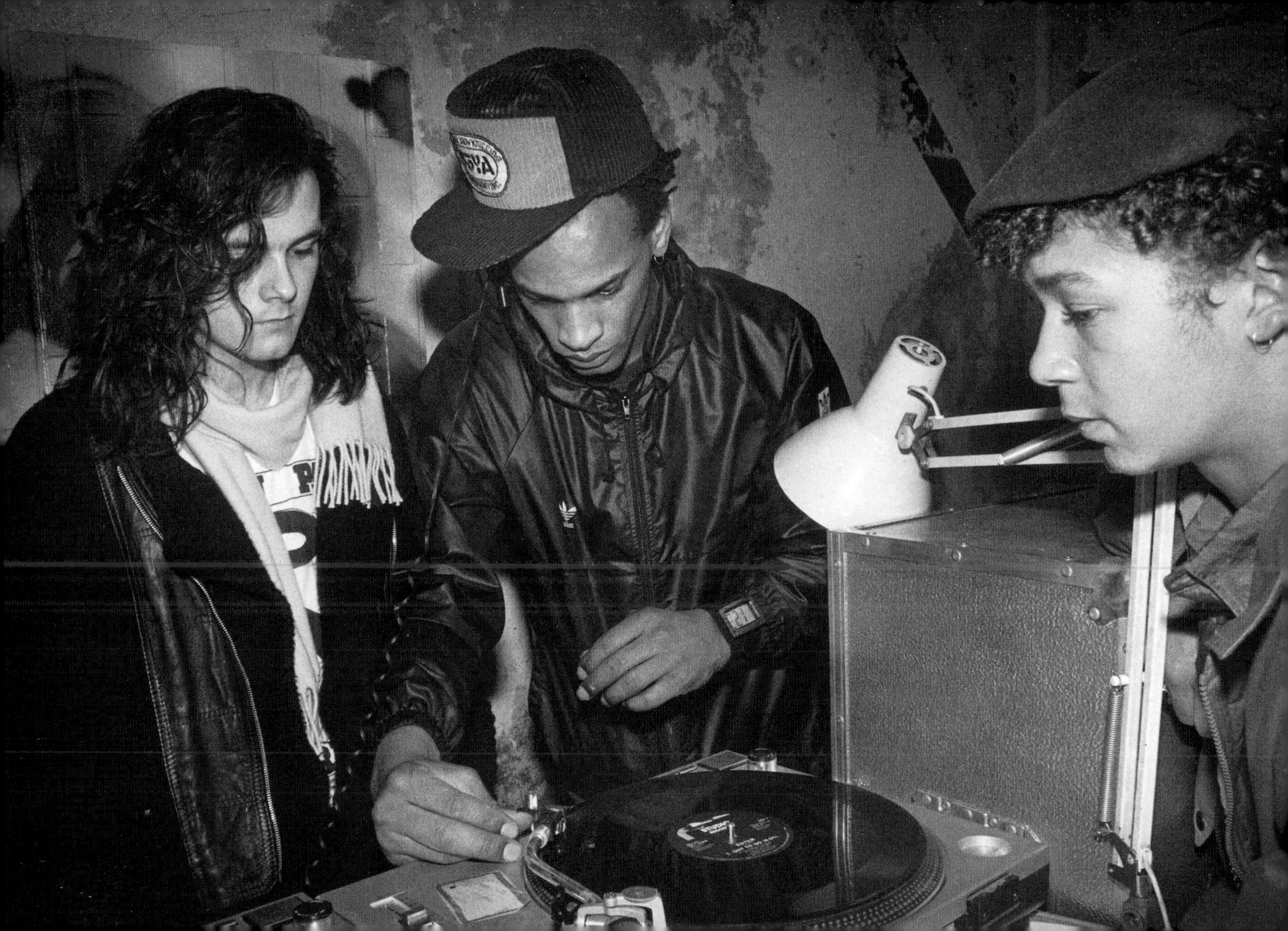

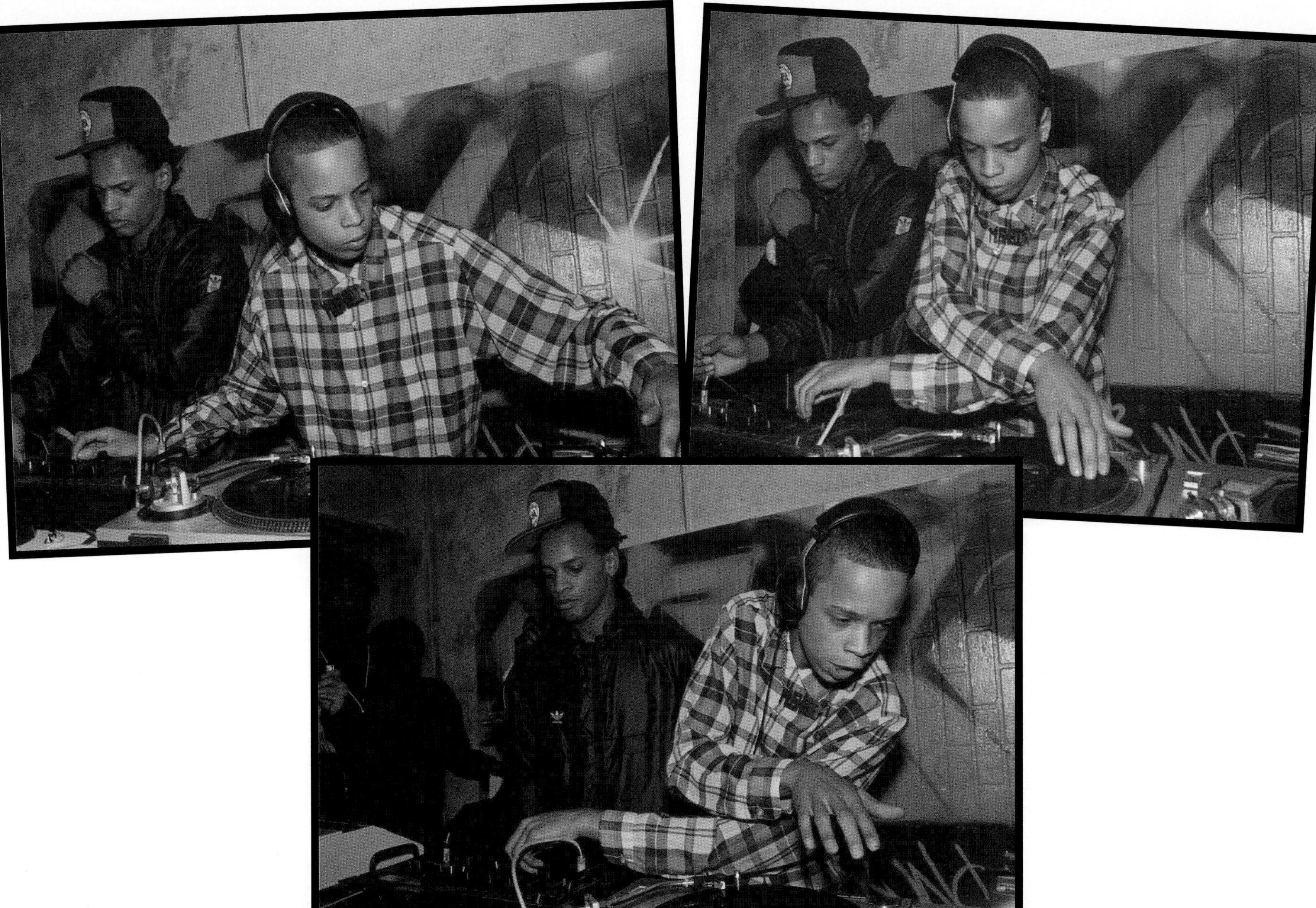

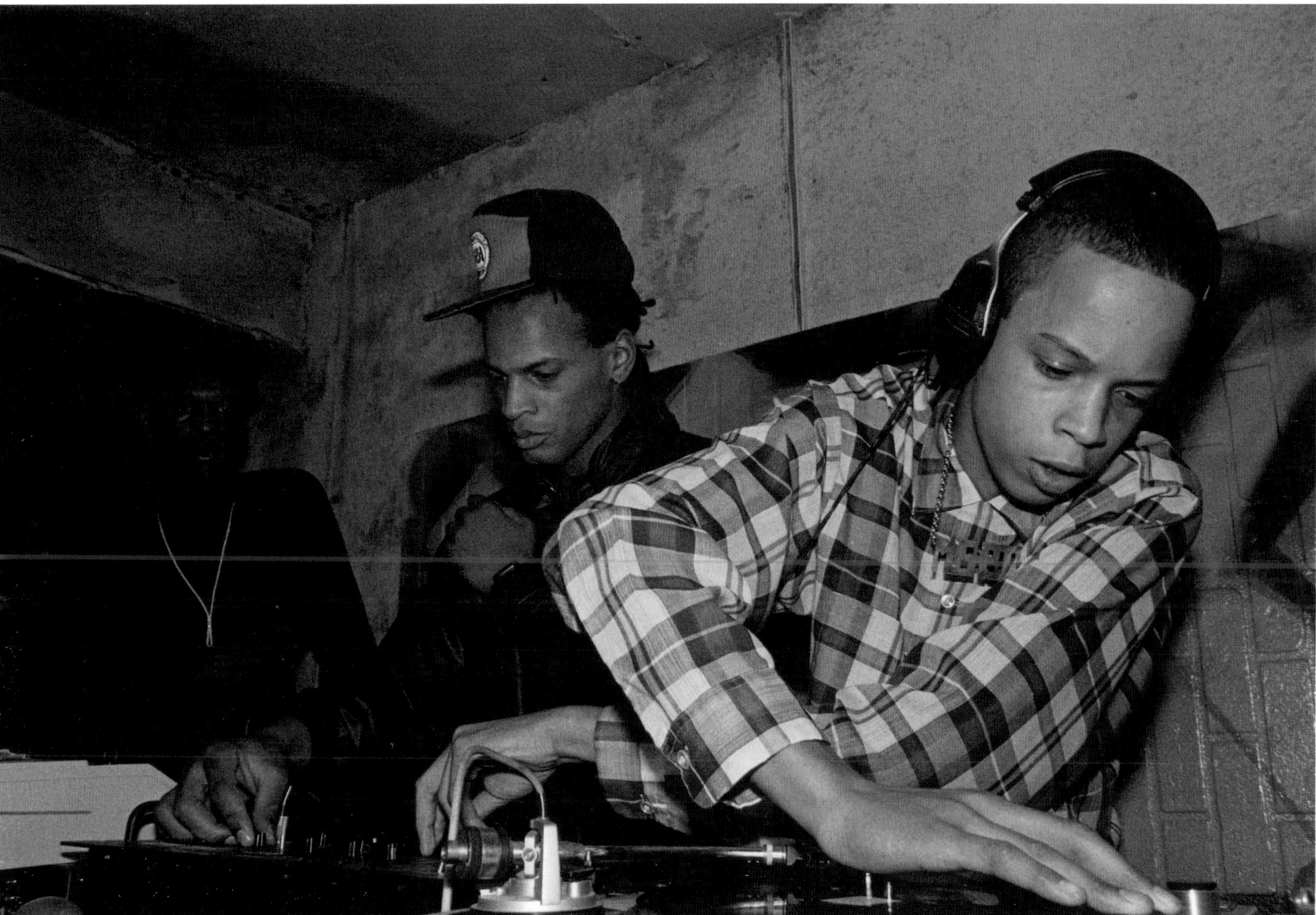

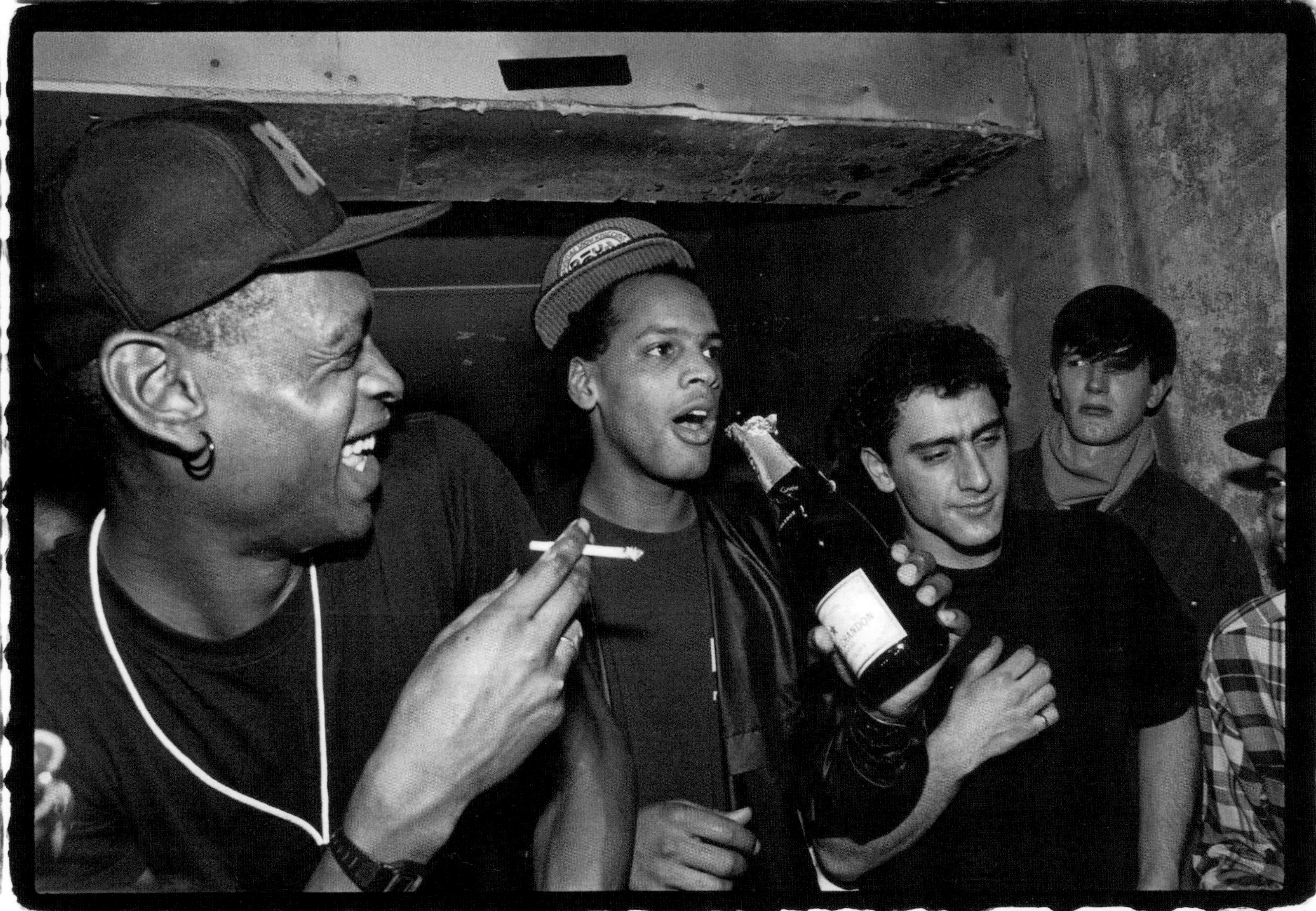

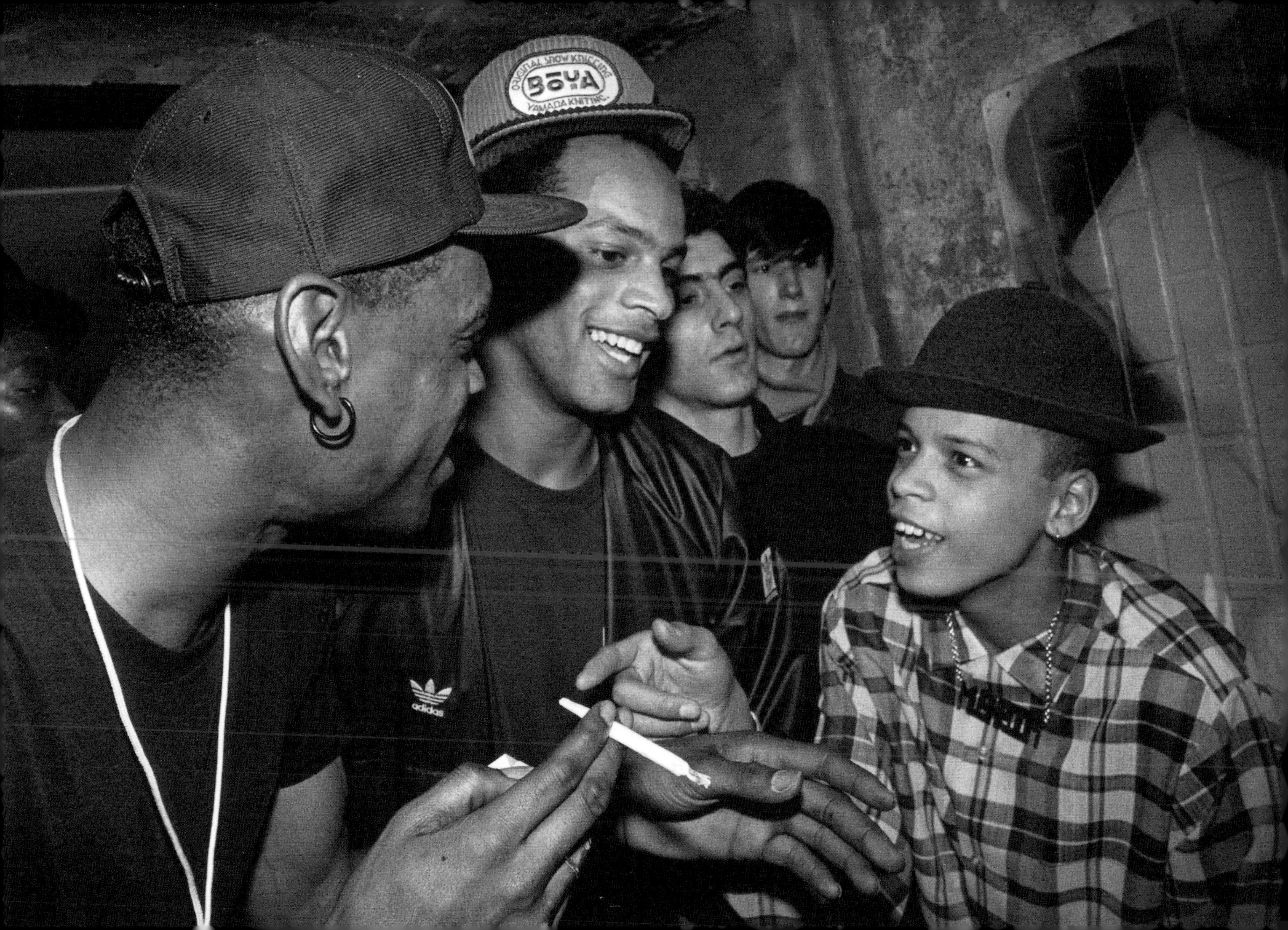

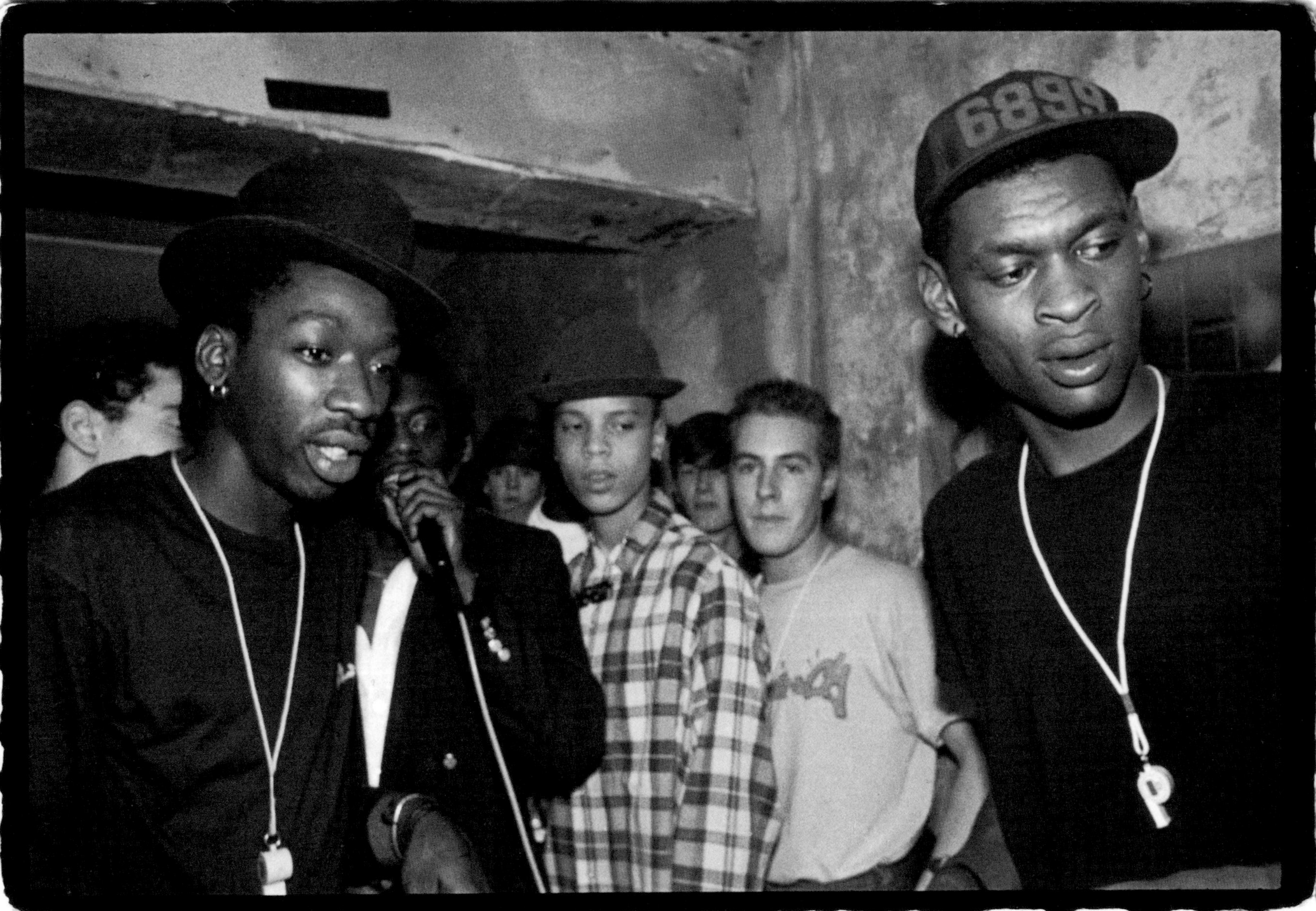

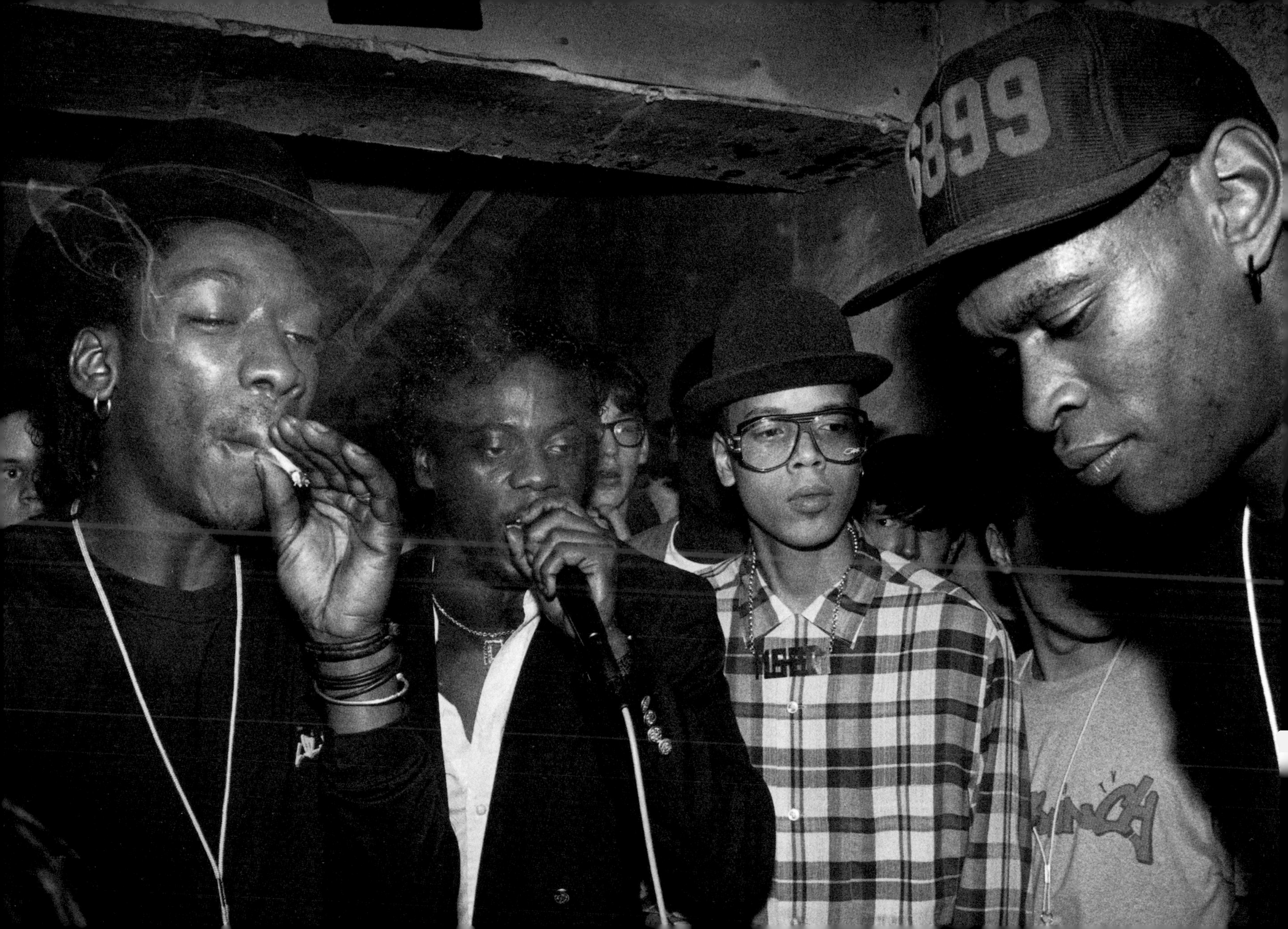
6899

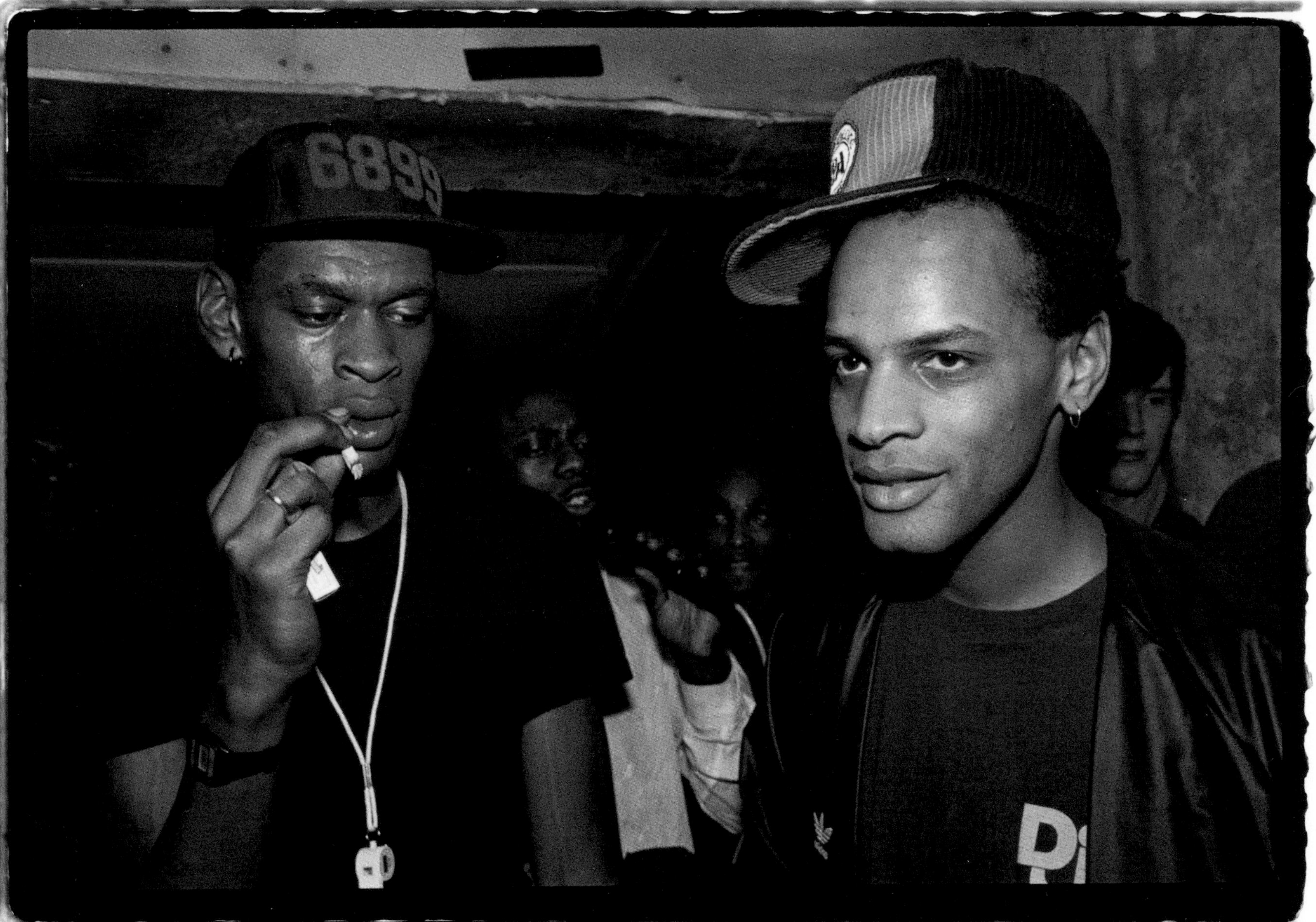

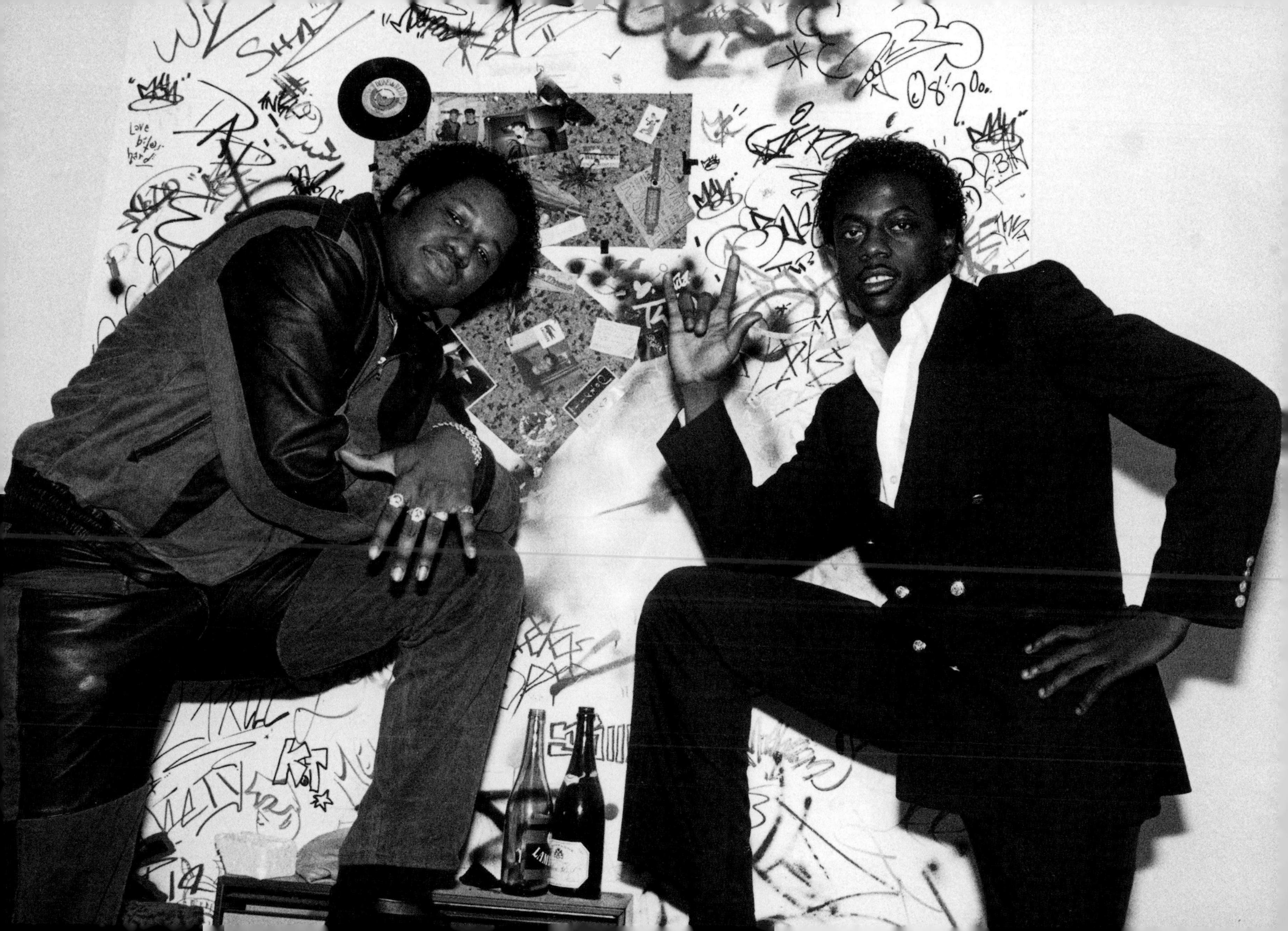

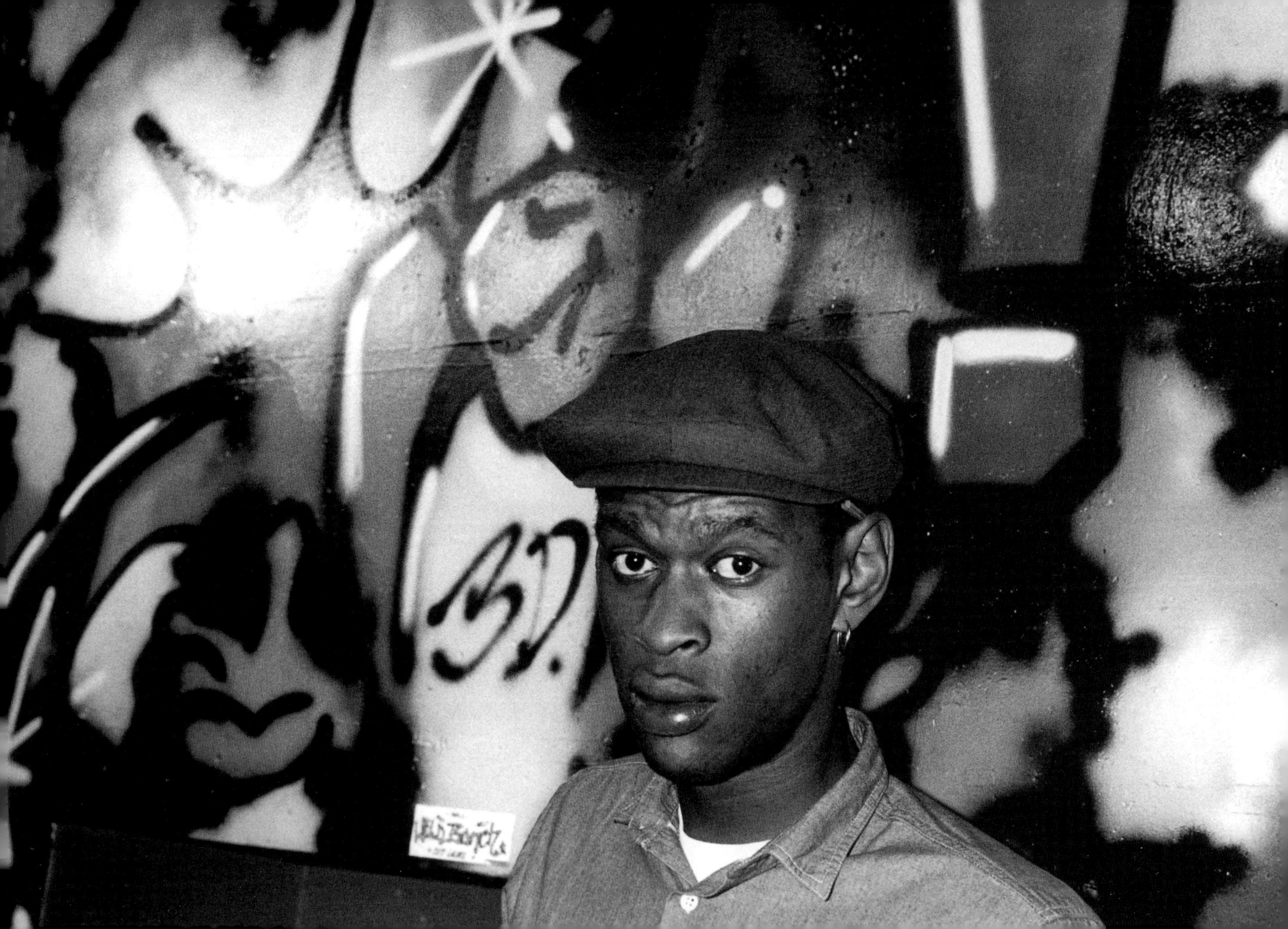
3D
Wild Bunch

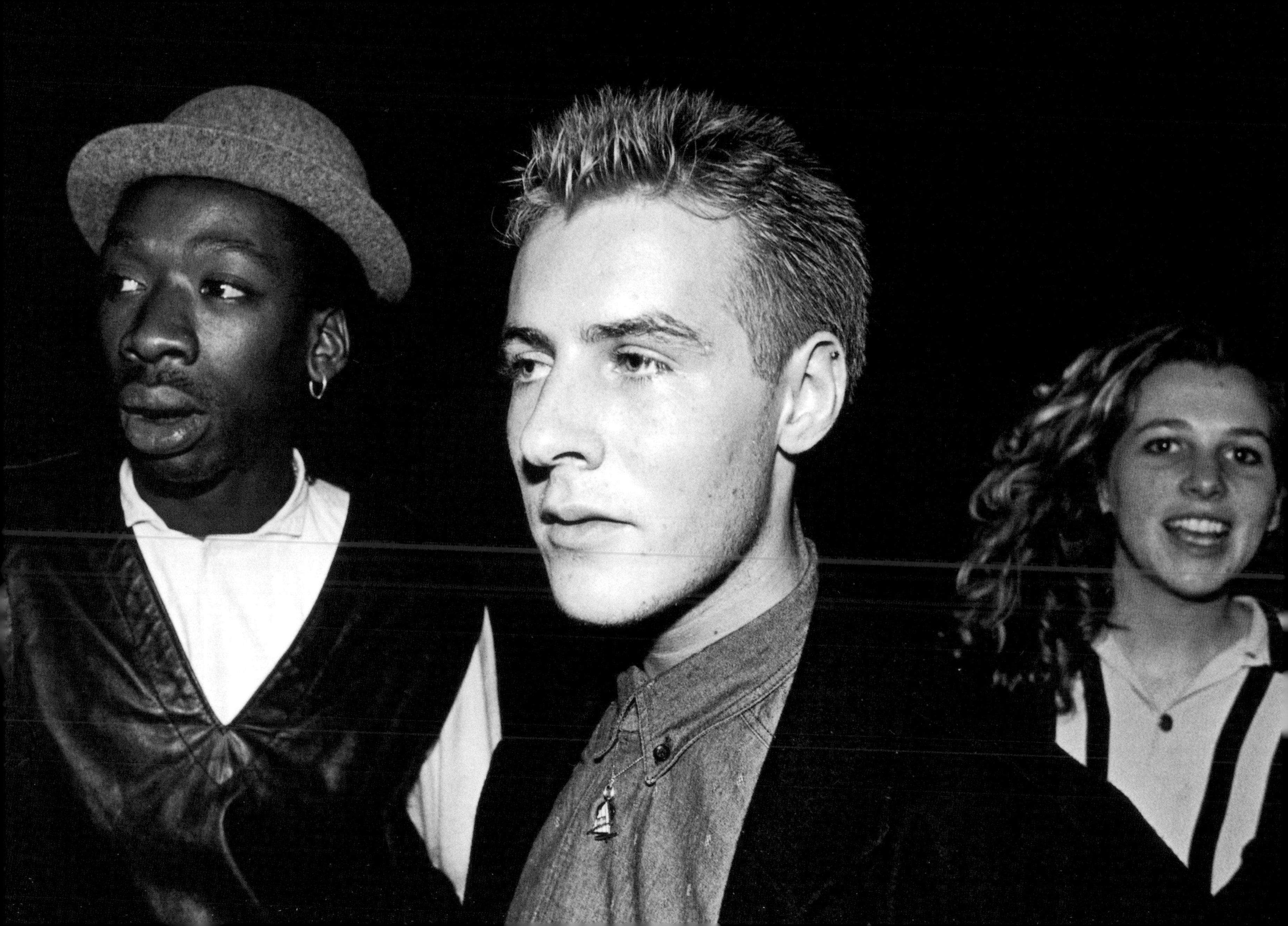

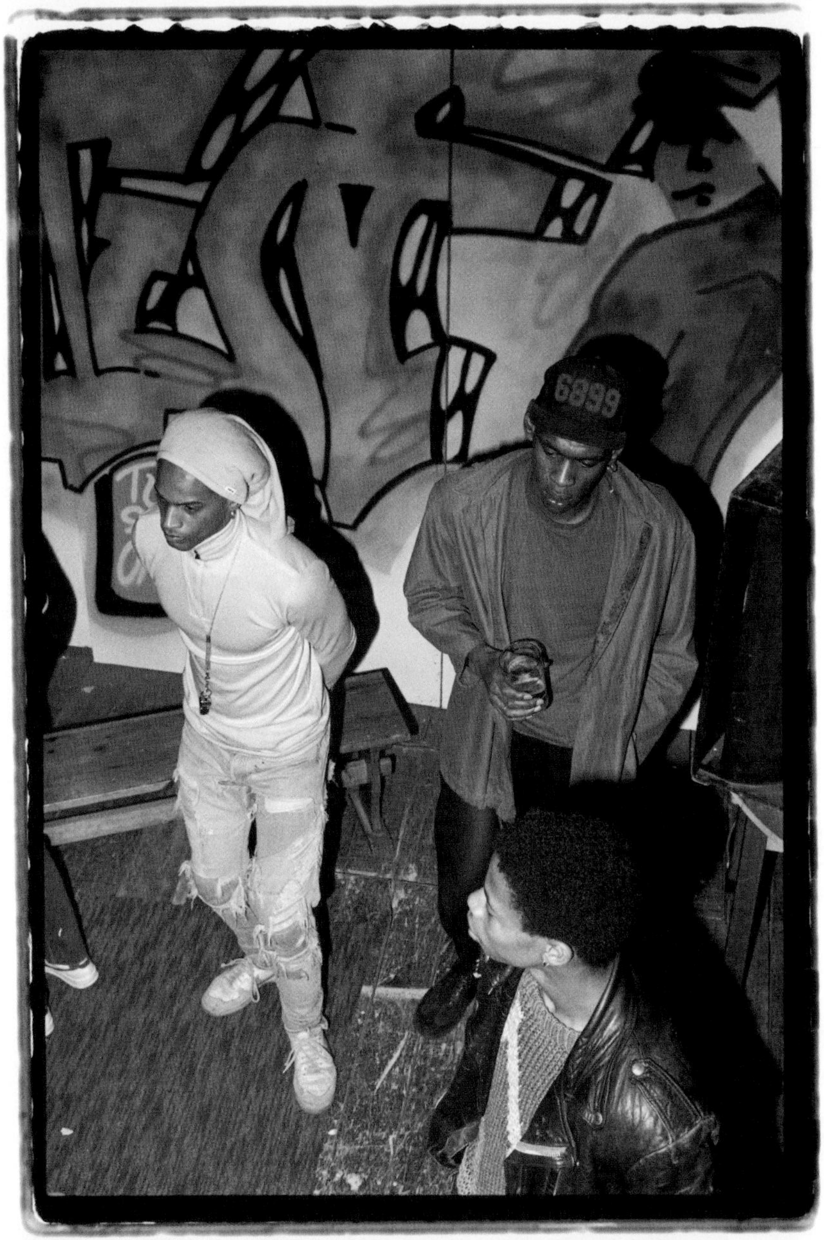

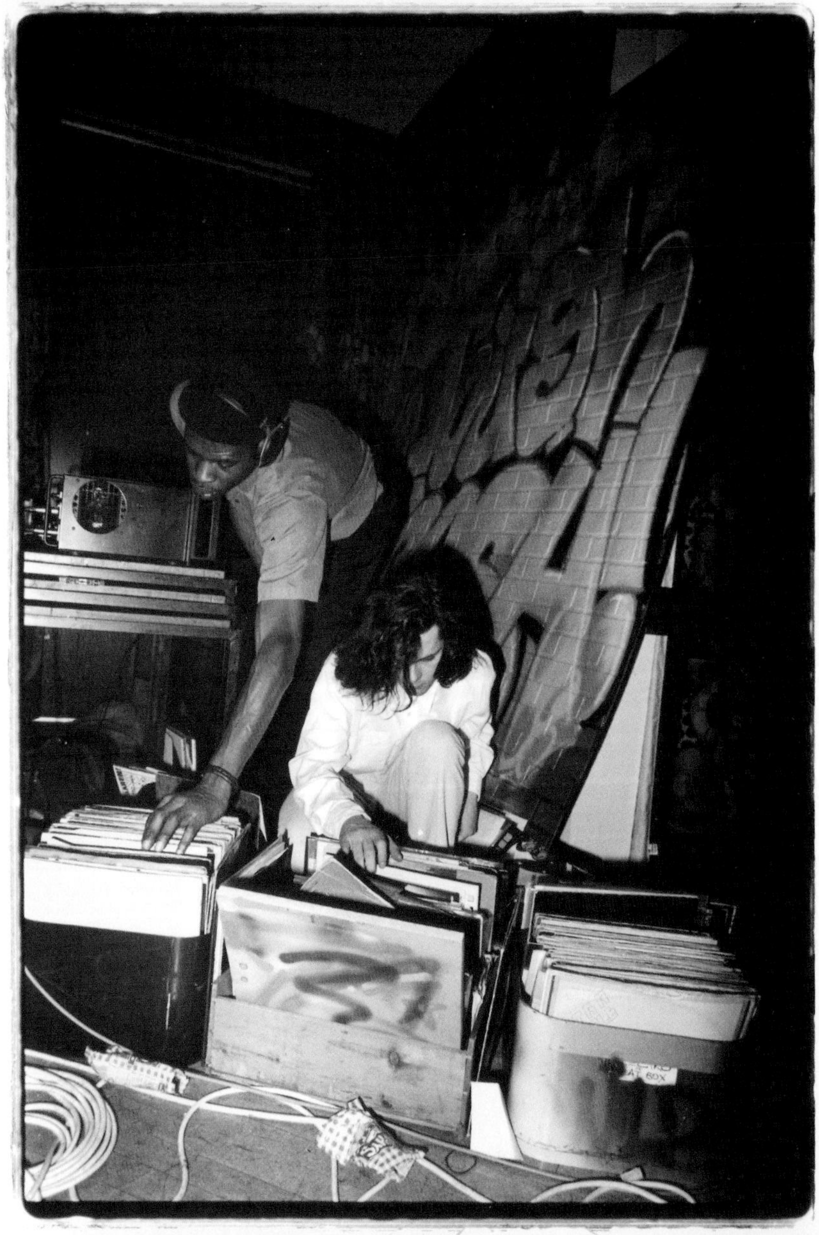

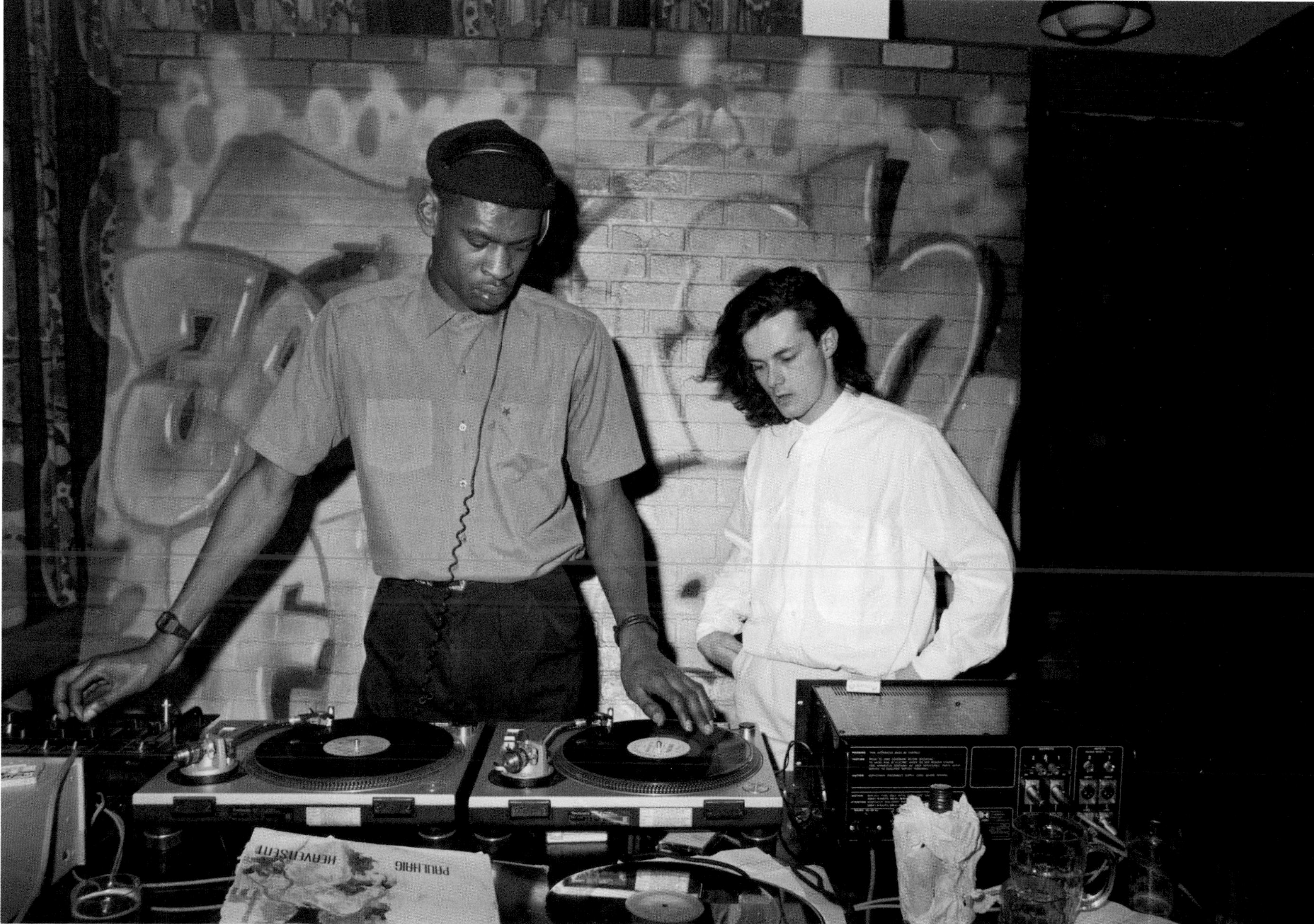

PAUL HAIG
HEAVENSENT

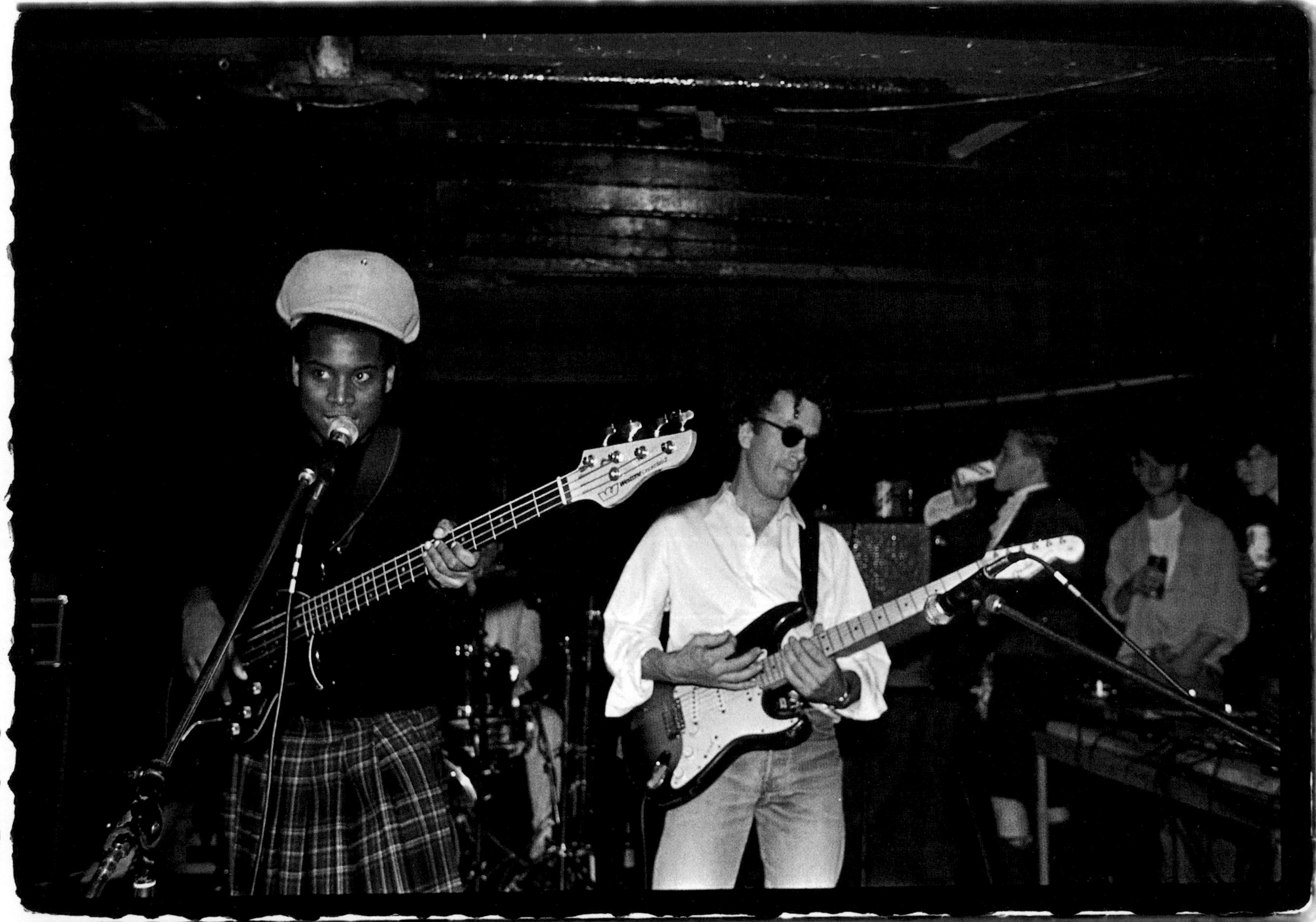

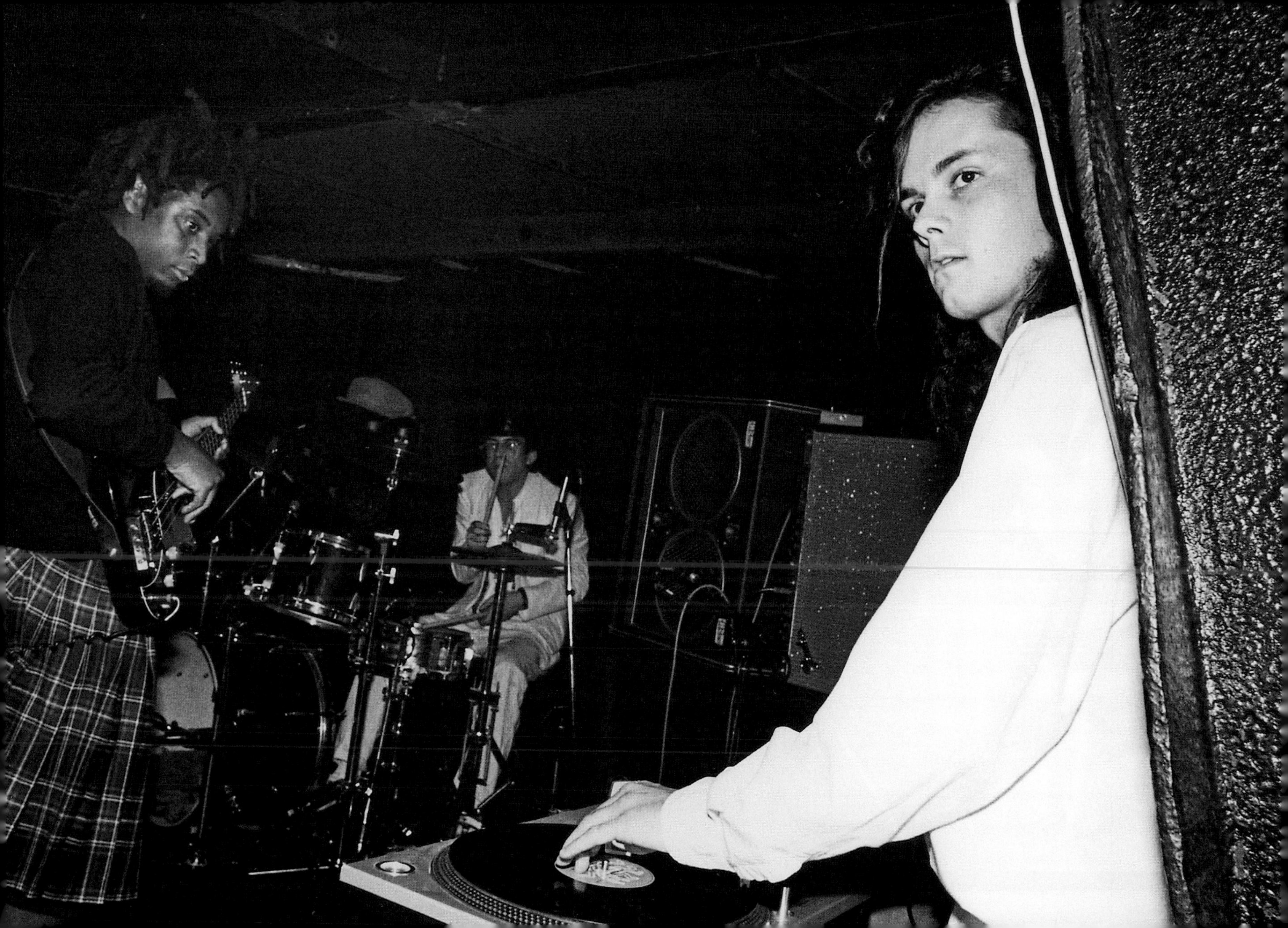

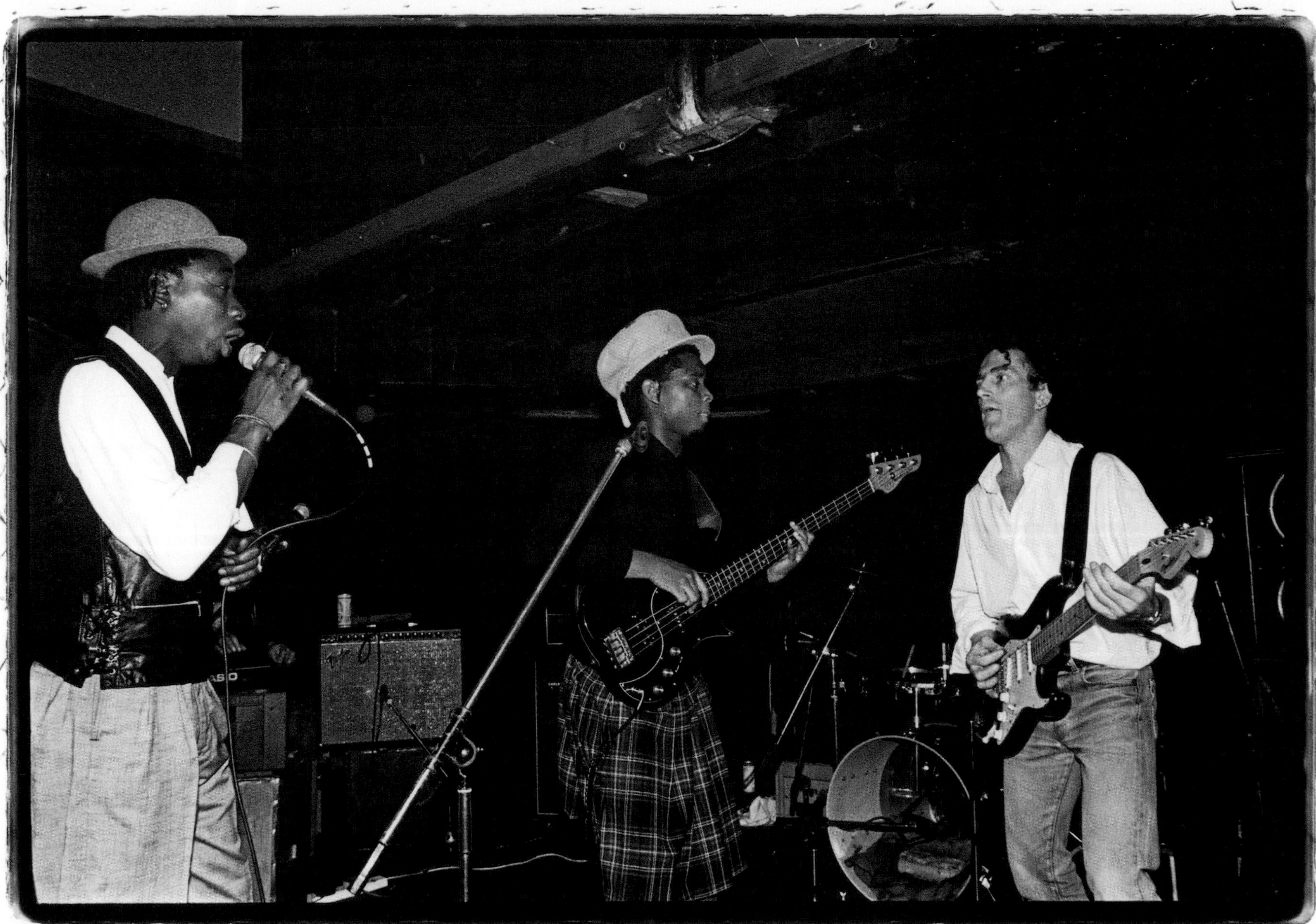

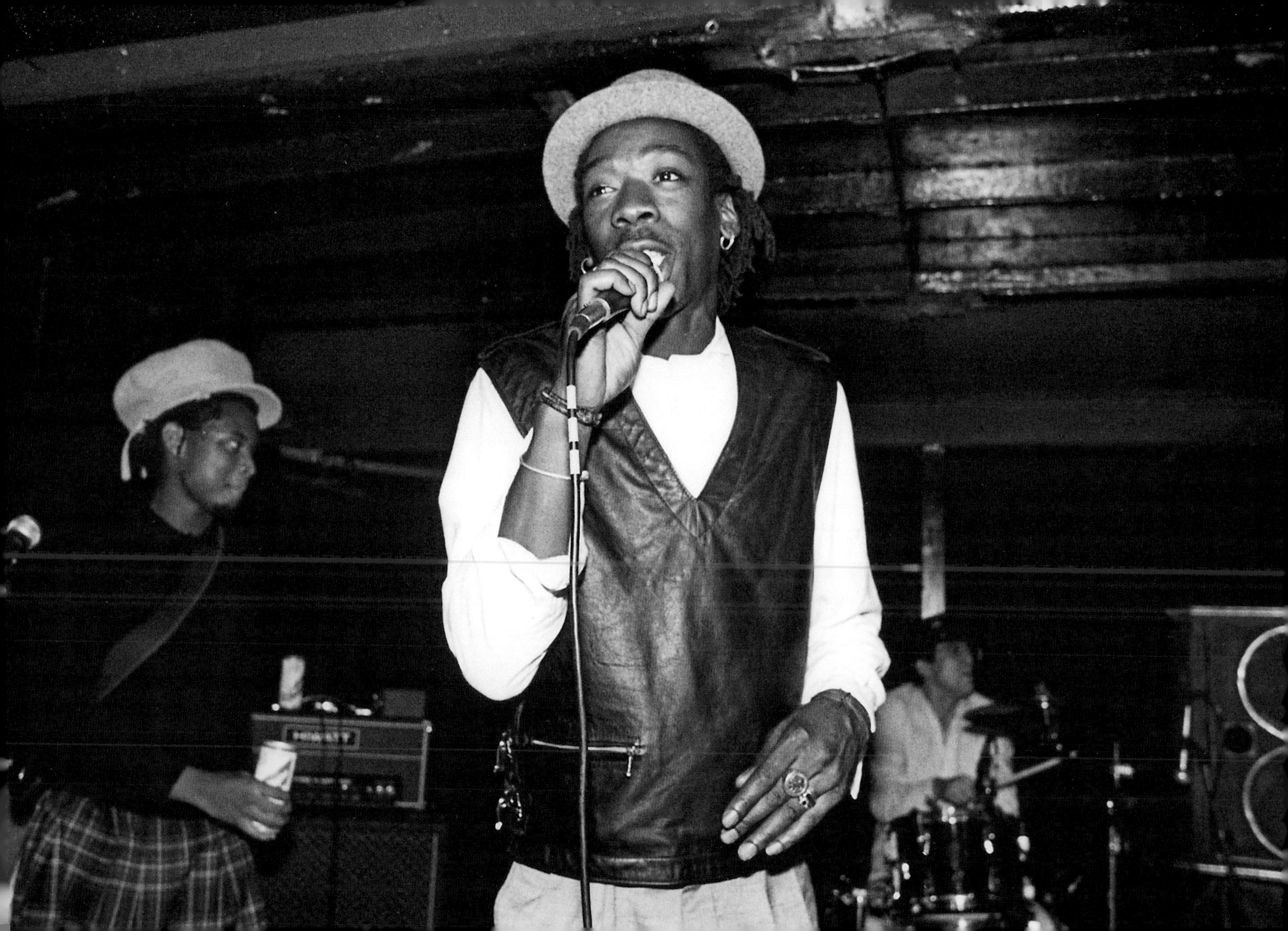

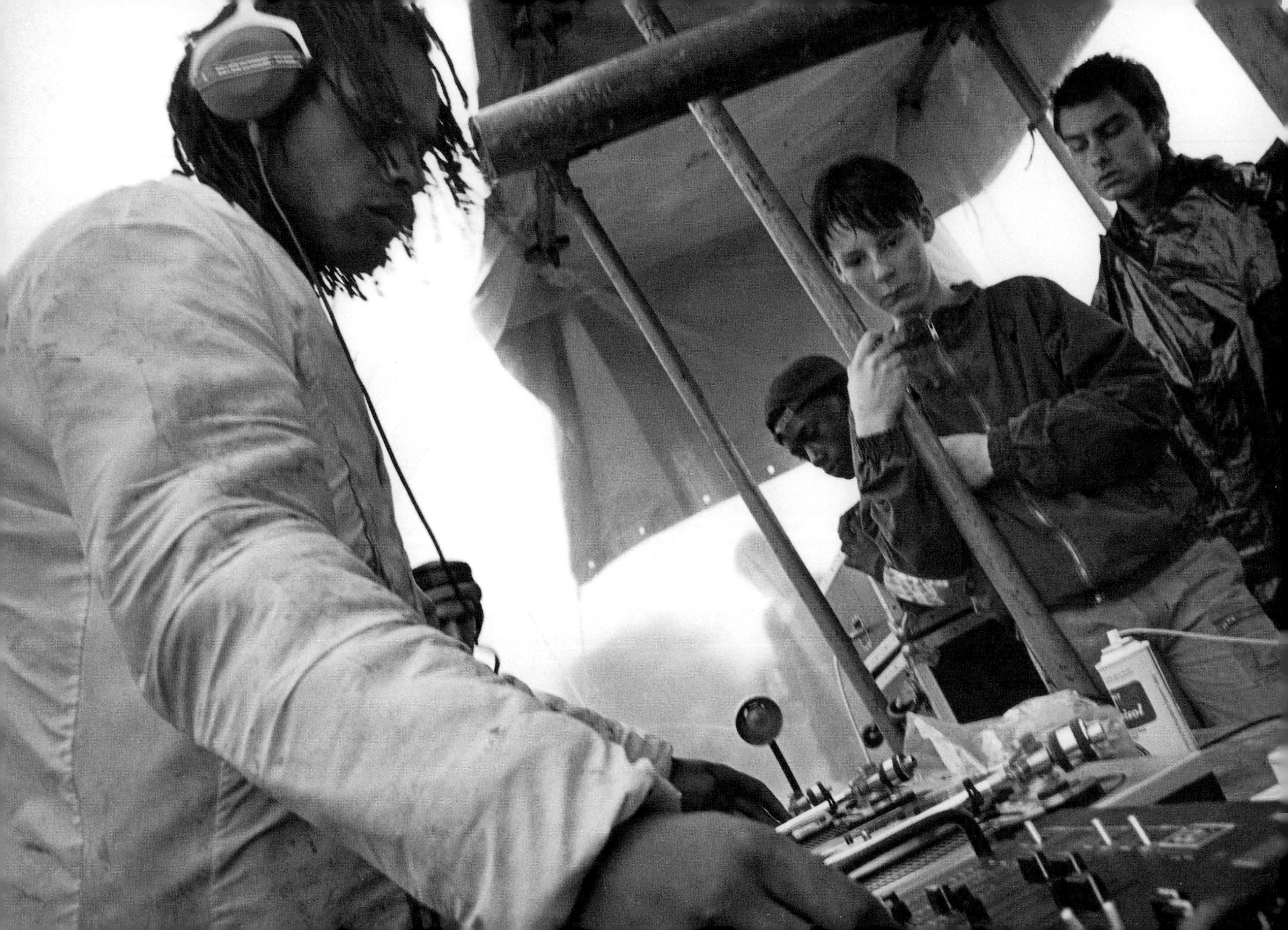

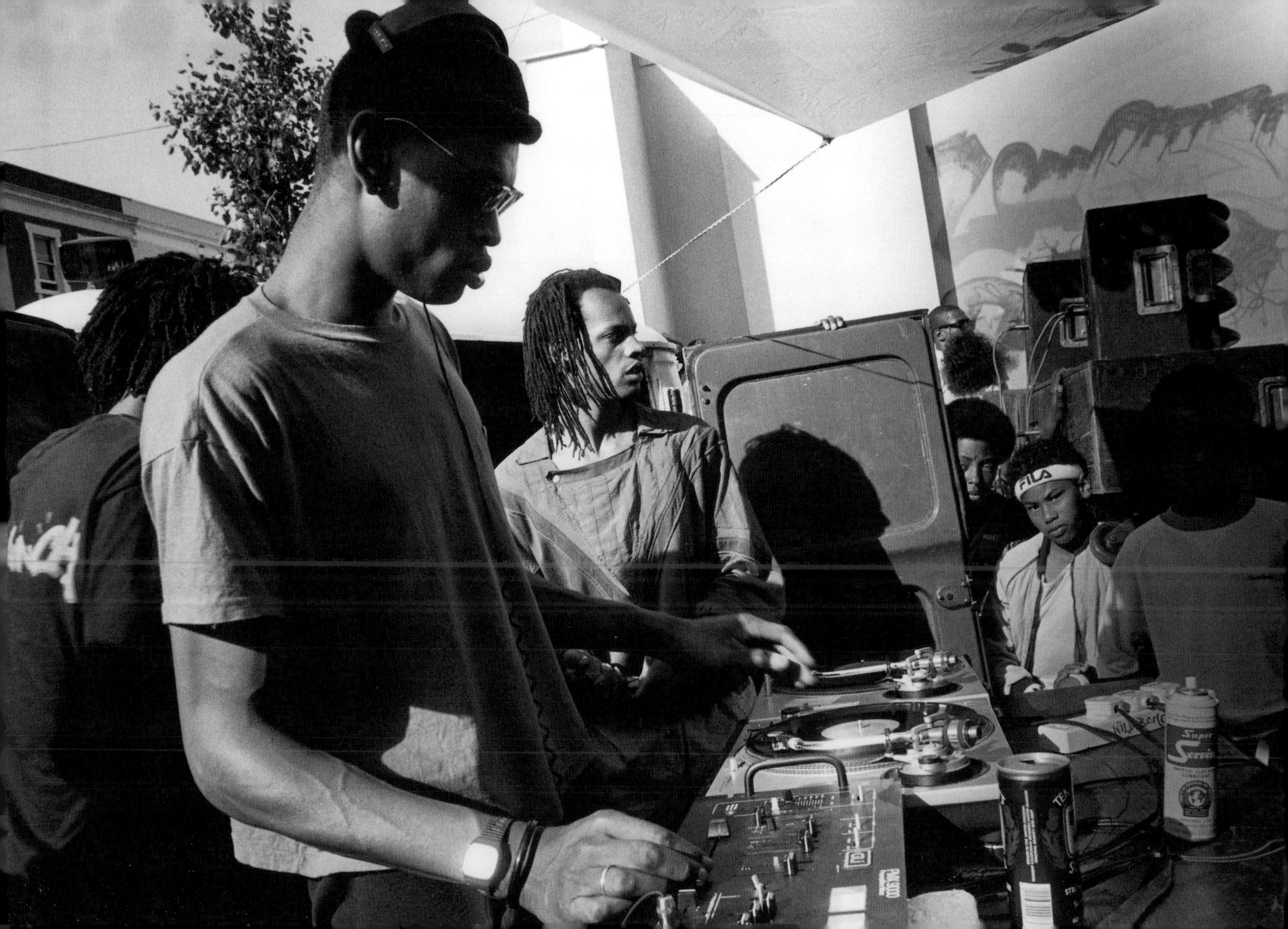

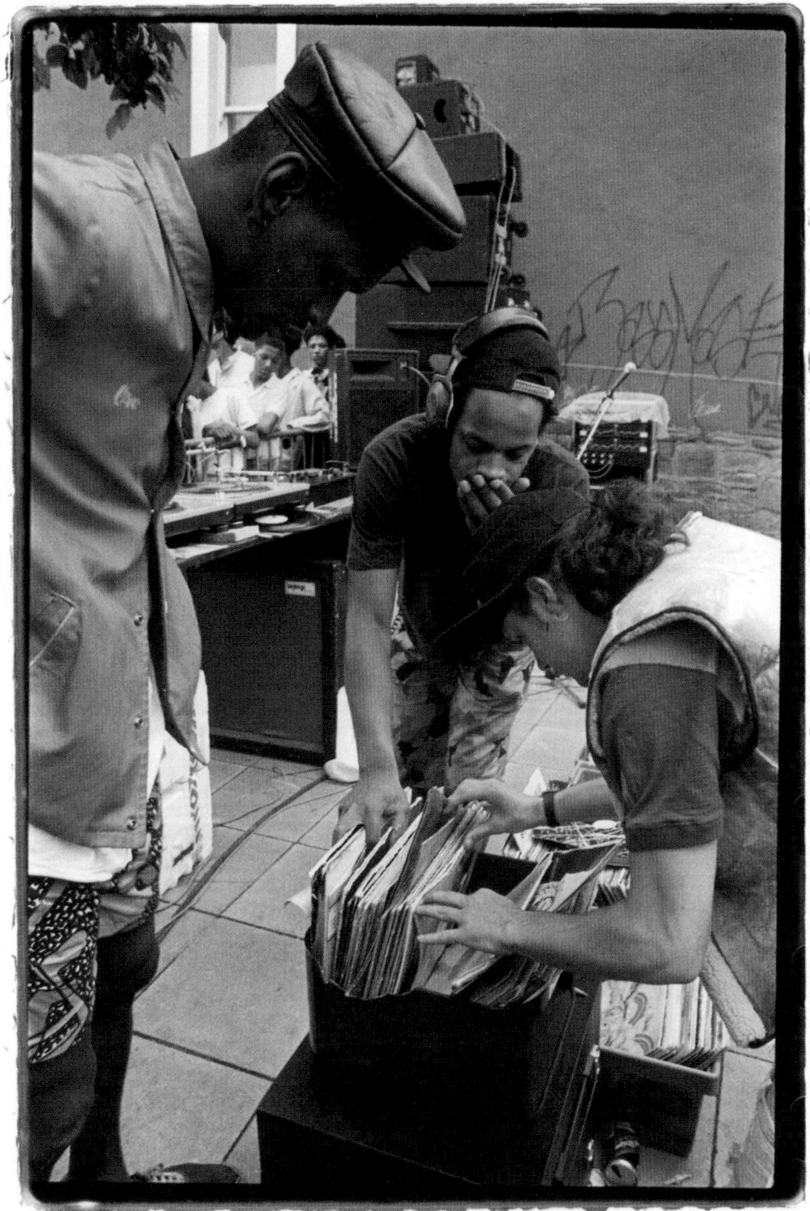

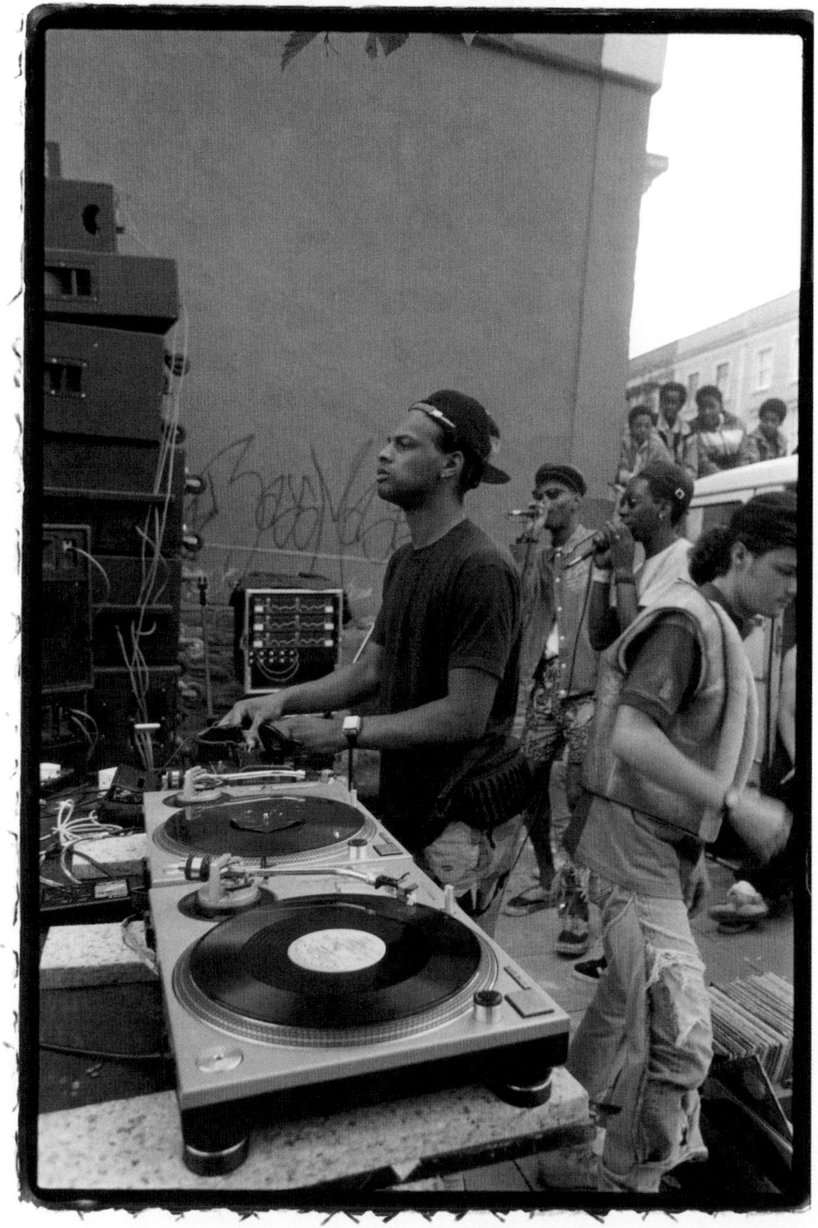

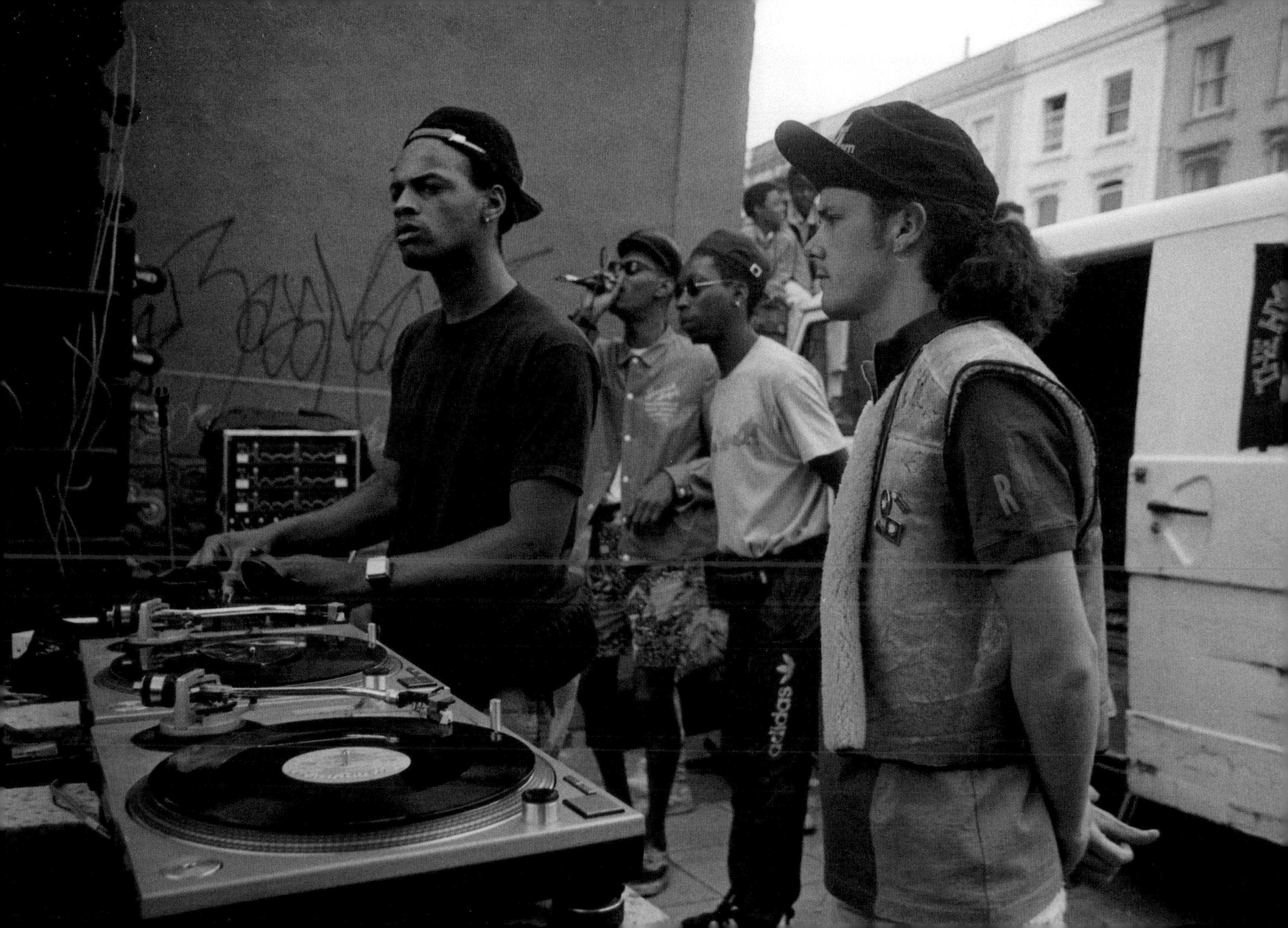

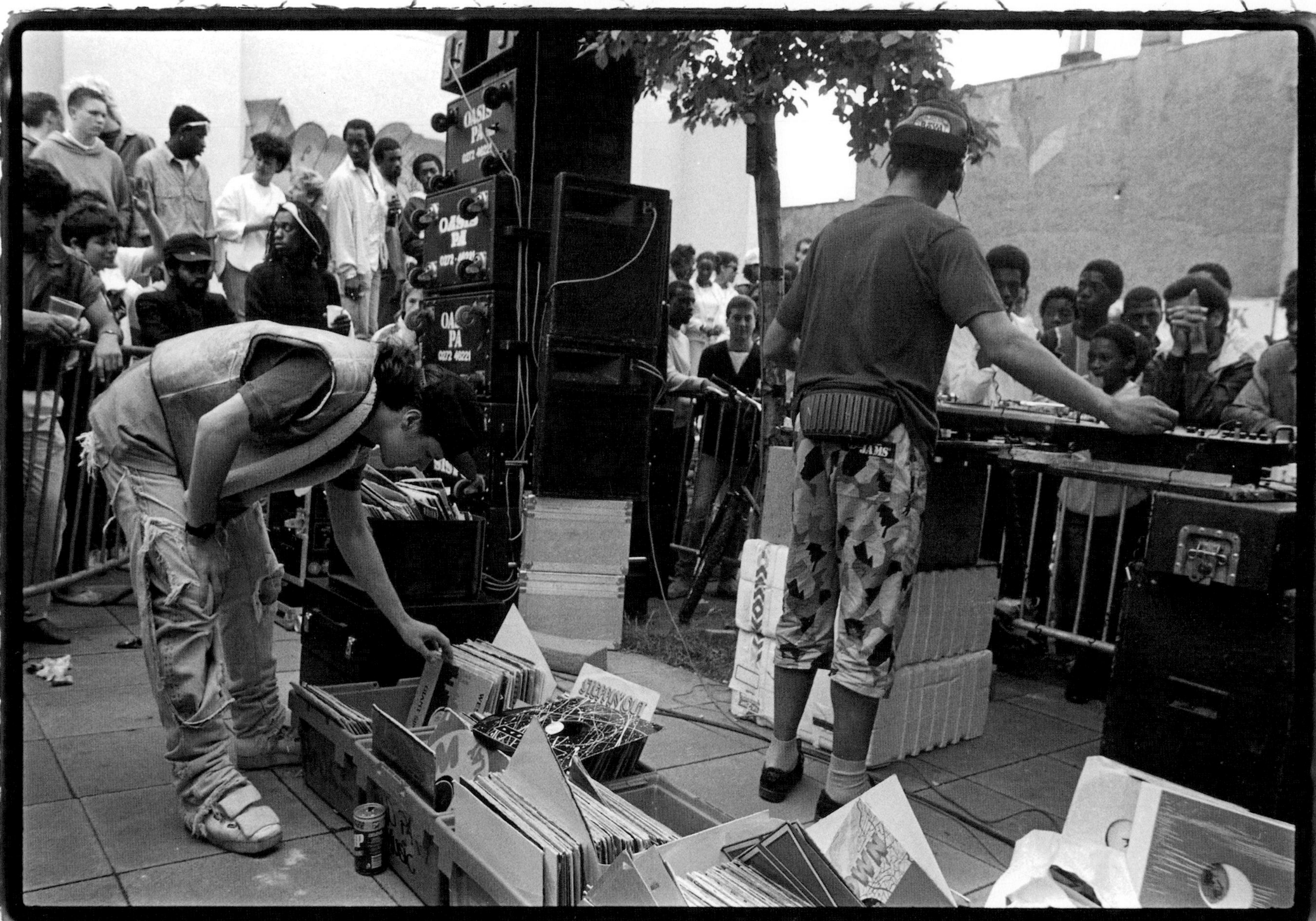

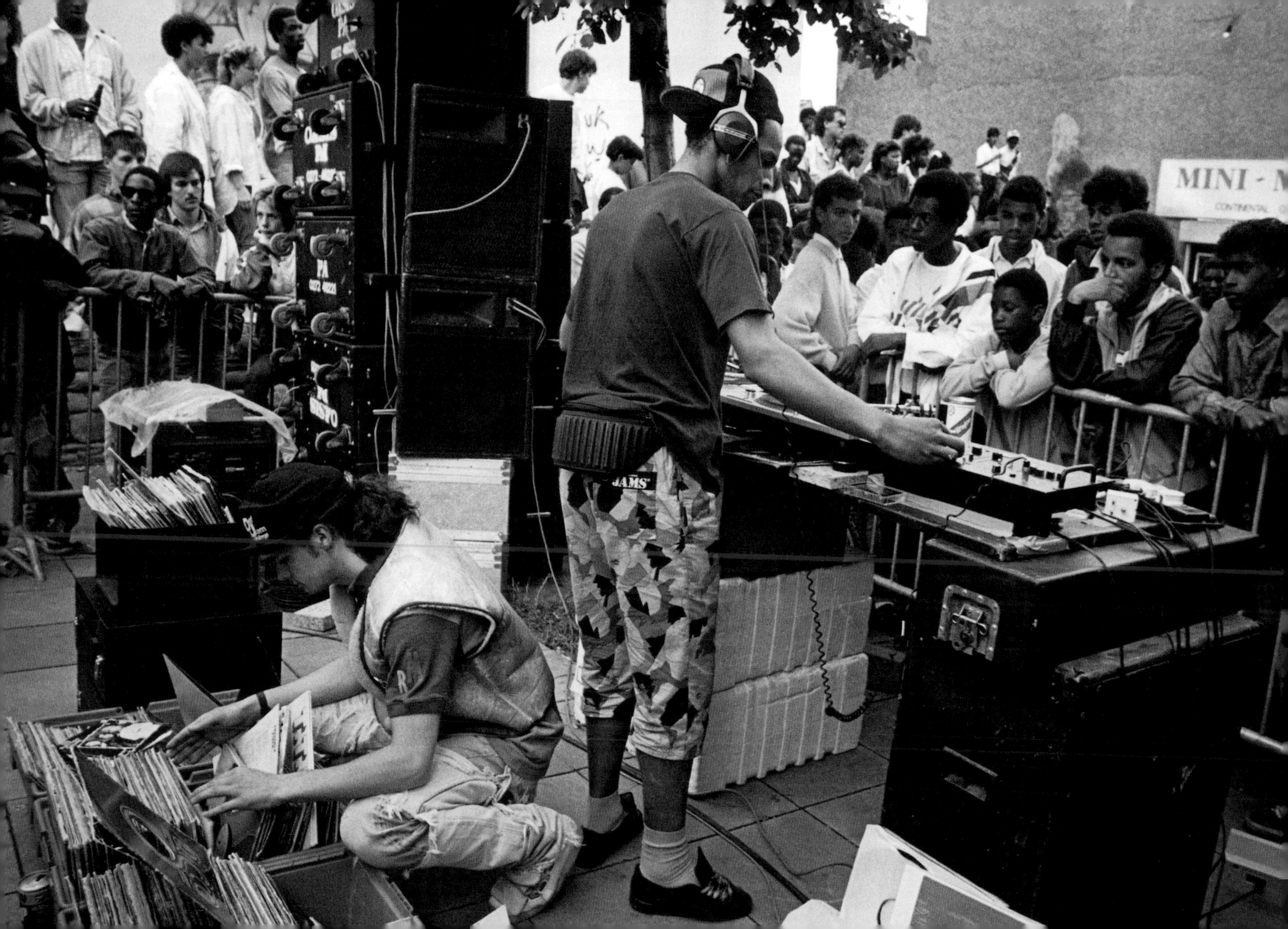

MINI - M

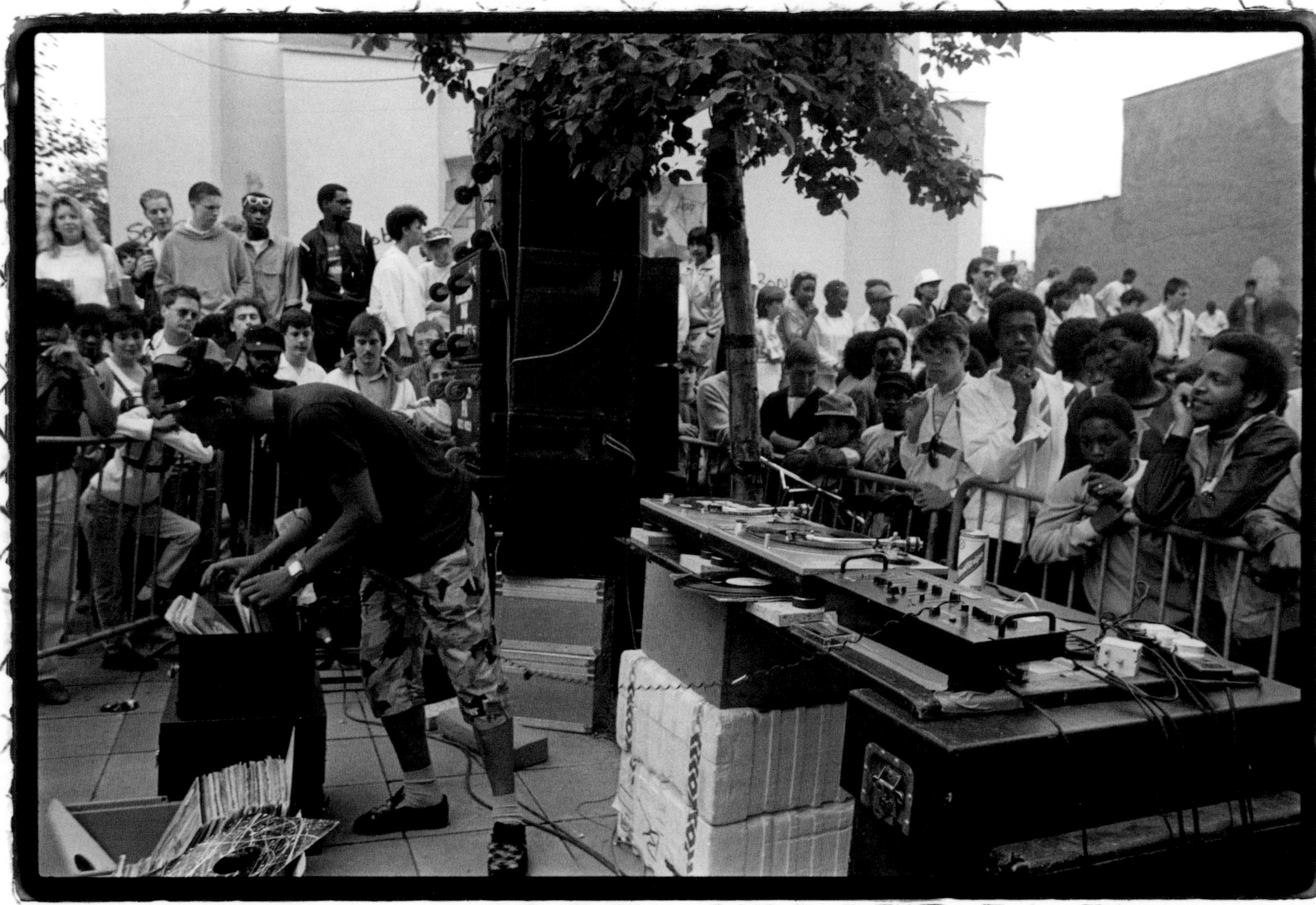

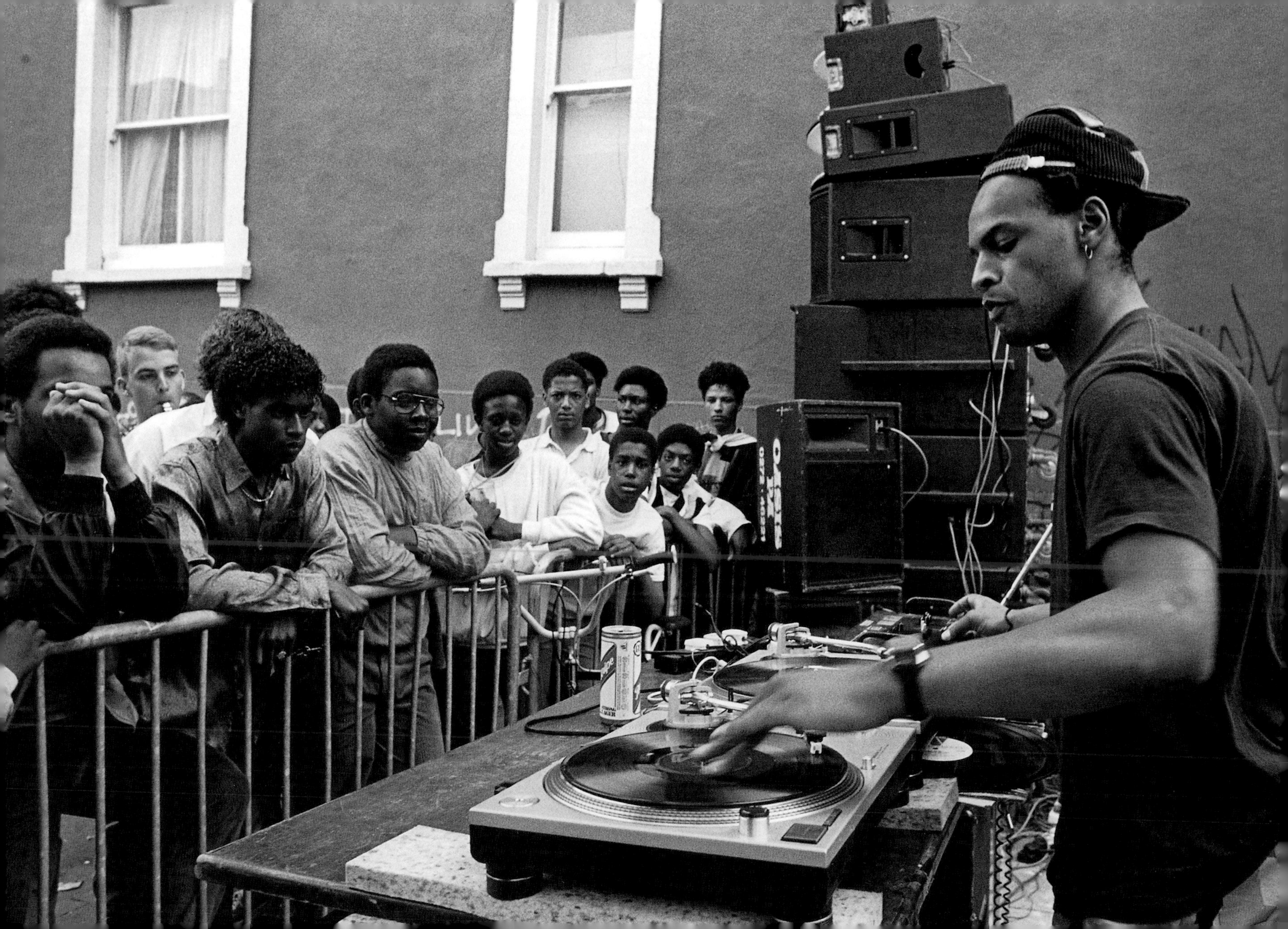

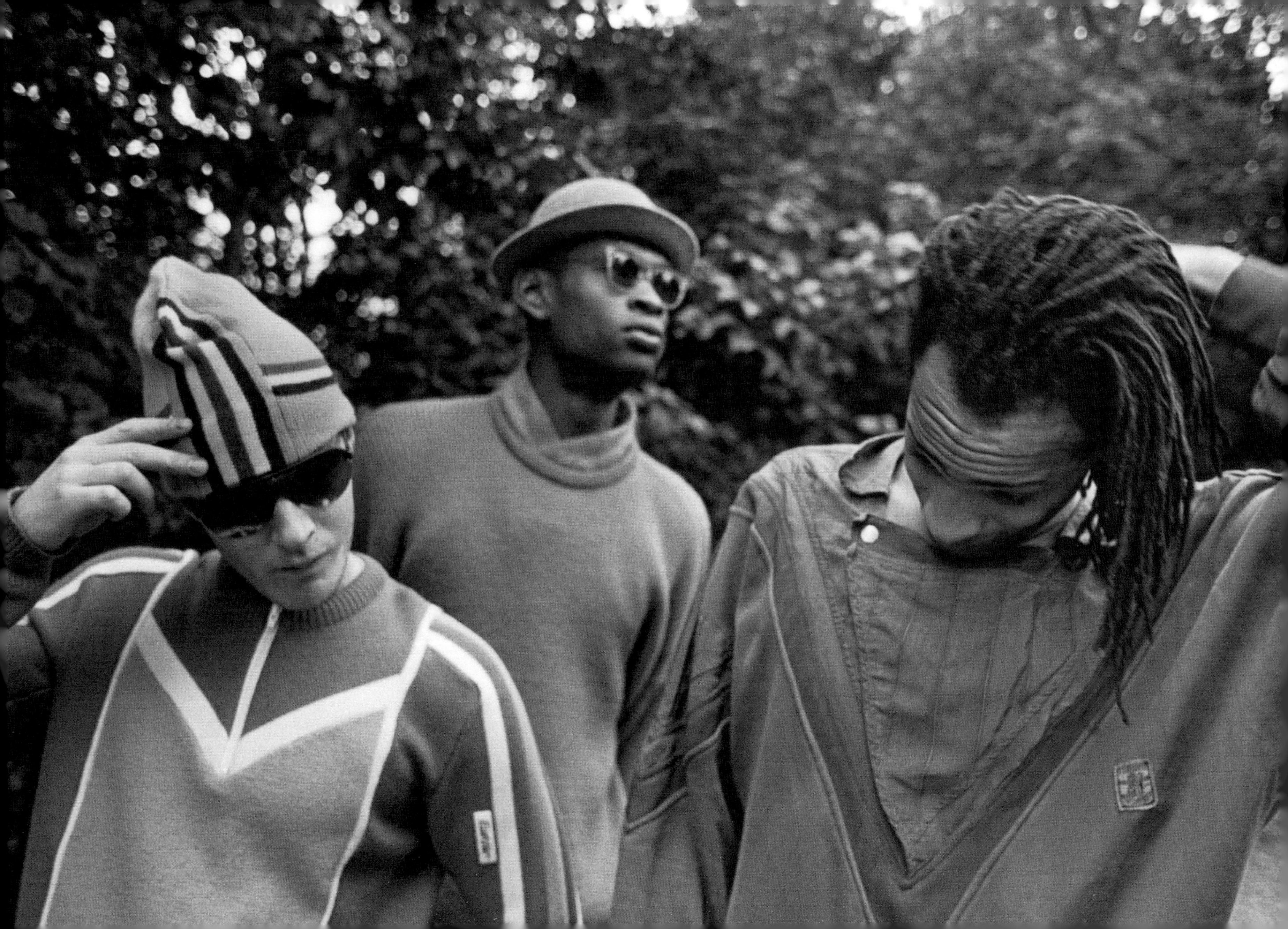

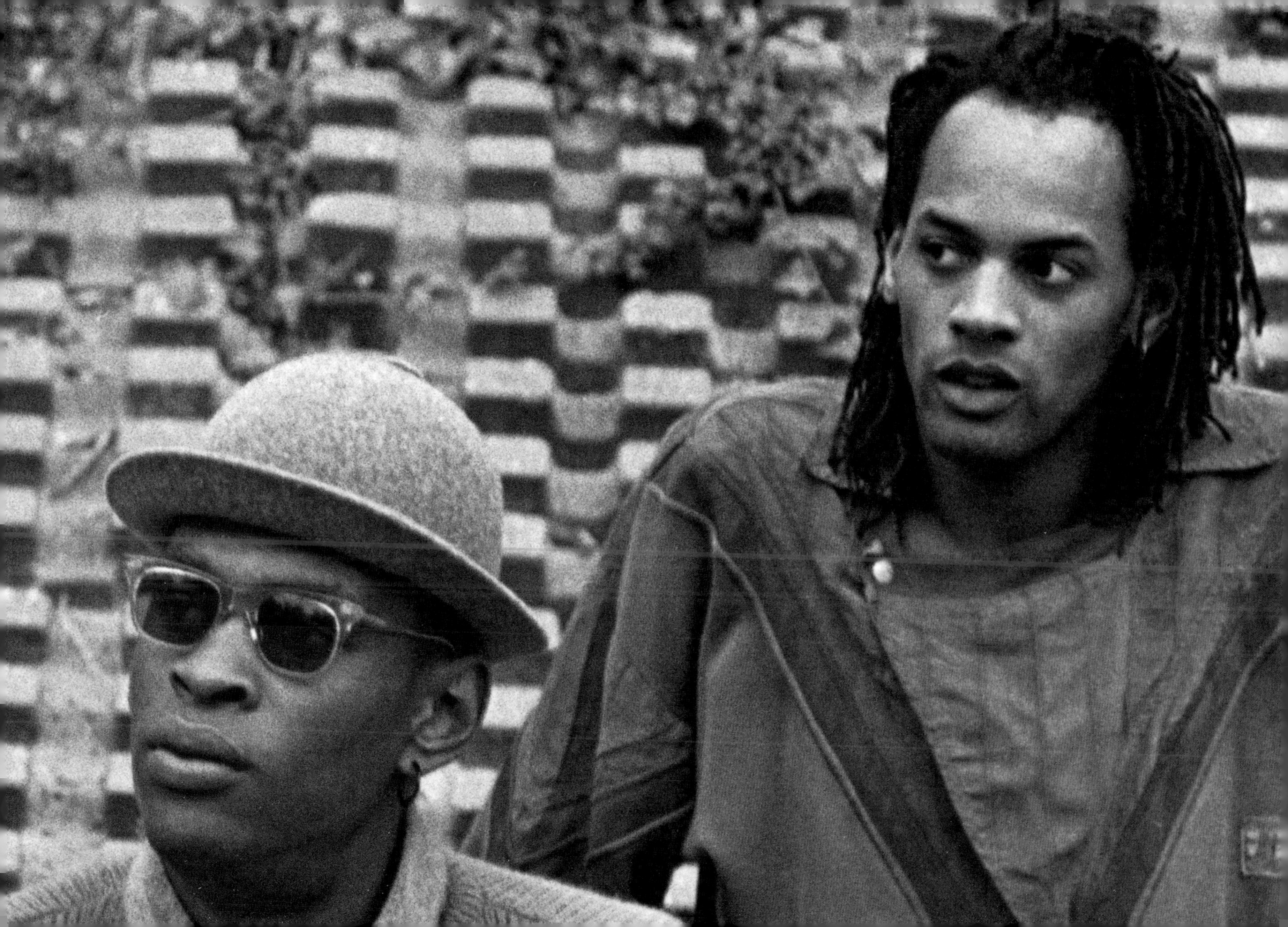

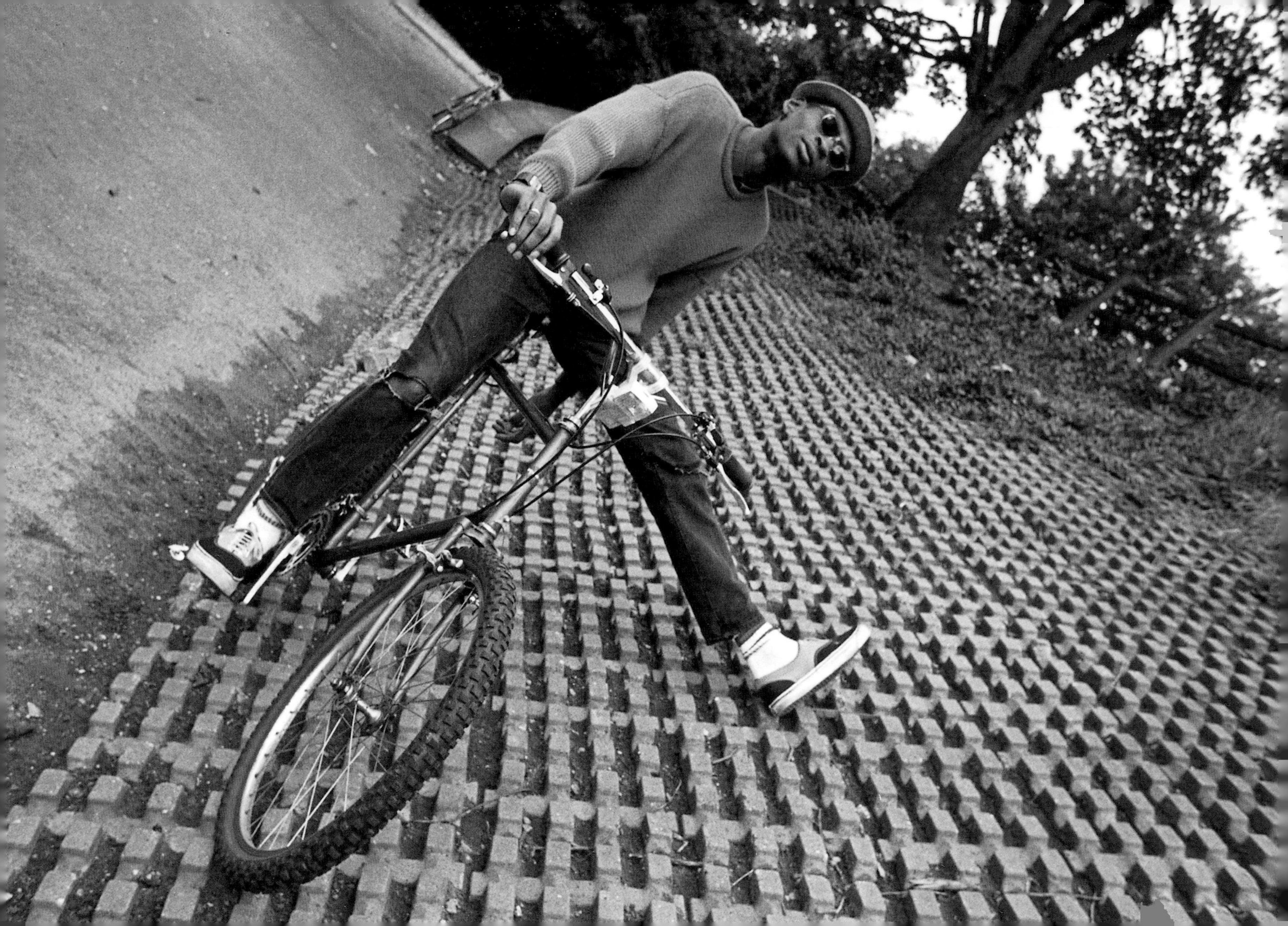

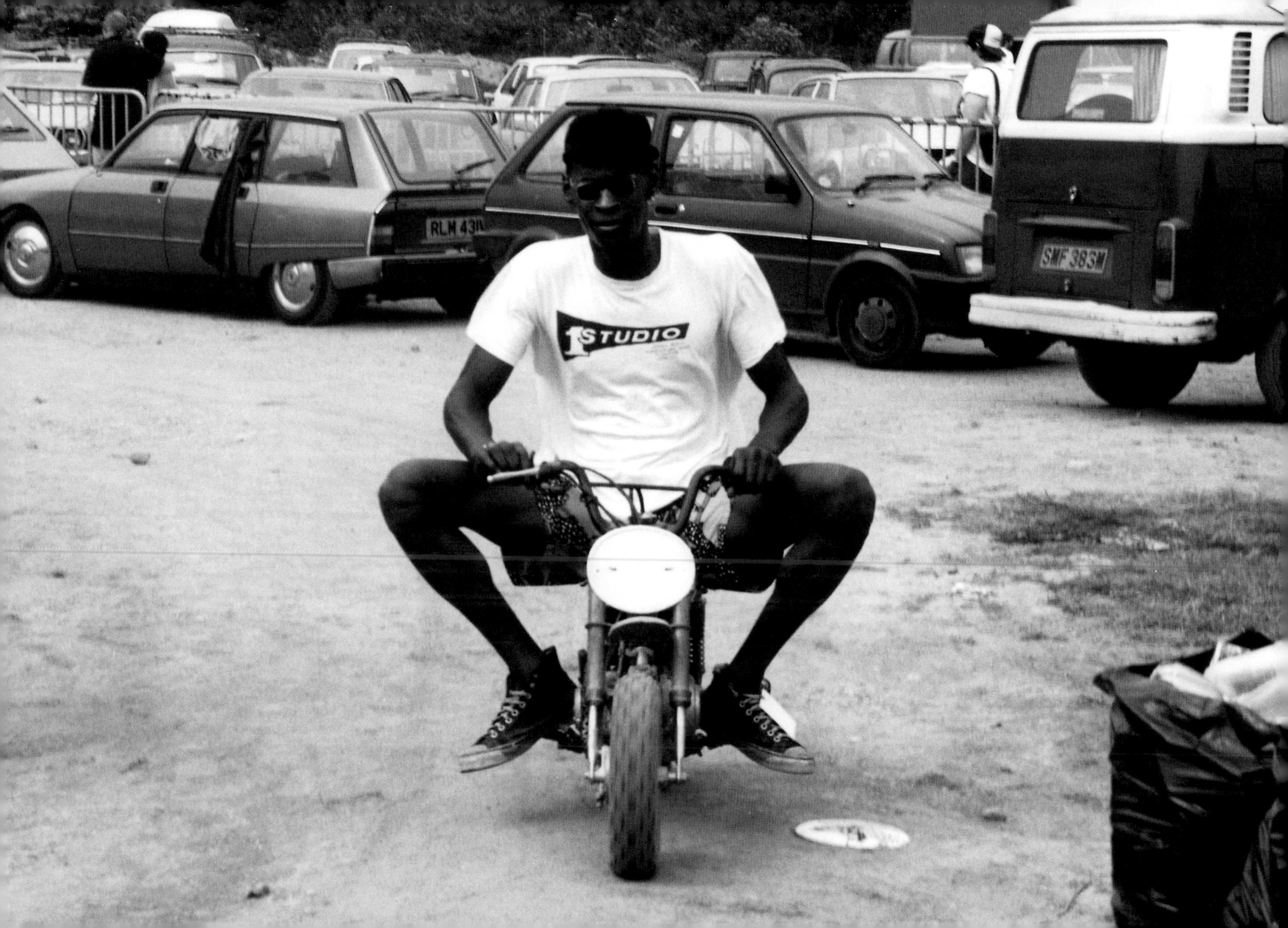
1 STUDIO
RLM 431
SWF 38S

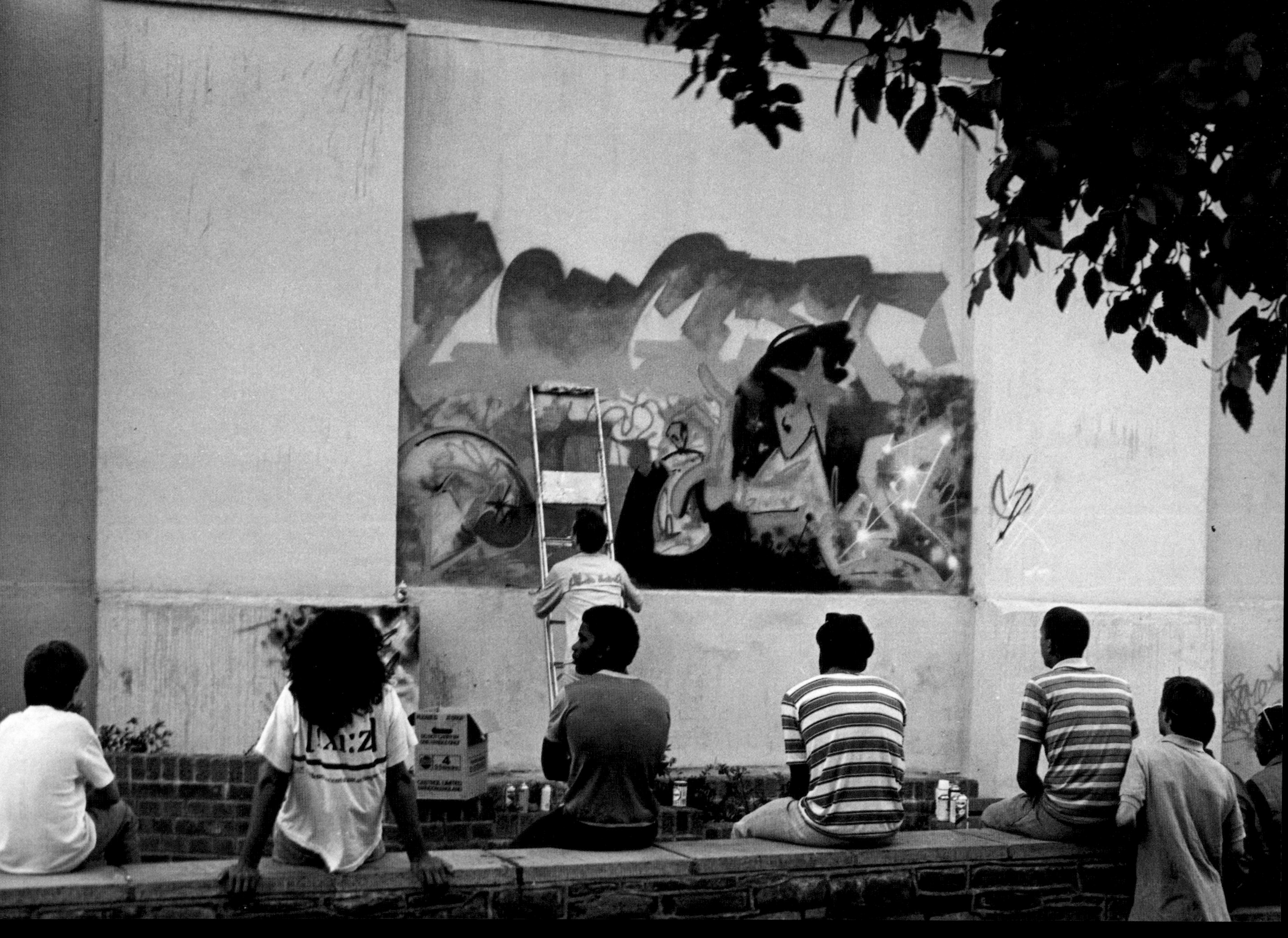

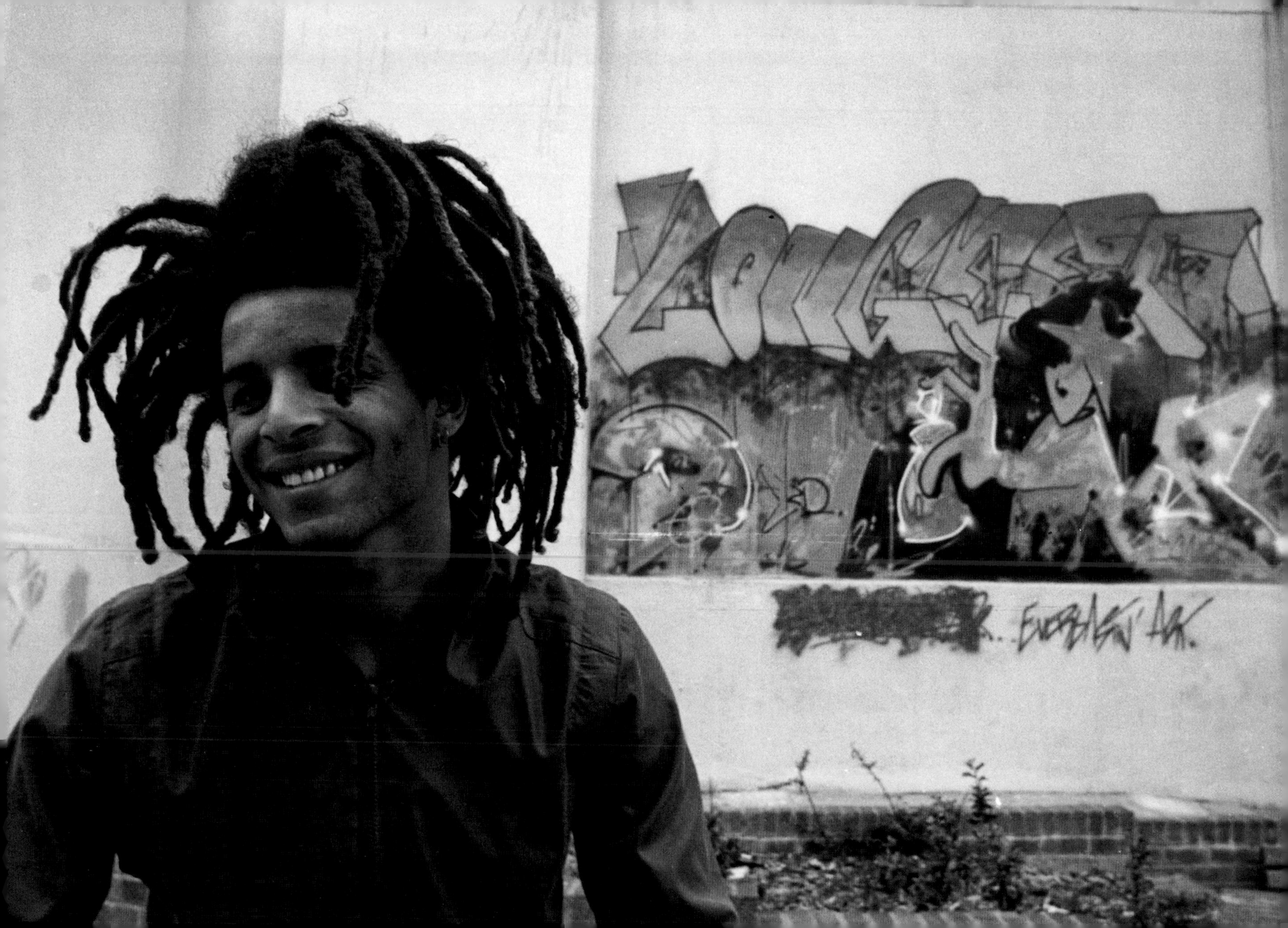

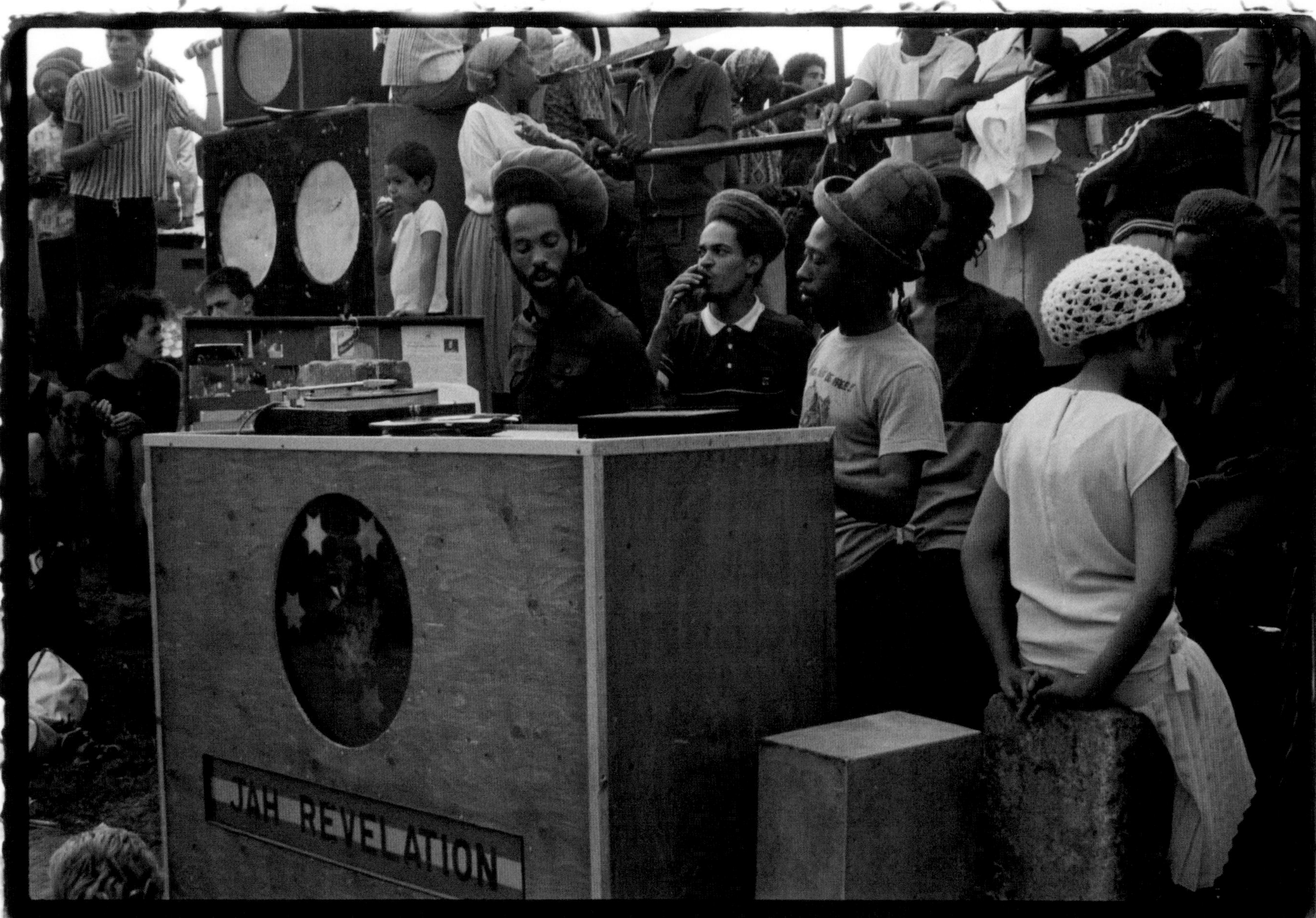
JAH REVELATION

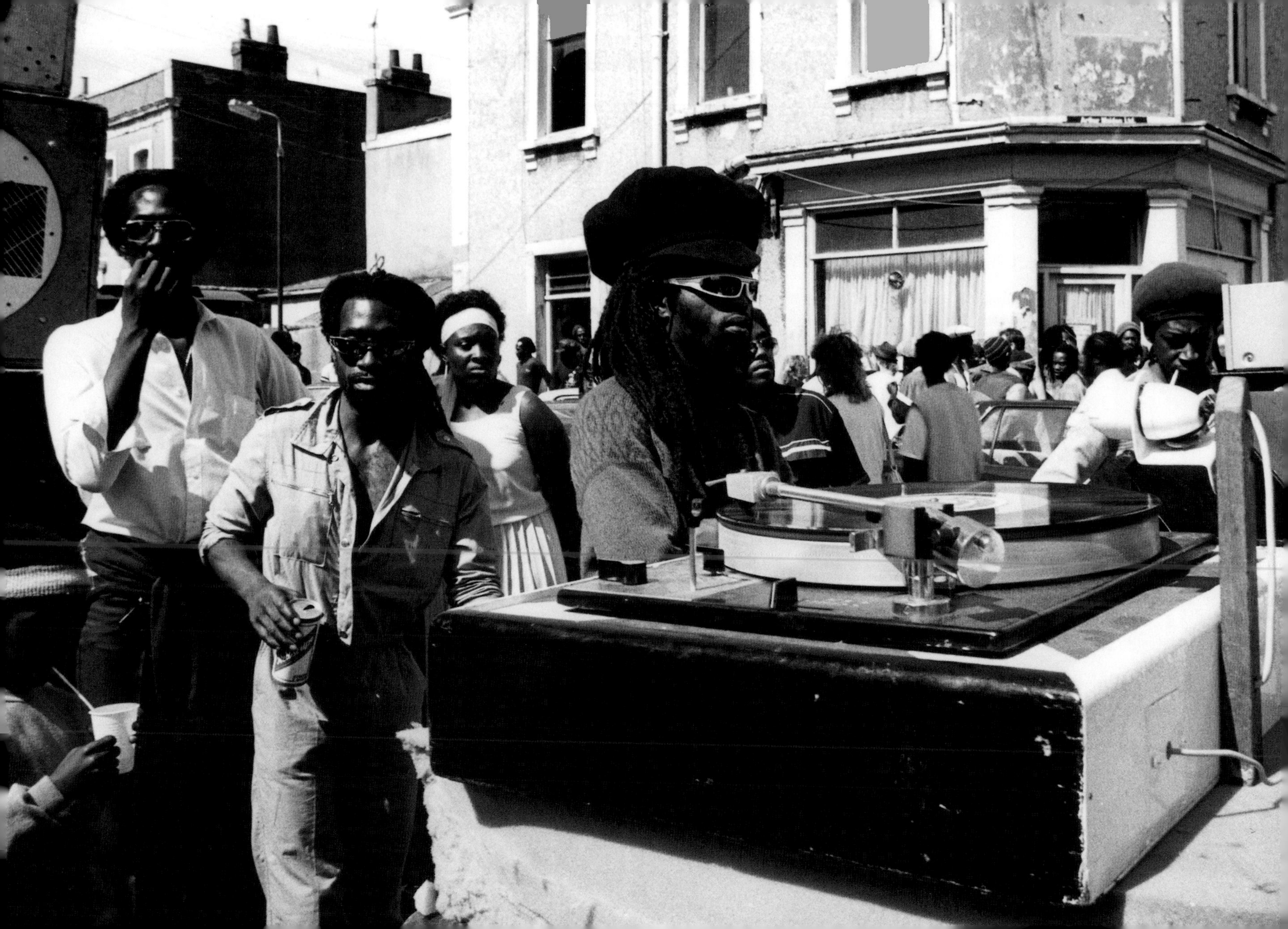

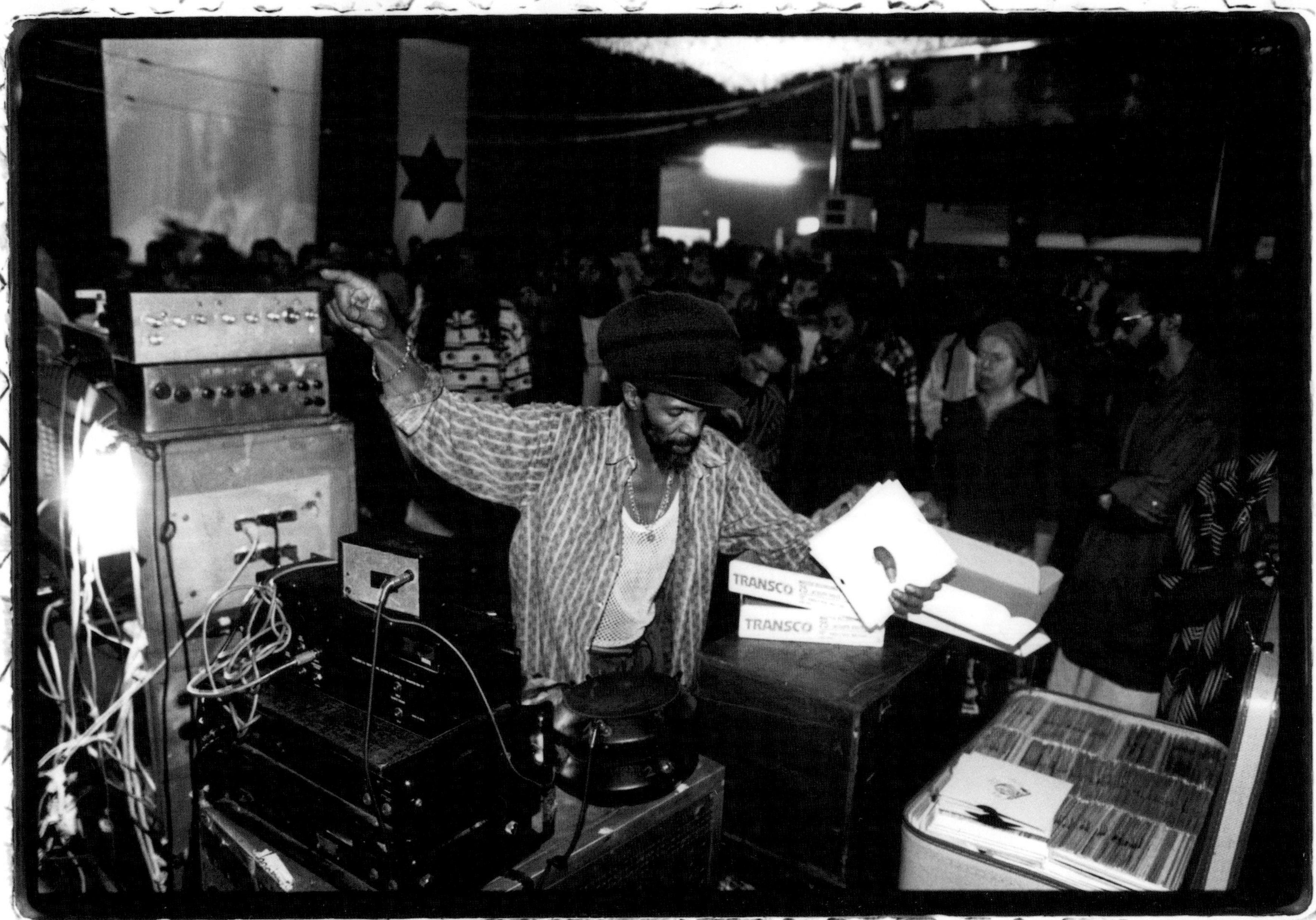

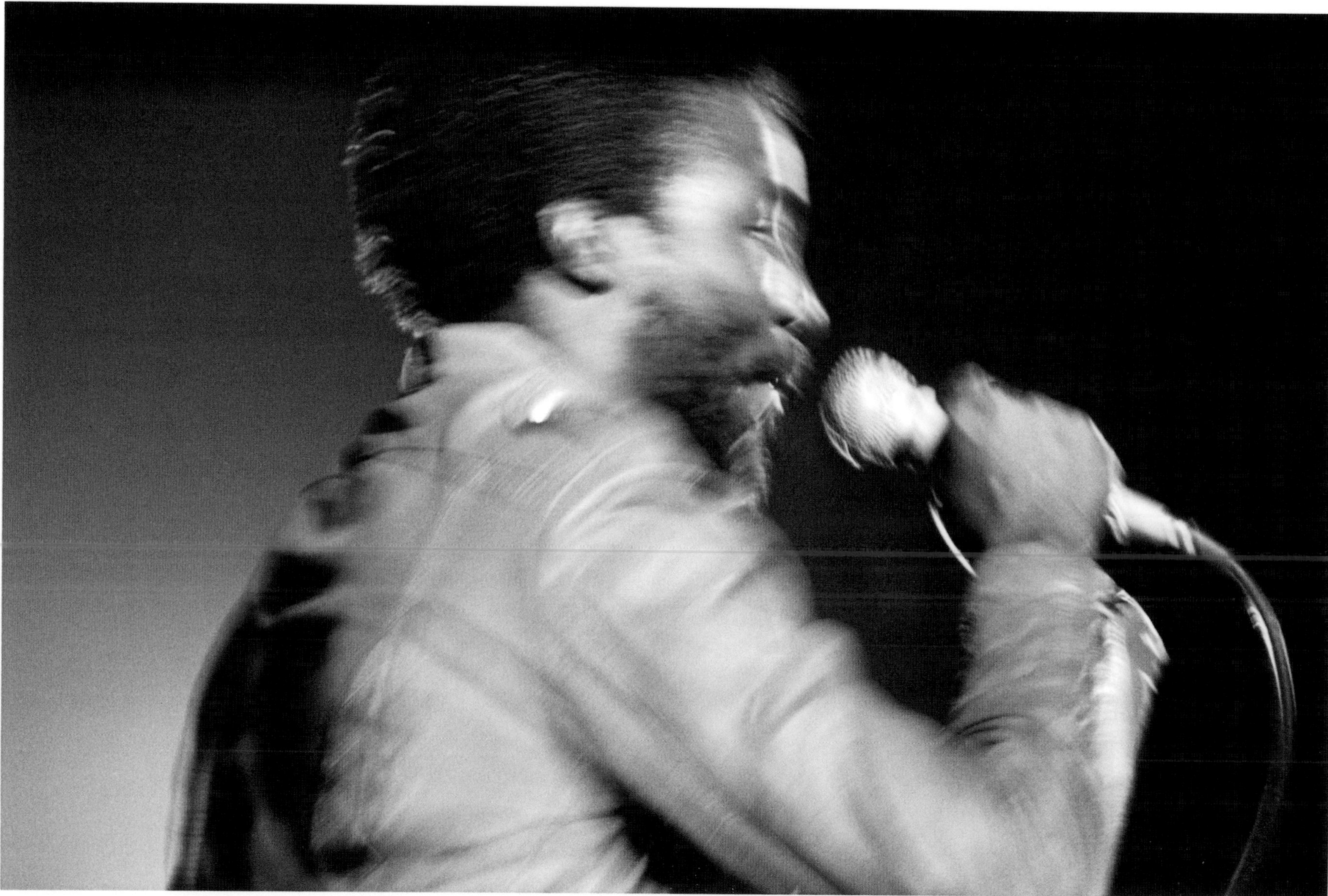

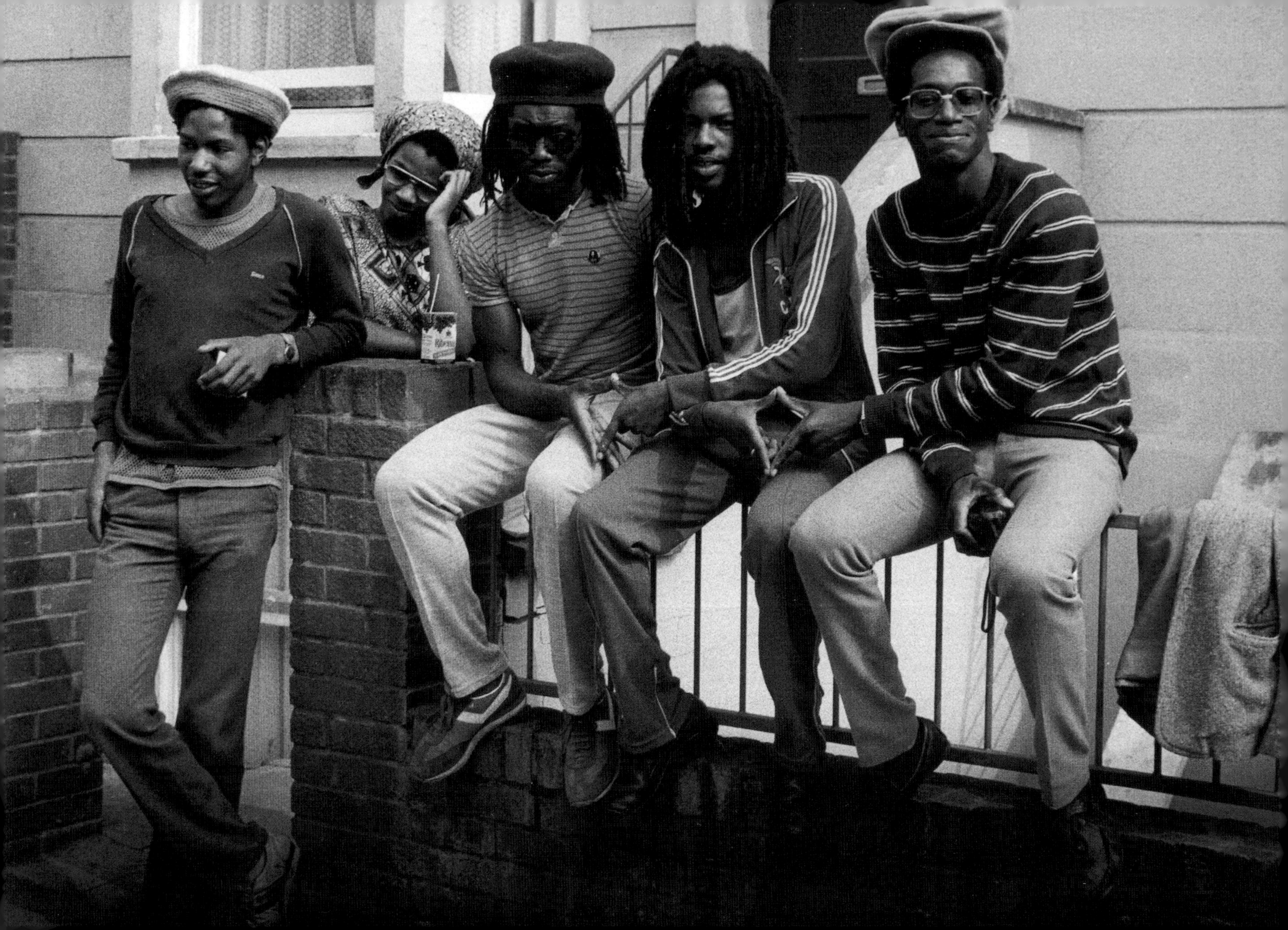

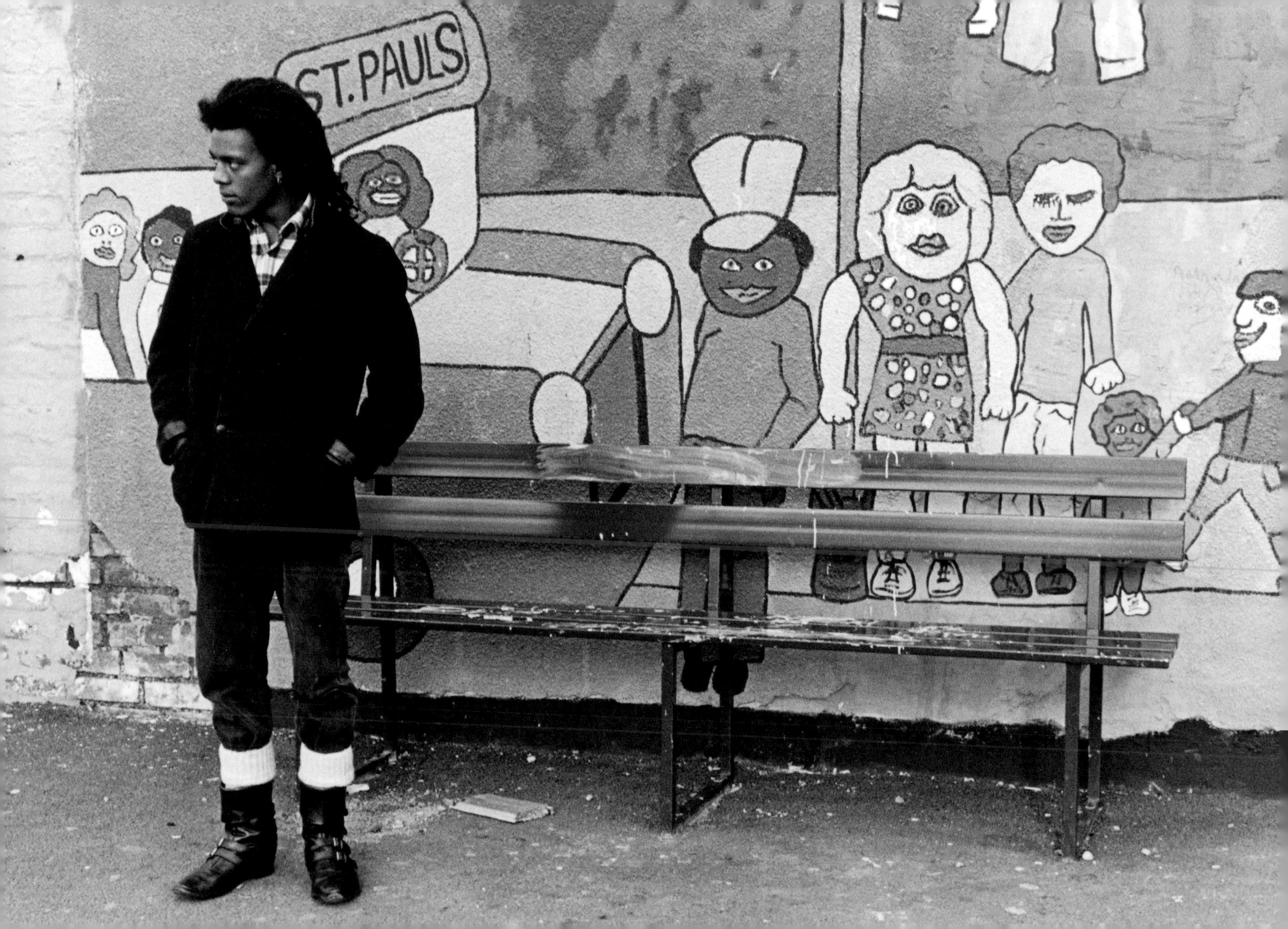
ST.PAULS

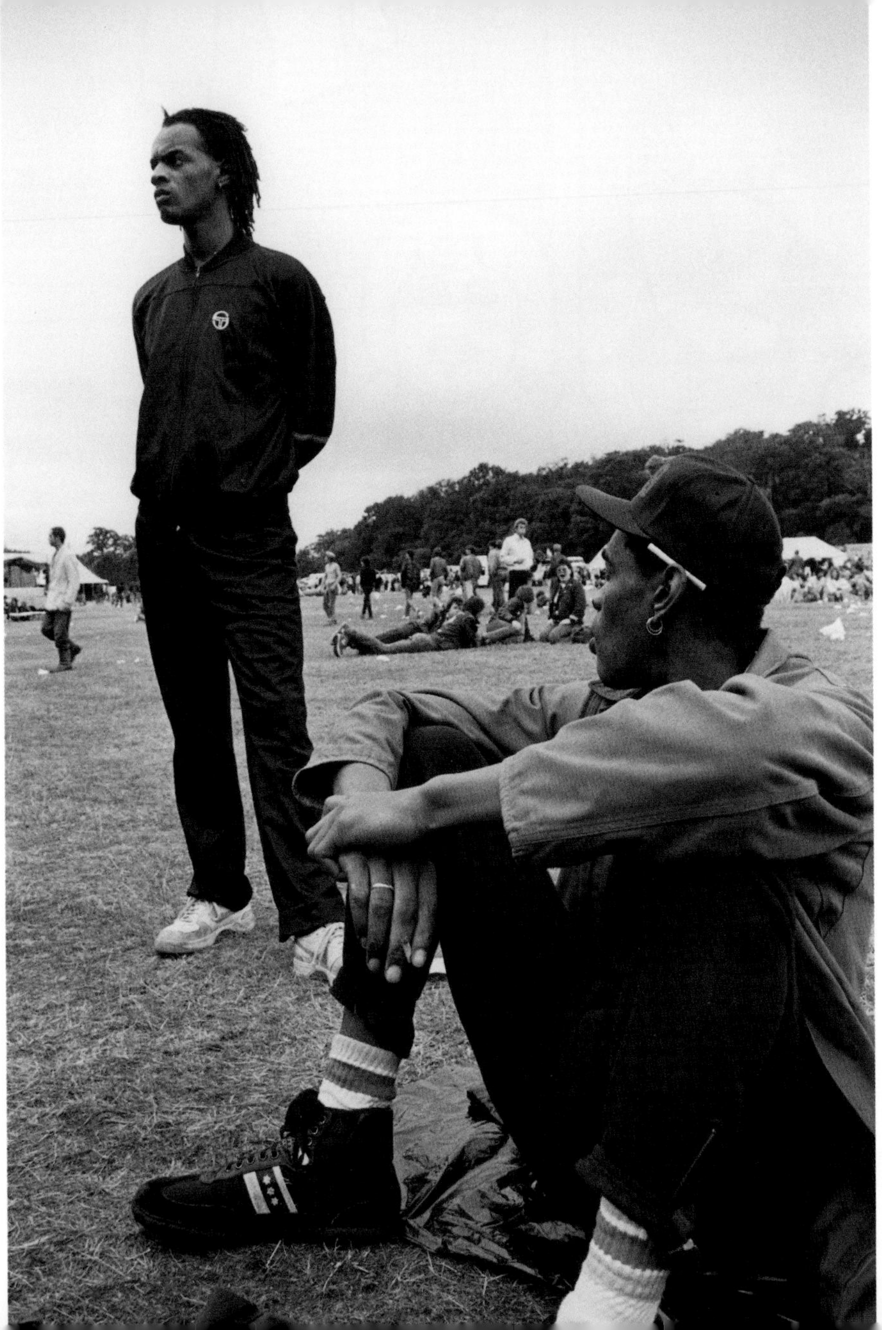

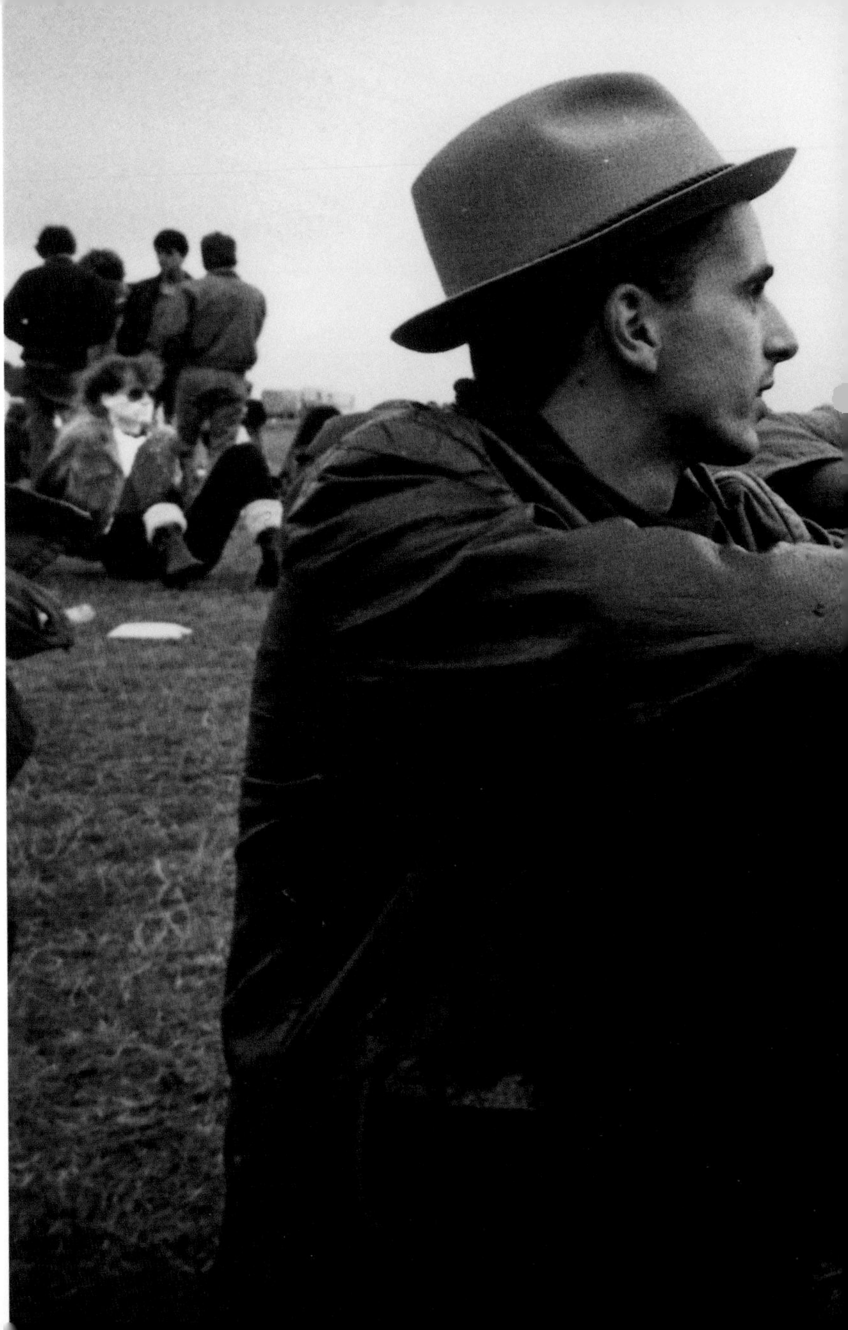

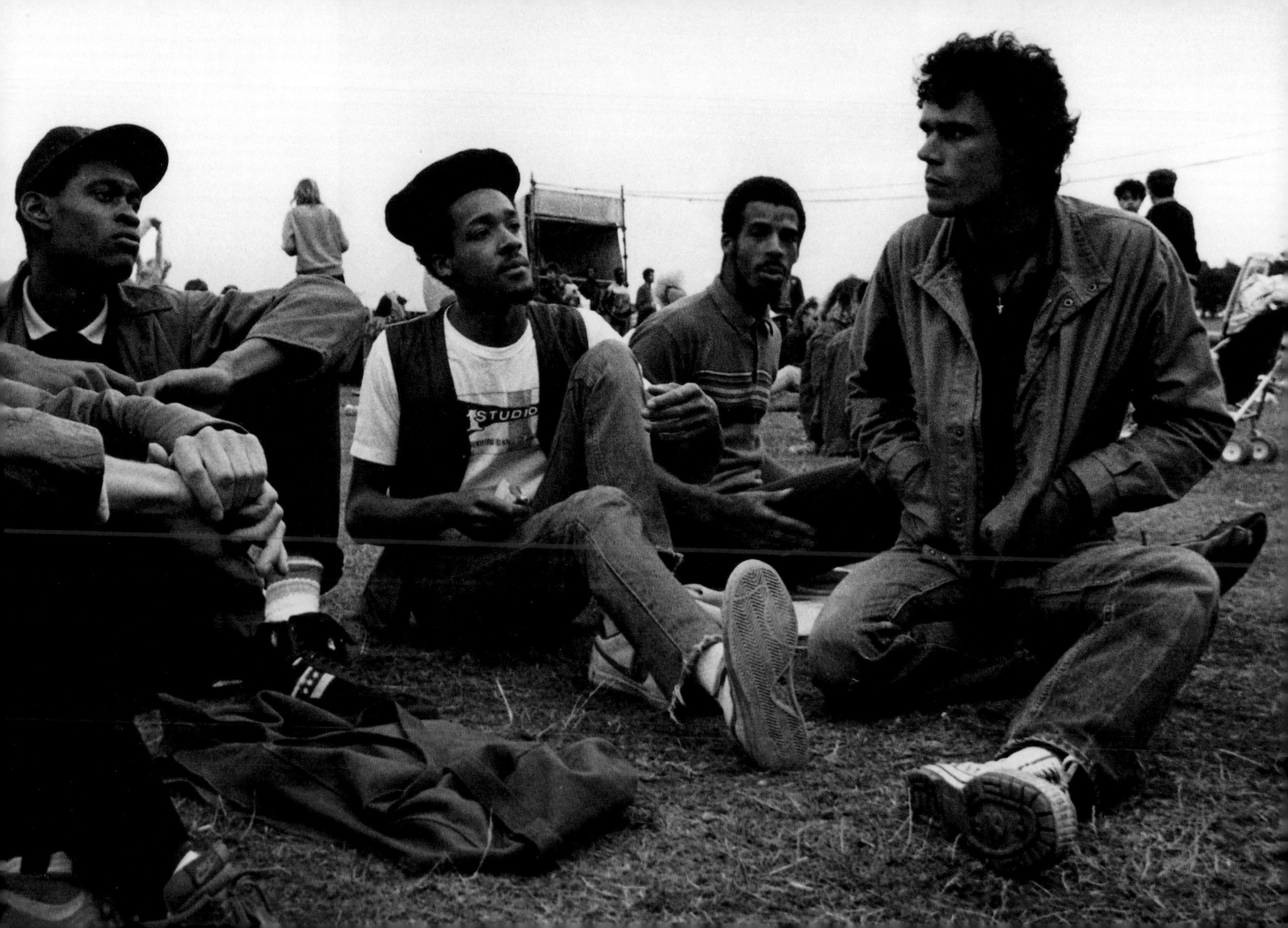

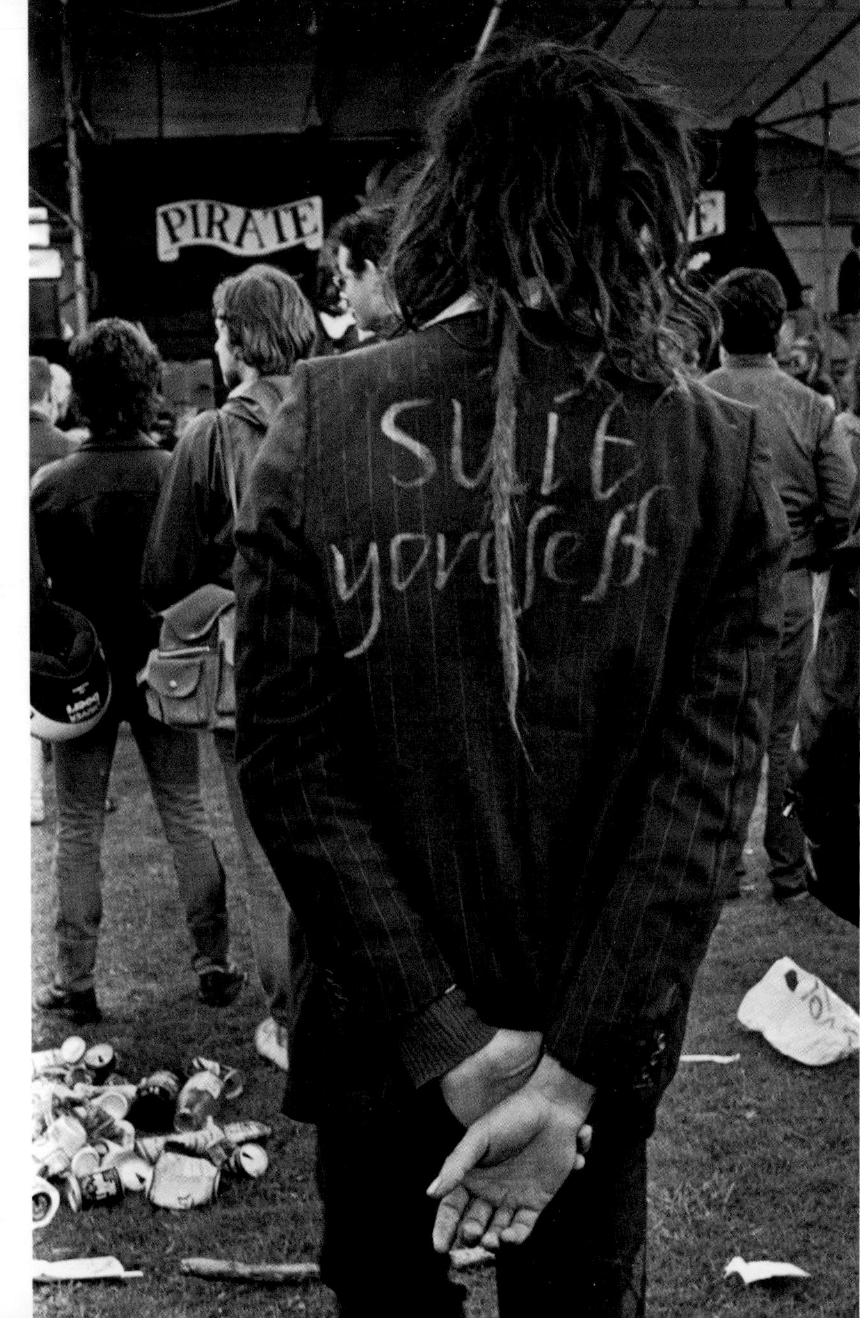

PIRATE
suit yourself

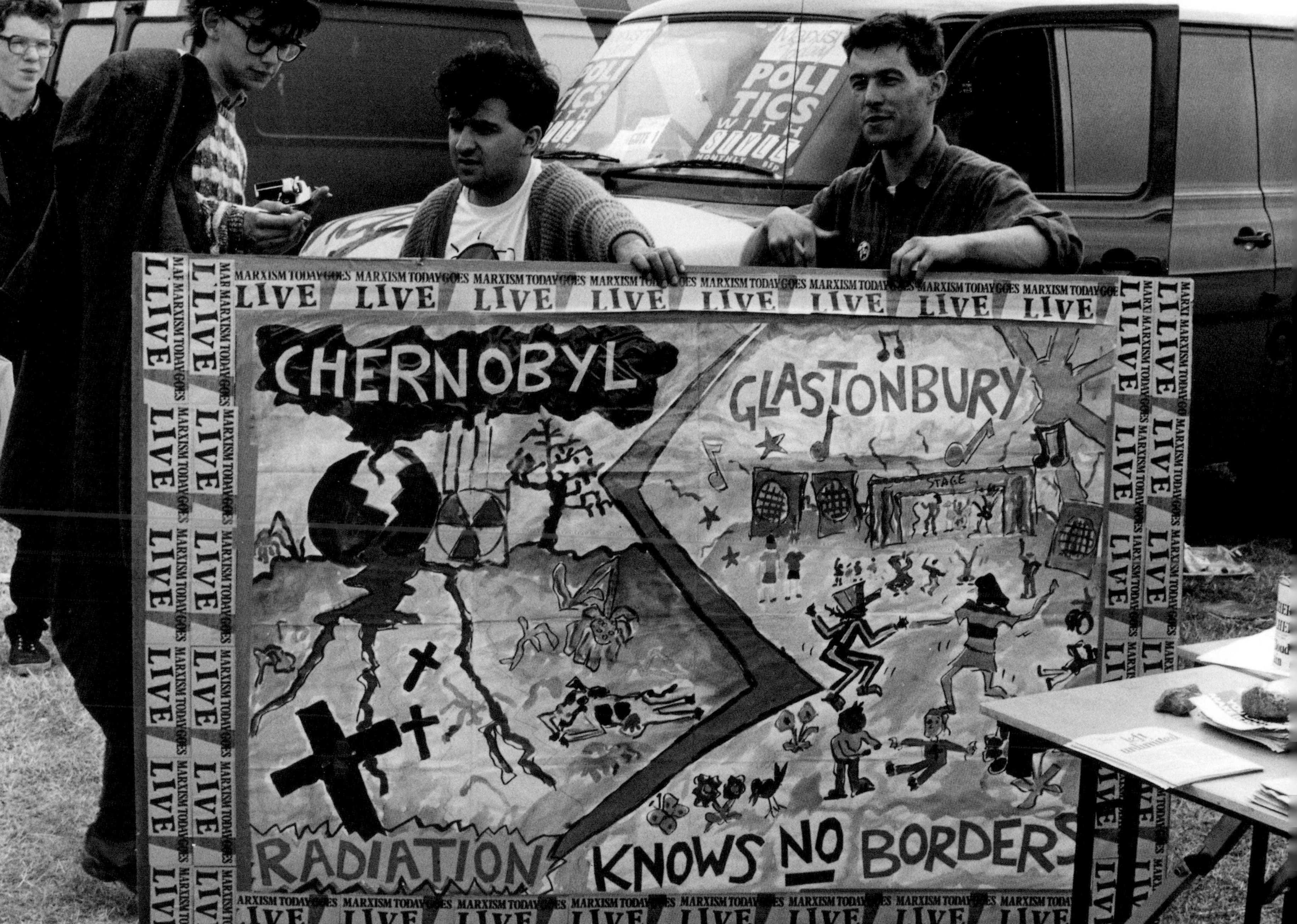

POLITICS WITH SOUL
MARXISM TODAY GOES LIVE
CHERNOBYL
GLASTONBURY
STAGE
RADIATION KNOWS NO BORDERS

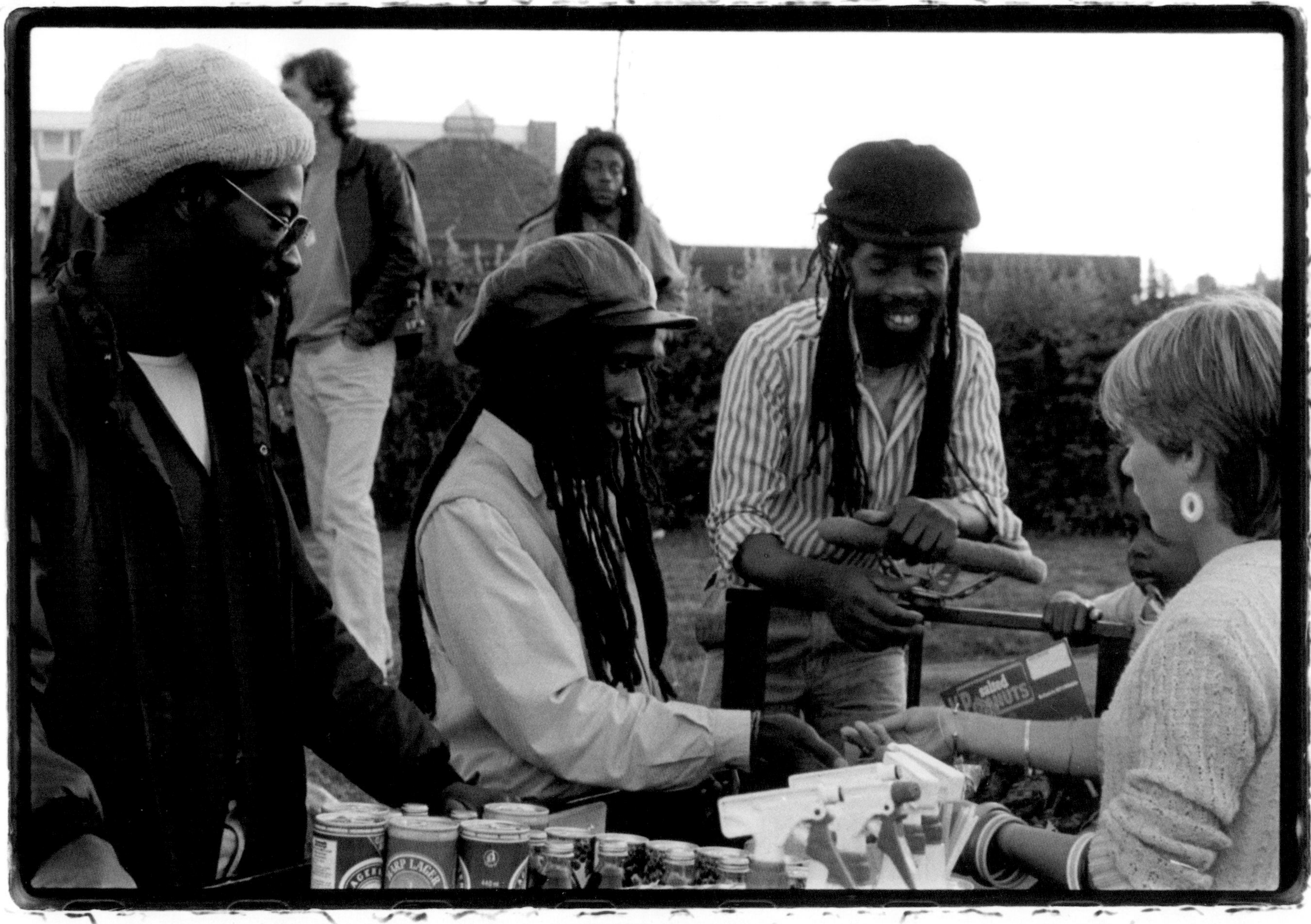

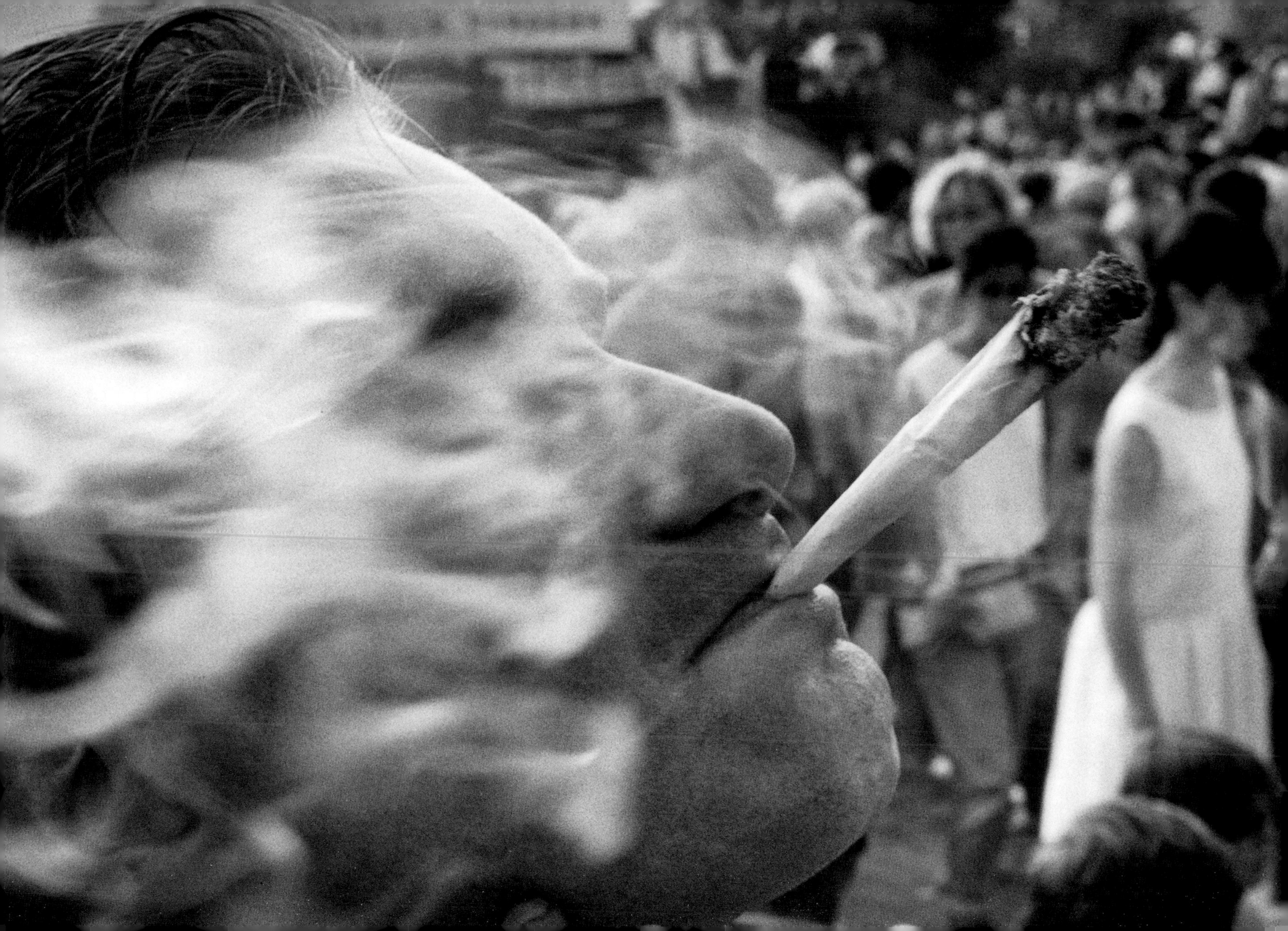

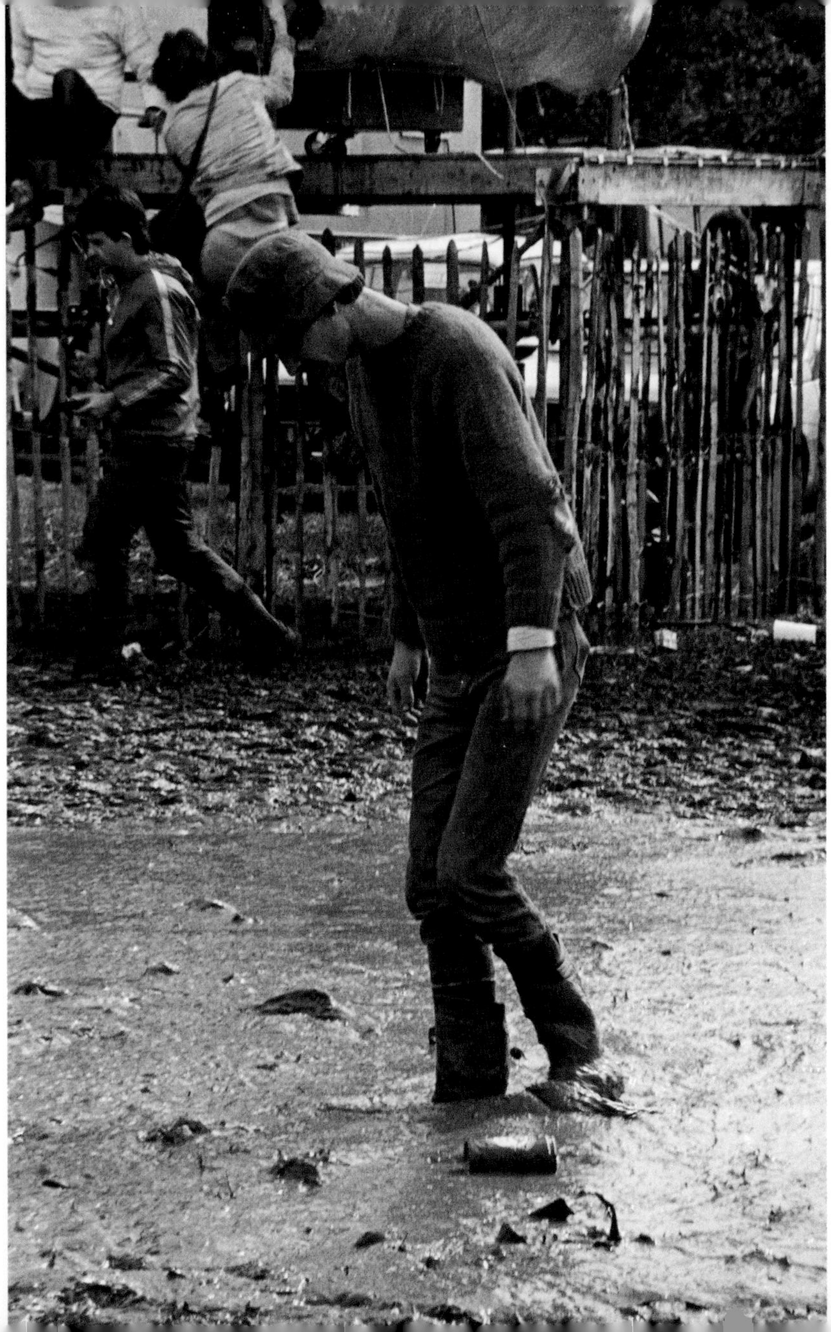

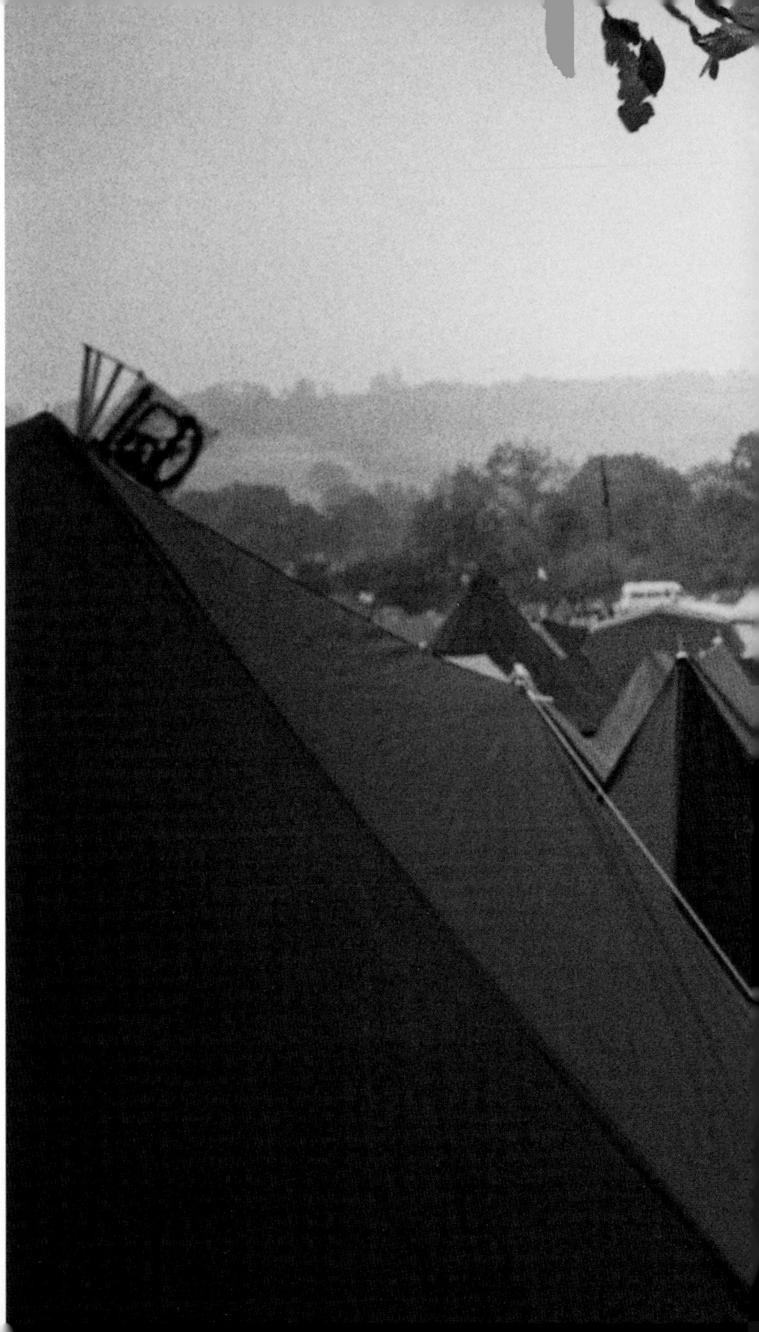

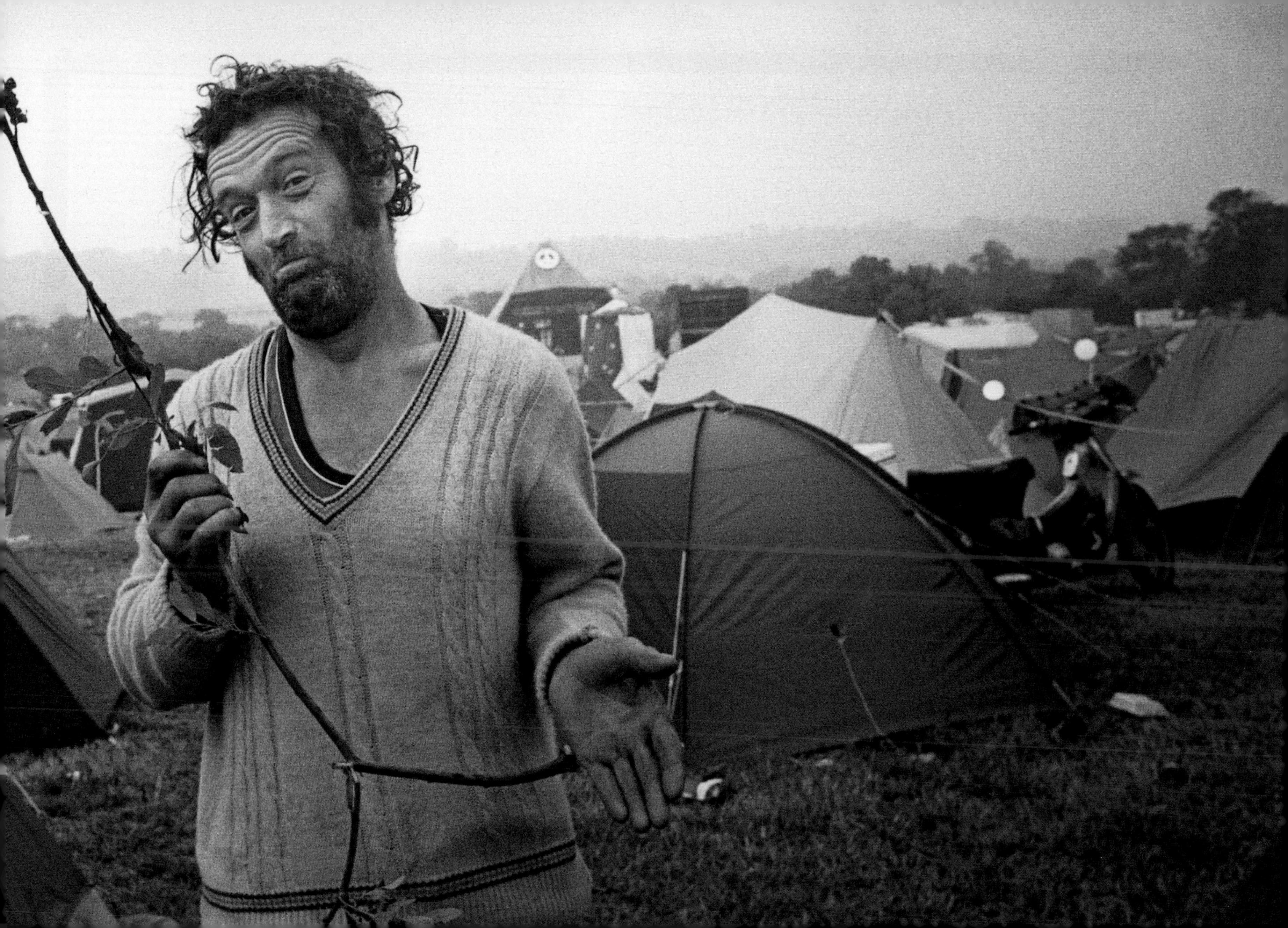

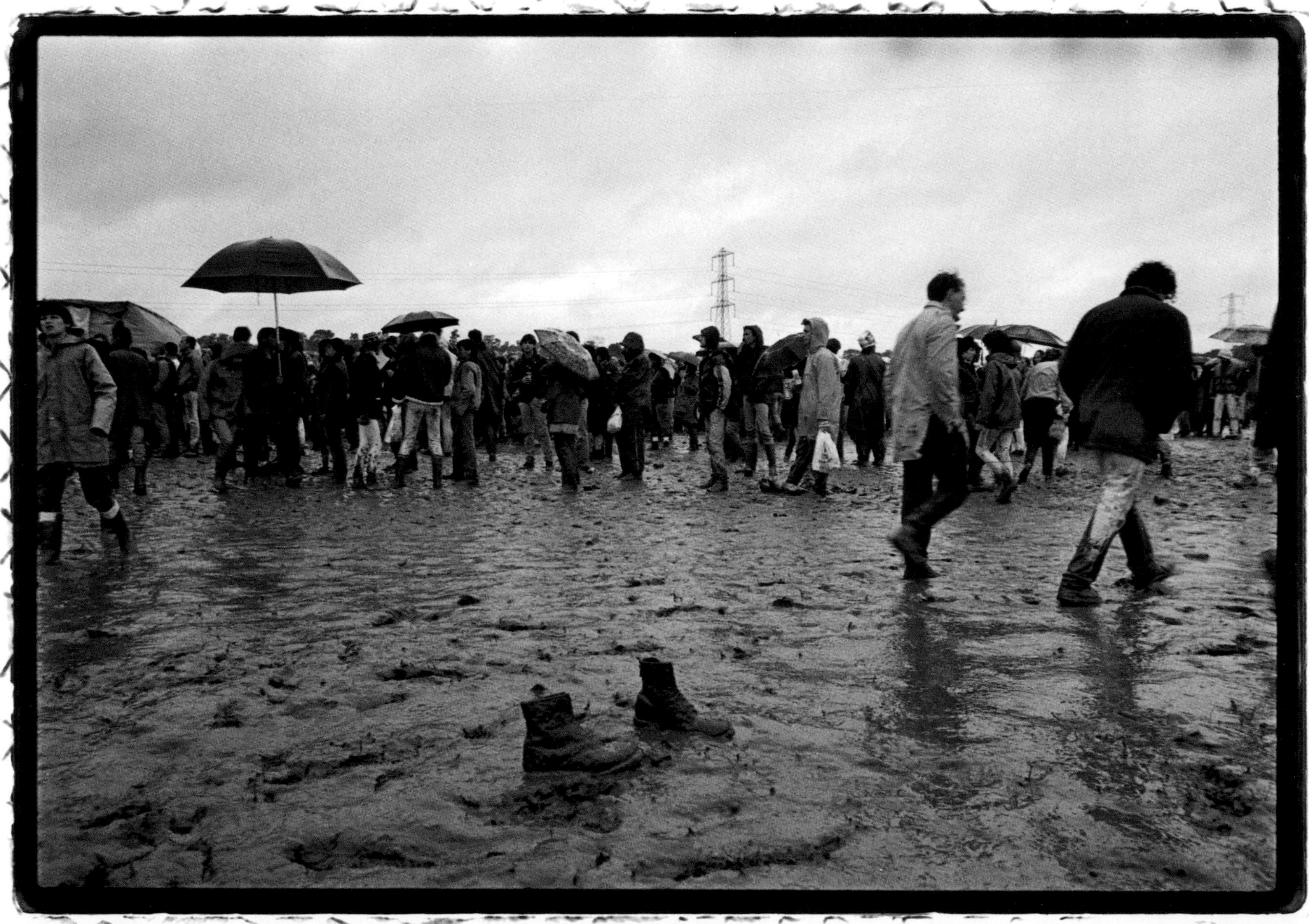

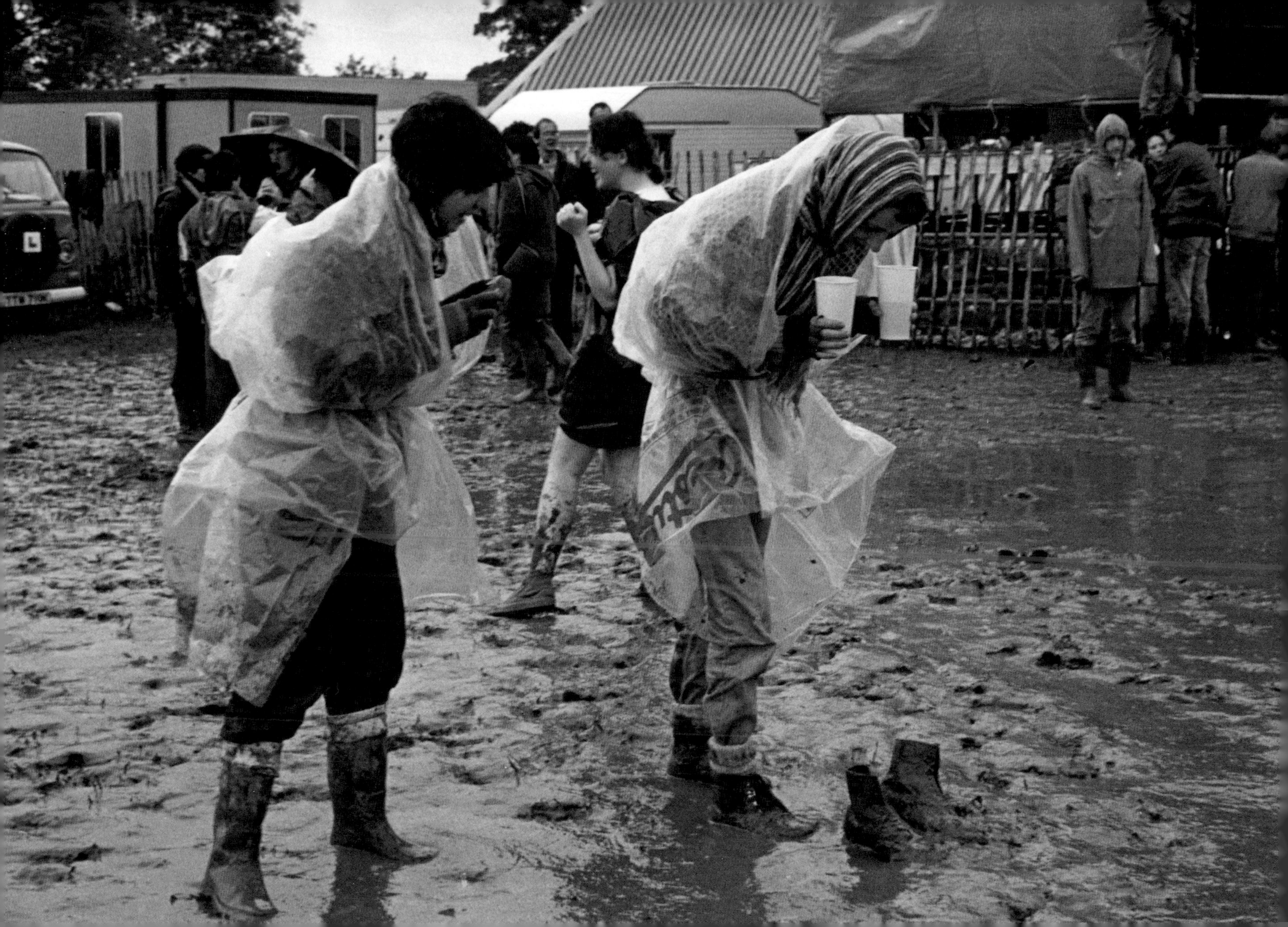

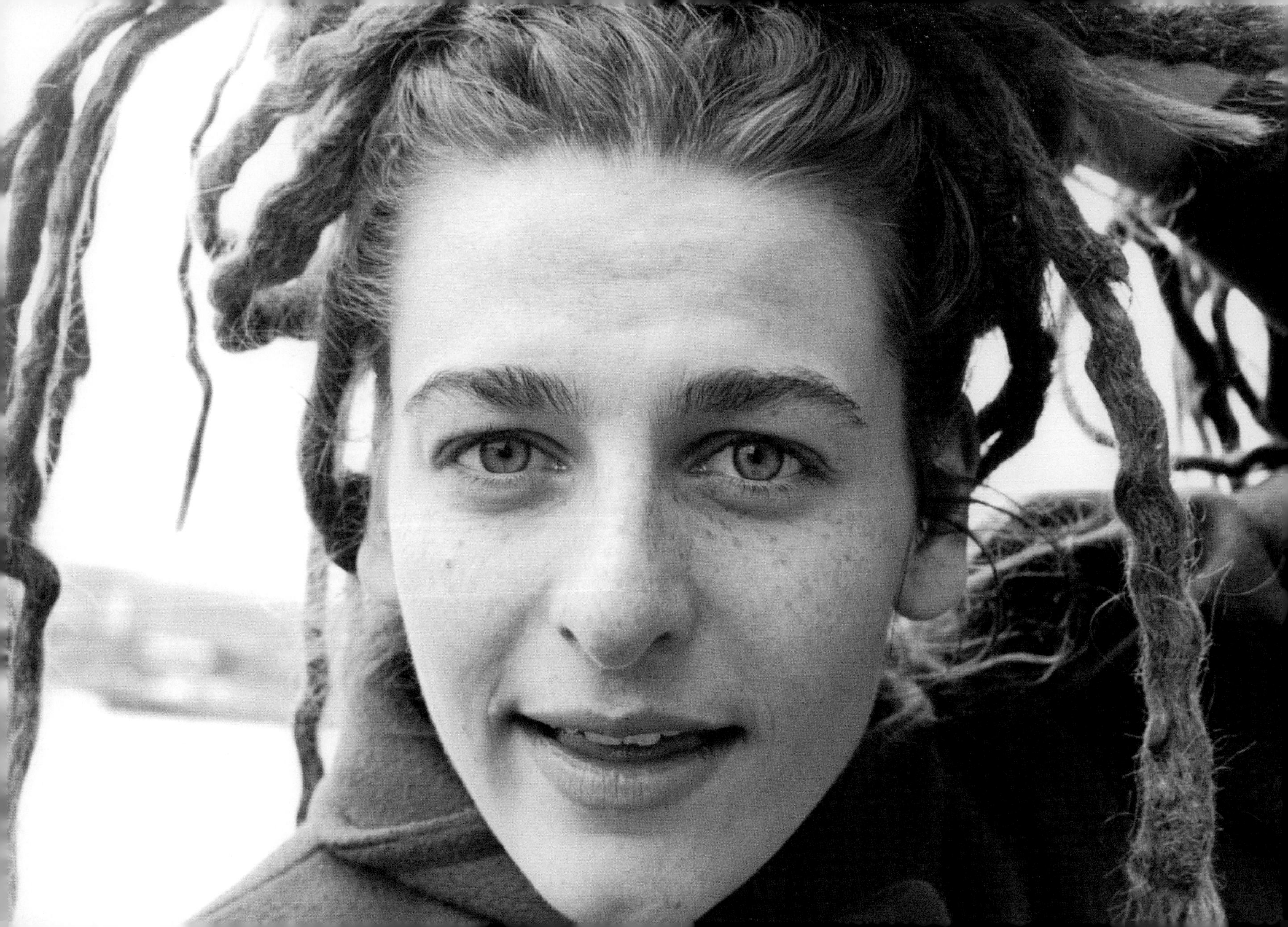

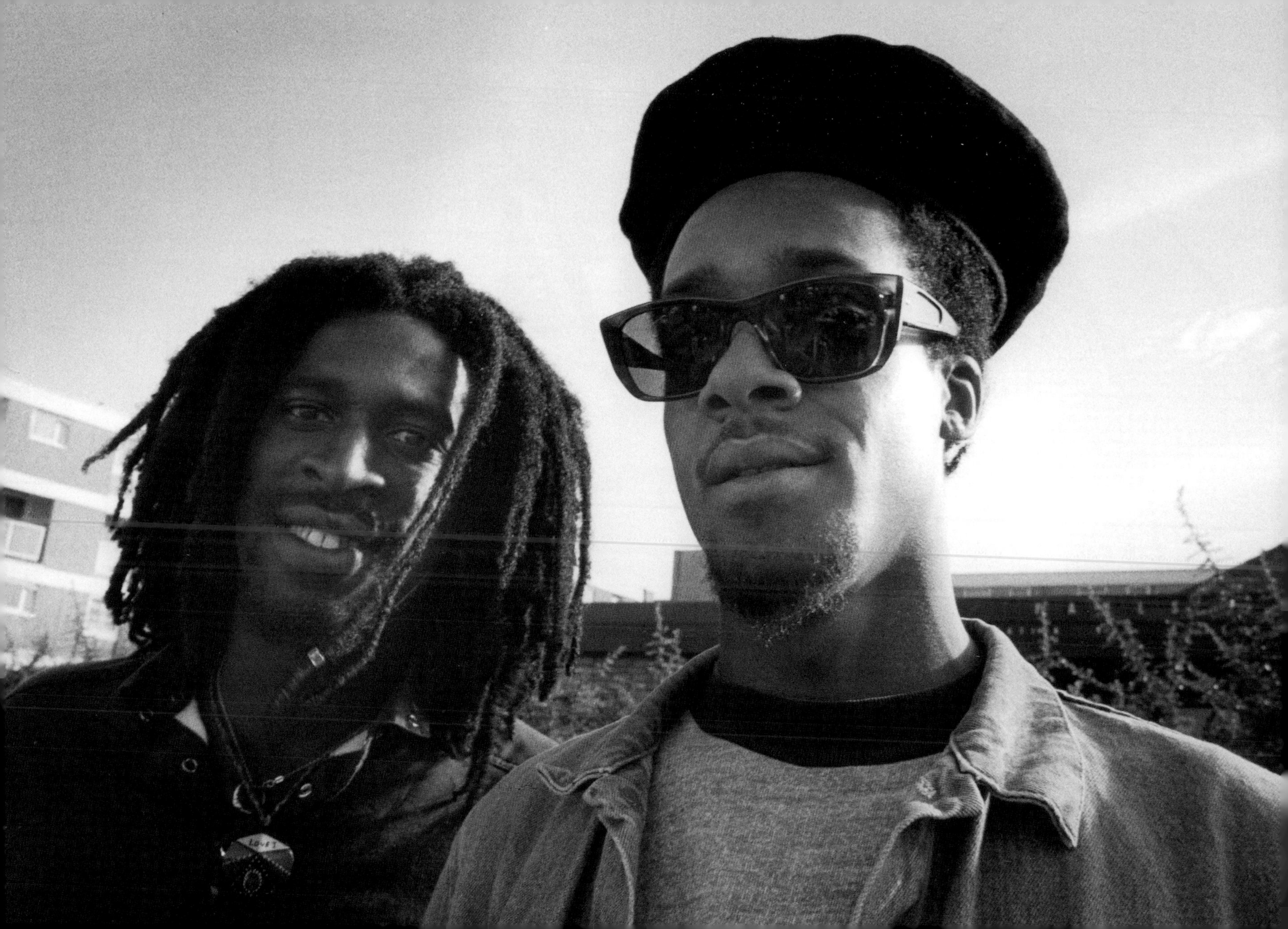

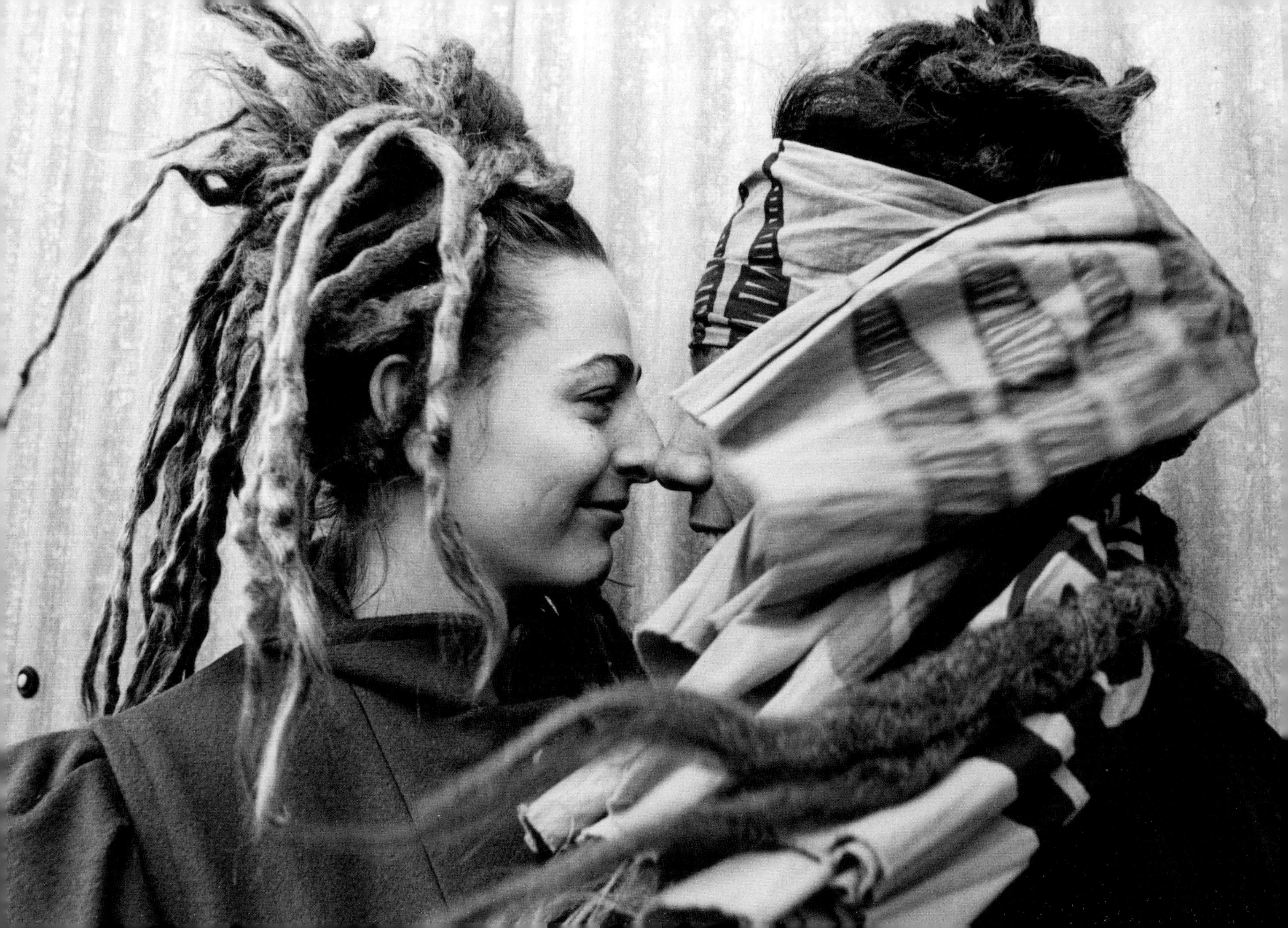

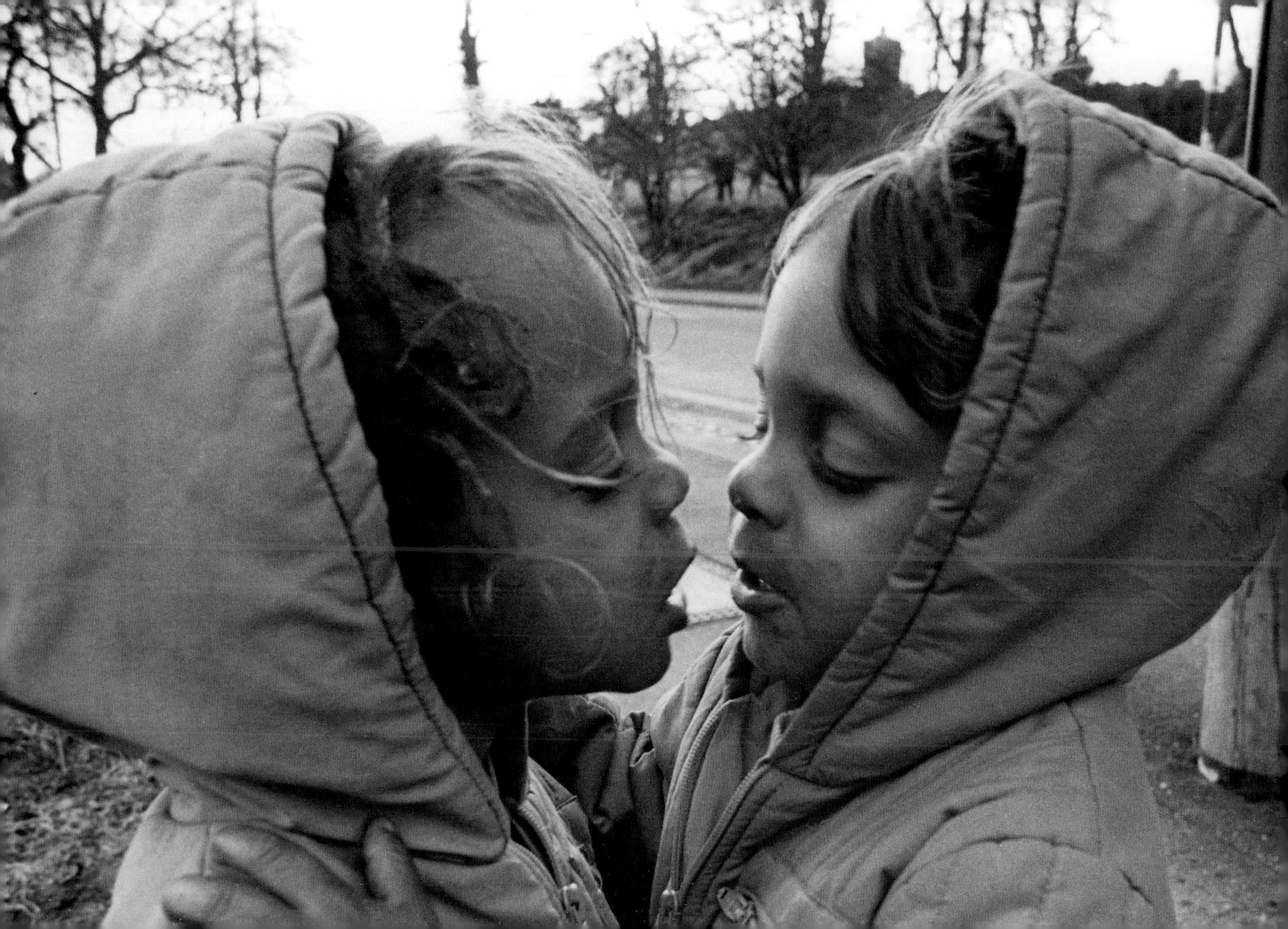

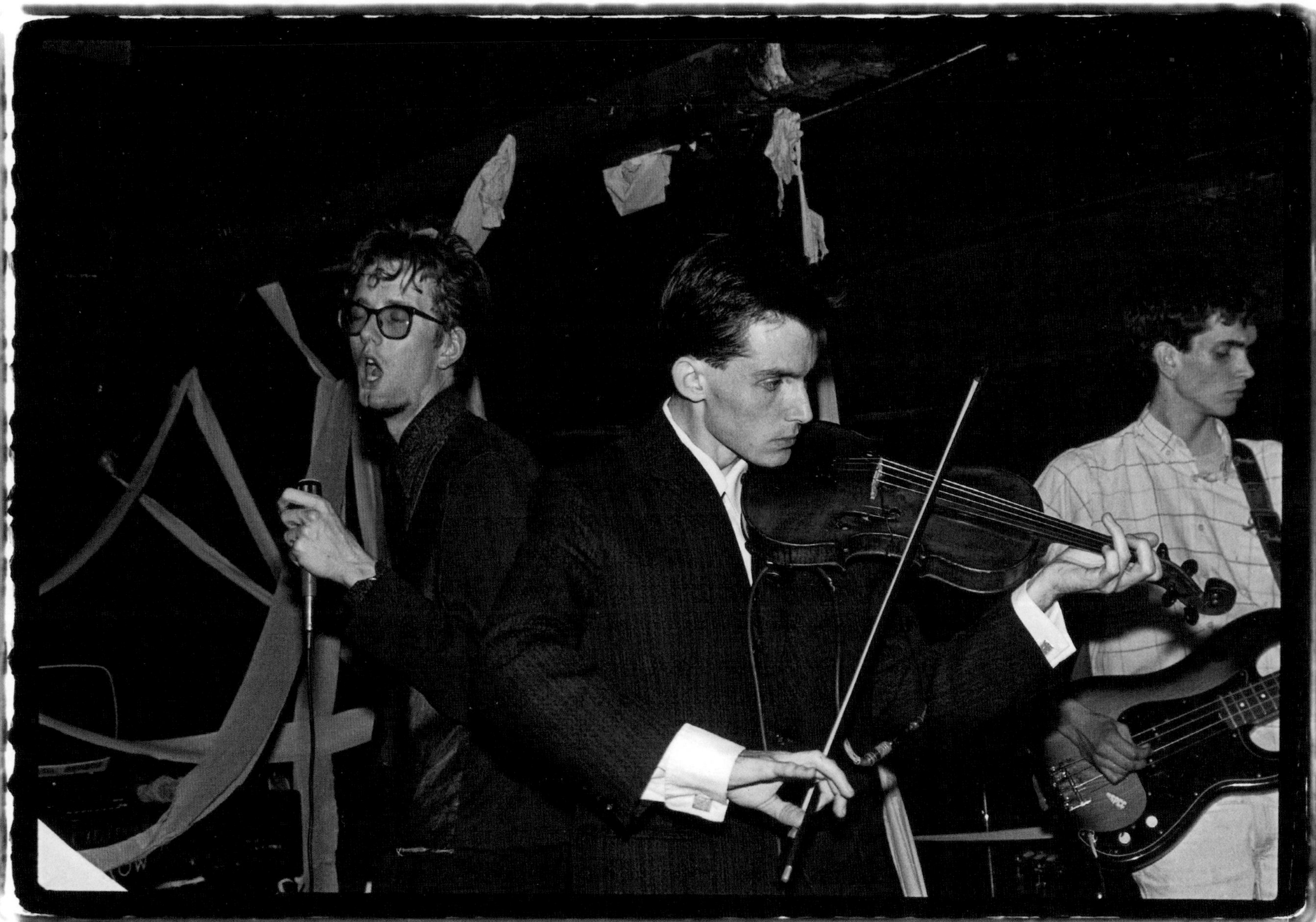

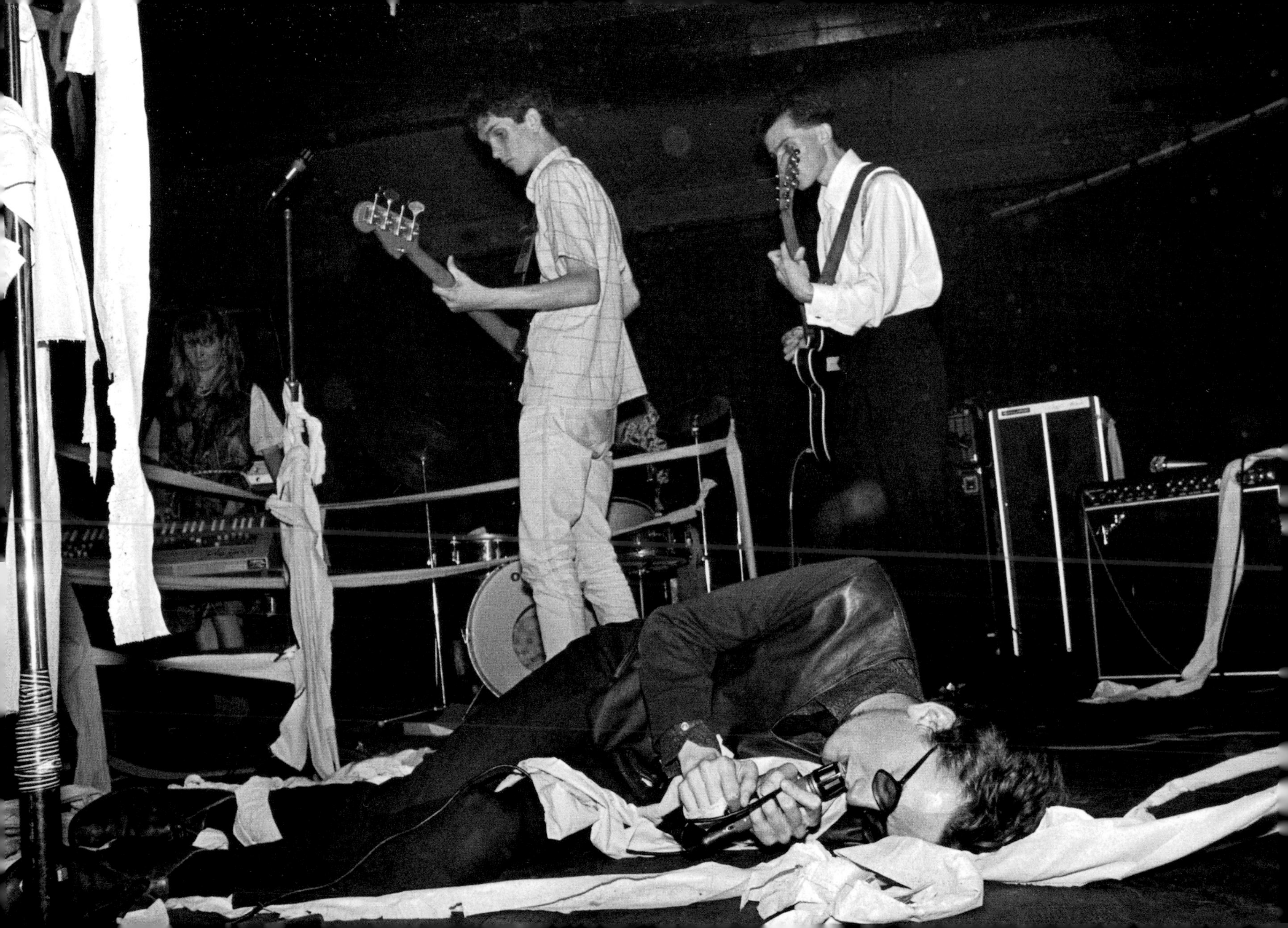

Wild Dayz

diggin in the crates
cuttin out the negatives
erasin the fakes
this ain't no catwalk

stalkin predator
no piranha paparazzi
he puts the b in b-boy
beezer pure posse

the lens is dripping attitude
it's street cinema verite

he documents all the different
mutations of the bass nation

new york tokyo rio
it's that bristol state of mind
when the bass line electrocutes
your spine
it's like a future god

plucking power lines
so when u want that
deep and dirty funk
call beezer

there's none more punk
rewind selector
see the sound boy skanking
to the low end theory
he's got a degree in ghetto-o-logy

i remember those crazy summers
those days of rage
then as now we manned the
barricades

kiss the future
protest and survive
this is one camera that never lies

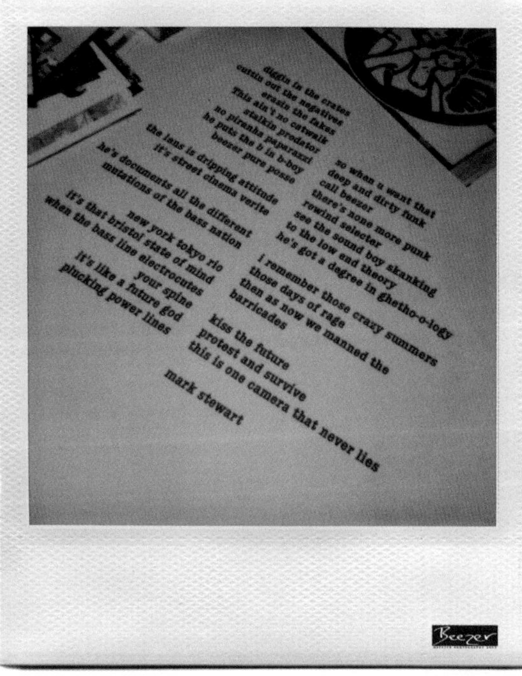

mark stewart

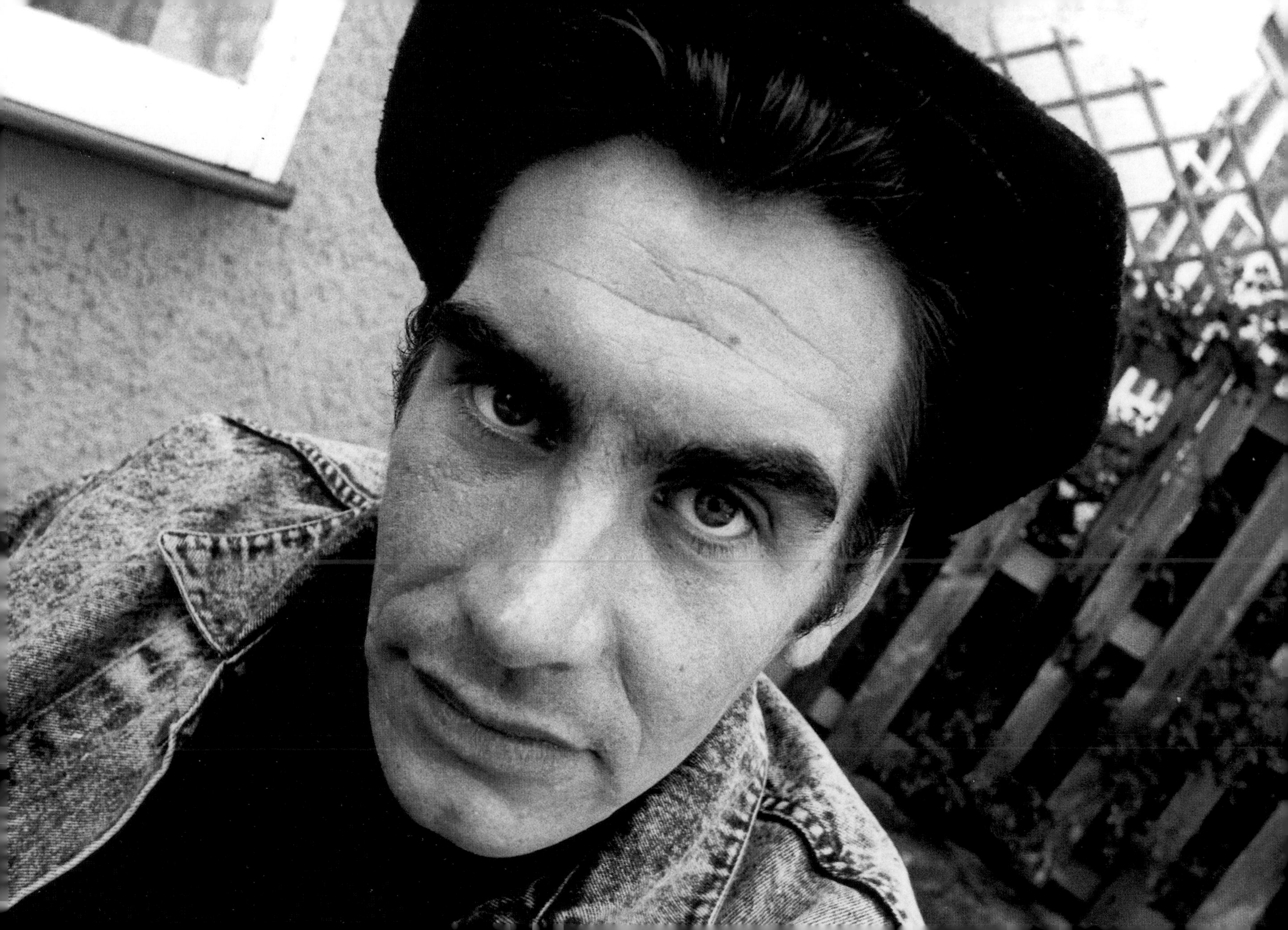

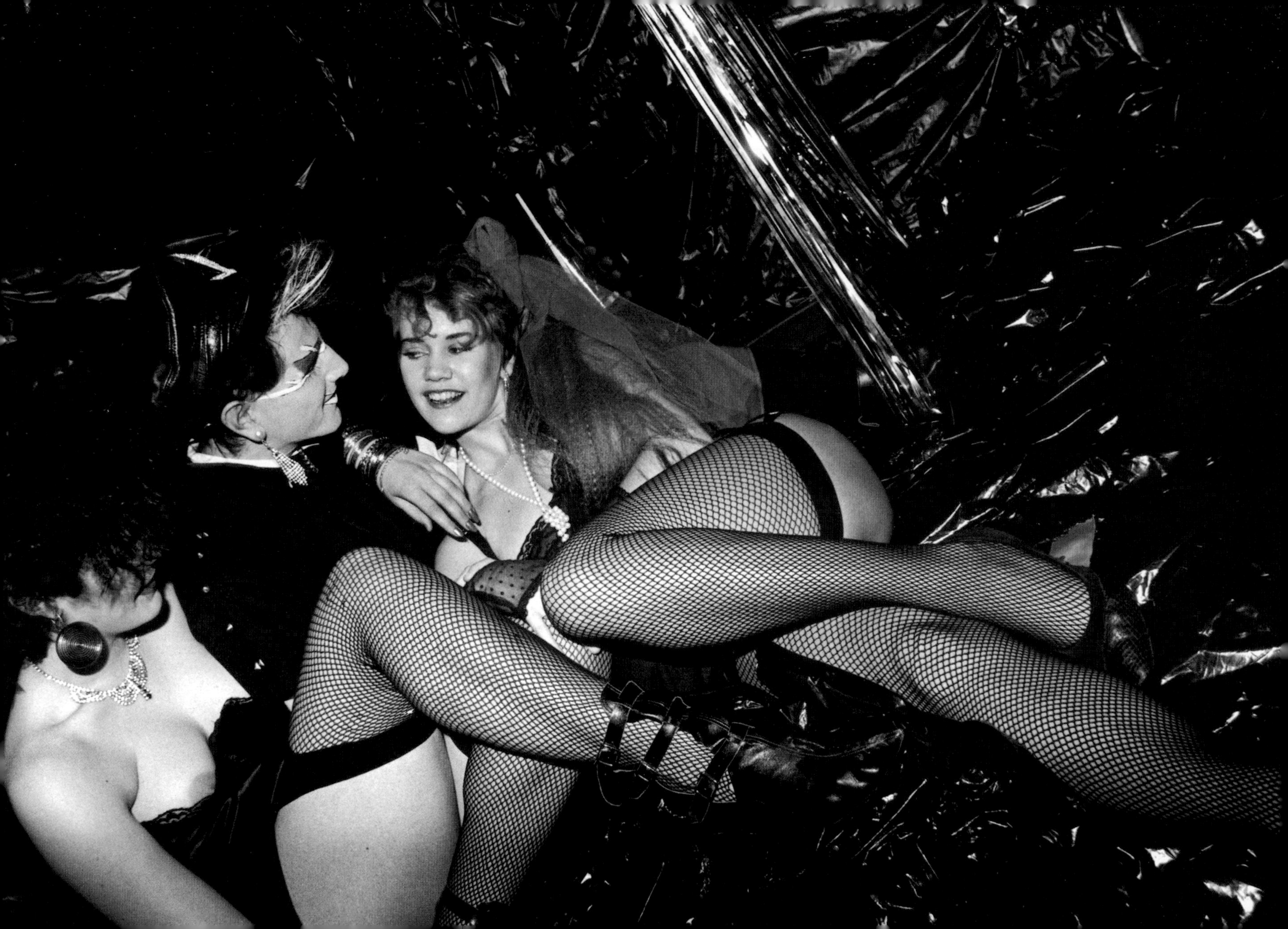

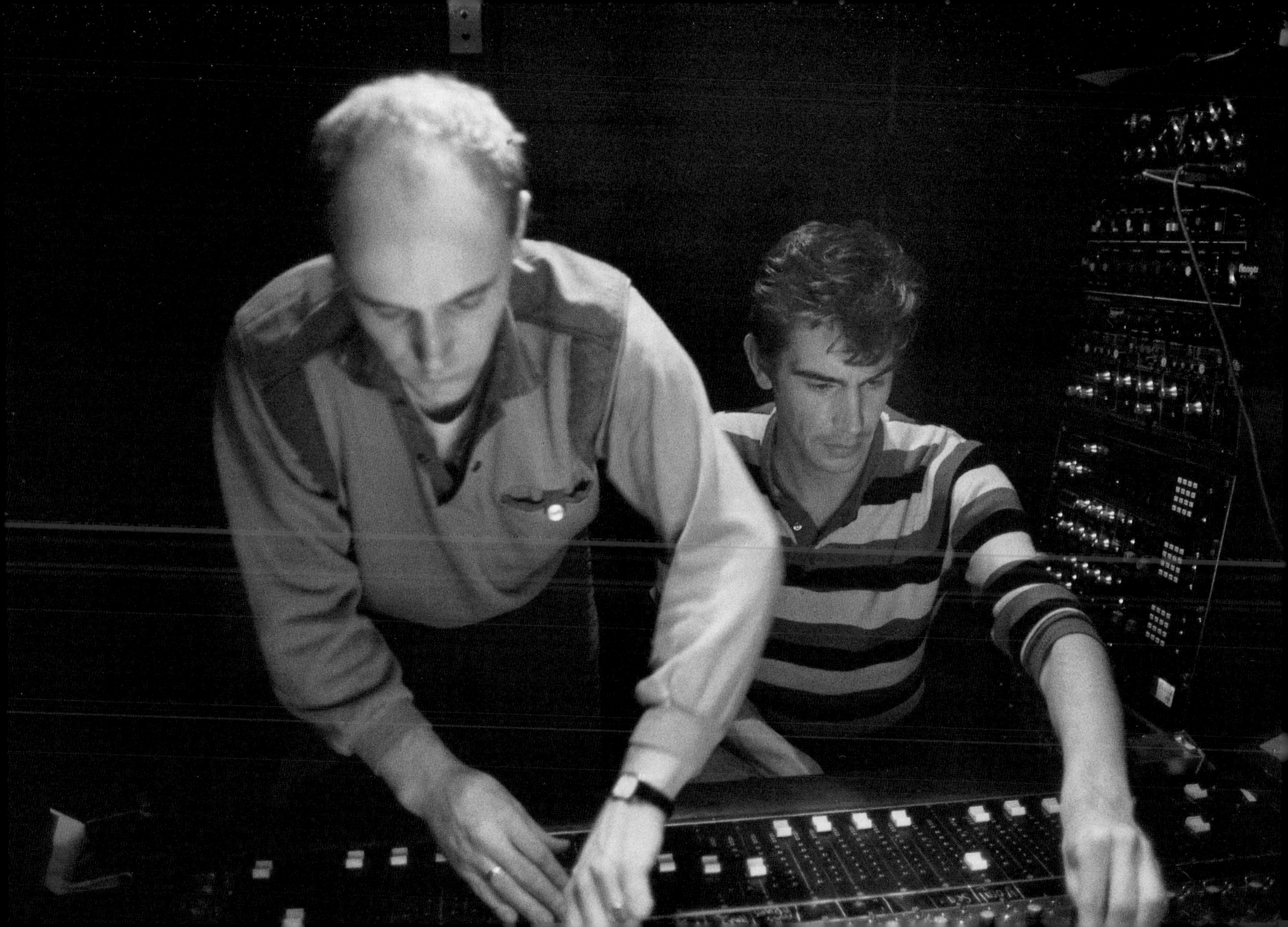

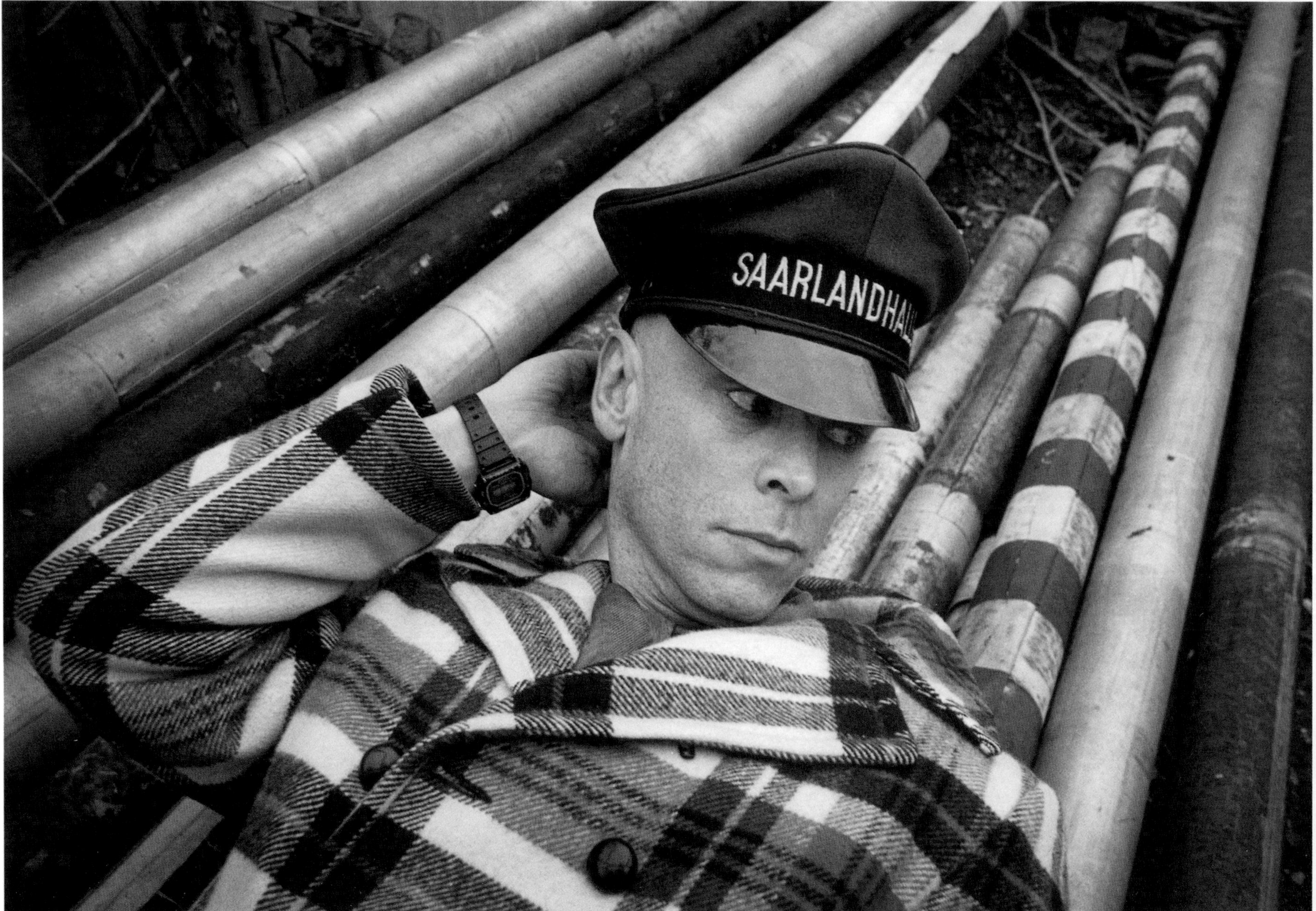
SAARLANDHALL

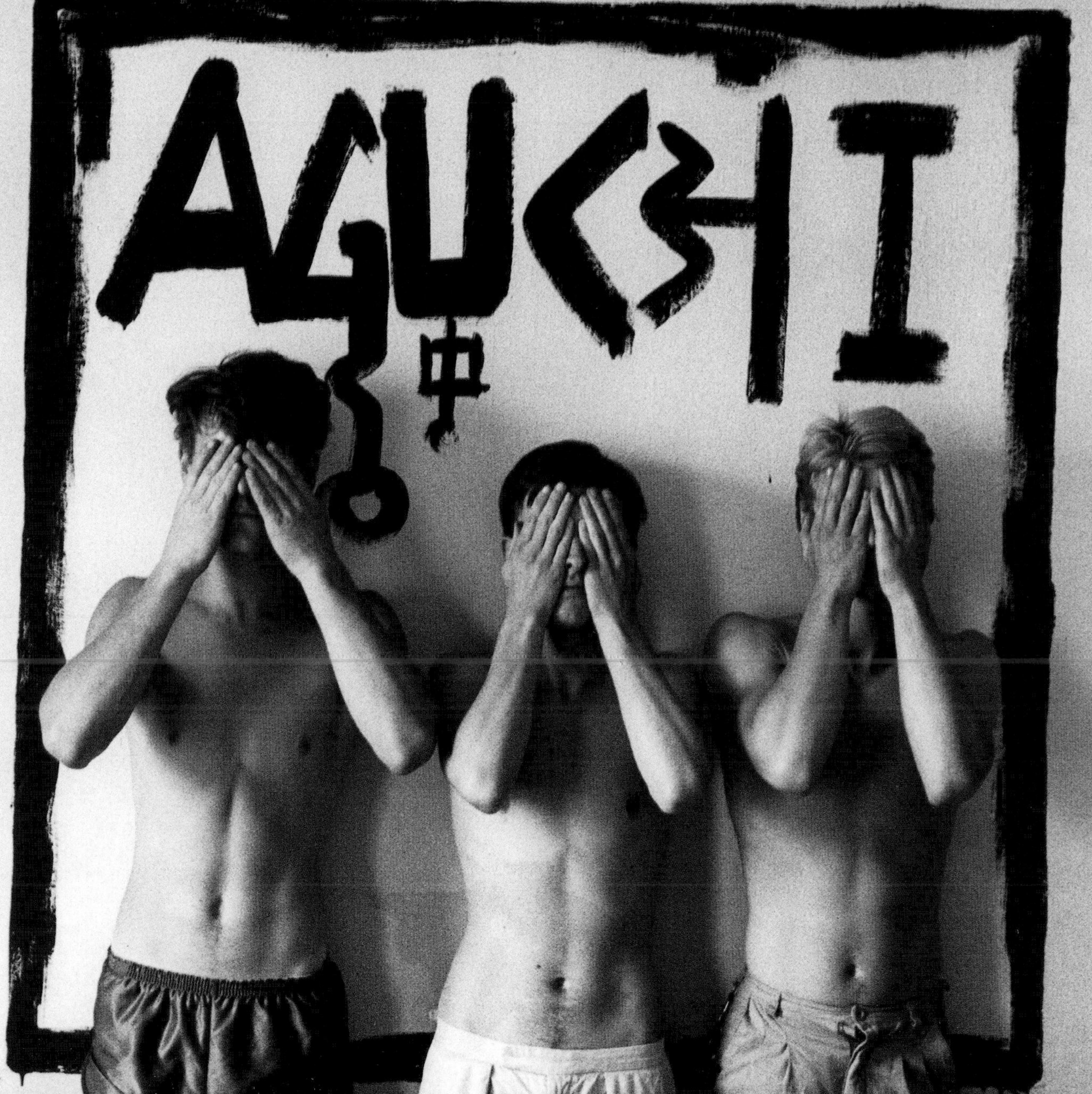
AGUCHI

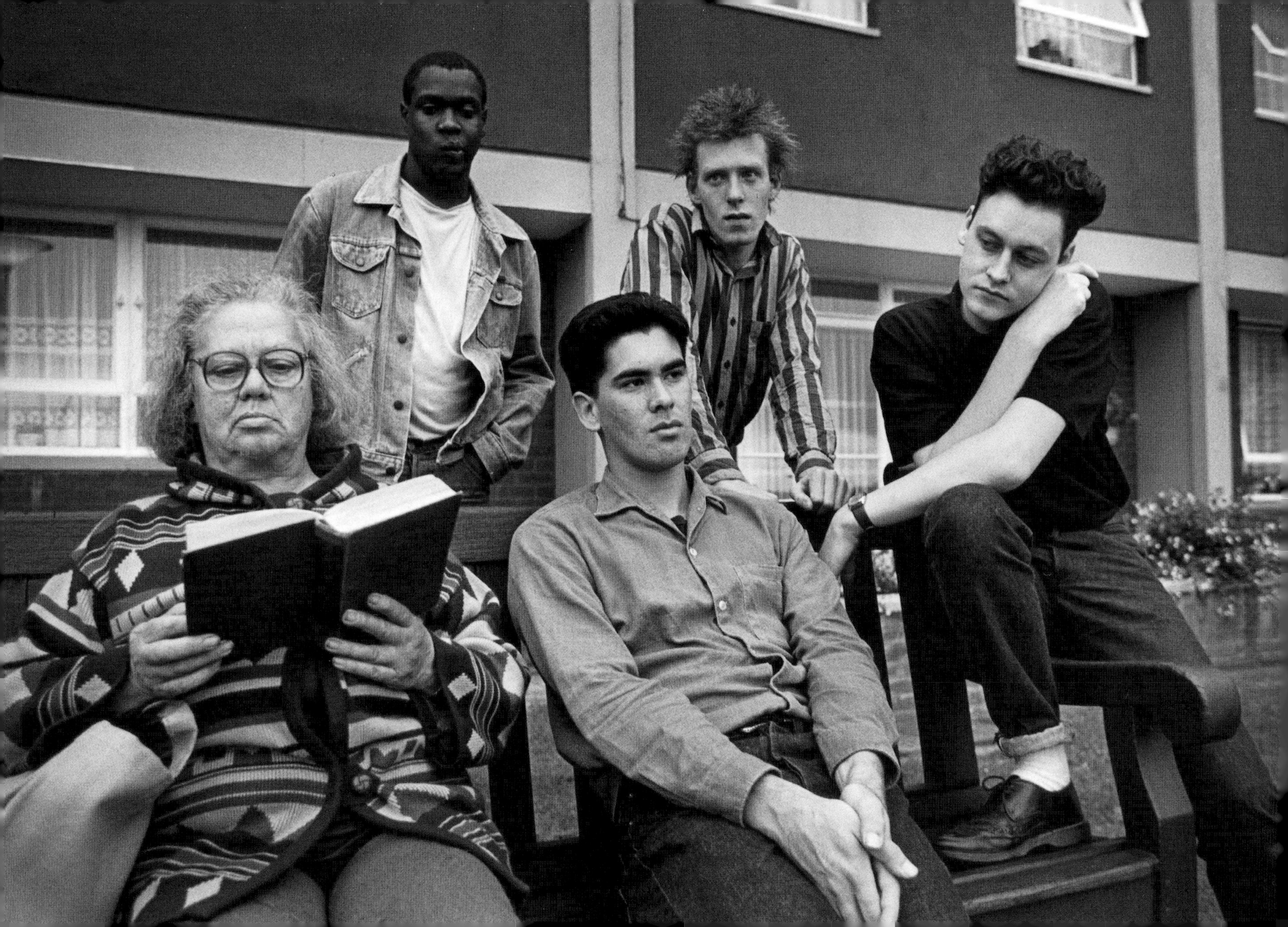

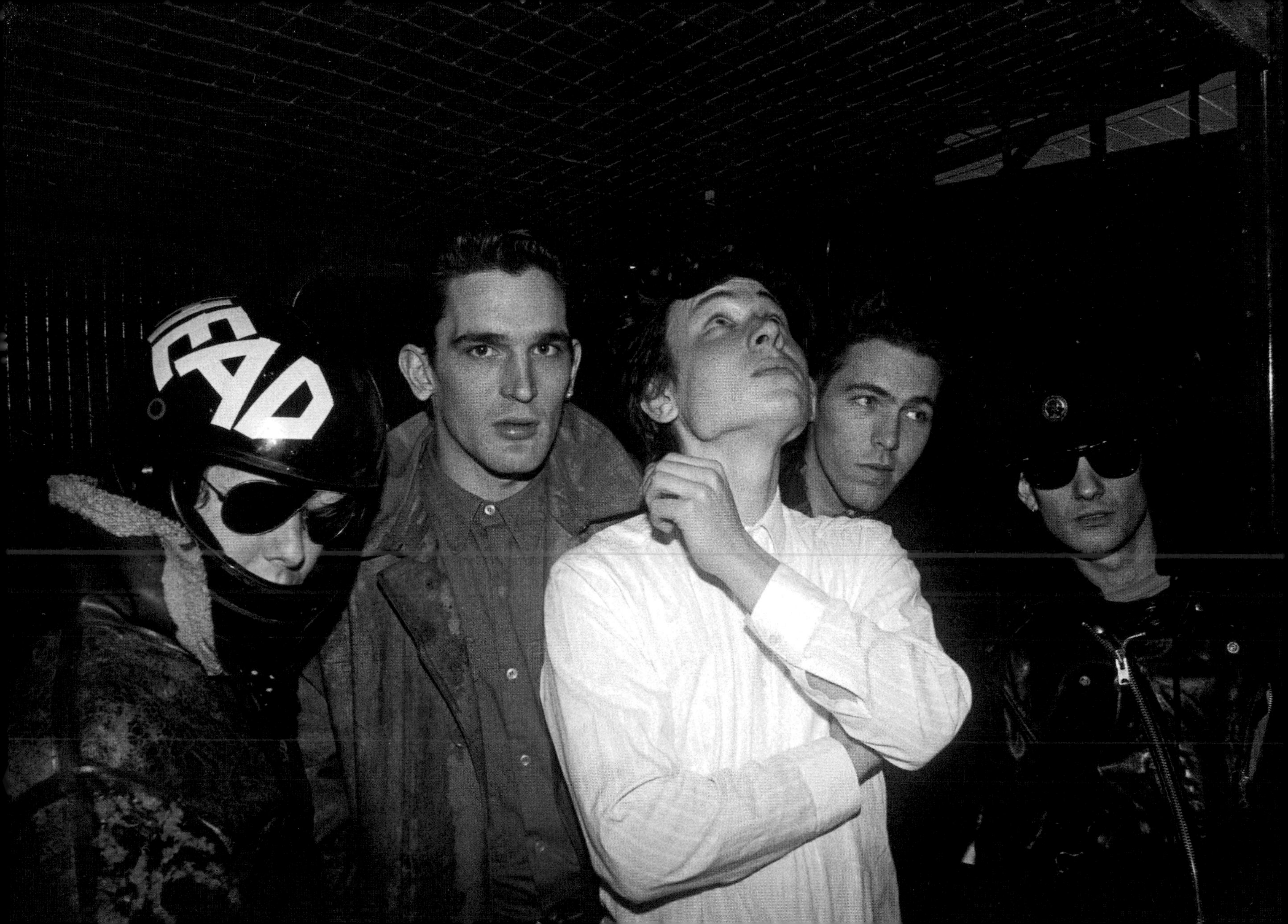

EAD

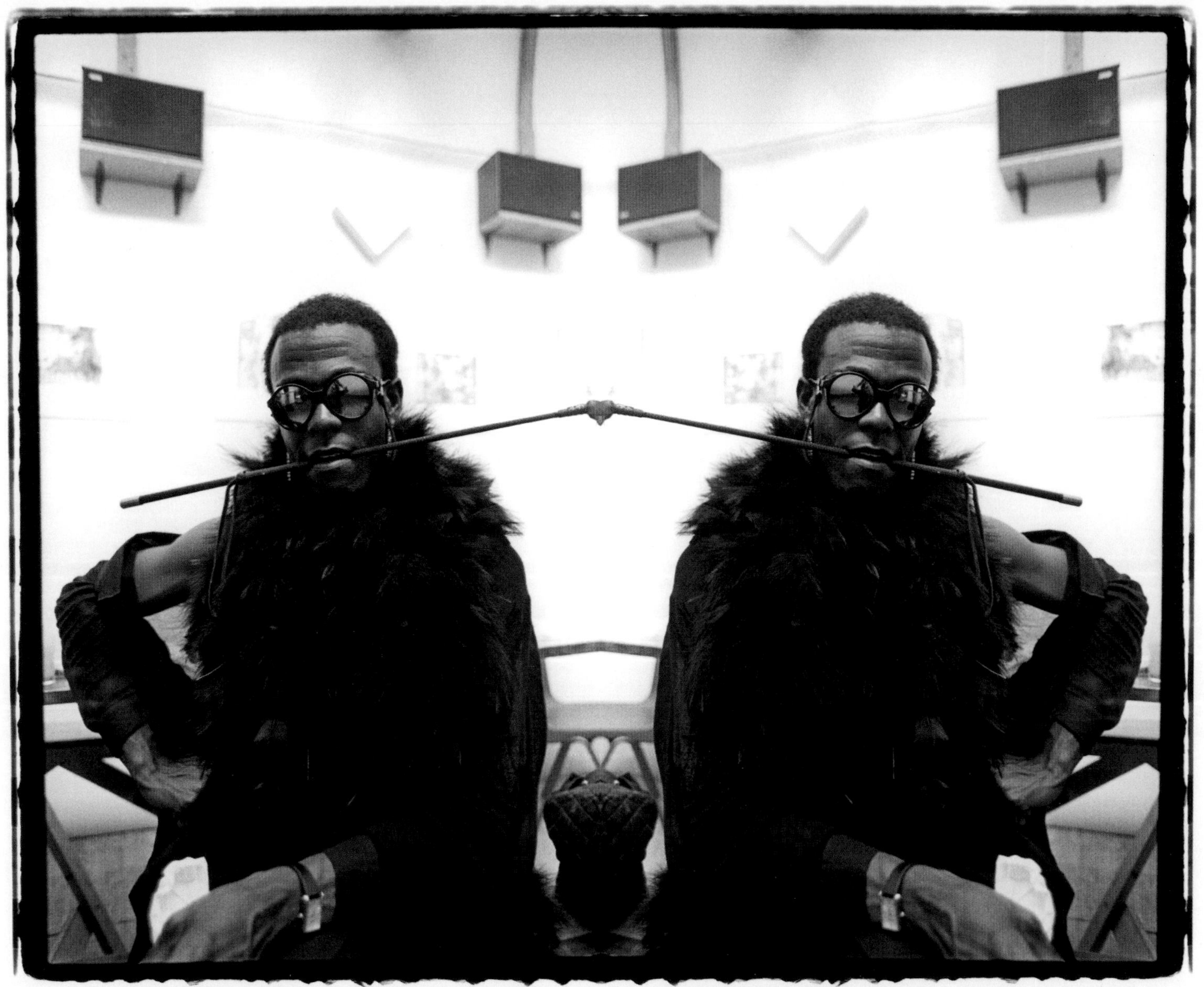

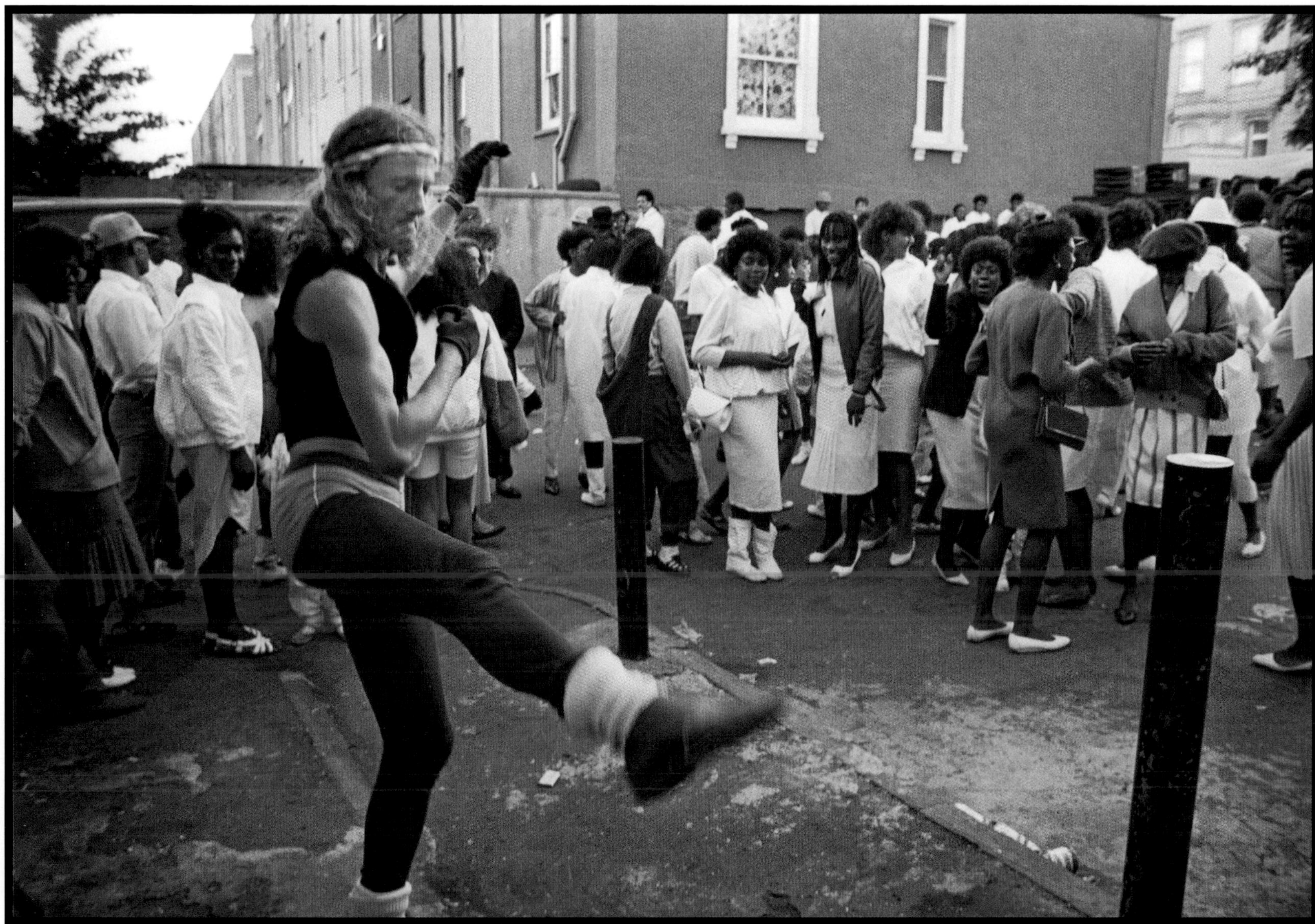

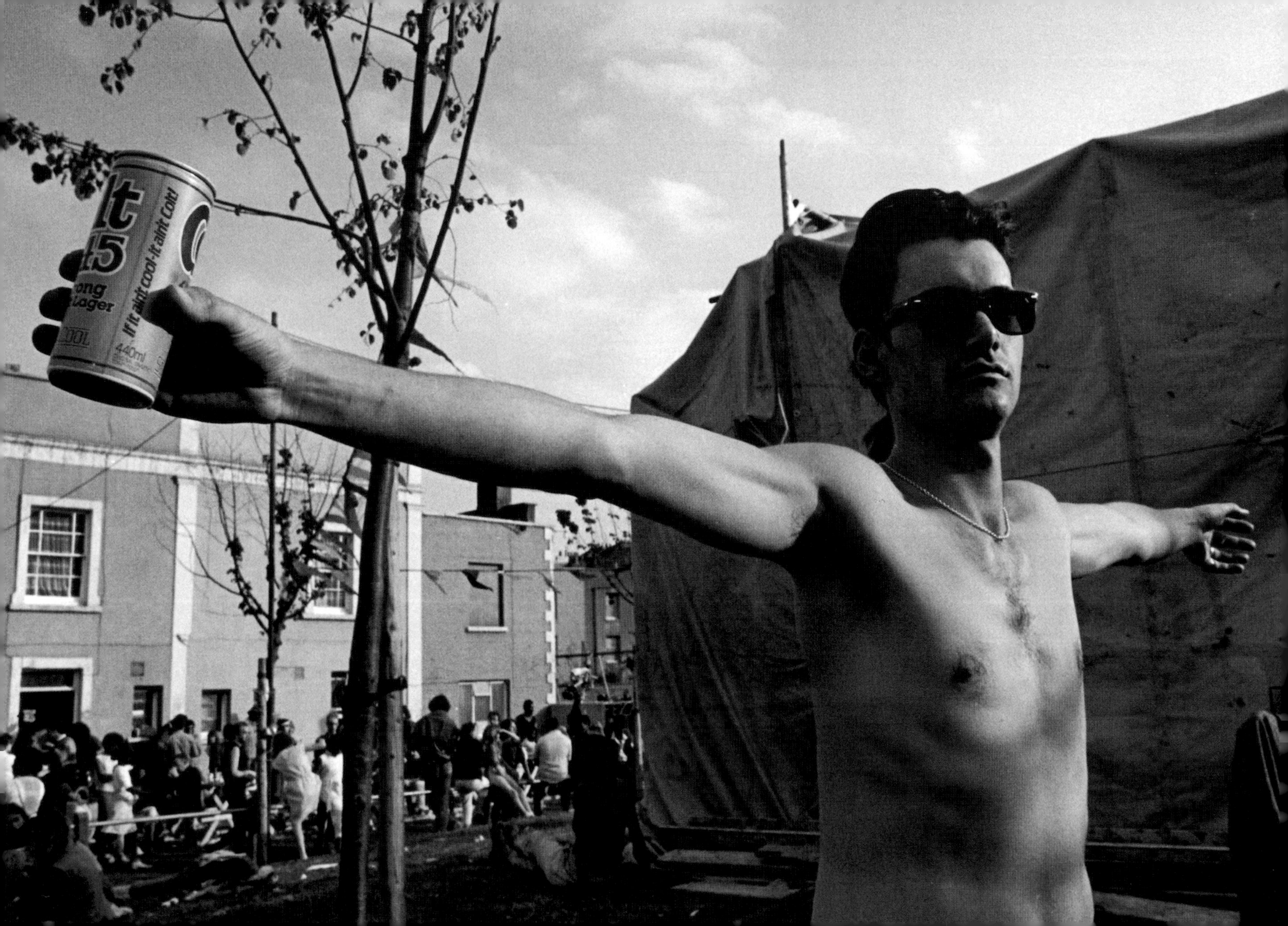

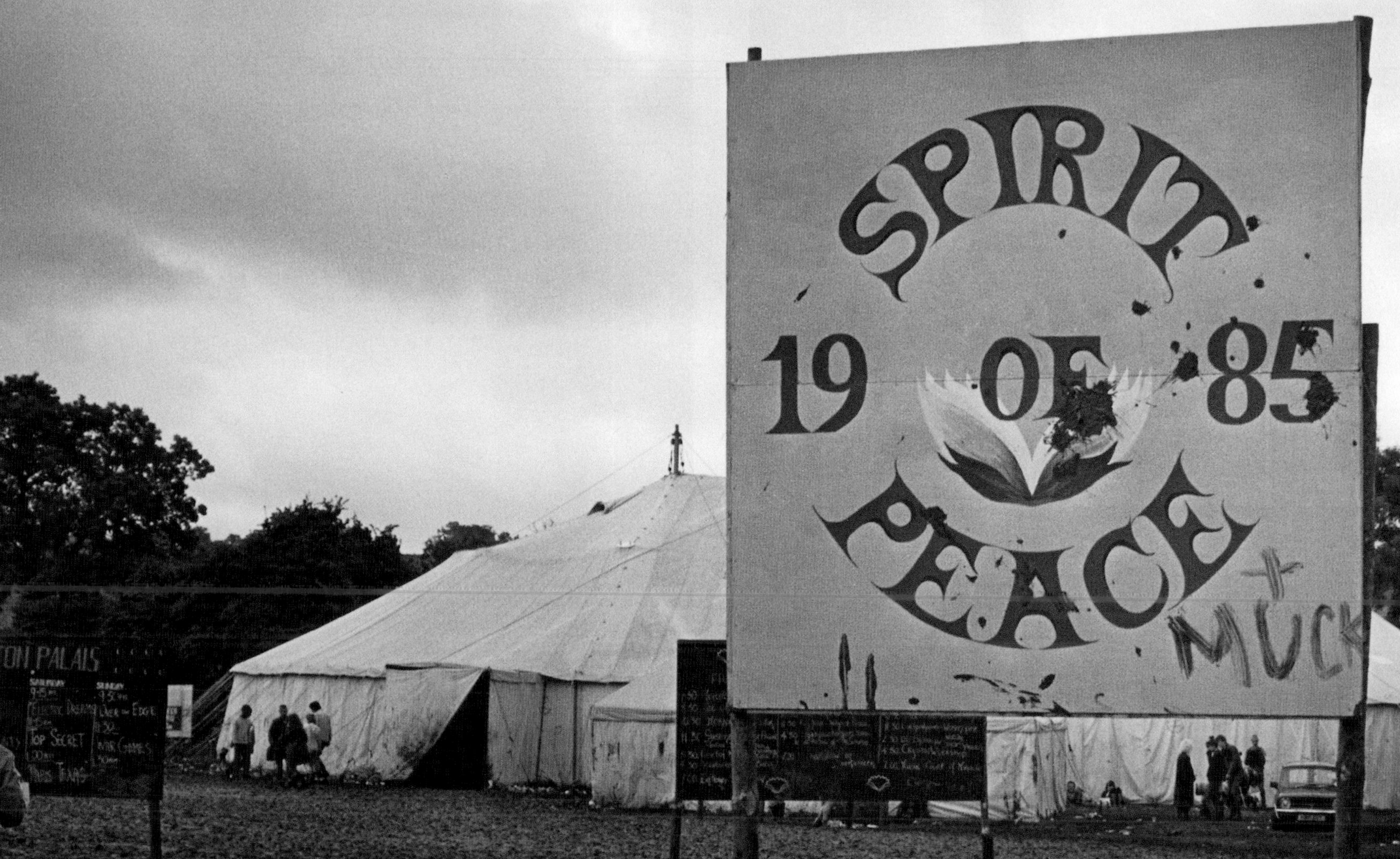

SPIRIT
19 OF 85
PEACE
MUCK

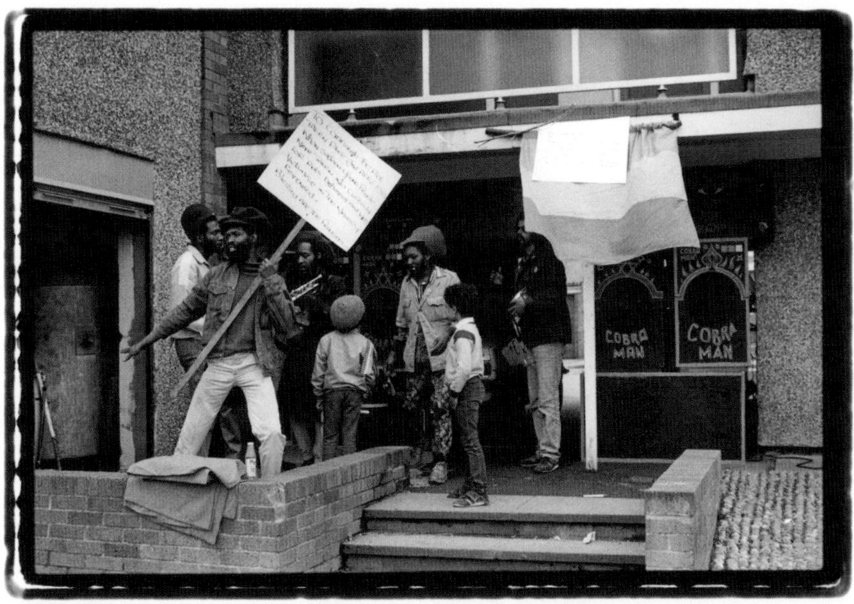

COBRA MAN
COBRA MAN

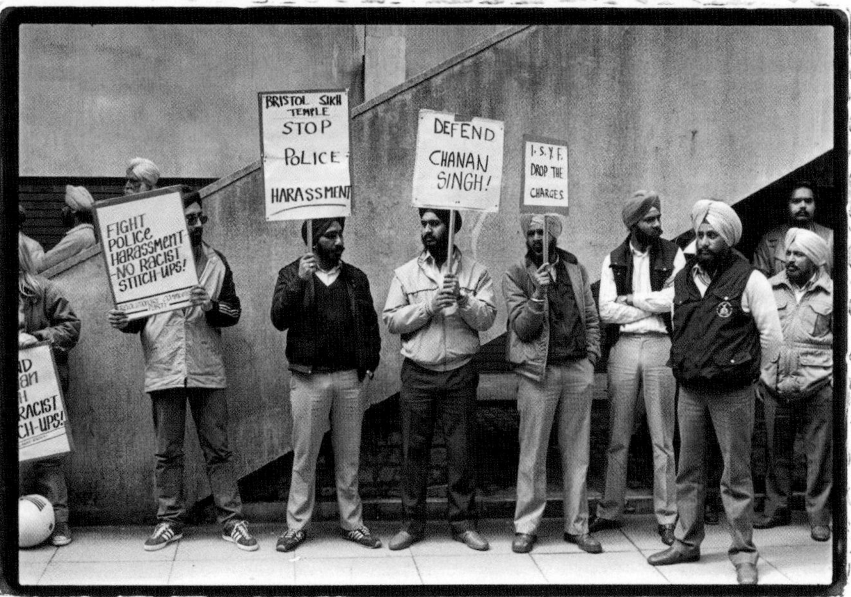

BRISTOL SIKH
TEMPLE
STOP
POLICE
HARASSMENT
DEFEND
CHANAN
SINGH!
I.S.Y.F.
DROP THE
CHARGES
FIGHT
POLICE
HARASSMENT
NO RACIST
STITCH-UPS!

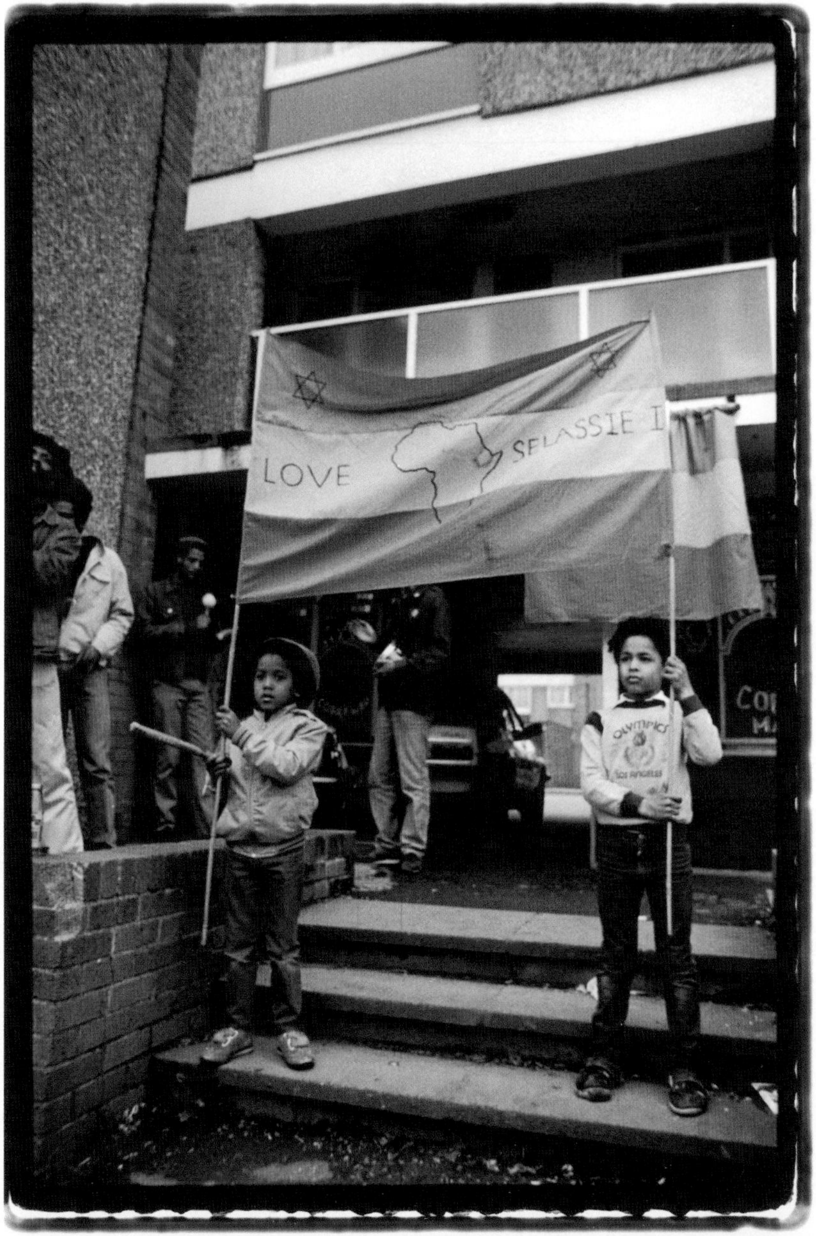

LOVE   SELASSIE I
COBRA
MAN
OLYMPICS
Los Angeles

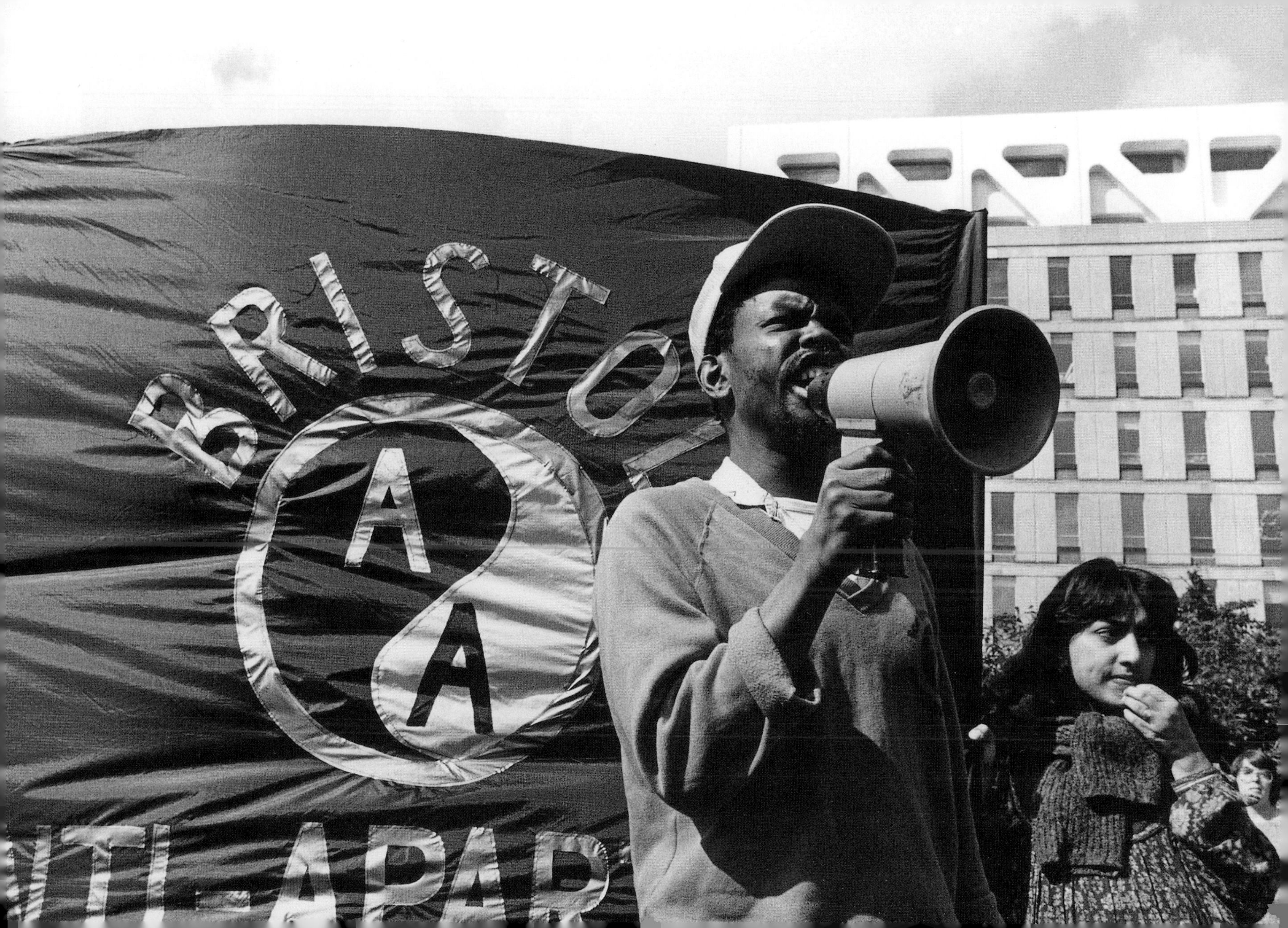
BRISTOL
A
A
A
A
NTI-APAR

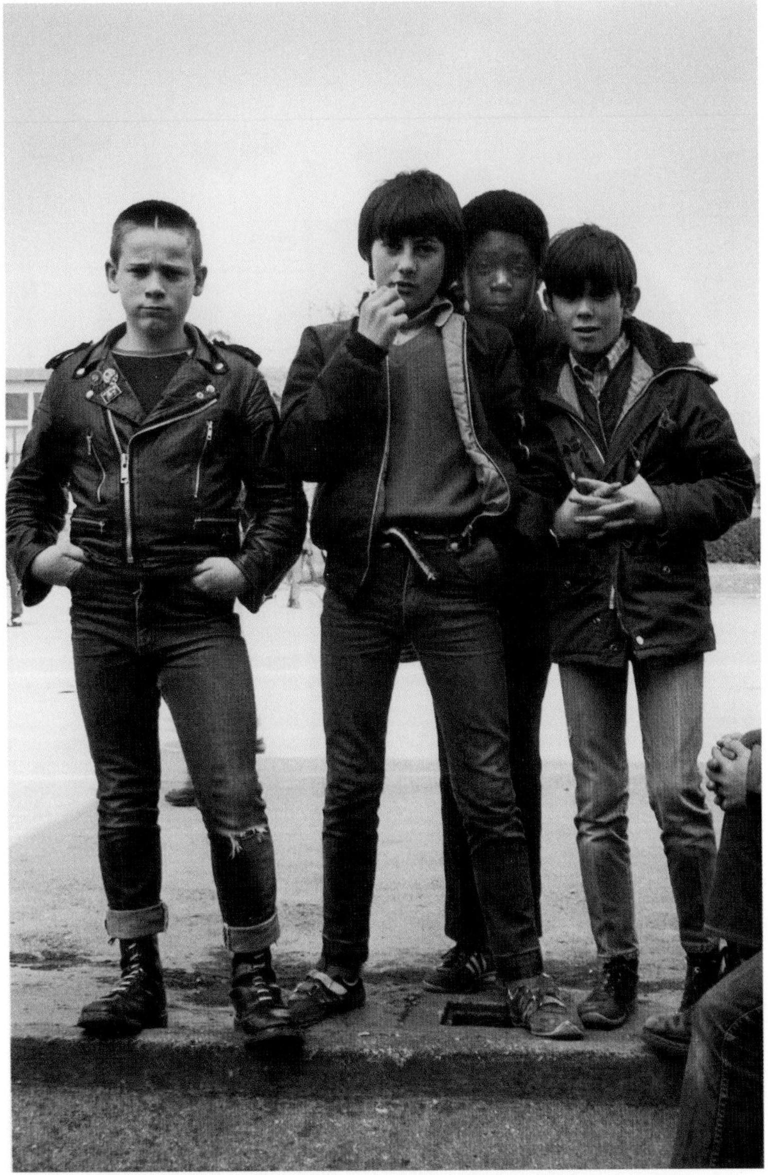

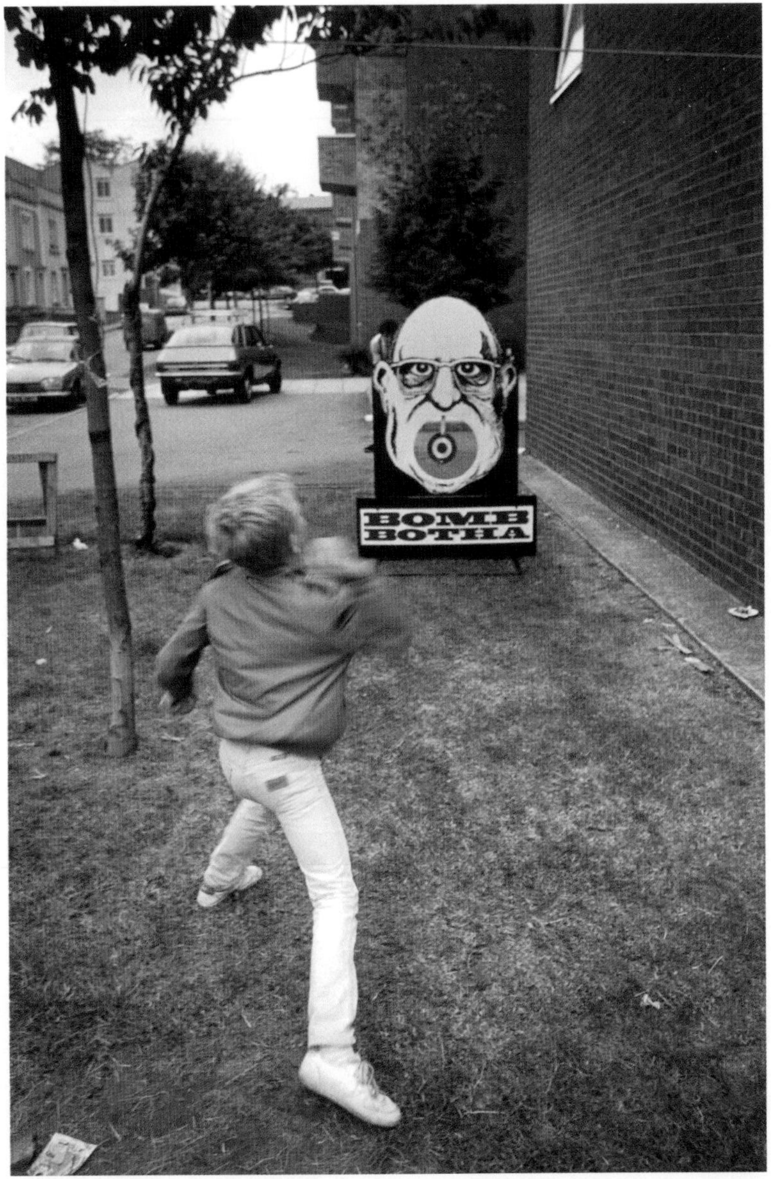

BOMB
BOTHA

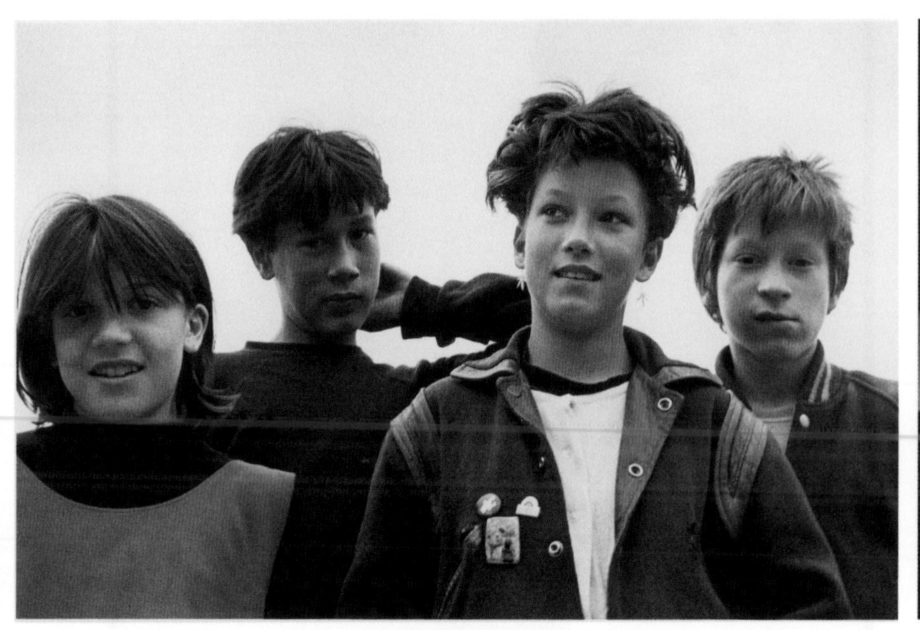
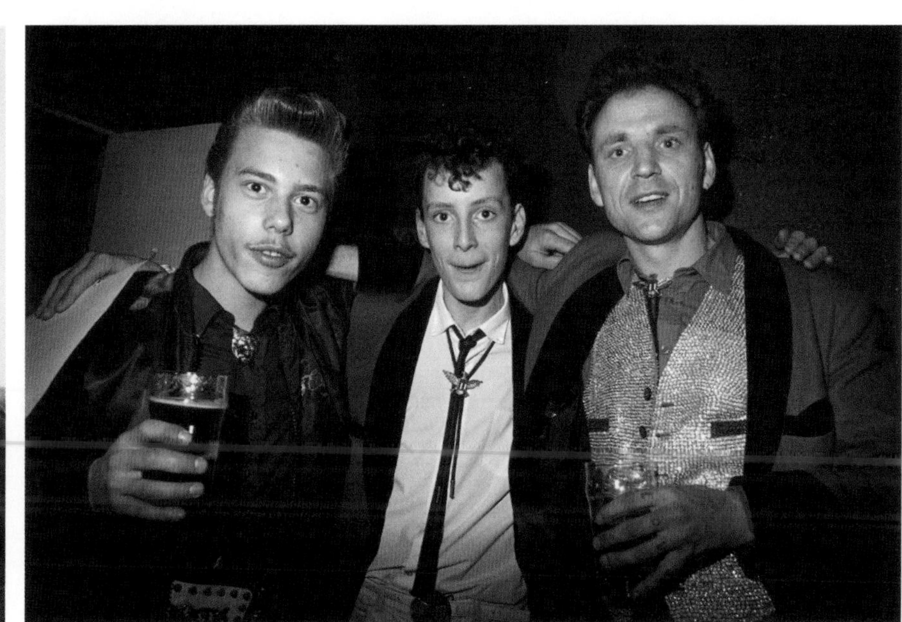

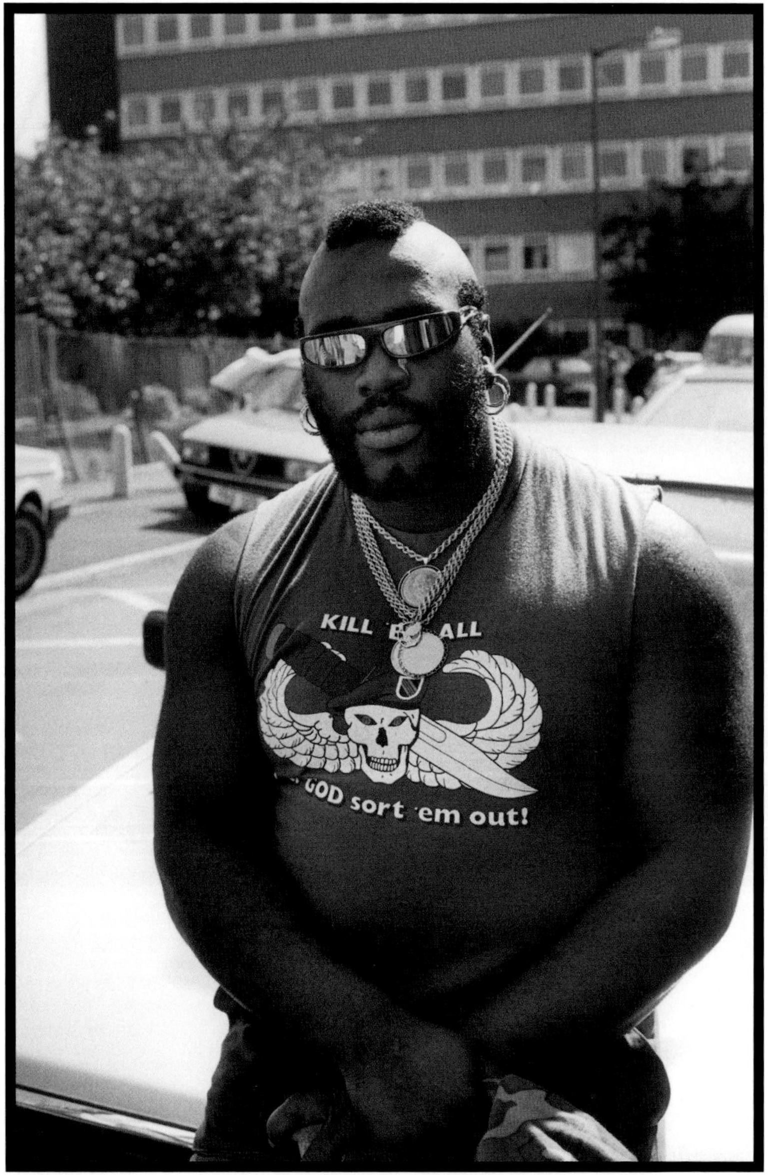

KILL 'EM ALL
GOD sort 'em out!

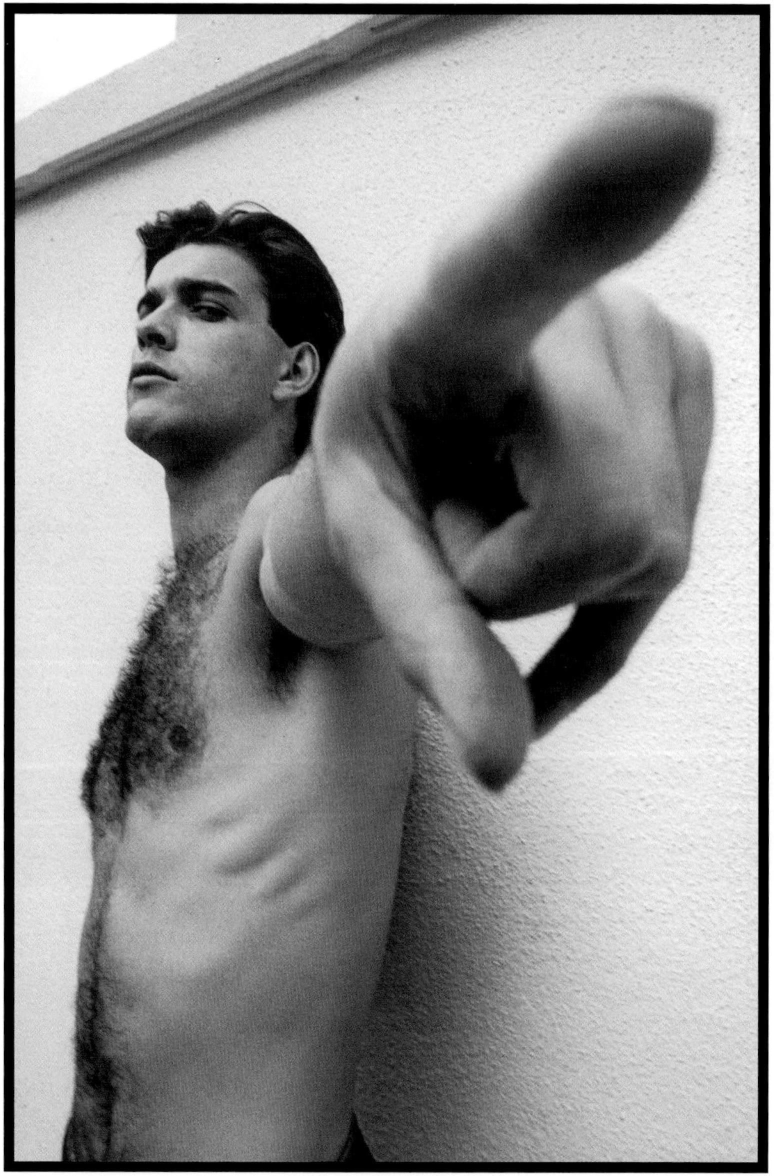

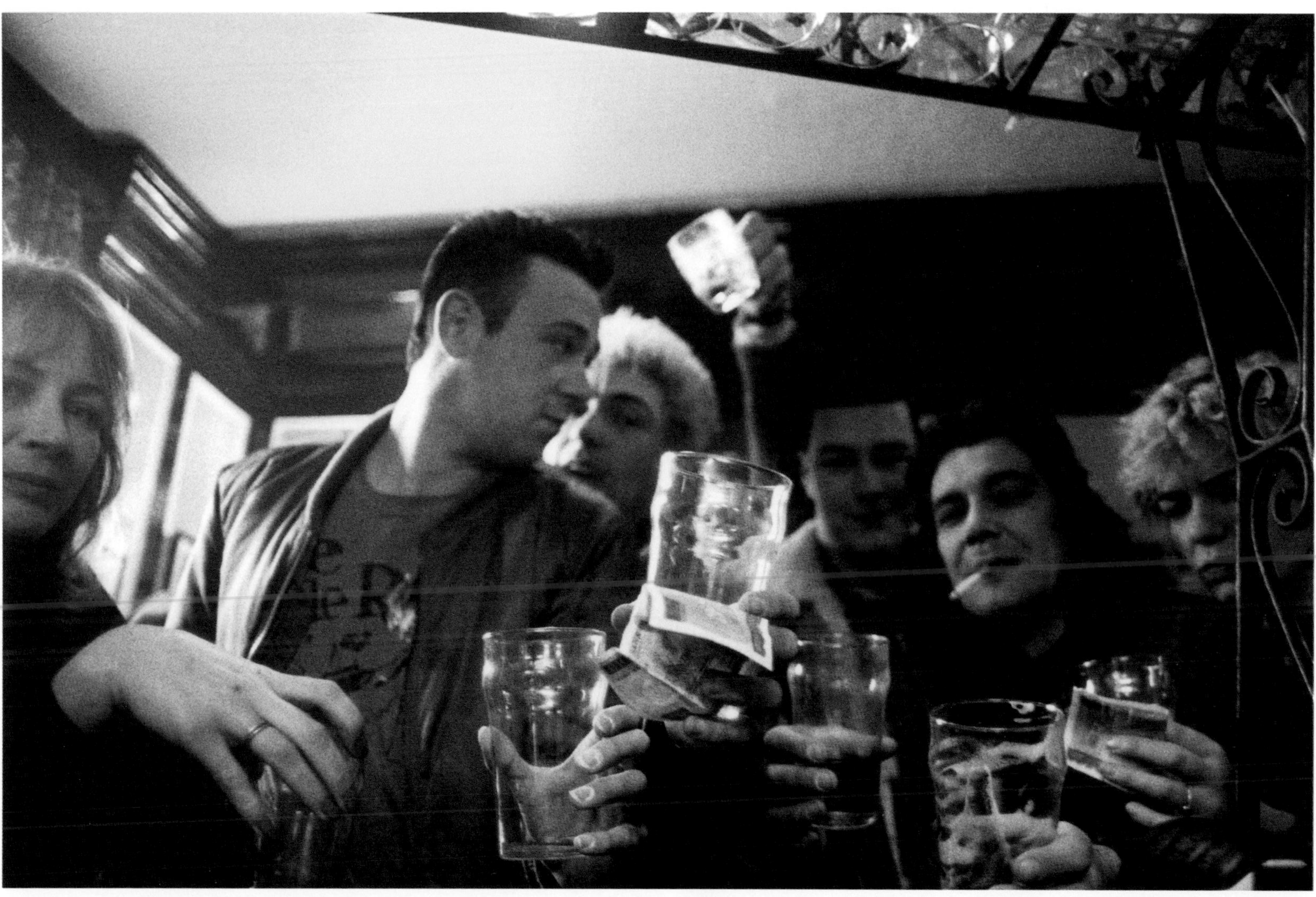

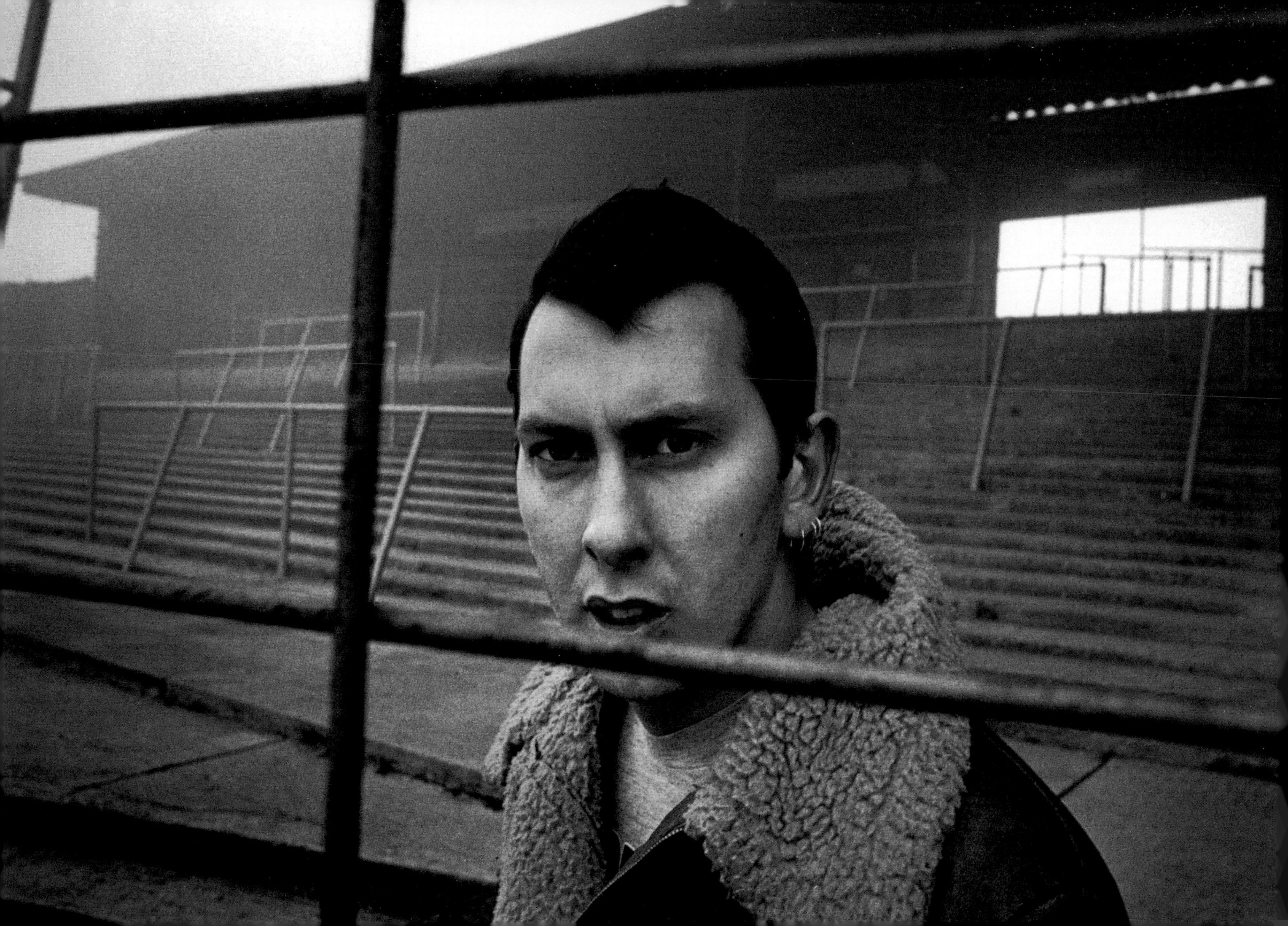

The Wild Dayz

In the mid 80s, as a teenager growing up in the city of Bristol, Southwest England, I would never have imagined that by simply 'hanging out with a camera' and shooting the events surrounding my life at that time they would have such a global impact in the years to follow.

It was at the age of 16, when I left school with fairly low grades, that I accidently discovered my love for the camera. Uncertain of the job prospects that lay ahead, I applied to Bristol's Brunel Technical College for a place on their audio-visual course. They requested me to bring a portfolio of photos to the interview, so, with absolutely no knowledge of a camera, or its functions, I borrowed a mate's camera and hastily put together my first collection. I was luckily accepted and chose to specialise in photography

From the early age of 11, I was actively involved in the local music scene and was especially motivated by the punk scene – the year being '77. I went to many different clubs and was fortunate enough to watch the scene change from the early days of punk through to reggae, hip hop/electro and dance. This may well have contributed to my low school grades at the time!

In '82, the year that coincides with the early days of British hip hop, most of my mates developed a huge interest in DJing. So at the end of most days when many of my friends would go for a night on the town with their decks, I would always have my camera around my neck!

Most pictures in this book were shot between '83 and '88, before I moved to London and then to live and work in Tokyo in 1993, and it was only on a recent visit to the UK that I discovered I had 20 rolls of processed yet unprinted negatives from those Wild Dayz. I realised I had come across an exclusive and important collection of work from that time and really wanted to share it with others.

Looking back, I feel very proud that a lot of amazing talent came out from what I was able to see, listen to, and photograph at the time. Possibly we had it easier in those days since there wasn't a 'crack' problem like in the United States. Teenagers just seemed to have one thing on their minds: GMPF – Girls, Music, Puff, Fashion – in no specific order. Everyone also seemed happy to have me taking their pictures. Some of the genres of music were under-represented by the music press at the time, especially British hip hop artists.

Looking back, I realise that I am incredibly lucky to have such a fantastic collection of visual memories from those great times. I hope you too will enjoy sharing some of these magical moments from those ever so 'Wild Dayz.'

I would like to dedicate this book to my father, who unfortunately never quite got to see why his son was always blacking out his bedroom windows; and to my son, Arthur Ryuichi Beese. I hope his experiences will be as memorable as mine and hope you too will feel inspired.

October, 2009

Beezer

Cheers & Kampai

To firstly my family, especially my mum Irma, Anita, Emma, Eddie, Helen, Richard, Carly, Pat, Margaret (RIP), Jazzino, & Heidi, and to all Bristolians & Austrians who are far away, but always close to me.

Huge thanx in no particular order to Tom da mom (always in trouble!), Mark Stewart & family, Daddy G & family (easy!), 3D, Mushroom, Milo, The "Nellee Hooper", Massive Attack Crew, Willie Wee, Ari Up, Geoff D (for supporting me like no other), Neneh Cherry, Smith and Mighty, Andy Scholes, Adrian Sherwood, Tim Simenon, Pete D, Roni Size, Krust, DJ Die, Andy & Corin-Alpha, Andy the Greek, Matt Black-Coldcut, George & Kate@thisisrealart, James Lavelle. Richard Jones, Nick Law, Marc & Nicky @ Tangent Books.

Hiroshi Fujiwara, K.U.D.O - NIGO - Kan Takagi@Ape Sounds, Toshio Matsura, Gota Yashiki, Moichi Kuwahara, Tatsuo Sunaga, Takeo Kikuchi, Mori² - Natural Calamity, Mr. Okamoto & Mr. Nishio@ relax magazine, Mr. Egaitsu & Mr. Kurihara Michiharu Shimoda - Silent Poets, Mintos, Eugene Otsuka, DJ Alex from Tokyo, Mimi kobayashi@UMU Productions, Tomoki Ohno, Mr. Hamada@ollie magazine, Mr. Suzuki & Mr. Matsuyama@Takarajima-sha, Naoki & Miwako@Disc Shop Zero, Mr. Koizumi@remix magazine, Mr. Noda, Mr. Wakano, Daizo Murata & Yoichi Nishimura@AIR, Liquid Room, Nobu & all @ Hysteric Glamour, Yellow, Mr. Shimizu@ Manhattan Records, Ms. Koga@BEAMS Records, Mr. Uemura@Bonjour Records, Beezer Photo School Students, Yoko & Rune, Kimiko Hanari, Mr Ikeda @ Life Design, Yasushi @ Rush Productions.

Kosta & Flora, John Waddinton, little Sue, Jamie Hill, Dave Lewis, Tony Wrafter, Glaxo Babies, Pop Group, Slits, All my friends' kids, Elena & baby Arturo in Madrid, Eddie in NY, Koji Yamashita (Visual Sky King of the future), Bertram (Newtrament), David Lefevre, Nigel Dewar Gibb (the best bengoshi in the world!), Sharon & Alexi John, Dick Jewell & Family, Froggy, Roz, Jeremy Hirsch, Sean Oliver (RIP) & Andrea, Janine Rainforth, John Shelley (Illustrator Originator!), Mark, Mary & Aran Devlin, Teresa 'Squeezer!!' Harrow, Rene, Annette & Stacy Martin in Paris, Arnaud & David@ Bandol, Gill, Kerry Vegemite!, Miho fleas, Yves & Maya & La Fabrique posse, Angie & the Renatos, Rod Iverson, Etsuko, Venue Magazine, Monty (Tokyo's No.1 club organiser), Francois, Chink, Carlton Romaine, Malcolm, Sapphire, Money Mark, De La Soul, Colin Hope, Redman, Keith Murray, Kev Petri, Danielella, Andy Fairly(RIP), Dexter D, Paul Stewart, Ben Young, Danny Krilly, Des Murray & the Totterdown Posse (who always took the little white boy to the blues!), Jah Shaka, Fatman, Jah Tubbys, Moa Ambassa & sound systems back then (where those dub plates now?), Quid Twists, Shebeems/blues, Dug Out, Dungeons on Lee Bridge Road, RAW, Aux Bachanelles, Battle Bridge Road, (RIP and thanx for all the memories), Tri X, Cider, the good Sensi!, Sonoma & the Ruby Room Crew, Metropolis - Japan's No.1 mag, Sebastian Boyle, Rizlas that stick, Brian, Colin Charles, Thai Matt (be a good Godmum!), Dan & Mrs. G, Annie & McGanns, Sara Dunn, Sandra (bacon sarnies), Rankin, Dahlia Favreau, Paz (RIP), Loud Magazine, Polly (Plug), Rich Denman, Tony Hawkins, Sean Liu, Aya Nakamegz xx, Andy Vining, Fergy, Ebbow, Jacqueline Taylor (the extreme nun!), JJ (RIP), Diablo bros in Rome, Patrick Ryan & the Yab-Yums, Aki Wanatabe (Tokyo's No.1 Cutter), Scouse Dave & Sue, Jo Mac, JB, Punk Rock, High Heels, DJ Yukalicious, Piwi, the Barlow sisters, Leo & Baldhead Steve, Brunel Technical College, Fuji (moto), Gary@Nig Music NY, Al Mack, Lord Barnzley, & The Child of Jago, Sunny Day, Wigan, Sean McLusky, Special K's, Joe & Madoka in NY, Lucky Jeff Klein, Michel Teman, Morikawa family, B-Boys & Fly Girls, Guy Perryman, Lisle, Kawakami family, Dirk Kreft, Franco, The Nemeths, Judith Sullivan (Tokyo's PR Queen!), Joshua in NY (always thanx for my stays), Ole in Berlin, Wieland (RIP) & Ricarda (I'll never forget those Saigon River Boat Parties!), Linzi Baker, Anna Seabourne, David Jones, Jose Stefan, Patrick, Dora, Arnold, Dimitri from Paris, Estelle Lordonne (mon cheri!) my french connections!, Chelsea FC & the girl (love you both!), Esther (you old slapper!), John 'Leroy' Best, Marcellus, Nikon FE's, multigrade paper, England as I left it, Dom T, Andro Genius, Jah Rastafari, Shibuya, Soho, Sir Arthur C. Clarke, Soti, Claire & Bio, Luke & Nikki@Phuture Trax, Roy the Roach, Jon 'pleased' Wimmin, Carlos Gibbs (Red Box), Mark Oxley, Chrissy, George & Sunny, Life with a meaning, Ivan Drake, Mr. Hosokawa, Chris Orchard, Marbo, Burro, Brad B, Sayako, Greg Natali, James Vyner, Raphael & yabe (U.F.O), Matt Broad, the twin sisters (you know who you are!) Alice Perera, Rasha, Patrick Simmons & family, Gregory Gordon and Cyril Roy - I thank you with all my heart.

Thanx and sorry to all those I've missed... **Beezer**

First edition published November 2009 (9781906477318)
Second edition published December 2009 by Tangent Books
This edition published 2018

Tangent Books
Unit 5.16, Paintworks, Bristol, BS4 3EH

0117 972 0645

ISBN: 9781906477332

www.tangentbooks.co.uk

email: richard@tangentbooks.co.uk

Copyright: Andrew 'Beezer' Beese/Tangent Books 2009

Images: Beezer, www.beezerphotos.com
All photos are the copyright of Andrew 'Beezer' Beese/
Beezer Photos
Images of 3D artwork on p.34 (rt), p.36 and pp. 42–51
copyright Robert del Naja
Beezer Management: John Boreland, Soulful Management
System, soulfulmanagementsystem@gmail.com
Publisher: Richard Jones

Design: Nick Law
Marketing: Marc Leverton
Office Manager: Nicky Johns

Andrew 'Beezer' Beese has asserted his right under the
Copyright, Designs and Patents Act of 1988 to be
identified as the photographer of this work.

This book may not be reproduced or transmitted in any
form or in any means without the prior written consent
of the publisher; except by a reviewer who wishes to quote
brief passages in connection with a review written in a
newspaper or magazine or broadcast on television, radio
or on the internet.

Printed in Poland
www.lfbookservices.co.uk

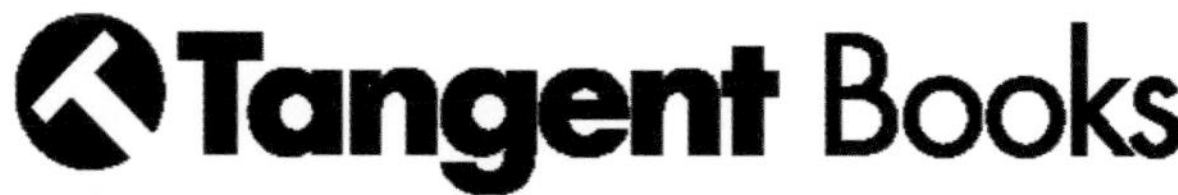

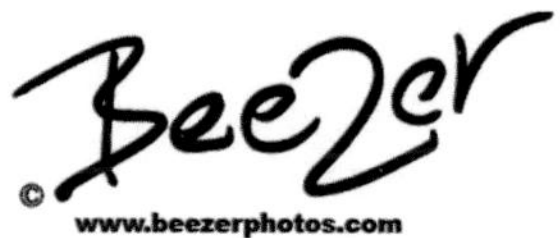

Wild Dayz (revisited)

beezer an alice of/in the underground
takes us on a trip of

reclamation/excavation of the
denied/the buried the scarcely known

he opens doors to the power of the
imagination/the unconscious/
stressing the links between the
individual and collective

he elucidates (posse) archetype a/one
of the few children of the lens

giving it life and light

the strange fertilising power of this
particular machine

He has multi vision opposing the
situational 'primary' allegiance

to the letter of the law...

to objects with restricted boundaries

wild dayz is a call to encourage the uprising of...

Mark Stewart, Berlin

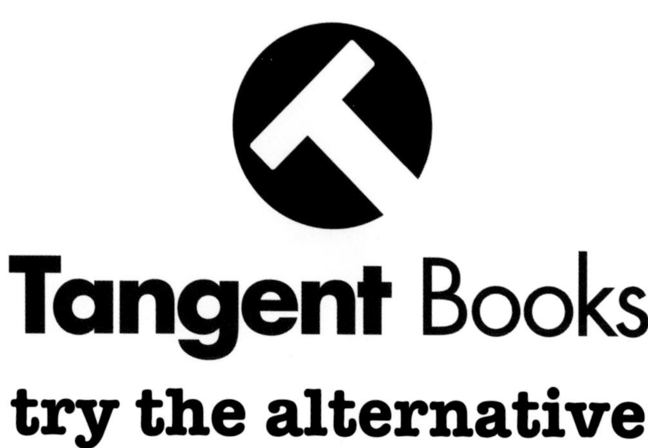

Tangent Books

try the alternative

www.tangentbooks.co.uk

gallery

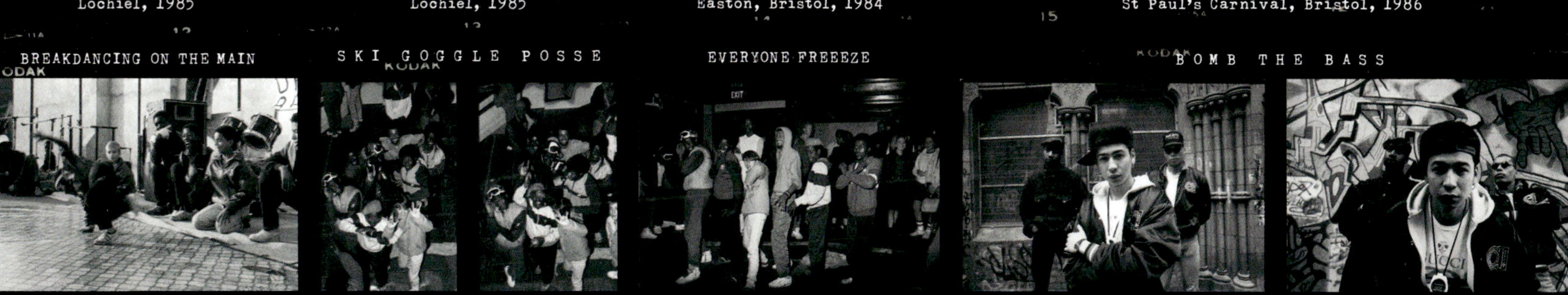

WILD BUNCH
LIFE ON THE BRIDGE (SEE NOTE 1) 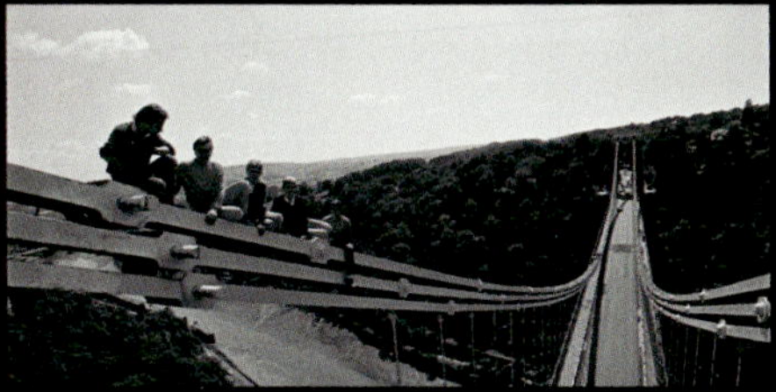
ENTER THE DUGOUT
3D AND BRIM
BRIM AND THE KIDS
Camden, London, 1985
Workers on Clifton Suspension Bridge, 1986
The Dug Out Club, Bristol, 1983
Arnofini Graffiti Exhibition, 1985
Arnolfini, Bristol, 1985
WALL POSSE 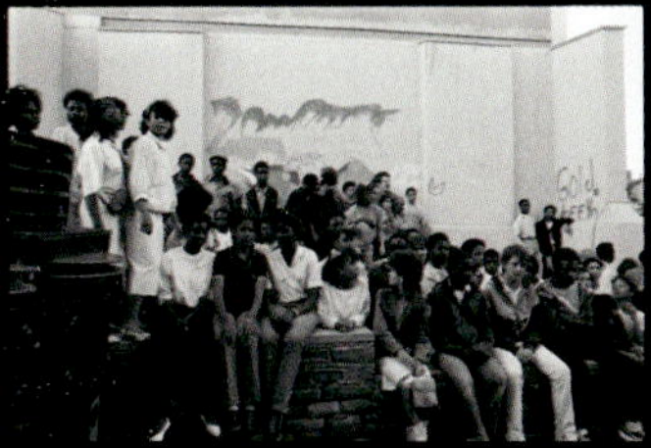
WALL POSSE B-GIRL
OLDER WALL POSSE
UP & COMING BREAK DANCERS
BODY POPPIN'
St Paul's Carnival, 1986
St Paul's Carnival, 1986
St Paul's Carnival, 1986
Arnofini Graffiti Exhibition, 1985
Lochiel, Bristol, 1985
BODY POPPIN'
BODY POPPIN'
LAYIN' DOWN THE LINO
BREAKDANCING ON THE MAIN 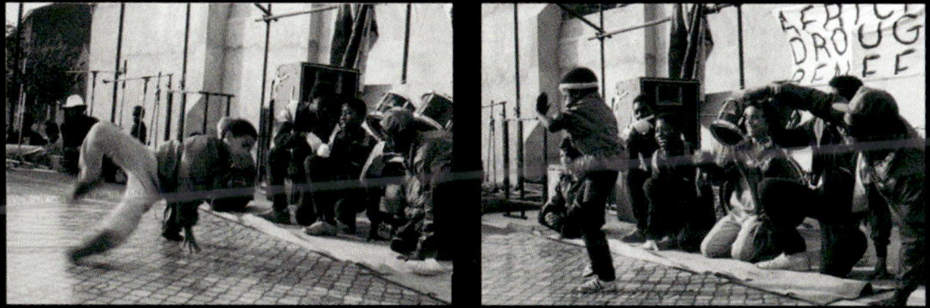
Lochiel, 1985
Lochiel, 1985
Easton, Bristol, 1984
St Paul's Carnival, Bristol, 1986
BREAKDANCING ON THE MAIN
SKI GOGGLE POSSE
EVERYONE FREEEZE
BOMB THE BASS
St Paul's Carnival, 1986
Thekla, Bristol, 1985
Thekla, 1985
Tim Simenon, Tabernacle, London, 1986

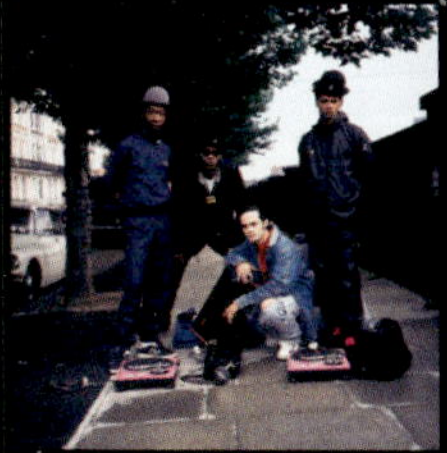

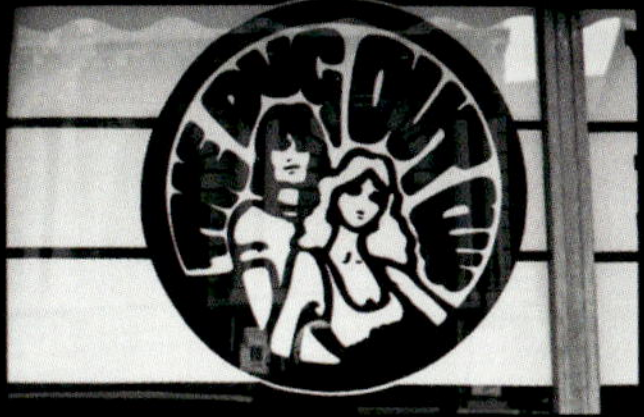

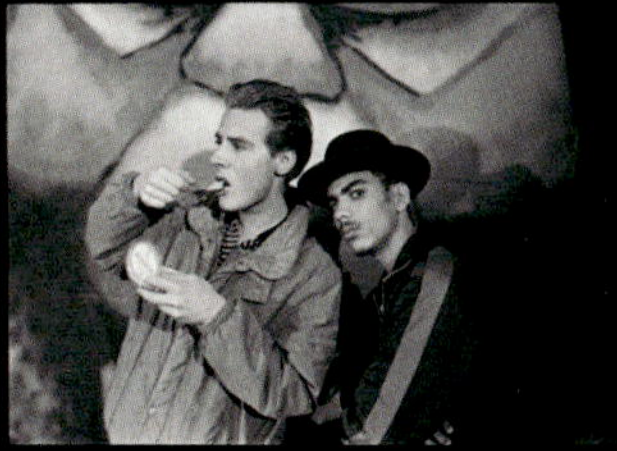

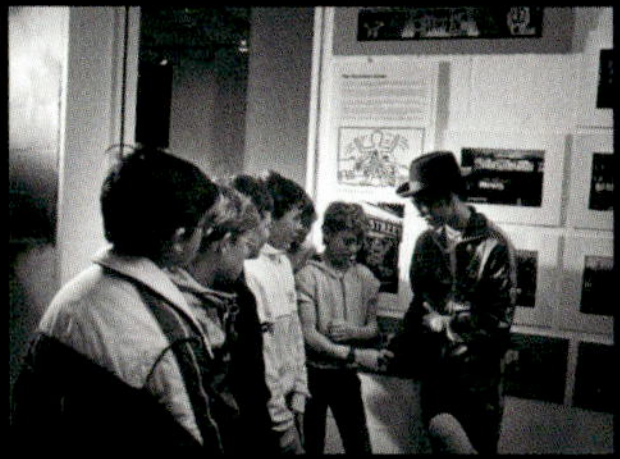

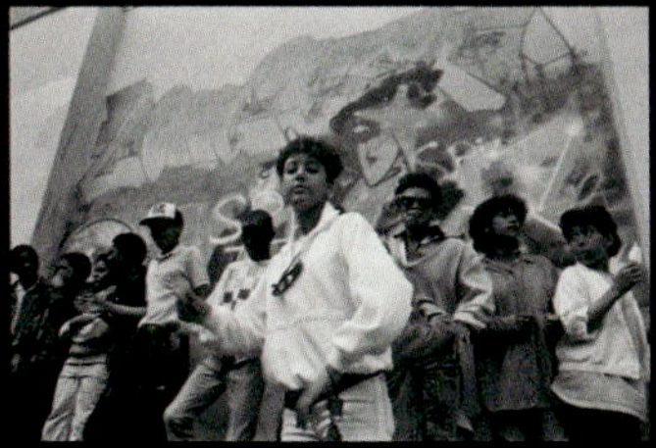

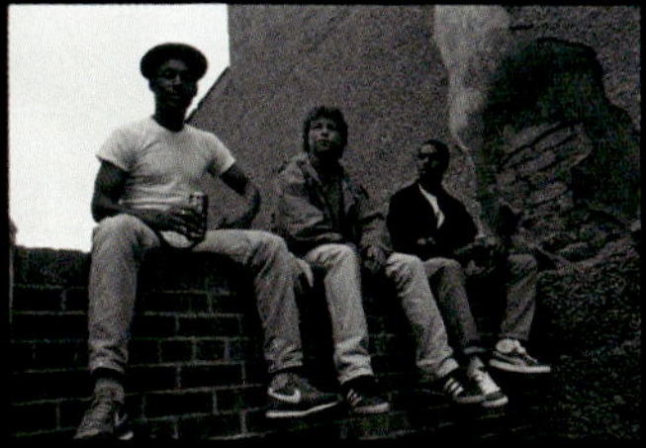

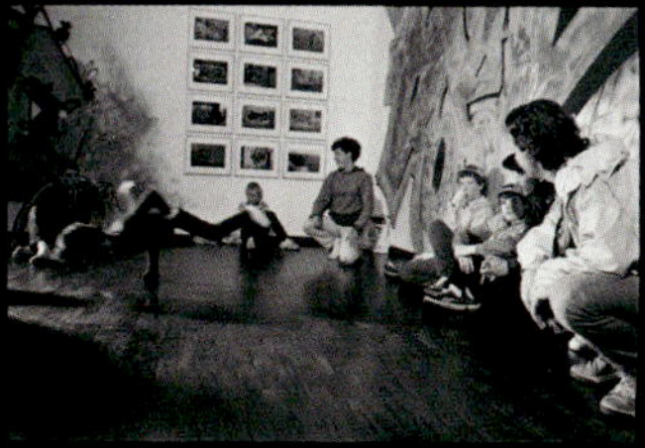

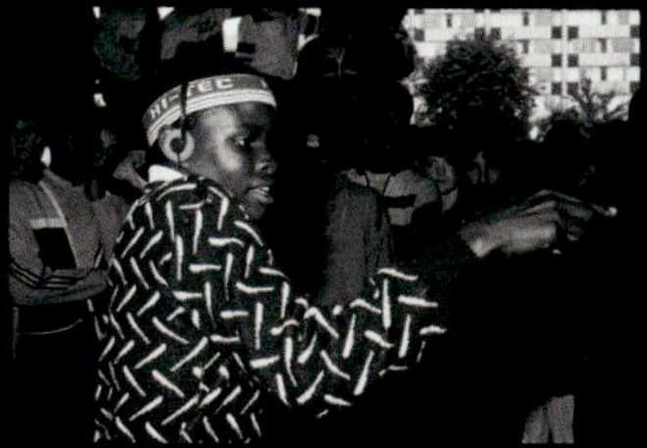

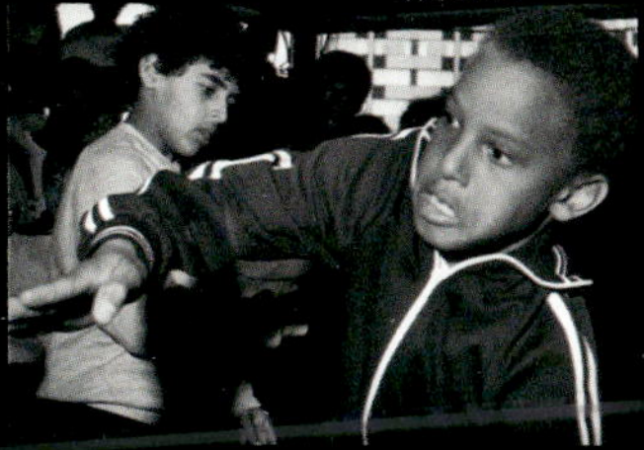

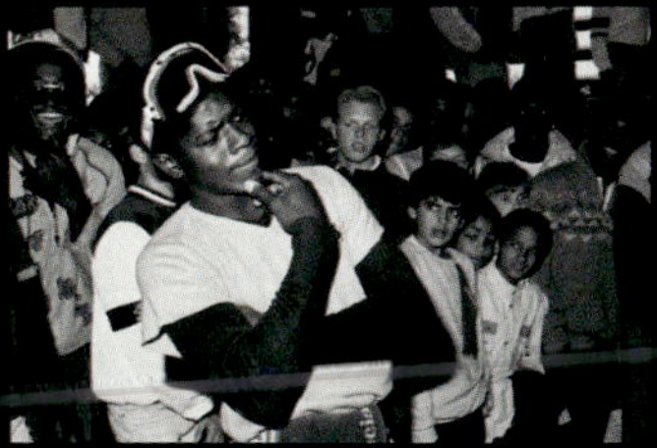

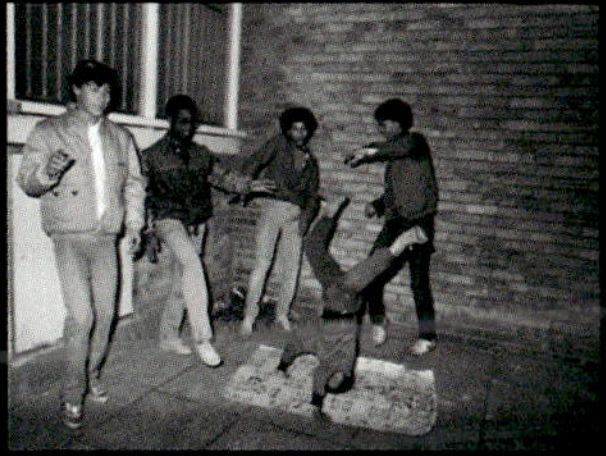

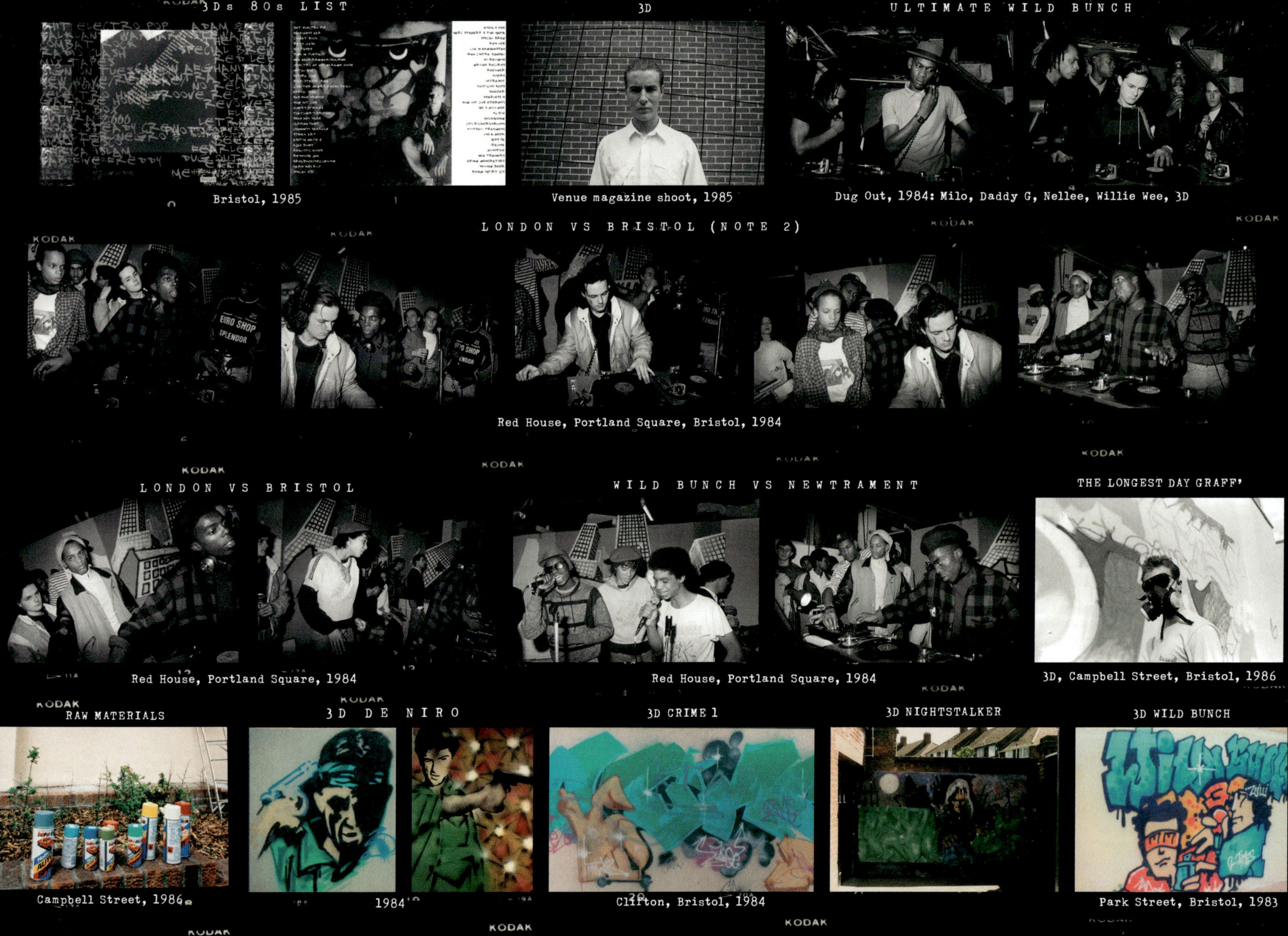

Bristol, 1985

Venue magazine shoot, 1985

Dug Out, 1984: Milo, Daddy G, Nellee, Willie Wee, 3D

Red House, Portland Square, Bristol, 1984

Red House, Portland Square, 1984

Red House, Portland Square, 1984

3D, Campbell Street, Bristol, 1986

Campbell Street, 1986

1984

Clifton, Bristol, 1984

Park Street, Bristol, 1983

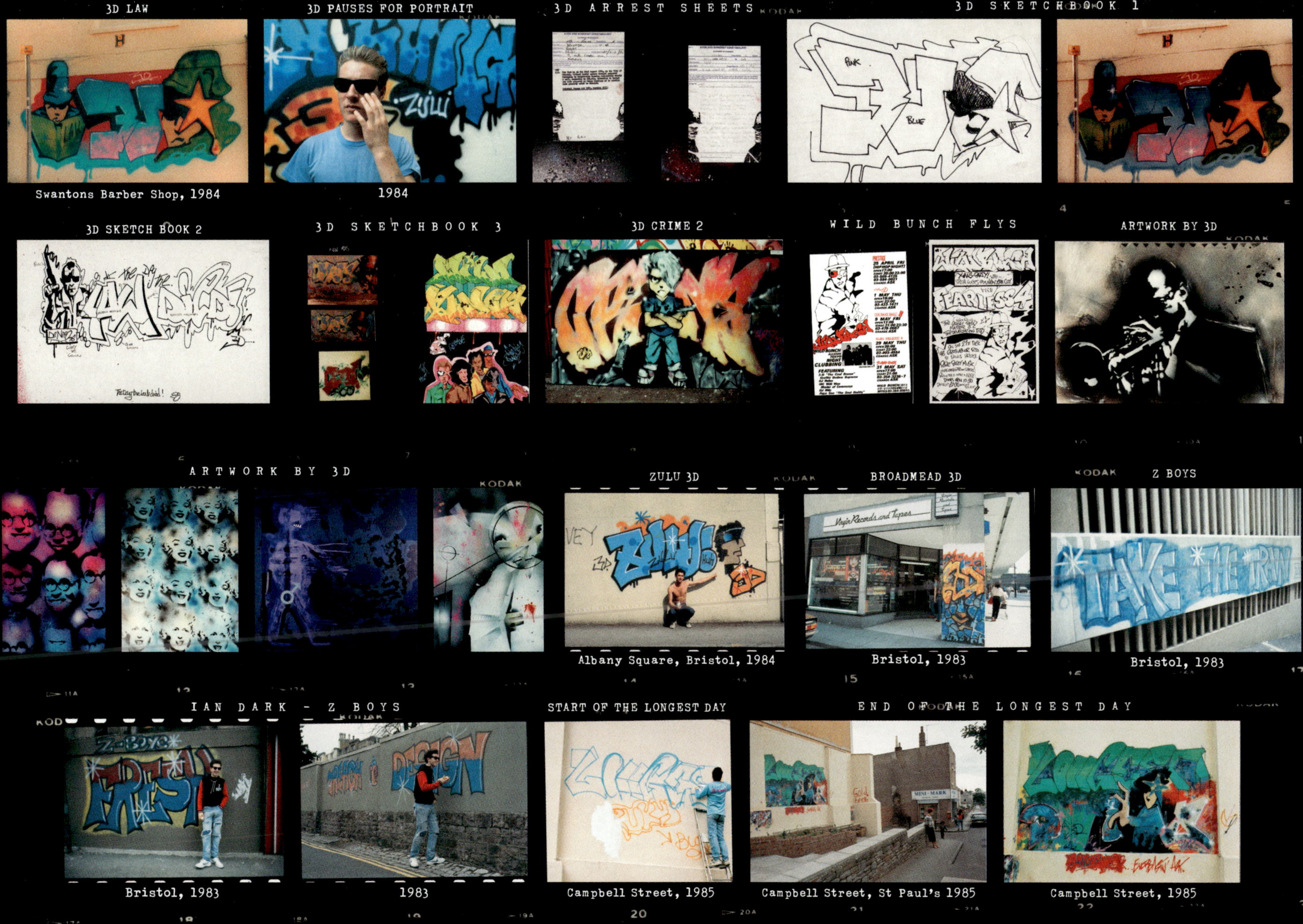
3D LAW
3D PAUSES FOR PORTRAIT
3D ARREST SHEETS
3D SKETCHBOOK 1
Swantons Barber Shop, 1984
1984
3D SKETCH BOOK 2
3D SKETCHBOOK 3
3D CRIME 2
WILD BUNCH FLYS
ARTWORK BY 3D
ARTWORK BY 3D
ZULU 3D
BROADMEAD 3D
Z BOYS
Albany Square, Bristol, 1984
Bristol, 1983
Bristol, 1983
IAN DARK - Z BOYS
START OF THE LONGEST DAY
END OF THE LONGEST DAY
Bristol, 1983
1983
Campbell Street, 1985
Campbell Street, St Paul's 1985
Campbell Street, 1985

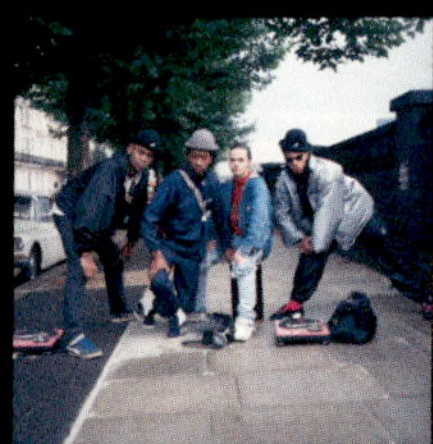 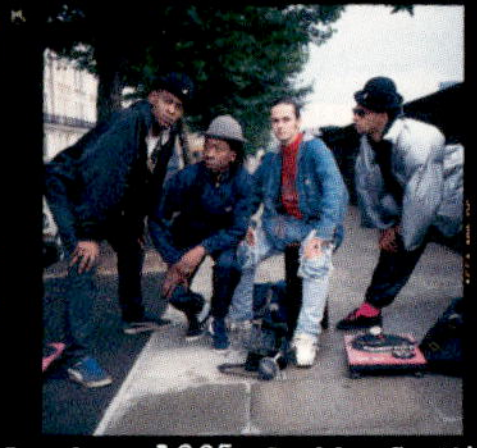 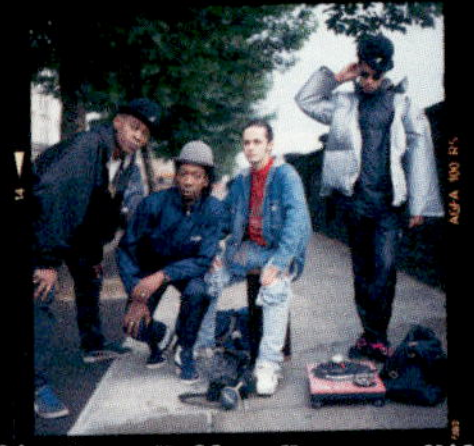 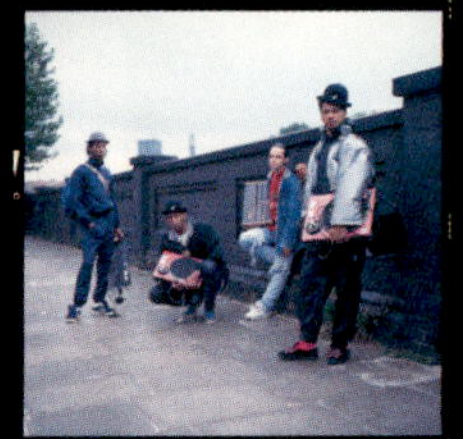

Camden, London, 1985, Daddy G, Willie Wee, Nellee Hooper, Milo Johnson

Red House, Portland Square, 1984

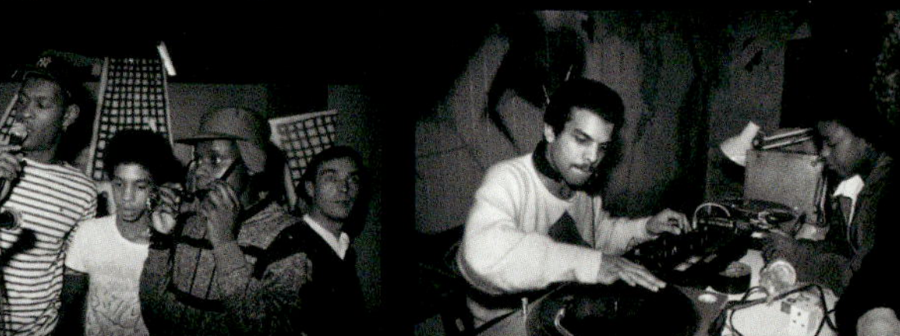 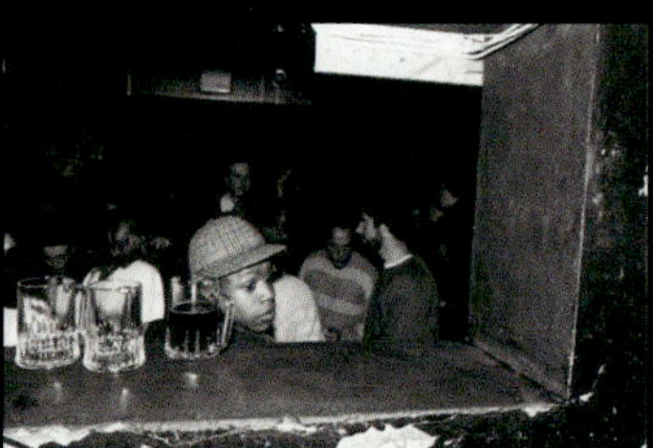 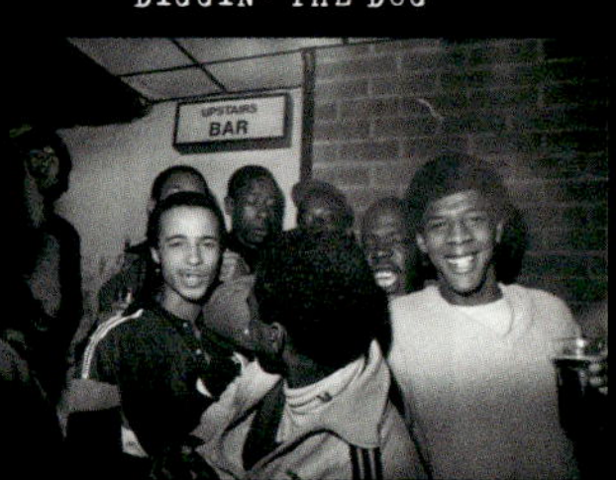 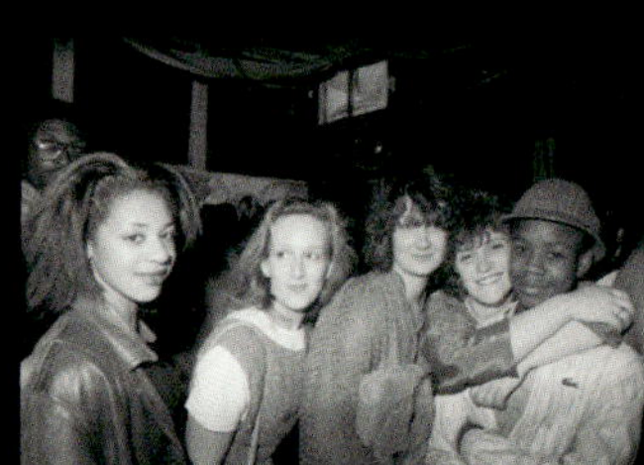

Red House, Portland Square, 1984　　The Crypt, Bristol, 1985　　Dug Out, 1985　　Dug Out, 1985　　Dug Out, 1985

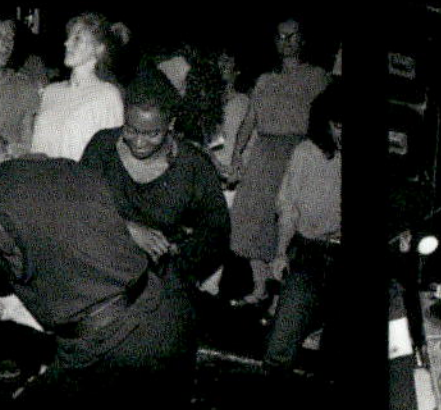 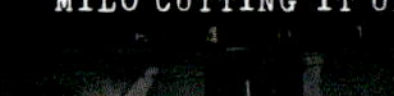 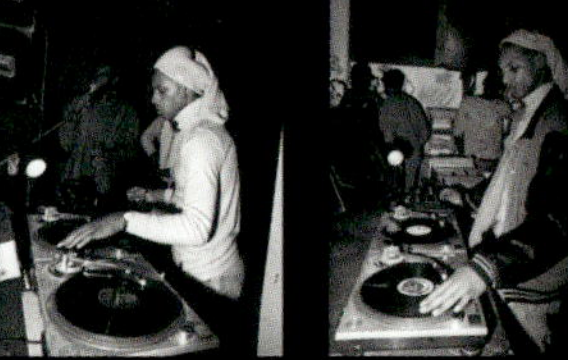 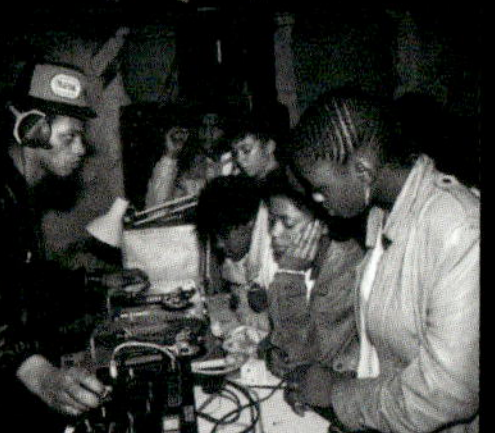 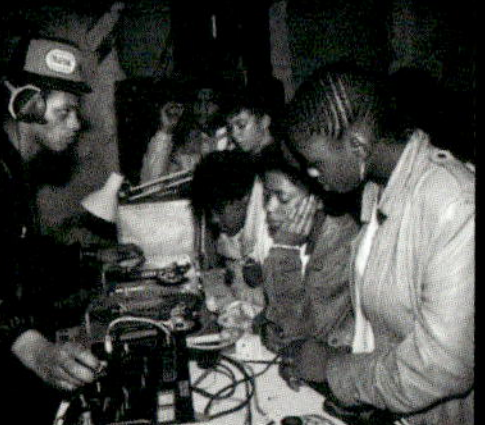 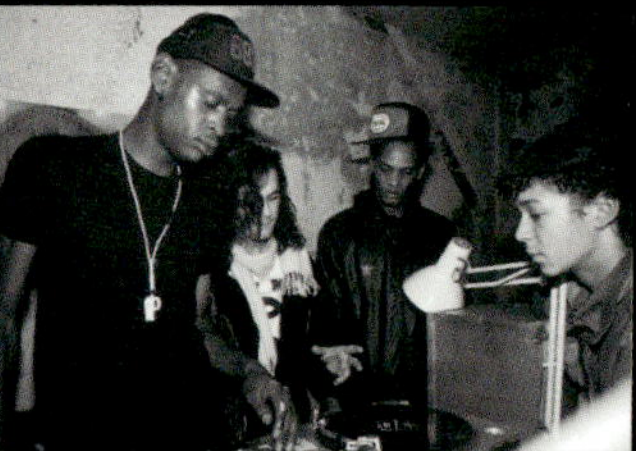 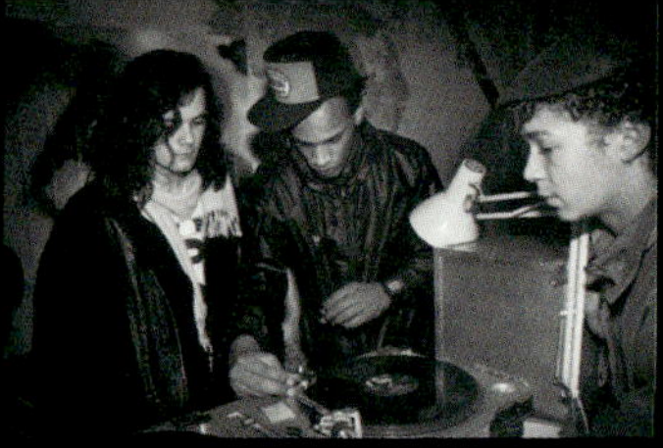

Thekla, 1985　　The Red House, 1984　　The Crypt, 1985　　The Crypt, 1985　　The Crypt, 1985

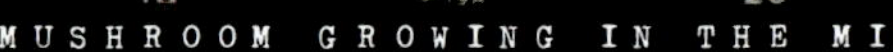 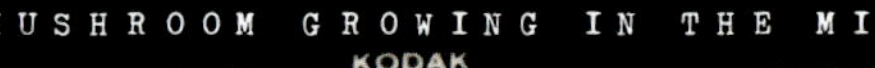 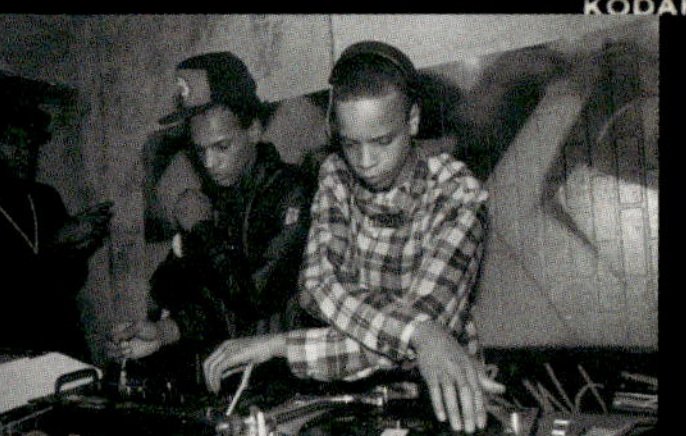 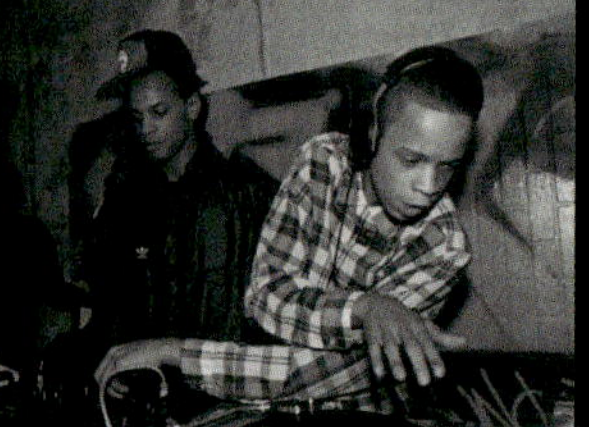 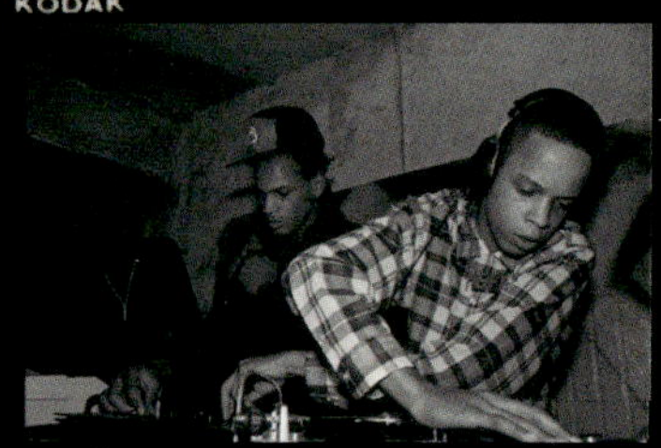

DJ Mushroom at The Crypt, St Paul's, Bristol, 1985　　The Crypt, 1985

ROLLIN' & SPINNIN'

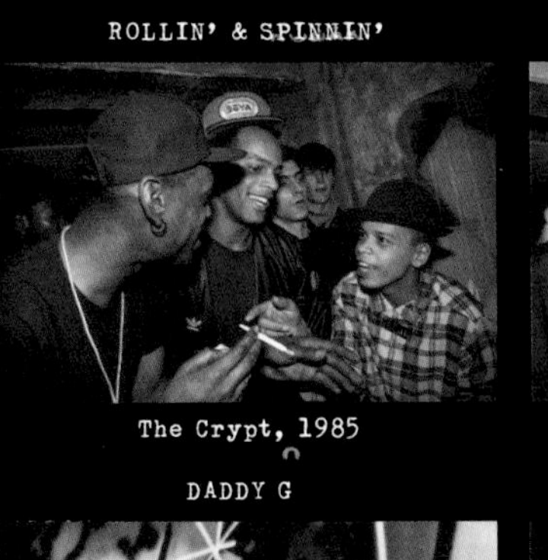

The Crypt, 1985

GLARE TO THE RIGHT

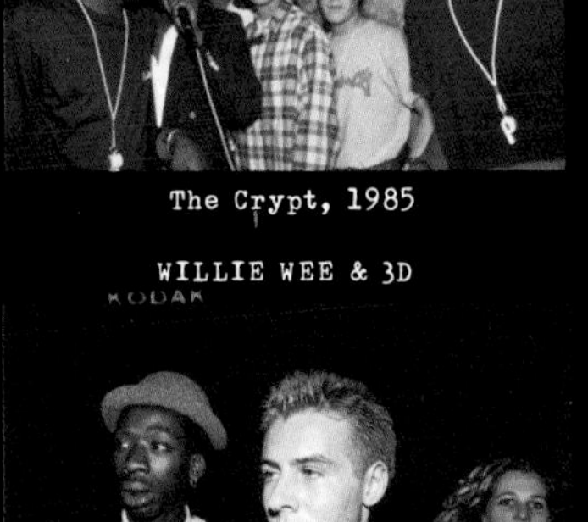

The Crypt, 1985

SMOKIN' DA MIC

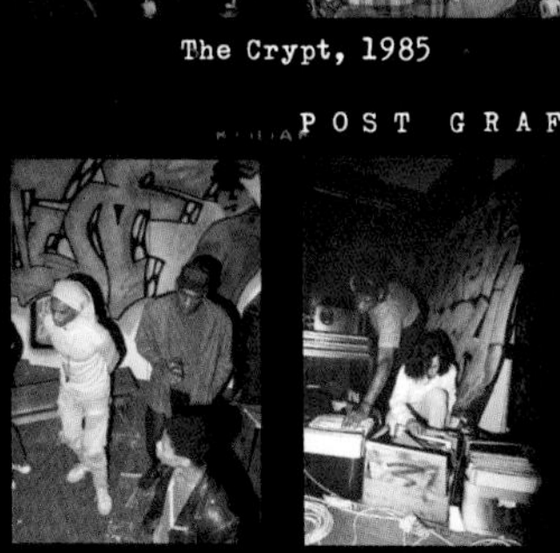

The Crypt, 1985

PAUSE FOR A CAUSE

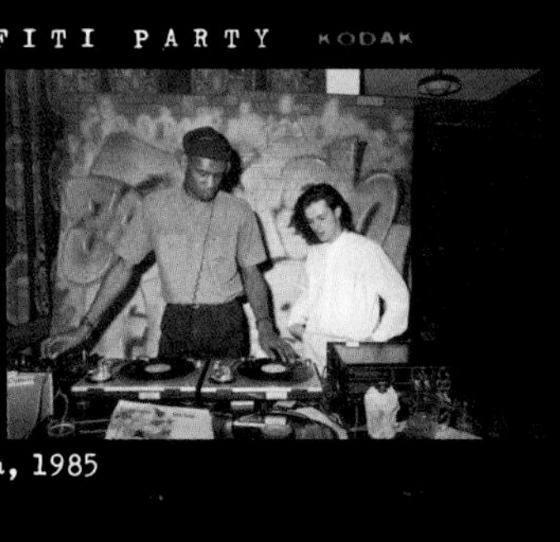

The Crypt, 1985

MASTER O.C & DEVASTATING TITO

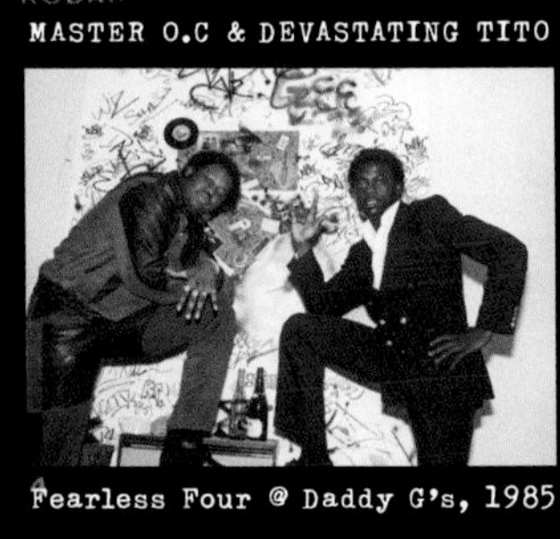

Fearless Four @ Daddy G's, 1985

DADDY G

Revolver Records, Bristol, 1984

WILLIE WEE & 3D

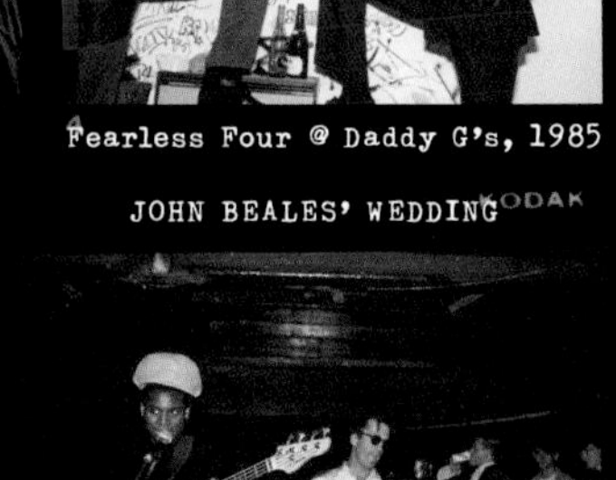

The Dug Out, 1984

POST GRAFFITI PARTY

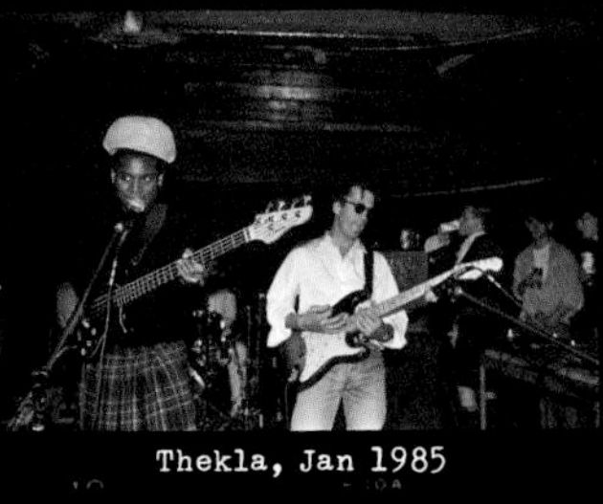

Thekla, 1985

JOHN BEALES' WEDDING

Thekla, Jan 1985

J O H N   B E A L E S'   W E D D I N G   (N O T E 3)

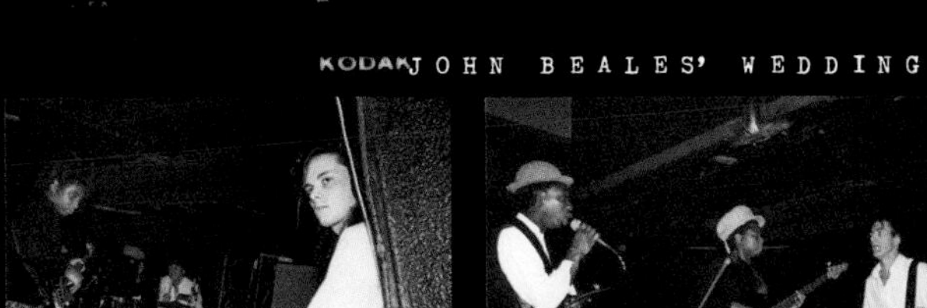

Thekla, Jan 1985

MILO IN TENT

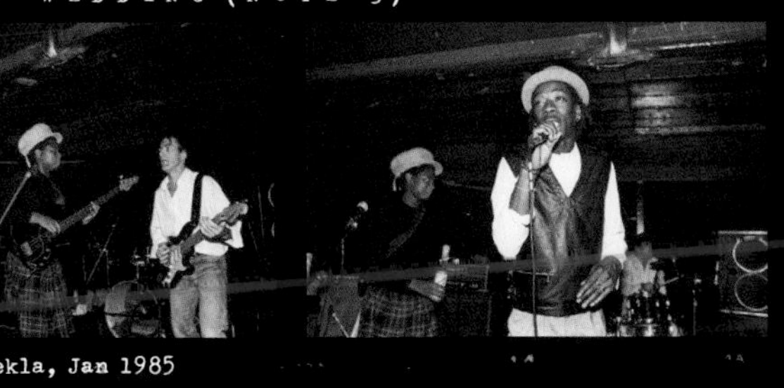

Glastonbury, 1985

DADDY G IN THE SHADE

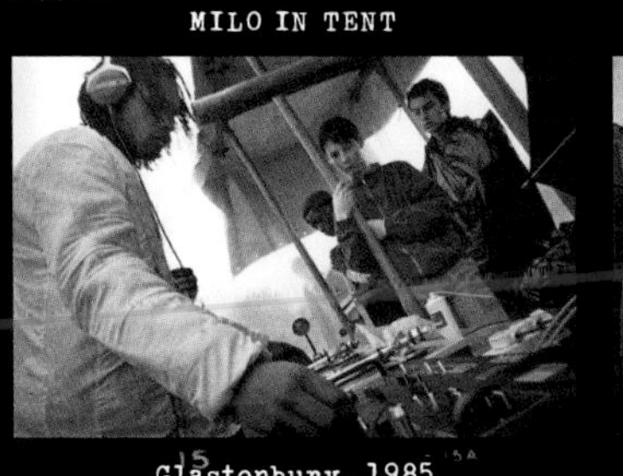

St Paul's Carnival, 1985

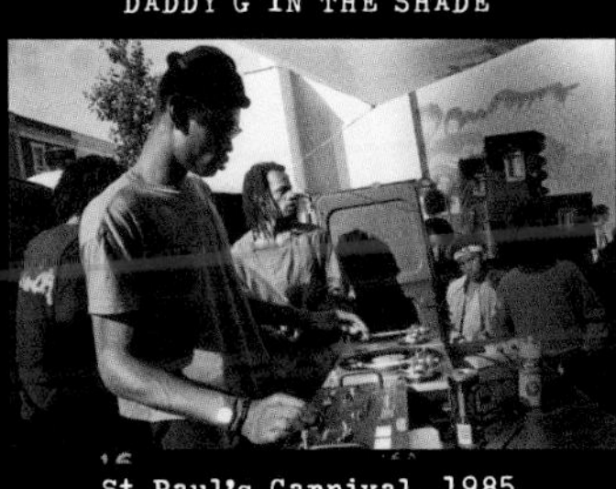

N E L L E E   I S   M Y   S E L E C T A

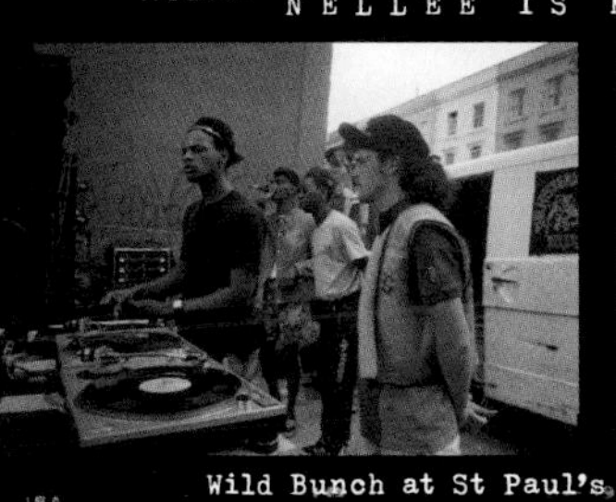

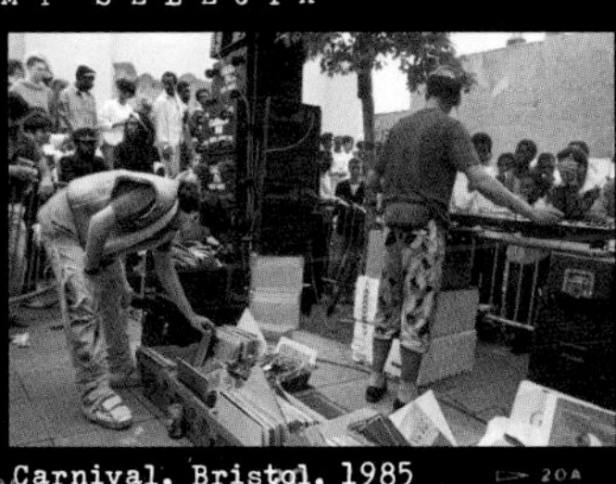

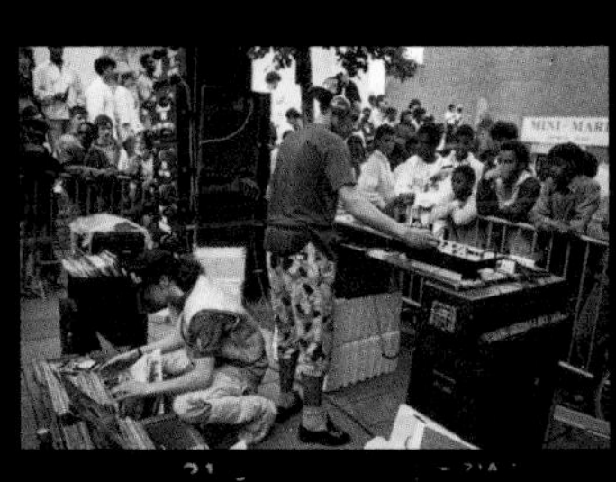

Wild Bunch at St Paul's Carnival, Bristol, 1985

ROCKAS

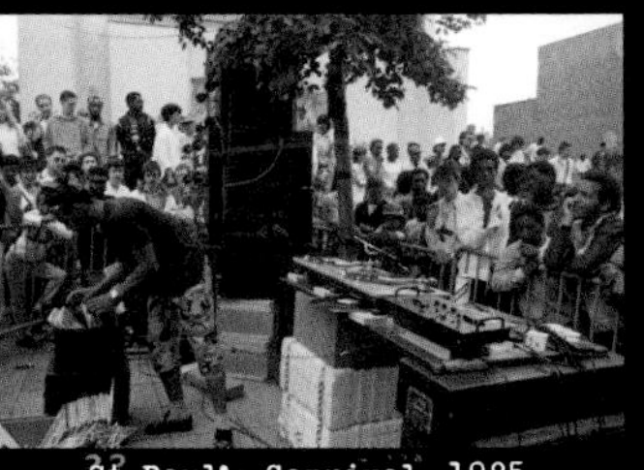

St Paul's Carnival, 1985

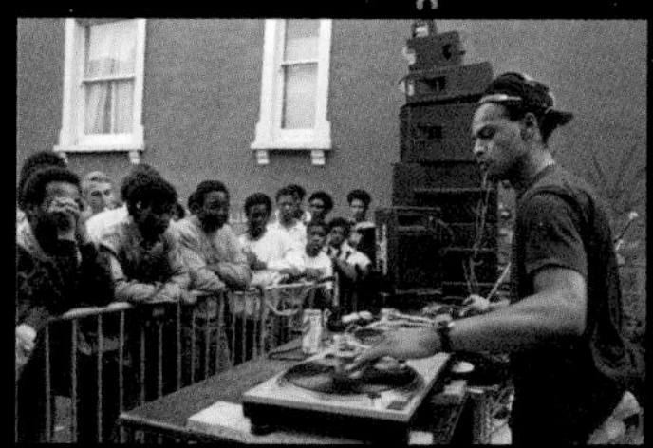

St Paul's Carnival, 1985

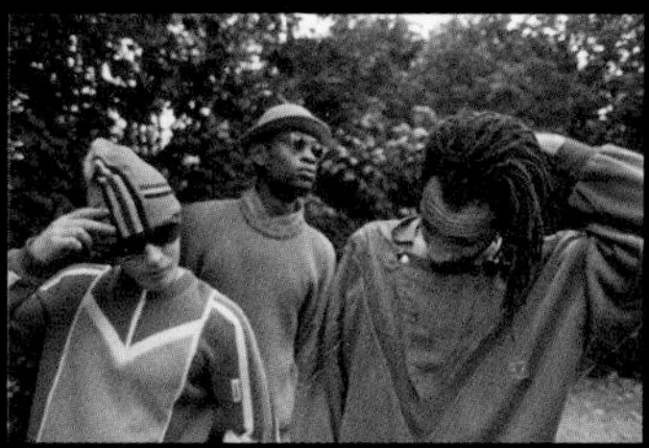
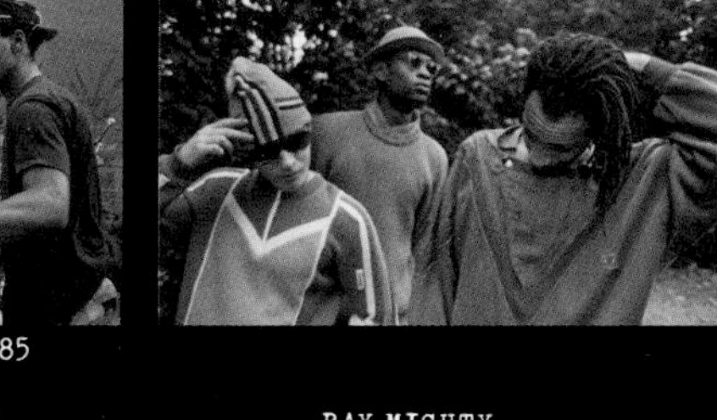
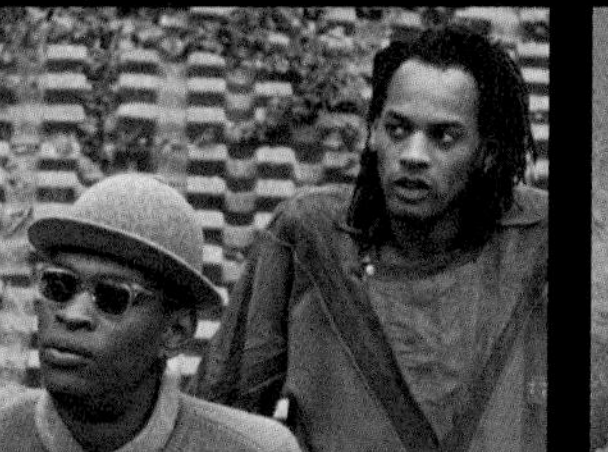

Montpelier Park, Bristol, 1986

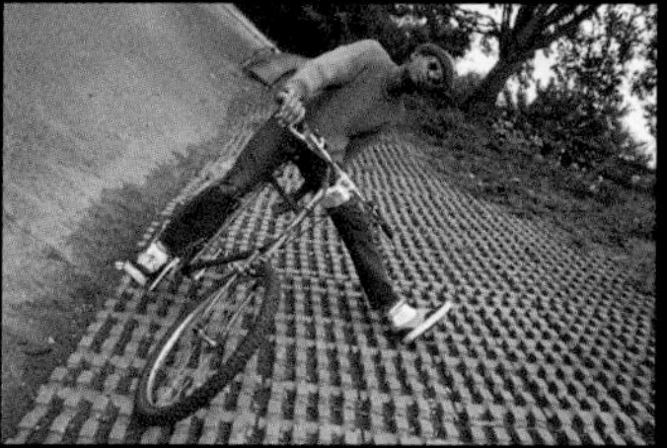

WOMAD 1987

WATCHIN' THE DAY GO BY   RAY MIGHTY   ROOTS STYLE N' FASHION   ENTERPRISE SOUND SYSTEM   JAH SHAKA

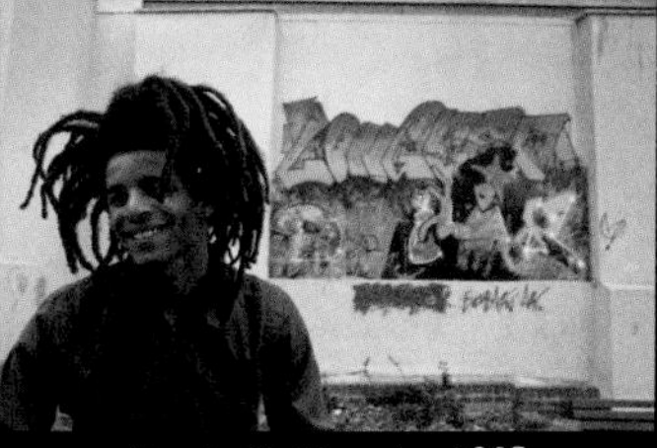

Campbell Street, 1985

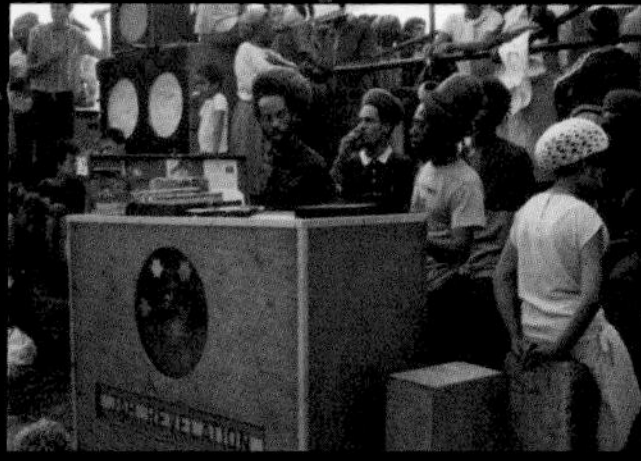

Campbell Street, 1985

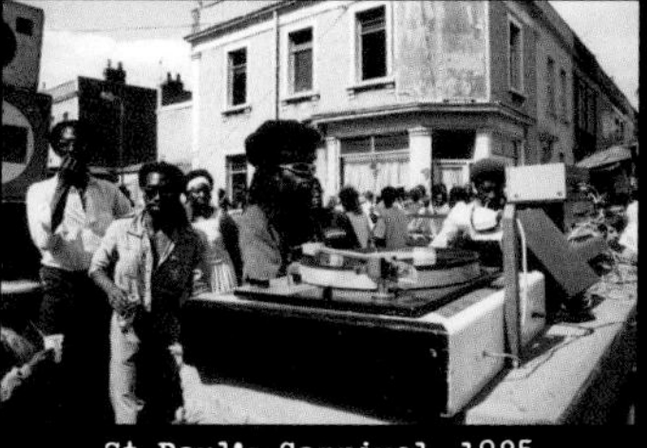

Notting Hill, London, 1985

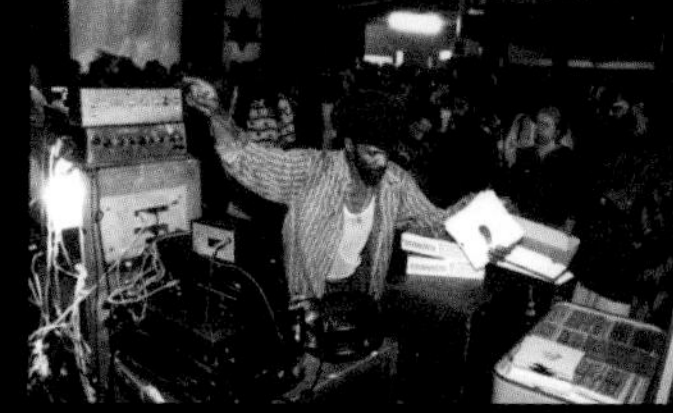

St Paul's Carnival, 1985

London, 1986

TOOTS OF THE MAYTALS   BRISTOL 12 TRIBES POSSE   T.C OUTSIDE STAR & GARTER   ASHTON COURT FESTIVAL

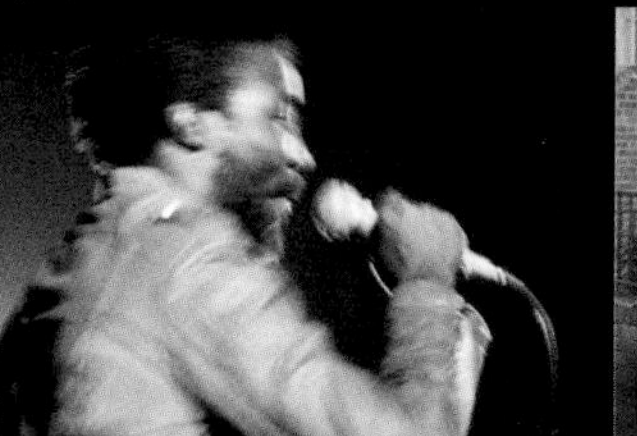

WOMAD, 1985

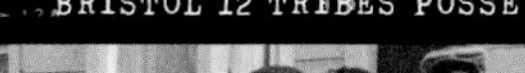
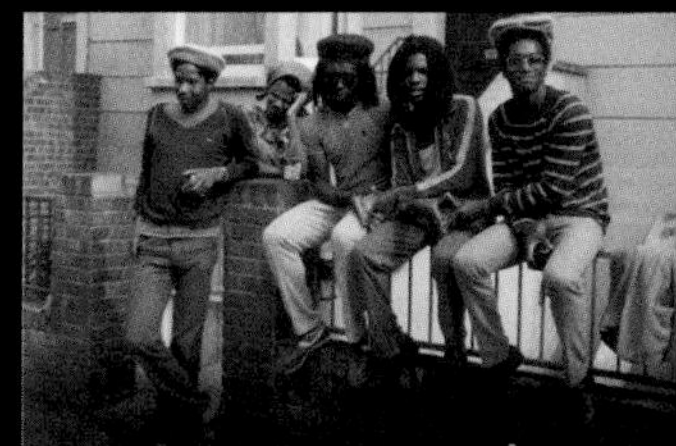

City Road, Bristol, 1984

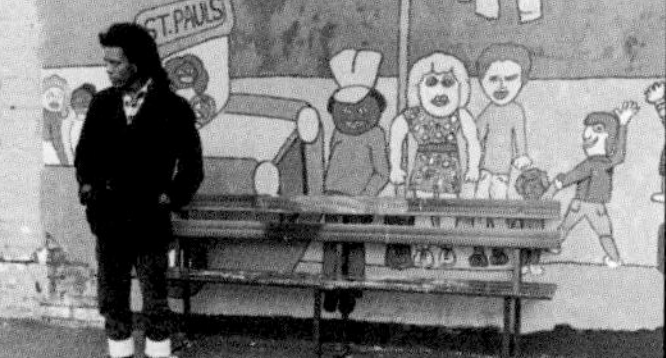

Bristol, 1985

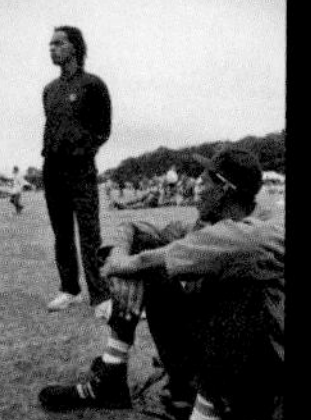
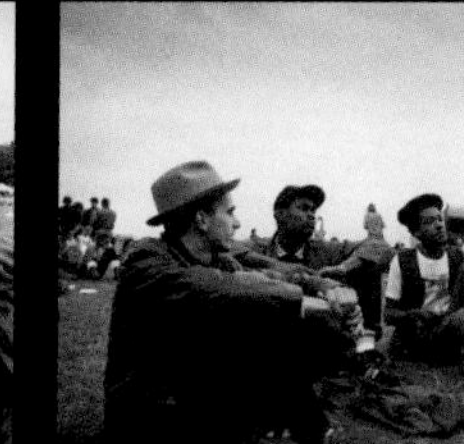
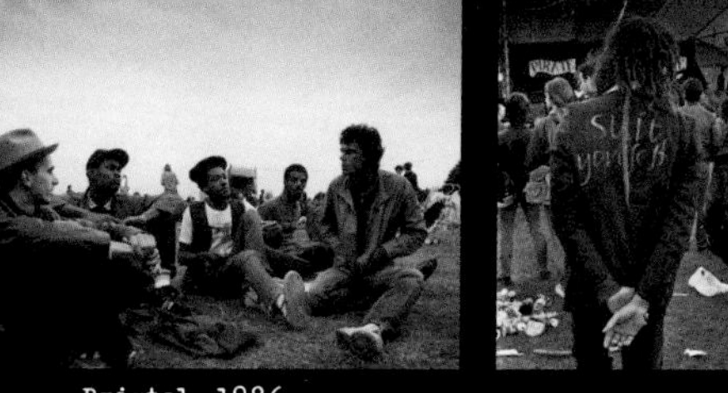

Bristol, 1986

GLASTONBURY   ROOTS VENDORS   SMOKE 'TIL I CHOKE   MUDSTUCK   SOMEBODY'S DAD

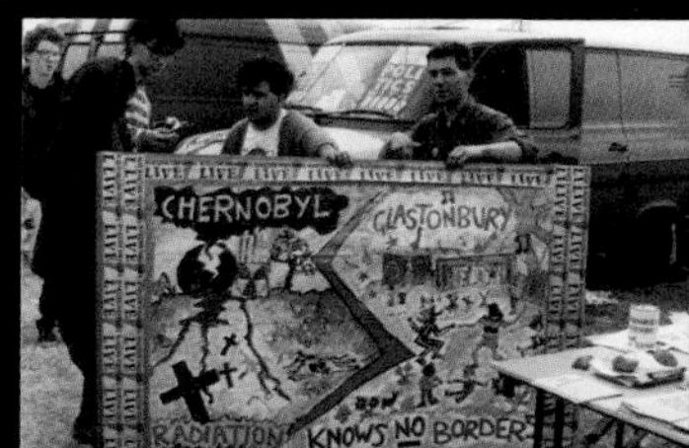

1983

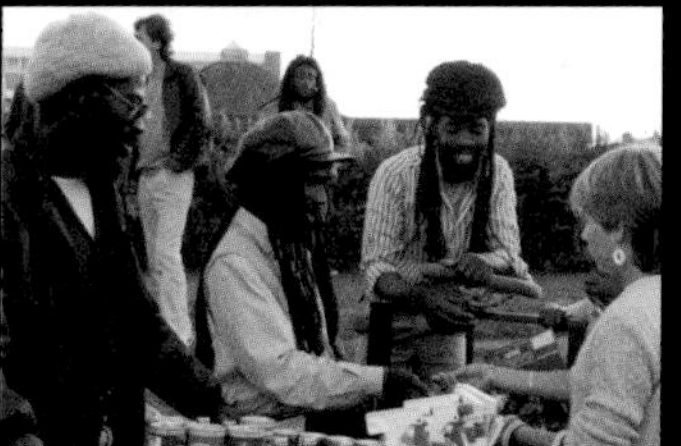
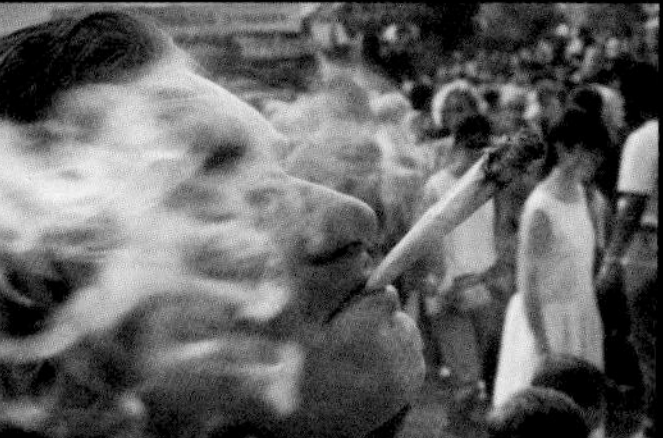
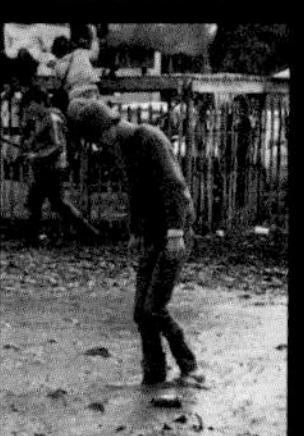

St Paul's Carnival, 1986

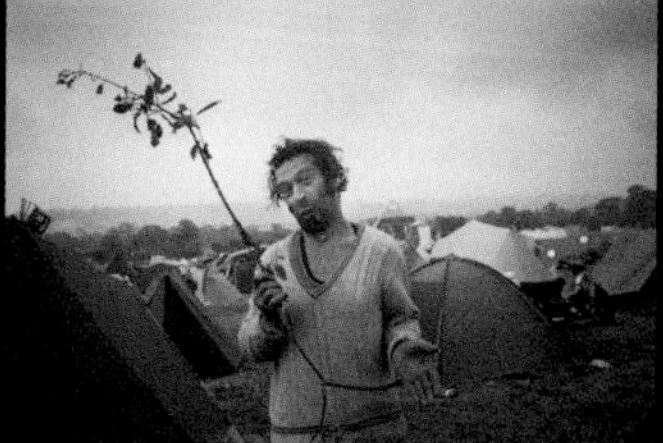

Glastonbury, 1985

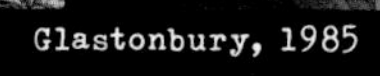

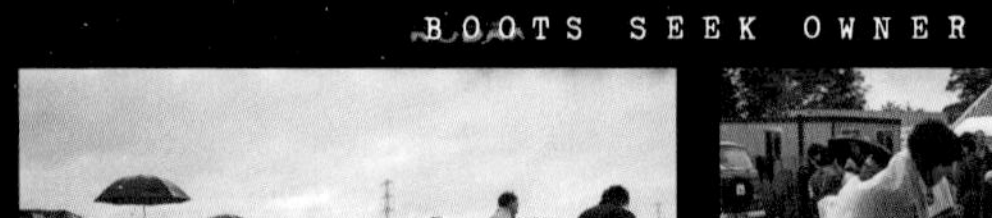

BOOTS SEEK OWNER

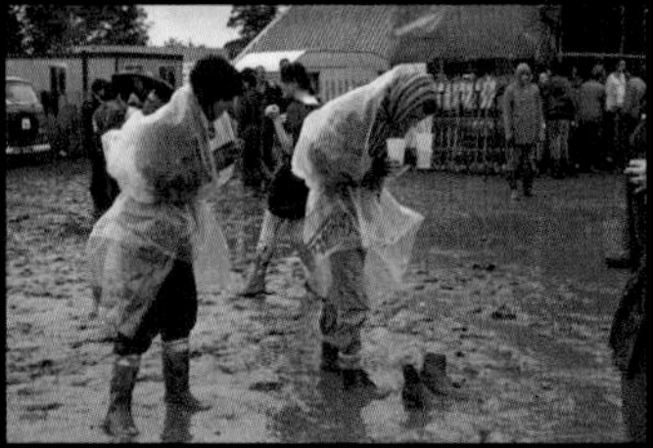

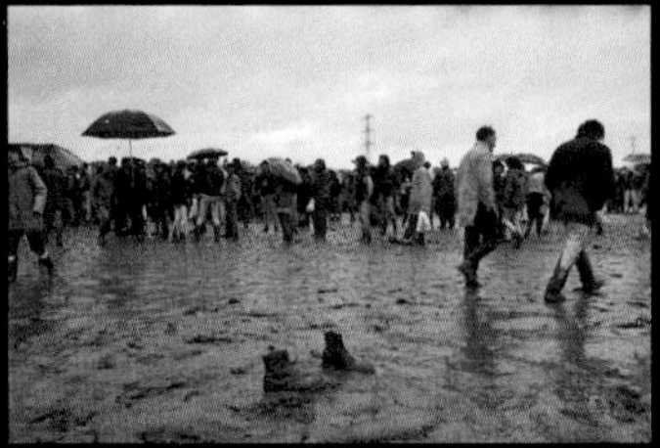

Glastonbury mud field 1985

ARI UP

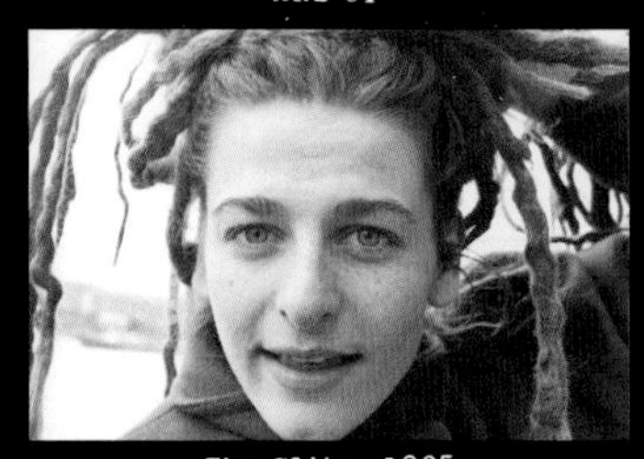

The Slits, 1985

BASIL & SIMEON

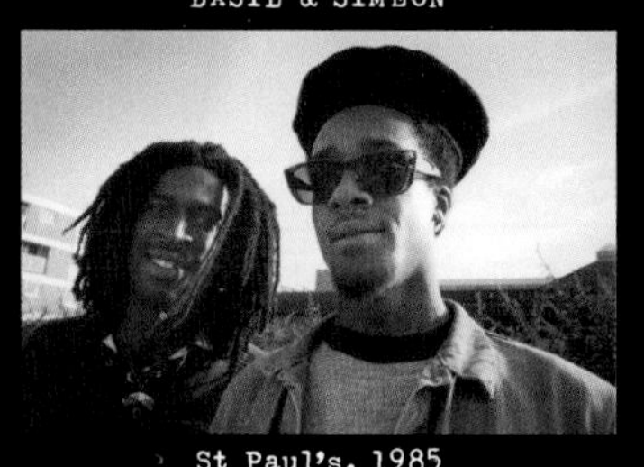

St Paul's, 1985

ARI & CHARLY

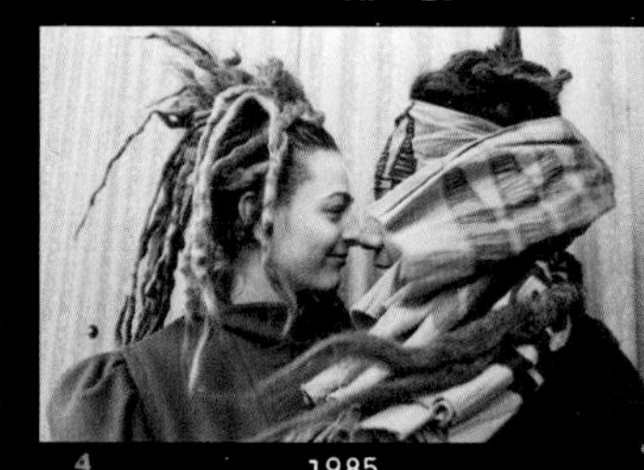

1985

PABLO & PEDRO

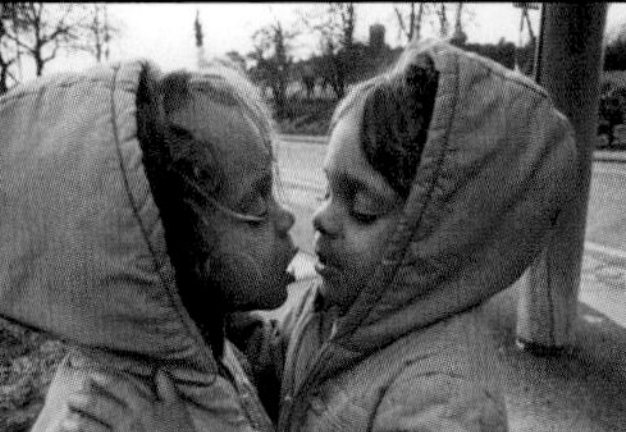

1984

PULP @ THE THEKLA

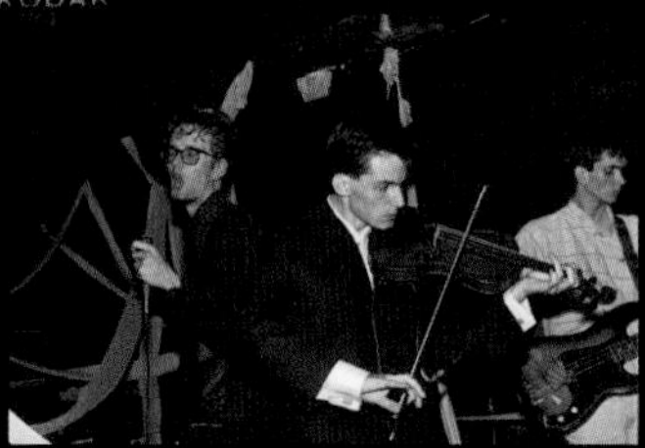

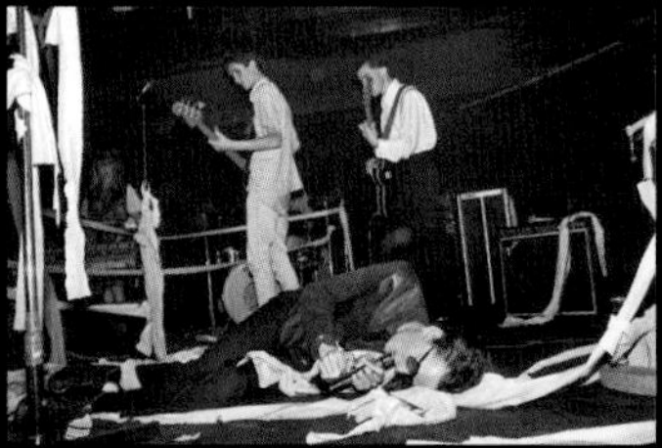

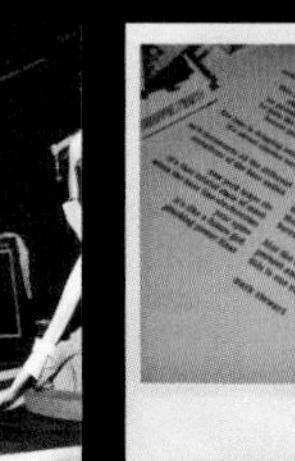

Bristol, 1986

MARK MY WORDS

MARK STEWART

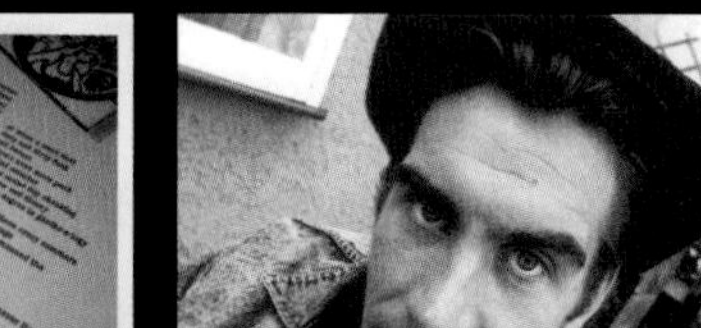

Redland, Bristol, 1984

NO COVER UP

Goth Night, Studio, Bristol, 1984

ADRIAN SHERWOOD & MARK STEWART

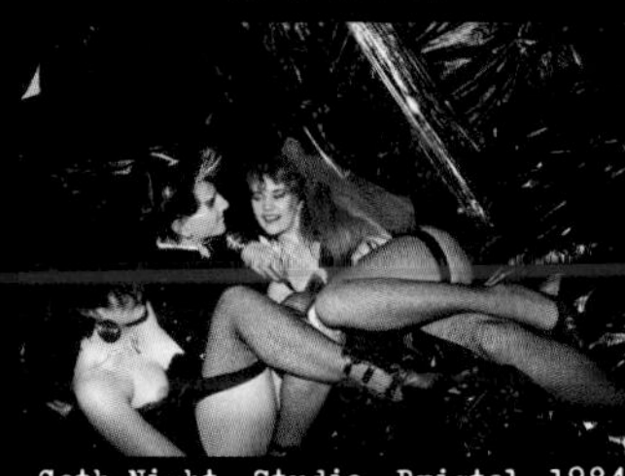

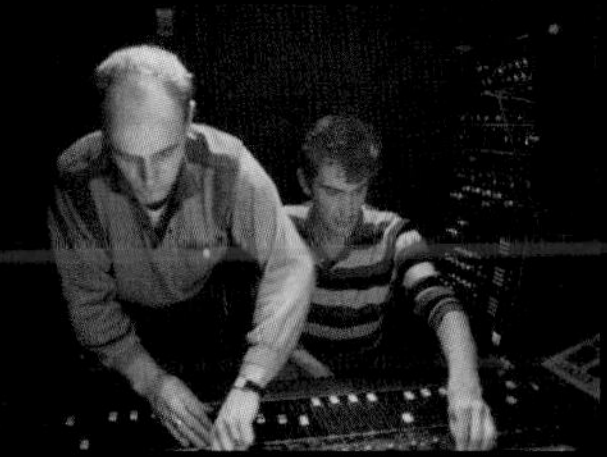

London, 1985

TED MILTON OF BLURT

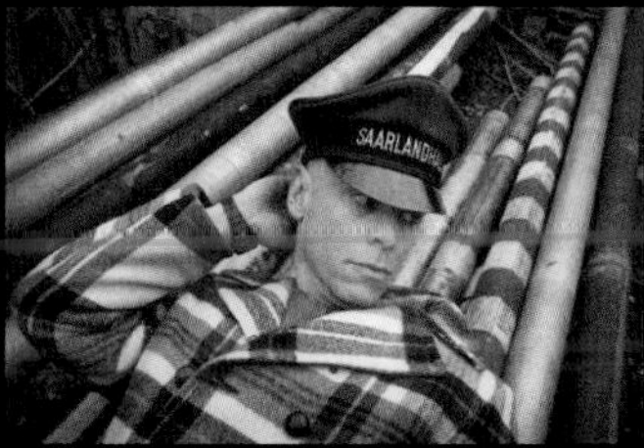

Jamaica Street, Bristol, 1985

AGUCHI

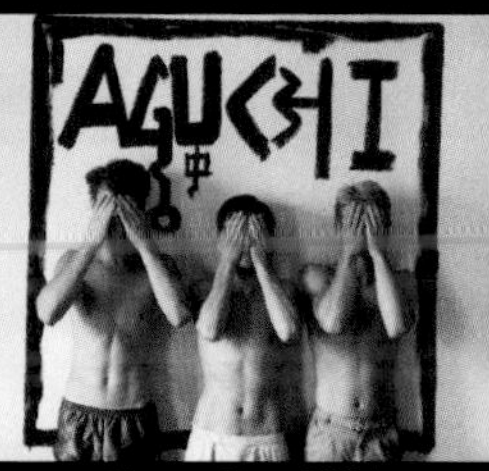

St Paul's, 1984

BRILLIANT CORNERS

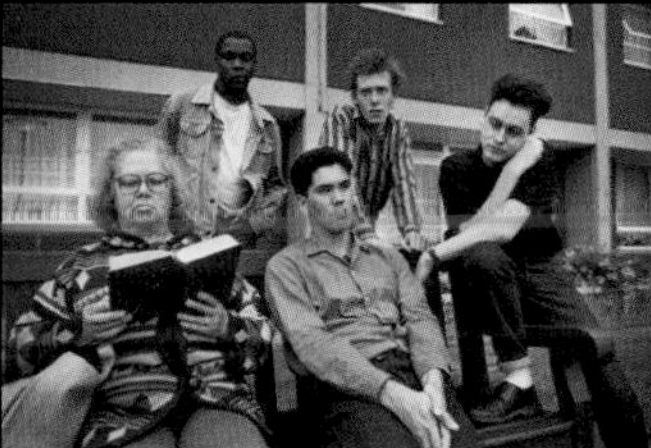

NME shoot, Kingsdown, Bristol, 1985

HEAD PHOTO SHOOT

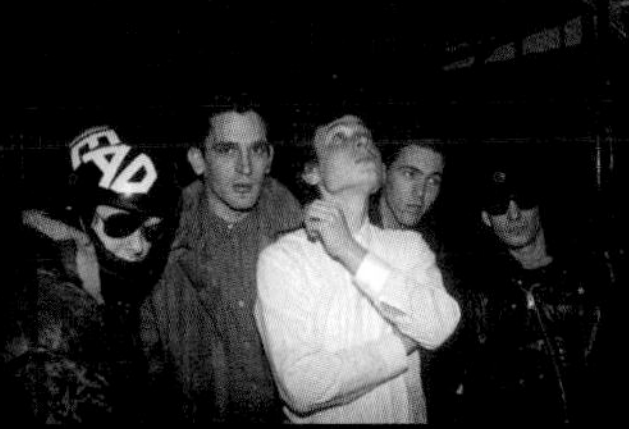

Bristol Docks, 1984

SAPPHIRE

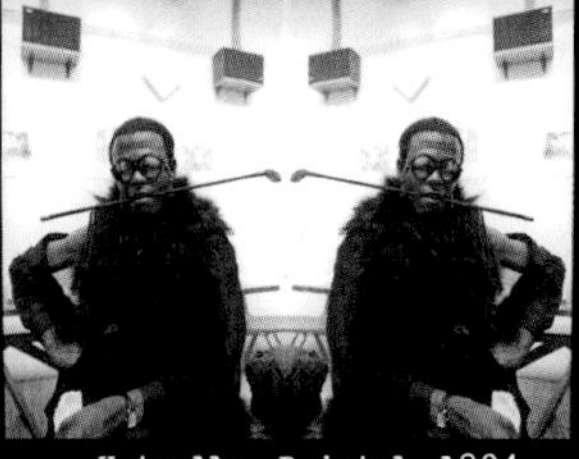

Hotwells, Bristol, 1984

STAN THE MAN

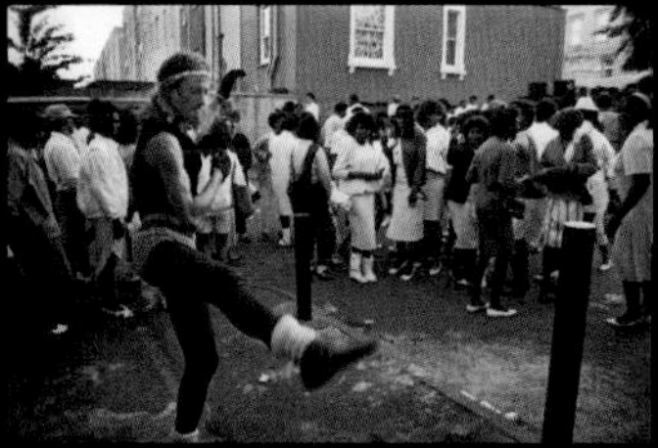

St Paul's, 1985

MICK THE SPIC

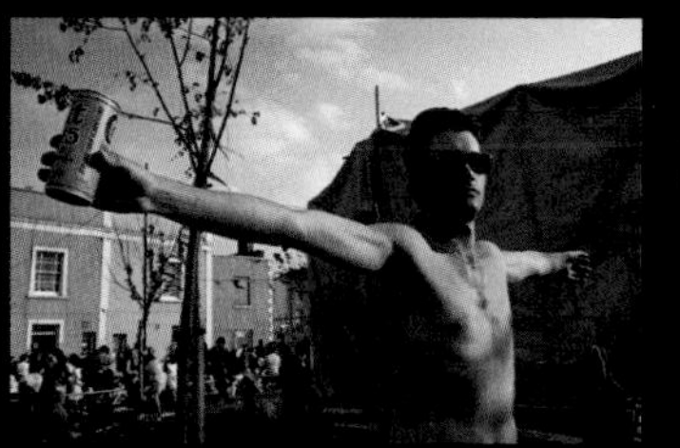

St Paul's, 1986

SPIRIT OF PEACE & MUCK

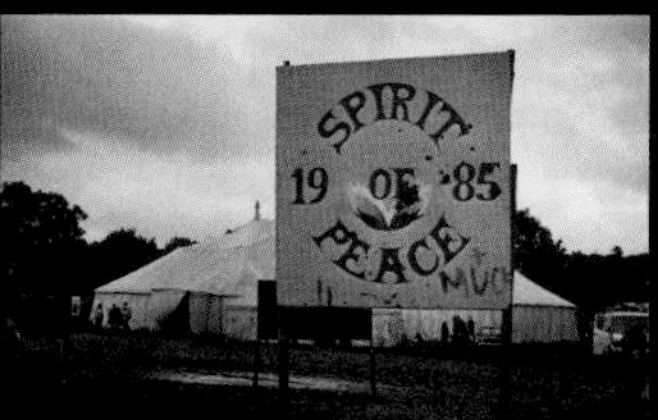

Glastonbury, 1985

ANTI-APARTHEID DEMO   GREENWAY BOYS   BOMB BOTHA

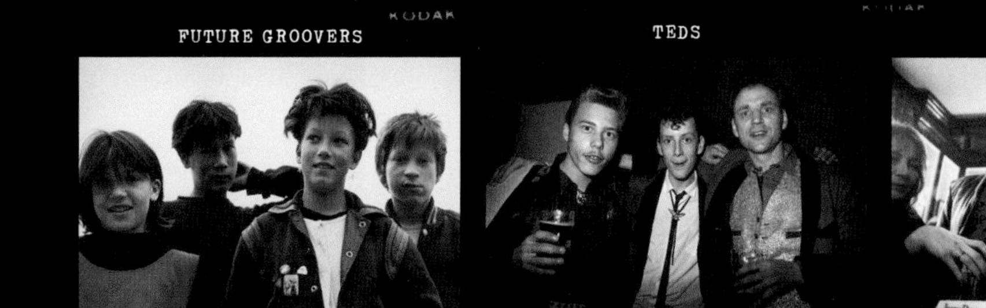

Nelson St, Magistrates Court, 1984

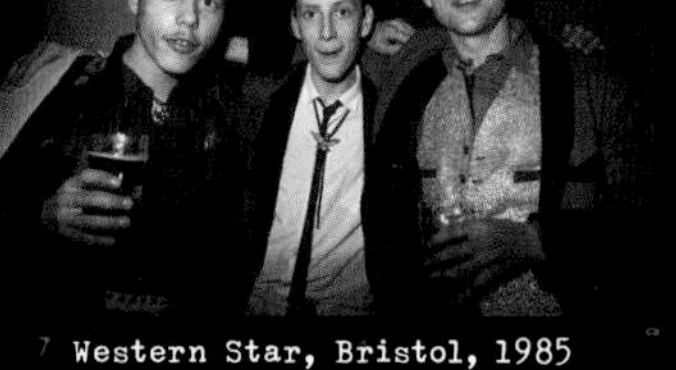

St Paul's Flats, 1985

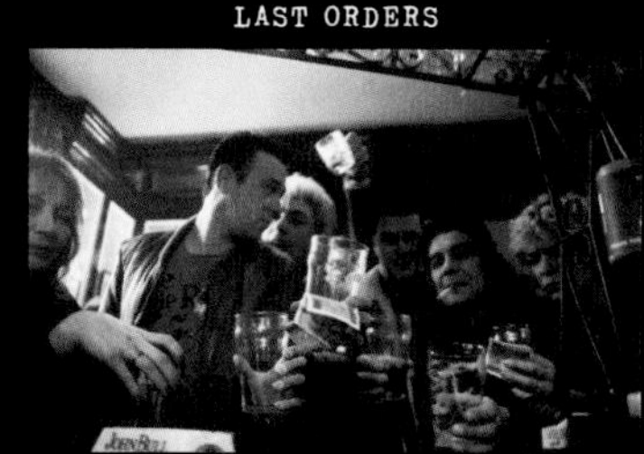

The Bearpit, Bristol, 1985

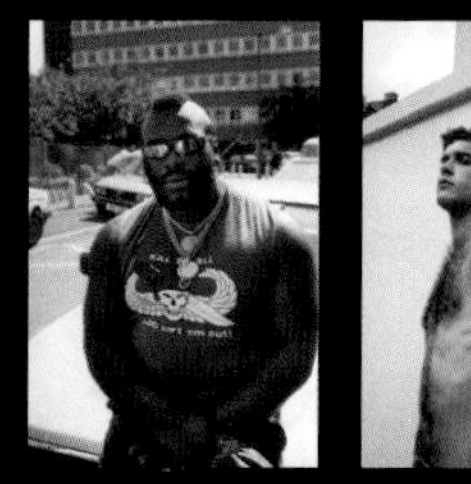

Bristol, 1983

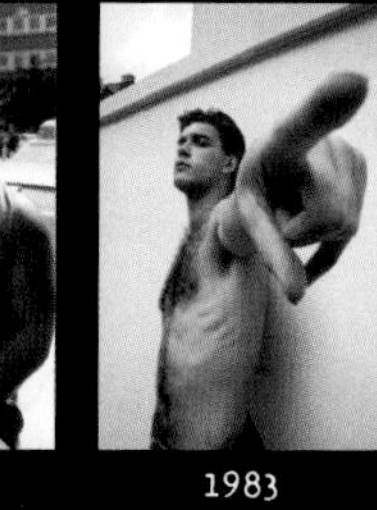

St Paul's, 1985

FUTURE GROOVERS   TEDS   LAST ORDERS   MR. T. TWIN   MALLY BENNETT

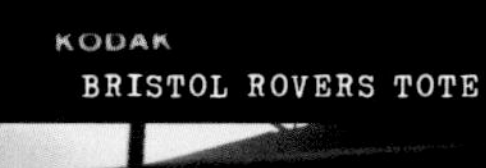

Ashton Court, 1986

Western Star, Bristol, 1985

Old England pub, Bristol, 1984

1985

1983

BRISTOL ROVERS TOTE   SELF-PORTRAIT   NELLEE & ME   VICTORY TO THE MINERS   3D SPRAY

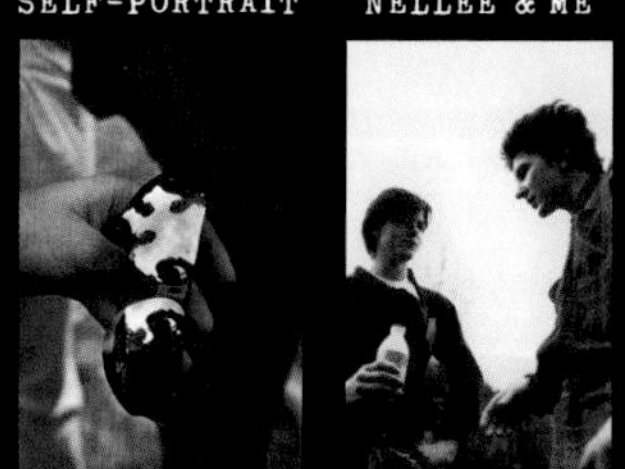

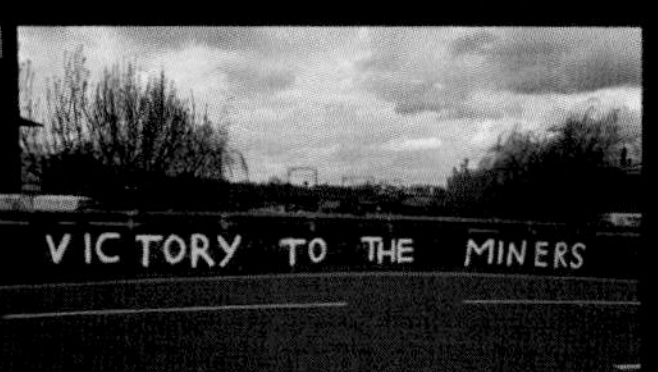

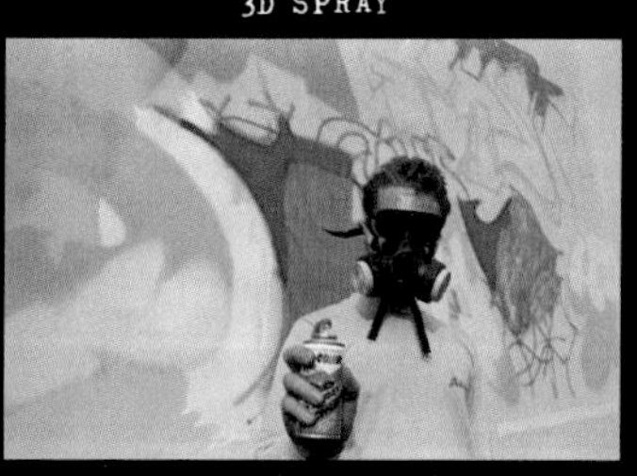

Eastville Stadium, Bristol, 1984   Ashton Court, 1984   Camden, London, 1984   St Paul's, 1985

NOTES: 1. Maintenance workers take a break and pose for a shoot for Venue magazine, Bristol.

2. The record visible in these photos is a 12-inch by the New York band LIQUID LIQUID. The track CAVERN was notable for its bass line which was later used on the Grandmaster & Melle Mel 1983 hit WHITE LINES (DON'T DO IT)

3. Sean Oliver on bass (Rip, Rig & Panic), Roger Pomfrey on guitar, Bruce Smith on drums (Pop Group), Nellee on the cut, MC Willie Wee